Ritual and Music of North China, Volume 2: Shaanbei

STEPHEN JONES
SOAS, University of London, UK

ASHGATE

Published by
Ashgate Publishing Limited
Wey Court East
Union Road
Farnham
Surrey, GU9 7PT
England

Ashgate Publishing Company
Suite 420
101 Cherry Street
Burlington
VT 05401-4405
USA

www.ashgate.com

British Library Cataloguing in Publication Data
Jones, Stephen, 1953 Sept. 23–
  Ritual and Music of North China, Vol. 2: Shaanbei. – (SOAS musicology series)
  1. Folk music – China – Shaanxi Sheng – History and criticism 2. Bands (Music) – China – Shaanxi Sheng – History
  I. Title II. University of London. School of Oriental and African Studies
  781.6'2951'05117

Library of Congress Cataloging-in-Publication Data
Jones, Stephen, 1953 Sept. 23-
  Ritual and Music of North China, Volume 2: Shaanbei / Stephen Jones.
     p. cm. – (SOAS musicology series)
  Includes bibliographical references (p.   ) and index.
  ISBN 978-0-7546-6590-8 (alk. paper)
  1. Folk music – China – Shaanxi Sheng – History and criticism 2. Bands (Music) – China – Shaanxi Sheng – History Shaanxi Sheng (China) – Social life and customs. I. Title.

  ML3917.C6J66 2007
  784.8'9095117–dc22

                                                                2007008135

ISBN 978-0-7546-6590-8

Bach musicological font developed by © Yo Tomita.

Mixed Sources
Product group from well-managed forests and other controlled sources
www.fsc.org Cert no. SA-COC-1565
© 1996 Forest Stewardship Council
FSC

Printed and bound in Great Britain by
MPG Books Ltd, Bodmin, Cornwall.

Contents

List of illustrations and tables   *ix*
Foreword   *xi*
Acknowledgements   *xiii*
Terms used in the text   *xv*
Preface: perspectives and sources   *xvii*
Map *The Yulin region of Shaanbei*   *xxviii*

Part One: Introduction
1 Shaanbei society and its musics   3
       1.1 Setting the scene; 1.2 Shaanbei and its sub-regions;
       1.3 Shaanbei in the twentieth century; 1.4 The film *Yellow Earth*;
       1.5 Shaanbei musics in change; 1.6 Contexts; 1.7 Performers

Part Two: Turning a blind ear: bards of Shaanbei
Prelude   29
2 The tradition   31
       2.1 Social background; 2.2 Contexts; 2.3 Rituals for healing and
       protecting children; 2.4 Ritual equipment, stories, and music;
       2.5 Origin legends and early history
3 The Yan'an period   43
       3.1 A village bard; 3.2 Han Qixiang's early life; 3.3 The Yan'an
       reforms; 3.4 The training bands; 3.5 Li Huaiqiang in the
       Yan'an period
4 The bards after Liberation   55
       4.1 The new troupes; 4.2 The folk–state standoff continues;
       4.3 Li Huaiqiang under Maoism; 4.4 Han Qixiang after Liberation;
       4.5 The Cultural Revolution, and Guo Xingyu;
       4.6 Themes and music; 4.7 New stories fail to catch on
5 The reform era   73
       5.1 The teams decline; 5.2 Han Qixiang experiments; 5.3 New
       research and images; 5.4 Cassette culture 1; 5.5 Blind bards;
       5.6 Sighted bards; 5.7 A story for well-being; 5.8 A story for a
       temple fair
Conclusion: narrative-singing and healing   87

Part Three: Lives of Shaanbei blowers

Prelude   91

6 *Chuishou* before Maoism   95
      6.1 Terminology; 6.2 Caste, opium, and disability; 6.3 Contexts;
      6.4 The Chang family and the 'official blowers' story;
      6.5 Drum shops; 6.6 Other celebrated *chuishou*; 6.7 Yangjiagou
      under the landlords; 6.8 Instrumentations and priests

7 *Chuishou* under Mao   113
      7.1 The 1950s; 7.2 Drum shops in Suide; 7.3 Back in Yangjiagou;
      7.4 The official connection 1; 7.5 Loss-assessment; 7.6 The Cultural
      Revolution

8 The early reform era   127
      8.1 The commune system is dismantled; 8.2 Local research;
      8.3 Chang Wenzhou eats off the state; 8.4 Instruments; 8.5 Music

9 Modernization and the 'big band'   143
      9.1 The official connection 2; 9.2 Conservatory style;
      9.3 Cassette culture 2; 9.4 Following fashion: the Shaanbei
      big band; 9.5 New and old repertories

10 *Chuishou* around 2000   155
      10.1 Mizhi town; 10.2 Little Hong Kong; 10.3 Status since
      the reforms; 10.4 Changing economics; 10.5 Rivalry and violence;
      10.6 Changing learning processes; 10.7 Keeping up, dropping out;
      10.8 Not following fashion; 10.9 A village struggles

11 *Chuishou* in action   175
      11.1 A village funeral, 1999; 11.2 A village funeral, 2001;
      11.3 A town wedding; 11.4 A small temple fair; 11.5 The White
      Cloud Mountain

Conclusion: ritual and order   192

Part Four: Urban music in Shaanbei

12 Musics of Yulin city   197
      12.1 Yulin shawm bands; 12.2 The Yulin 'little pieces';
      12.3 The Yulin Folk Arts Troupe

Conclusion: local ritual cultures   212

Bibliography   217
Glossary-Index   229

DVD ⊙ *Notes from the Yellow Earth* (44')

  A Temple fairs

    1 Opera; 2 Offerings; 3 Crossing the Passes; 4 White Cloud Mountain and bard

  B Shawm bands and funerals

    1 Shawm bands; 2 Inviting the Soul; 3 Daytime suite; 4 Displaying the Road Lanterns; 5 Burial; 6 Settling the Earth God

  C Singing and bards

    1 The official image; 2 Drinking session; 3 Bards; 4 Story for well-being

  D The 'big band' sound

    1 Shop opening; 2 Wedding; 3 Funeral pop; 4 Beggar; 5 Displaying the Road Lanterns

List of illustrations and tables

Illustrations

All illustrations are by the author, except 9 (courtesy Chang family) and 10 (courtesy Gao Wanfei).

1	A corner of Yangjiagou village from hills above, 2001	2
2	A story for well-being, Hongliutan 1999	28
3	Cloth pantheons listing the gods	39
4	Blind bard Li Huaiqiang, 1999	44
5	Remnants of landlord architecture, Yangjiagou 1999	46
6	Guo Xingyu with his master Wang Jinkao, 2001	57
7	Wang Jinkao's *pipa*, 2001	67
8	*Chuishou* playing for funeral at side of soul hall, Yangjiagou 1999	90
9	Elder Chang (1916–98), *chuishou* in Yangjiagou	110
10	Assembled shawm players from Mizhi county, 1981	129
11	Chang Wenzhou with some of his shawms, 1999	132
12	The 'big band' accompanies Receiving Offerings procession, Baijiayan funeral 2001	142
13	Li Qishan's band, Lijiagou 2001	157
14	*Chuishou* lead procession, Yangjiagou 1999	178
15	Wang Shifa's band nears the groom's home, Suide suburb 2001	190

Tables

1	Counties of the Yulin region	6
2	Occupations for blind men and contexts for narrative-singing	33
3	Performing contexts for *chuishou*	100
4	Fee division of three big bands, 2001	164
5	List of funeral helpers	183

Foreword

This book gives an impression of music-making in daily life in the mountainous region of Shaanbei, a poor and largely rural area of northwest China. I hope to convey some of the kinds of musical activities you could expect to find on a trip to Shaanbei around 2000, passing through the barrage of pop music blaring from speakers in the bustling county-towns, on the way to take part in life-cycle and calendrical ceremonies in poor villages in mountain gulleys. I also attempt to put all this activity in the context of modern history, with data on society before and during the Maoist commune system. My story is based on the practice of grass-roots music-making in daily life, not merely on the prescriptions offered by central ideologues or the performances of official state-funded troupes.

We need to pay attention to rural China, since even with massive urban migration since the 1980s, two-thirds of the vast population still live there. In areas like Shaanbei, the population is predominantly (around 90%) rural and agrarian. The rural focus, even if largely based on recent observation, also pays dividends in showing the depth of historical China, with pre-Communist traditions still being maintained – whatever one's take on their constant recreation under changing conditions.

This is really a third volume on ritual and music in north China, including my 2004 book on a ritual association in a village of Hebei province. My main theme is the continuity of local folk ceremonial practices in a chosen region of rural north China – the painful maintenance of ritual and its music under Maoism, their revival with the market reforms of the 1980s, and their adaptations since the 1990s under the assaults of TV, pop music, and migration. This study has common features with my volume on Shanxi province (2007) – such as temple fairs, funerals, and shawm bands – but regional and local variation is always evident, and even these three case-studies are but tiny dots on the map.

The text is in four parts. Part One gives background to the area and its music-making in a changing society. Parts Two and Three discuss the lives of blind bards and shawm bands respectively, describing modifications in their ceremonial activities through the twentieth century. Part Four acclimatizes us to the modern world with some glimpses of different types of musical life in Yulin city, the regional capital, illustrating the contrast with the surrounding countryside.

The DVD is intended both to illuminate the text and to stand on its own. It shows bards performing at a temple fair and to bless a family in distress, and shawm bands performing at a wedding, at funerals, and a shop opening – including their pop repertory with the 'big band'. Also featuring as part of these events are opera troupes, geomancers, and performing beggars. By contrast, the film also shows a glimpse of the official image of Shaanbei culture as presented by a state ensemble in the regional capital.

Rather than explaining how the music 'itself' works, or exploring the riches of vocal texts, I mainly discuss the lives of musicians and their roles in society. Though the material is piecemeal, I believe it suggests some important perspectives, given the paucity of fieldwork data in English on music-making in rural China. In the interests of accessibility, and in order to stress the human dimensions of music-making, I try to steer clear of more arcane technicalities, sometimes offering informal vignettes of the tribulations of fieldwork in rural China. As with my work on music-making in Hebei and Shanxi, Ruth Finnegan's (1989) work on the 'hidden musicians' of an English town is an apt inspiration here, as the musicians of the poor Chinese countryside, long the bedrock of society, have remained anonymous, and their labours, their social necessity, unrecognized. Music-making is a vital part of ritual and society, and the diverse performers of local communities cannot be discussed separately from society or modern history.

Acknowledgements

I am most grateful to local musicians and families, including bards and shawm band musicians, and particularly to 'Older Brother', Zhihui, and Runlin in Yangjiagou. Local scholars and officials have also been most supportive.

My work on Shaanbei music-making was carried out mainly while based at the Music Department of SOAS, London University, on a research grant from the Chiang Ching-kuo Foundation. My 1999 and 2001 field-trips were funded by the British Academy and SOAS respectively. The British Academy also funded the making of the DVD. I am grateful to them all.

In China, Qiao Jianzhong, former Director of the Music Research Institute in Beijing, first inspired me to visit Shaanbei, and his extensive family in Yulin looked after me affably. Anthropologists Guo Yuhua and Luo Hongguang, then of the Chinese Academy of Social Sciences, gave me valuable background on the area. Guo Yuhua accompanied me there in 1999, and Zhang Zhentao and Tian Yaonong, colleagues from the Music Research Institute in Beijing, in 2001; where I write 'we' in the text below, this refers to these joint fieldtrips. Xiao Mei, Adam Yuet Chau, and Iguchi Junko also kindly shared their experiences of Shaanbei with me. Adam Yuet Chau, Rachel Harris, Rowan Pease, and Jan Chmelarcik have offered insightful suggestions on parts of the draft. Susi Arnott made a fine editor of the DVD; Jeremy Glasgow from SOAS assisted with voice-over engineering.

A more succinct version of Part Two appears in *Chinoperl* 27 (Jones 2007a).

Terms used in the text

Transliteration and pronunciation: some basic guidelines follow to pronouncing the *pinyin* system of romanized Chinese, and some of its local variants.

c	as in i*ts*
q	as in *ch*oose
x	between *ss* and *sh*
z	as in bi*ds*
zh	as in *J*oe
a	as in b*a*r
e	as in h*e*r
i	ee: *di* 'dee'; but when preceded by c, ch, r, s, sh, z, or zh, then shorter than er. Thus, *dizi* 'deedz'
o	as in l*o*rd: *bo* 'bore'
u	as in b*oo*
uo	(after c, d, l, n, r, s, sh, t, z, zh) same as o above: *luo* 'lore'
ü	as in German umlaut; after x or q, the u is also effectively an umlaut
ao	as in n*ow*
ian	*ee-en*: *jian* 'jee-en'
ie	*ee-yeah*: *die* 'dee-yeah'
ou	*oh*
ui	*way*: *shui* 'shway'

Below are some very approximate clues to how Shaanbei dialect varies from standard Chinese:

pinyin	Shaanbei dialect
hao	hou
hei	he
bei	bie
he	huo
shi, chi, zhu	si, ci, zu
xia	ha
qu	ka
bo	ba
duo	de

Thus *xiashou* (player of the lower shawm part) is pronounced like *hashou*; *heshang*, Buddhist priest, resembles *huosang*; Heilongtan sounds like Helongtan. I use standard *pinyin* in the text, with one exception, choosing local *ha* instead of national *xia* (*hashou*). Where an 'r' is commonly added to a term, I add it without punctuation: *haidir*.

I use English terms for two major temples, Black Dragon temple (Heilongtan) and White Cloud temple (Baiyunguan, often known as Baiyunshan, White Cloud Mountain), as well as for one of our kindest informants in Yangjiagou, known as 'Older Brother' (Dage). I leave village names untranslated, but many begin with 'X family (jia)', followed by a suffix tellingly describing the hill landscape, such as *gou* (gorge: hence Yangjiagou, Yang family gorge), *yan* (ridge), *ping* (gulch), *ban* (hillside), and so on (for a fine list, see Zhang Junyi 1993: 111–15).

Ages are given in terms of *sui* 'years'; since one is 1 *sui* old at birth, and one year older with every Chinese New Year, these ages generally translate into Western ages of one year less. Even where the word *sui* is not used, I have adhered to Chinese ages, leaving the reader to subtract one from the number. Where we have firm dates of birth (often when the subjects mention under which of the Twelve Animals of the Chinese calendar they were born) and death, they are cited as such.

Calendar: dates are often given in terms of the Chinese lunar calendar, still used throughout rural China. The Chinese New Year (1st day of the 1st moon) generally falls around late January–early February.

Currency: 1 *yuan* (colloqially *kuai*) equals 10 *jiao* (colloquially *mao*); 1 *jiao* equals 10 *fen*. Around 2000 there were *c*15 *yuan* to the pound sterling.

Distances: 2 Chinese *li* (*huali*) = 1 kilometre.

Land: 1 *mu* = 1/6 acre (1,000 sq.m., 1/15 hectare).

Weights and measures: 2 *jin* = I kilogram; 1 *sheng* = 1 litre; 1 *dou* = 10 litres.

Preface: perspectives and sources

Here I outline some of the issues involved in studying local Chinese expressive cultures, including politics, ritual, and history.

Culture and politics

China, particularly under Communism, is sometimes assumed to represent a case of close state control over 'the arts'; meanwhile traditional ritual practices, as 'feudal superstition', might seem to have been banished. Thus 'arts policy' and official prescriptions have been much discussed, largely in the context of state-supported ensembles rather than grass-roots music-making. Since the liberal reforms of the 1980s, 'the arts' are also discussed in terms of globalizing urban media culture (whether 'elite' or 'popular').[1]

These forms, like all expressive culture, are worth studying, but they are only a tiny proportion of expressive cultural activity in China, as in most societies. Hence the 'hidden musicians' – both urban and rural – might include amateurs like folk-singers, members of New Year's dance troupes and lay religious sects, and people attending karaoke bars, as well as occupational performers such as lay Daoists, shawm bands, spirit mediums, and bards. Apart from the state, the 'hidden patrons' might include temple committees and peasant households sponsoring rituals.

It was in Shaanbei, base area for the Communist Party from 1936, that they made early experiments in land reform and social revolution, earlier than in most other areas of China; this experience was to be crucial for policy under the People's Republic once the Communists came to power nationally. Cultural activities were an important aspect of official campaigns to mobilize the masses. David Holm's fine study on Shaanbei (1991), while largely about Communist cultural reforms in the 1940s' Yan'an period, was also a pioneering study in being enriched by his fieldwork in the early 1980s – before most Western scholars were venturing anywhere into rural China; he thus paid attention not only to official propaganda but to grass-roots practice. Yet today, so marginal may the influence of Maoism on music-making (and indeed on Chinese musicology) appear that a recent Chinese thesis on music in Shaanbei (Tian 2005) barely mentions its status as revolutionary base, instead citing ancient Confucian texts to illuminate the ideological base of music-making there.

---

[1]   See e.g. Perris 1983, Kraus 2004, and Hockx and Strauss 2005. For a summary of some relevant issues on ritual music and Communism, see Harris and Norton 2002.

Since the 1980s, scholars (mainly Chinese) have opened up the riches of the myriad local cultures in China, particularly in reference to ritual. Partly insulated against modernization by protective local cadres, both ritual and expressive culture turn out to have been resilient. Ironically, it is thus in rural China today that many of the traditions of imperial China, including its elite, are to be found. Nor is this some marginal survival: it is the life-blood of the majority of the population. One is understandably preoccupied with twentieth-century change, but looking at Shaanbei today, given its cultural resilience, maybe Tian's relegation of Communism is not so wilful: Shaanbei culture today retains strong elements of pre-Communist traditions. That is not to say that politics has no bearing on local culture; on the contrary, state initiatives, repressive as much as supportive, may be important. Local politics always bears on the maintenance of culture, as I showed for one Hebei village (Jones 2004).

In documenting the 'revival' of folk traditions in China since the 1980s' reforms, several scholars, both Chinese and Western, have aptly observed accommodation, negotiation, and collusion between local groups and local state officialdom in community rituals such as temple fairs.[2] Chau's case in Shaanbei of the accommodation between local elites and the local state is clear for a major enterprise like the Black Dragon temple. I find it less clear for the humble practitioners such as the 'hidden musicians' I listed above – who depend on that collusion inasmuch as their ceremonies rely on the local state's tolerance, but who themselves have few clear dealings or contact with the local state.

Indeed, my material suggests that collusion was always a part of the picture, even under Maoism, although the 1980s' reforms certainly brought traditional ceremonial culture out into the open again. And this is significant for the contexts of music-making: 'turning a blind eye' was always a feature of the local state's relation with folk culture. Thus although local ceremonial may be contrasted with central state power, it should not necessarily be seen as resistance.

But today, if the local state is visible in public ceremonial contexts, it is much less audible: music-making veers from traditional to pop with little trace of official state style. Throughout China, the high-profile urban state-supported performing troupes established under Maoism represent only a tiny proportion of amateur and professional musicians – and this was so even during the heyday of the state troupes in the 1950s. Apart from amateur music-making (for both ceremonial and entertainment) like singing or dancing, many peasant musicians make or supplement their living by performing for folk ceremonial.

Still, I am concerned to contemplate the influence of central official policy on music-making in Shaanbei. Local societies throughout China have seen radical change in the twentieth century, from the collapse of the imperial system through the unrest of the Republican period, and then through Maoism to the reforms. Along a continuum of places more or less heavily influenced by official (including cultural) policy, one might expect even rural Shaanbei to be rather near the official

---

[2]   Examples include Guo 2000; in English, Tan 2006, and for Shaanbei, Chau 2006.

pole, since although poor and remote, it was already the headquarters of the Communist movement in the years leading up to its national victory.

Whether typical or not, the very fact of Shaanbei's location as birthplace of the revolution makes the modern history of expressive culture there interesting. It both suffers and benefits from its revolutionary image. During the Yan'an period, folk-song, local opera, and *yangge* song-and-dance (Holm 1991, and §1.5 below) were highly politicized, and commodified, achieving a national reputation. Shaanbei music has already been the subject of much mythologizing: new works from the Yan'an period, such as 'The East is Red' and the Yellow River Cantata, formed a significant part of the state's cultural propaganda (Tuohy 2001). Since the 1980s' reforms, the 'Northwest wind' style of pop music and several films and TV programmes have fostered the wider media image of Shaanbei music.

But such mythologizing only tells a tiny part of the story. The Communist Party's degree of success in transforming local culture in such a rural and 'backward' area might be a good index of how successful their cultural (and social) policies were nationally. We should distinguish change as the direct or indirect result of cultural policy, and change as the direct or indirect result of other policies – social, economic, and political. How did successive Communist campaigns – in the Yan'an period from 1936 to 1947, and under the commune system from the 1950s to the 1970s – influence ritual and expressive culture in Shaanbei; and what has happened since the 1980s' reforms? Central policy could be unclear, unpopular, or deflected:[3]

> Although the Communist Party, in trying to improve life, both adapted to and transformed peasant values and social relations, Chinese villagers – including Party members – kept to their own agenda. Even when the Party brought economic gain and cultural healing, centre and hinterland were frequently at odds. [...] Villagers and their allies and patrons among officials also tried, as they had for many generations under various regimes, to dodge, deflect, and blunt the impact of demands detrimental to local interests and values. Those negative impacts gradually eroded the new state's popular legitimacy.

Indeed, below I document considerably more contacts between folk musicians and state troupes than I have in my previous work on Hebei or Shanxi. But if anything, my discussion gives such official connections undue prominence: they remain utterly marginal in this vast barren landscape. Fleeting contacts of rural musicians with state initiatives only illuminate the resilience of local folk cultural networks.

In Shaanbei, as elsewhere in China, one may partly relate the persistence of pre-Communist belief systems (like worship of the gods and ceremonial practices) throughout these periods to the inability of modern governments to transform

---

[3] Friedman, Pickowicz, and Selden 1991: xv. Along with Chan, Madsen, and Unger 1992, this work is a basic source; Hinton 2006, a scathing attack on the book, is his final defence of the revolution.

the environment. The largely agrarian society has remained poor and partially dependent on divine blessing, even since the 1980s when some parts of the area made clear economic progress. It is precisely Shaanbei's position in the Communist myth that throws the maintenance of tradition there into yet starker light. While modern politics are an immediate element, the varied local conditions we find throughout China today are a complex heritage of longer historical processes, the results of factors such as ecology, economy, and lineage customs, as well as local politics and personalities – further complicated by their histories in republican and Maoist eras and since.

Ritual and ceremonial

While we have substantial data on political, social, and economic changes in rural society in modern China, both under Maoism and since the reforms (see n.19 below), we have very little about expressive culture there – which is firmly based in ritual. Meanwhile the majority of scholarship on Chinese religion remains text-based and historical, rarely addressing the concrete practice of ritual in the modern period – as if Communism had rendered the topic obsolete after 1949.

However, since the opening up of mainland China in the 1980s, a great amount of ethnographic material, in Chinese, has emerged, revealing the maintenance of local (notably ritual) traditions.[4] In Western languages, scholars like Lagerwey, Dean, and Holm publish fine work. Such material mainly concerns south China, and still rarely addresses the expressive culture that is indivisible from ritual performance.

Thus ethnographies of rural China document bewilderingly varying roles for ritual in society, that I doubt can be explained merely by scholars' different focuses. In fine studies such as those of Chan, Madsen, and Unger (1992), Gao Mobo (1999), or Liu Xin (2000, for a village not far south of Shaanbei), the secular aspects of weddings and funerals are the only evidence of ritual practice; temples and their related activities, or religious specialists such as Daoists and mediums, appear almost entirely absent, again as if beaten into obsolescence by Communism. Conversely, Dean and Lagerwey document communities in southeastern China that, still today, appear dominated by religious activity; in Dean's work, we find that even one among several cults has over a thousand active temples in a mere two counties, and that a single village may hold between 45 and a staggering 250 days of ritual and theatre per year. North Chinese regions like Shaanbei appear to

---

[4]   Notably in the journal *Minsu quyi* and the series edited by C.K. Wang (1997–) and Lagerwey (1996–) (for English reviews of items in these series, see Overmyer 2002); see also Dean 1993, 1998. For Western-language bibliographies on popular Chinese religion, see http://web.missouri.edu/~clartp/bibliography_CPR.html and http://website.leidenuniv. nl/~haarbjter/chinPRCbibtext.html. For music, see also the two series edited by Tsao Poon-yee. For some issues in this section, cf. Jones 2003: 321–5; Jones 2004: 344–54 and 363–6; Jones 2007: ix–x.

be somewhere in the middle of this secular–religious continuum, but as yet our material does not suffice to explain such variation.

Still today, people in Shaanbei – as in much of rural China – persist in enlisting divine powers in their chronic struggle with the elements and their need for healthy crops and children. In my work on music-making in Shanxi (Jones 2007), I used, for convenience, the terms 'ritual' to refer narrowly to religious ritual, and 'ceremonial' to describe the broader range of customary practices.[5] The broader usage includes all kinds of performance at life-cycle ceremonies (for the household) and calendrical observances (for the wider community, notably temple fairs), as well as at occasional events such as the consecration of a new dwelling, or the pledging of a vow in order to be granted a healthy son by the gods. Such 'ceremonial' performances, indeed, may include religious 'ritual'.

Those who are aware of religious practice in modern China may know of the ('institutional') ritual of priests resident in the major Buddhist and Daoist temples, in cities and on the major mountain sites; those a little more informed may know of the 'diffused' activities of lay Buddhist and Daoist ritual specialists – groups of ordinary peasants performing for life-cycle and calendrical ceremonies, often with the aid of hereditary ritual manuals. And apart from such temple and lay ritual specialists, other religious performers include geomancers, spirit mediums, bards, and lay sectarians; not to mention, of course, ordinary folk drawing lots, burning incense, and pledging vows to the gods.[6]

Thus the topic of the elite 'classical' religion of Daoism is itself broadening: from early textual and doctrinal history to living ritual performance, from temple to lay Daoists, and thence to the total performance and activities of Daoists in society. And a yet broader field of study is that of the whole social activity involved in 'doing religion': for Shaanbei, Chau stresses vernacular social practices such as 'hosting', and the wider ritual context might include the behaviour of geomancers, worshippers, and cooks. One is led to study what we may call 'local folk NGOs', such as temple committees, groups of lay Daoists performing rituals for the community, and shawm bands – all working outside the state institutional system.

Throughout China, the cast of divine intermediaries commonly includes individual geomancers and mediums. But the term 'ritual specialist' in China is often applied more narrowly to groups of Buddhist and Daoist practitioners, whether full-time priests or laymen. In much of China, despite the decline of temple priests under Maoism, groups of lay ritual specialists – ordinary peasants with hereditary traditions of ritual manuals and liturgical practice – have continued to fulfil duties such as reciting scriptures for mortuary rituals and temple fairs, sometimes

---

[5]   For one among a plethora of definitions of ritual, see Grimes 1990: 9–15; Bell 1997 is a fine survey.

[6]   Fine studies on Chinese popular religion (indeed for Shaanbei) are the works of Adam Yuet Chau; note his list of five 'modalities' for 'doing religion' (2006: 75–6). The convenient concepts of 'institutional' and 'diffused', taken from C.K. Yang (1967: 20–21, 294–340), have now been questioned: Chau 2006: 143–6, cf. Dubois 2005: 193–5.

further enacting ritual drama.[7] These groups, with their complex ritual sequences including vocal liturgy, percussion, and melodic instrumental music, have long attracted Chinese musicologists, and me. They are common in north China, such as occupational lay Daoists in Shanxi or amateur ritual associations in Hebei, but in Shaanbei they seem quite rare.[8] Amateur pilgrim associations attend Shaanbei temple fairs, but liturgical recitation has not been documented. In their absence, the geomancers, mediums, and funeral managers take on a more prominent role as 'ritual specialists'. And with this broader definition of ceremonial life, and popular religion, my musical focus turns towards bards and shawm bands.

Performance, ritual, and music

Given the major role of all kinds of music in Chinese ritual events – from the performance of opera and parades of dance groups, to the chanting of geomancers, to the vocal liturgy and melodic and percussion music of ritual specialists – music is strangely absent from studies of Chinese religion. The study of Chinese ritual so far has been largely 'silent', like attending a ritual with earplugs in, or watching a video with the sound switched down. This is all the more perplexing since studies of religion in China – which, as we saw, with access to fieldwork have expanded from text-based historical research – have begun to pay attention to performance and its implications. Like religion, music is something that people *do*.[9]

A good instance is the study of 'precious scrolls' (*baojuan*), liturgical manuals in 24 chapters belonging to sectarian groups since the Ming dynasty (Jones 2004: 267–9, 363–4). Sinologists and scholars of Chinese religion have described in detail the textual and doctrinal history of these volumes, using texts found in libraries. But these are manuals for performance; the texts alone do not begin to show how they are performed, with their use of 10-word lines sung with complex solo-chorus alternation, ending with unwritten refrains invoking Amitabha Buddha at the end of lines, the percussion accompaniment, the *qupai* melodies that punctuate the chapters.

Nor do *baojuan* studies show how they are *only* used for performance – before which the ritual specialists wash their hands, unwrap them from their blue cloth, light incense, and kowtow before the god images. And they are still performed by

---

[7] C.K. Wang's series (1997–) shows the ubiquity of such ritual specialists throughout south China.

[8] For lay Daoists in Shanxi, see e.g. Jones 2007; for Hebei, see Zhang Zhentao 2002c, Jones 1999, 2004, Dubois 2005. For temple Daoists in south Shaanxi, see Herrou 2005. For a detailed study of lay Daoist vocal liturgy in Changwu, southwest of Shaanbei, see ANS 1559–1684. For elsewhere in north China, the instrumental vols. of the *Anthology* offer leads; citings of Daoist groups in the vols. for Gansu and Ningxia, just west of Shaanbei, also suggest that the scarcity of Daoists in Shaanbei is exceptional (cf. §1.7 below).

[9] For ritual and performance, see Dean 1998: 30–46, Sutton 2003. For 'doing religion', see Chau 2006, esp. 59–76; for 'musicking' see Small 1998.

sectarian groups and lay ritual specialists over a wide area of north China (not, as far as I know, in Shaanbei, but in Gansu just west, as well as Hebei and Shanxi). The sinological study is valuable, but without fieldwork on performance it is, as one might say, academic.

Meanwhile, anthropologists also manage to consign music to a separate field of research. However, the documenting of music in rural China almost inevitably leads to the study of ritual. While we may be interested in all kinds of music-making, including music for entertainment, yet in the countryside, most types of performers – folk-singers, narrative-singers, opera troupes, instrumentalists, dancers – depend largely on ritual, as may now be seen in the monumental *Anthology* (see below). Even if the direct relevance of music to the ritual event is not always clear, vocal music (including all points on the speech–song continuum), percussion, and melodic instrumental music are ubiquitous aspects of ritual performance. The broadening of focus from elite to popular religion is paralleled in studies of Chinese music by the two major series edited by Tsao Poon-yee. It has been a learning process for me, and my Chinese colleagues, to expand from the melodic instrumental music of 'ritual specialists' in the narrow sense (itself less crucial to their performance than their vocal music and percussion) to the practices of shawm bands and bards, and to the diverse activities of all the participants.[10]

Focuses of time and space

The modern history of China may be simply discussed under three headings: the pre-Communist period, the Maoist commune system from the 1950s to the 1970s, and the period since the liberal economic reforms of the 1980s. As both imperial and Maoist periods recede, and as Western studies of Chinese music focus ever more on urban institutions and globalization, work on rural China, where daily music-making in the post-Mao era reflects both imperial and Maoist periods, is all the more necessary.

The fine recent studies, cited above, of local Chinese ritual cultures suggest a potential confusion between historical and contemporary description. On one hand are 'idealized' prescriptive accounts of elderly informants, which may refer to the pre-Communist period, itself far from static. Some such studies tend to a somewhat simplistic agenda of 'rescuing imperial culture before it is too late'; some others consist of synchronic documentation of observed traditions that appear to have seen little long-term modification despite sweeping waves of social change.[11]

---

[10]   For music in Chinese ritual, note the two major series edited by Tsao, including Zhang Zhentao 2003; note also Xue 2003. In English, see e.g. Yung et al. 1996, Rees 2000, Tan 2002, Ruizendaal 2006.

[11]   For the nostalgic view, see the Lagerwey (1996–) series on Hakka culture; for the synchronic approach, see e.g. the series of articles from Kevin Stuart's team on rituals of ethnic minorities in Qinghai.

In China since the end of the Cultural Revolution in 1976, much fieldwork on traditional music and local ceremonial has inevitably had an element of 'salvage' (*qiangjiu*). Meanwhile, Chinese scholars have tended to view living genres not merely as remnants of imperial traditions but as illustrations of arcane ancient treatises of music theory. Others, more concerned with music in society, document synchronically, describing rituals which they have observed since the 1980s; again, if these may appear to maintain pre-Communist traditions more or less intact, the process of maintenance since the 1930s is hardly documented. Still others recognize a partial revival since the repression under Maoism, but appear to see it as a pale reflection of pre-Communist traditions, preferring to interview elderly informants on the riches of the tradition before Communism. Some studies, including the *Anthology* and the notable series edited by C.K. Wang, seek to combine synchronic and diachronic approaches, though the two may be hard to disentangle.

This study mentions the pre-Communist tradition only briefly. One might attempt to document it, with all its temples and rich ceremonial life; ideally one would seek to periodize pre-Communist times for ritual and music – the Republican era was anything but tranquil or static, and if we had more local data, we might undertake a similar task for the late imperial period too. But material would be provisional and sparse compared to the riches of fieldwork, both observation and documentation of living memory.

Many studies address the issue of revival of tradition since the 1980s, after an assumed period of stagnation under Maoism.[12] My fieldwork in north China suggests that the revival was less of a reinvention than it may seem, once one documents the maintenance of traditions under Maoism (Jones 2004, 2007; cf. Tan 2006, for southern Fujian). Focusing on revival since the 1980s tends to dismiss the Maoist period too readily: though religious life was doubtless severely constrained then, our assessments of the post-Mao revival are often based on flimsy assumptions, not only about the privations of Maoism but about the preceding period, itself no 'golden age'. Through interviewing senior practitioners, a more nuanced view of twentieth-century ritual practice emerges.

If religious practice in mainland China, as in Taiwan,[13] has remained strong, despite periods of repression and the partial spread of modern secular values and economic progress, some scholars have suggested that ostentation is gaining ground over ritual expertise. While ceremonial life was undoubtedly of greater complexity before Maoism, some material suggests that with extreme poverty, ritual resources and expertise were in short supply even then.[14] Sure, the laicizations of monks through the 1950s and restrictions on folk ritual practice forced many occupational

---

[12]   Classic examples are Siu 1989 and Jing Jun 1996.

[13]   For a summary of issues in a substantial literature on religion in Taiwan, see e.g. Clart and Jones 2003.

[14]   A glance through the Lagerwey volumes (1996–), or, for north China, Johnson 1994, illustrates the complexity of pre-Communist ritual. Disputing the nostalgic view, see Jones 2004: 344–54; Chau 2006: 5–7, 45–8. For the growth of ostentation, see Siu 1989.

ritual practitioners like Daoists and shawm players to change trades. Yet traditions survived – especially 'household' ones like lay Daoists and geomancers, indeed even amateur sects; the ritual network of life-cycle and calendrical events was impoverished but not destroyed. Still, government campaigns surely contributed to a diminution of expertise, in ritual and music. If expertise was rare before the revolution, it was at least available to be re-inputted; now it is just harder to find.

The main contribution of this study to such debates, apart from drawing attention to the interdependence of music and ritual in rural China, is to attempt to place both in a firmer temporal frame, arguing for greater study of the Maoist period and seeking to perceive changing currents since.

As to space, our concepts of modern Chinese ritual practice are still dominated by the mass of research on southeastern China, including Taiwan; north China is a late arrival at the Chinese ritual studies ball, and much further work is needed before we can integrate it into our overall picture.[15] Of course, 'north' and 'south' are crude delineations, and local features obtain everywhere. As we see in §1.2 below, Shaanbei is part of the northwestern frontier of Han Chinese culture, far from its image as a cultural heartland that was fostered largely by its position as Communist base during the war of resistance against Japan. The literate culture of the imperial elite may seem to have an even more flimsy base here than in more central areas. However, even here both ritual and music constantly reveal a firm grounding in that culture, both in context (such as funerals) and in music (like the ancient stories of blind bards, or the titles of shawm pieces).

Having outlined my general rural focus, this study considers musical life not just in the poor villages, but also in the small towns that are the local hubs of the surrounding countryside. While the realities of rural music-making are certainly at a considerable remove from central official propaganda, local ceremonial and cultural networks extend, if not as far as a whole county, over an area of a few districts or townships (*xiang*) – what Dong Xiaoping has called 'mid-level research' between the individual village and some broader geographical framework.[16] Having myself lurched from an overview of instrumental ensembles in the whole of China (1998) to a detailed ethnography of ritual music-making in one village (2004), my work on ceremonial music in one small area of a couple of districts within one county (2007) seems quite a satisfactory subject to tackle. The present study of one larger sub-region can only give an overview, isolating a few cases. Note that I mainly discuss the southeastern counties of the Yulin region: while touching on other parts of Yulin, and of the Yan'an region, this is far from a survey of Shaanbei as a whole.

---

[15]   Recent ethnographies for north Chinese ritual, apart from the works of Chau, include Zhao Shiyu 2002, Tsao 2003, Qin and Bujard 2003, Jones 2004, Dubois 2005, Herrou 2005, Overmyer and Fan 2006–7, as well as articles in Guo 2000.

[16]   In Overmyer 2002: 347–57.

Sources

It has taken many years to complete this book, but it remains only a very partial impression, based on two brief field-trips (in 1999 and 2001) and background reading. I have continued to consult the Shaanxi provincial volumes of the *Zhongguo minzu minjian yinyue jicheng* [Anthology of folk music of the Chinese peoples, henceforth 'the *Anthology*'] – that most fundamental, if flawed, source for local traditions of Chinese music – as well as a variety of local publications. Still in Chinese, Tian Yaonong (2005) has published his thesis on music in Shaanbei, based partly on our joint fieldwork in 2001 – as is a major article from Zhang Zhentao (2002a). These two sources often contain more detail than my comments below, but we all reflect on the material in different ways. Tsao 2003, besides a version of Zhang's article, contains useful articles by Qiao Jianzhong and Xiao Mei. The 2006 CHIME international conference on Chinese music, held in Shaanbei, prompted a Chinese website, and a collection of articles is expected.[17] As to social material, although my work in Shaanbei has been rather wide-ranging, the county gazetteers (*xianzhi*) published since the 1980s (and their predecessors in imperial and republican periods) are a potentially useful source for such studies. But nothing can compare with talking to local inhabitants.

One famous village, Yangjiagou, in the hills east of Mizhi county-town, has been the object of study for a steady stream of Chinese and foreign scholars.[18] It is not necessarily typical, in that it was home to a dominant local landlord clan in the Republican period, and has been visited by sociologists since the 1930s; since Chairman Mao stayed there in 1947 it has become a minor revolutionary pilgrimage site. Sociologists with new agendas have made thorough restudies since the 1990s, and recently a Japanese team has published a book on its architecture, soundscape, and society. Today villagers have become all too accustomed to outsiders. However, the revolutionary connection has not protected it from poverty. Though only 18 kilometres from the main road, it was a difficult journey until 1999. The village gained electricity only in the early 1980s, and its first telephone only in 2000. Though Yangjiagou's musical traditions have been declining since the early

---

[17]   See http://www.anthromusic.com (all websites cited as of 01/01/2009) under Yuannei luntan, then click 06 nian 7yue, duozhong shiye xiade huangtu gaoyuan yinyue wenhua guoji yantaohui. For the *Anthology*, see Jones 2003, and on 'ritual music' therein, pp. 318–21; Shaanbei vols. are cited below under 'Abbreviations' at the head of the Bibliography. Tian's work gives useful detail on some social aspects, even if some might dispute its theoretical conclusions and musical analysis. Among many useful, if somewhat sanitized, Chinese websites on Shaanbei are http://www.dashanbei.com (under headings such as wenhua and minsu), and for music, http://www.sbctyyw.com and http://www.snwh. gov.cn/feiwuzhi, under Yulin and Yan'an. For a Japanese project on Shaanbei culture, see http://www.crec.org.cn/crec/index_jp.html.

[18]   See e.g. Rawski 1986, Esherick 1998, Guo 2000, Fukao, Iguchi, and Kurishara 2007 (below I cite this Chinese translation of the original 2000 Japanese edition), Iguchi 2005.

1930s, it has not lost its traditions. My modest contribution to Yangjiagou studies below is to attempt to put the lives of its bard and its shawm-band musicians since the 1930s in the wider Shaanbei context.

As to Western sources on Shaanbei, since Holm's major 1991 study of the political uses of song and dance there in the 1940s, I have been much inspired by Adam Yuet Chau's work on 'doing religion' in the Black Dragon temple, but little else has been published. More generally, apart from sources on ritual mentioned above, Western studies of local Chinese society constitute important background, including first-hand accounts of the early days of the revolution in north China, as well as more recent studies bringing the story into the reform period.[19]

---

[19] E.g. Hinton 1966, 1983, Myrdal 1967, 1973, Belden 1973, Crook 1959, 1979; Friedman, Pickowicz, and Selden 1991 (and Hinton's 2006 rejoinder; for religion and popular culture, see 183–212), Chan, Madsen, and Unger 1992, Huang 1989, Jing 1996, Seybolt 1996, Gao Mobo 1999, Liu Xin 2000.

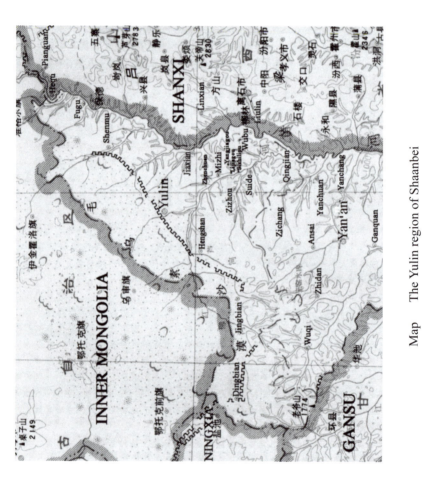

Map   The Yulin region of Shaanbei

PART ONE

Introduction

Illustration 1   A corner of Yangjiagou village from hills above, 2001

Chapter 1

Shaanbei society and its musics

'I simply fail to understand how people so close to Yan'an could remain completely untouched by the spirit of Yan'an.'

Xia Yan, commenting on the film Yellow Earth.[1]

This book depicts the life of music in the rural society of Shaanbei, the north of Shaanxi province in northwest China, through the changing times of the twentieth century. In this introductory chapter I first give a general outline of the region, and then sketch some forms of musical activity there, before focusing on two genres (bards and shawm bands) in Parts Two and Three.

1.1 Setting the scene

Early spring 1939, in Shaanbei after the beginnings of the socialist revolution and during the war of resistance against the Japanese. Cultural workers of the Communist Eighth Route Army set out through the countryside, still controlled by the rival Nationalist government, to seek Shaanbei folksongs to adapt for the revolution. 'In this ancient land the melodies of *xintianyou* songs hover in the air throughout the year.'

Hearing only the sound of the wind, we see a small figure of a man wearing an army uniform trekking alone, dwarfed by the barren mountainous landscape. He is Gu Qing, an idealistic Eighth Route Army cultural cadre. As he comes nearer, he hears a song in the distance:

Life is hard for seasonal workers
They're hired in the 1st moon, dismissed in the 10th moon.

Gu Qing listens and takes out his pen, but the sound evaporates just as he begins to write down the song in his notebook. Next we see a wedding procession crossing the scarred landscape, the bride carried in a sedan, a band of *chuishou* shawm-and-percussion musicians leading the way. On arrival at the village wedding, Gu Qing is invited to the feast. As he shares the paltry dishes with the peasants, a ragged peasant sings high-pitched wedding songs. If the peasants are nonplussed at the presence of a government representative, Gu Qing too is evidently taken aback at his surroundings.

---

[1]   Barmé and Minford 1986: 267. For the film, see §1.4 below.

These are the opening scenes of Chen Kaige's ground-breaking 1984 film *Yellow Earth*,[2] which I will introduce further below. For the fieldworker, it strikes a simple but deep chord: the obstacles one meets in finding and 'capturing' music – 'plucking the winds', as the Chinese term for fieldwork translates literally[3] – and the difficulties of 'becoming one with the masses', as the Communist cliché goes.

Still on a simple level, the film shows the vast problems faced by the Communists in their goal of reforming a poor feudal society. Poverty seems insuperable, accompanying 'backward' traditions such as the sale of brides and processions to pray for rain. The citation at the head of this chapter shows how Communist ideologues were affronted by the notion that the peasantry could be so resistant to change during what was supposedly a time of exciting revolutionary transformation. Sure, Chen Kaige's film was a fictionalized imagination of 1930s' Shaanbei, but his artistic licence contained a basic truth.

I first visited Shaanbei in 1999, with few romantic illusions of following in the footsteps of *Yellow Earth* fieldworker Gu Qing. My forays in other regions of rural China had shown that tradition was still strong there after the collapse of the commune system in the 1980s. I soon came across an itinerant bard performing a 'story for well-being', inviting the gods into a peasant household to bring the family relief from misfortune (see Illustration 2 below and ⊙**C4**):

> *On a dark night in a small village near the Black Dragon Temple, a bard performs a story for well-being. These bards are usually blind, though since the 1980s some sighted men have been encroaching on their 'food-bowl', like tonight's performer. As a bard arrives in a village, a family beset by misfortune, with a handicapped son or ailing livestock, may request him to set up his altar and invite the gods to bless the family as he performs a long historical drama of romance and suspense. He punctuates the story with the rhythmic click of clappers tied to his leg, strumming the* sanxian *lute to the rustle of slim strips of wood tied to his wrist. In return the family gives him a place for the night on the* kang *brick bed of their cave-dwelling, a couple of bowls of noodles and a few* kuai *in cash. Bards have continued to earn their living by walking from village to village to sing stories, tell fortunes, cure illness, and serve as godfathers by 'hanging the locket' to protect children from misfortune. TV may be replacing their stories as entertainment, but chronic hardships and persistent belief in divine efficacy still demand that families invite a bard into their home to perform.*

These bards are the subject of Part Two.

Another common occasion for music is at funerals, where again there is little trace of modern ideology; the officially-prescribed cremation with its secular 'memorial meeting' has never been observed outside the cities, earth burial being

---

[2]   Some of the above is adapted from Tuohy 1999: 43. The opening paragraph is adapted from the opening subtitles of the film.

[3]   Hence the title of my book Jones 2004.

universal. At a funeral I attend in a hill village, a *chuishou* shawm band leads the coffin and the wailing mourners on the procession to the grave; a geomancer performs his magic and later exorcizes the house. *Chuishou* no longer smoke opium or beg, but in some parts of Shaanbei they are still more or less outcasts. They are the subject of Part Three.

All this seems to echo Chen Kaige's picture of a backward area still handling chronic problems in age-old fashions, irrespective of Communist dictates. Perhaps this was fair enough, since the commune system had long since been dismantled: anyone with any experience of the reforms since the 1980s might expect Communist culture to be taking a back seat. But changes were indeed to be found emanating from the towns, along the main transport arteries – changes now more market-led than politically dictated. The new rampant capitalism in the shape of media-broadcast pop culture eventually inspired a development in the shawm bands – the 'big band' sound (jacket photograph, ⊙**D3**):

> *At another funeral in a poor village perched above a landscape of barren terraced mountains, grizzled Chang Wenzhou (most senior and illustrious* chuishou *in the area, from a famous lineage going back at least eight generations) leads his big band in a medley of brash pop hits, young sax and trumpet players in shades swaying around funkily, drummer proudly beating the hell out a drum-kit.*

This change did not reach Shaanbei until 1995, but now looks likely to take root more efficiently than the 'revolutionary' culture of Maoism ever did.

1.2 Shaanbei and its sub-regions

Shaanxi province (classically known as Qin after the ancient kingdom there), along with parts of Gansu and Ningxia, forms the northwest frontier of the Han-Chinese-dominated territory of the People's Republic. Further to the west and north lie the minority-dominated areas of Gansu, Qinghai, Xinjiang, and Inner Mongolia. Shaanxi consists of three regions: the central area Guanzhong spreading out from the capital Xi'an; the southern area Shaannan; and the northern area Shaanbei, subject of this book. These three regions are very different physically and culturally. Shaanbei as a whole has less in common with the central Shaanxi plain of Guanzhong to the south than with areas to the east (Shanxi province, east of the Yellow River, from where many Shaanbei people migrated) and west (eastern Gansu and Ningxia).

Shaanbei has such a reputation as a kind of heartland of Chinese culture that it is worth reminding ourselves that it is something of a frontier backwater – unlike central Shaanxi and Shanxi, which are indeed ancient cultural centres. Its reputation derives largely from its position as base of the Communist resistance after 1936. Physically, the whole area is characterized by its dusty yellow soil, known as loess, and the terraces carved into the rolling hillsides by generations of peasants to create what arable land they can.

Shaanbei consists of two regions, or prefectures: Yan'an and Yulin. The Yan'an region, the southern part of Shaanbei, centred on Yan'an municipality, contains 13 counties. Before the 1935 arrival of the Communists, the area was severely prone to banditry. Its northern area, bordering on the Yulin region, including counties like Zichang, Ansai, and Zhidan, has much in common with the area discussed in this book.

Following Chinese scholars, I focus on the northern half of Shaanbei: the 12 counties of the Yulin region (see Map, and Table 1), whose official population in 1998 was over 3.1 million. This region, in turn, may be divided into three areas. My main base is the area southeast of Yulin municipality; while the survey includes material from the counties of Jiaxian, Wubu, Hengshan, Zizhou, and Qingjian, I mainly discuss Mizhi and Suide counties – already a large and diverse field.

Table 1   Counties of the Yulin region

County	area (km²)	townships	villages	population
Yulin (municipality)	7053	32	488	398,000
Mizhi	1212	15	396	207,000
Suide	1878	23	661	335,000
Jiaxian	2144	24	653	236,000
Wubu	428	10	221	76,000
Zizhou	2043	22	550	289,000
Qingjian	1881	18	639	208,000
Hengshan	4084	21	357	301,000
Fugu	3212	23	362	204,000
Shenmu	7635	22	978	346,000
Jingbian	5088	26	206	259,000
Dingbian	6920	30	333	283,000

Source: Shaanxi 1999, figures applying to 'administrative villages' (larger than 'natural villages') in 1995.

Also part of the Yulin region, still further northeast, in largely desert land leading to Inner Mongolia, the counties of Shenmu and Fugu are even more sparsely populated; musically too this area is quite distinct. Thirdly, the western part of the Yulin region (known as Sanbian, 'the three borders') includes the counties of Jingbian, Dingbian, and Hengshan, with closer cultural links with Ningxia province and the eastern protuberance of Gansu. This extensive sub-region, also largely consisting of desert lands, has also remained relatively isolated from development, and its music is even less known.

But everywhere, considerable differences persist between areas on the narrow river plains or on the main transport arteries, and the more remote villages deep in the mountains – not to suggest that the latter have been isolated from the revolution. Taking a look at Table 1, even one single county contains several hundred villages, all with their own ritual and musical traditions – their singers, spirit mediums, temples, and annual and occasional ceremonies. Far from the commodified repertory of modern urban professional arrangements of traditional music that confront the newcomer to Chinese music, the historical depth of Chinese culture is revealed in such local traditions.

Further relevant statistics: a regional government agency estimated that there were nearly 20,000 temples in the Yulin region in the early 1960s, and well over 10,000 temples by the mid-1990s – both, I believe, referring to temples where worship periodically took place.[4] In Shaanbei, temples are often single-room buildings on a hilltop, unstaffed except when a ritual is to be held. But temple fairs, held over two or more days several times annually to honour a local deity, are a common occasion for various types of expressive culture in China.

The population of mountainous Shaanbei is more scattered than that of areas on the plains of north China. It is sparsely populated by any standards, although Suide and Mizhi counties have a higher population density. Suide and Mizhi have poor districts, but may not seem too poor on one's initial journey along the busy main road running south from Yulin by the Wuding river. Of the main centres, as one travels south, Zhenchuan township, locally known as 'little Hong Kong', is bustling, perhaps more so than Mizhi county-town; Suide county-town is larger, modern, and city-like. Just west of Suide, away from the main transport artery, Zizhou county-town is noticeably less developed, and to the east, bordering the Yellow River, the county-towns of Jiaxian and Wubu are disturbingly poor and grim. For peasants in the remote villages in the ravines that rise either side of the few main roads, urban life may be more accessible than it was during the Maoist period, but it is still another world.

Since the terrain is mountainous and arable land scarce, houses are built into the hillside, making arched cave-dwellings, usually comprising three caves in a row in front of a large courtyard, facing south; unlike the more dense villages of the north China plain, these dwellings are quite spread out, dotted around the landscape. The rear of the cave-dwelling is occupied by a *kang* brick-bed, next to which is the stove for cooking, which also heats the *kang* in winter. As to diet, staples are noodles and steamed buns; fried vegetables and *doufu* bean-curd are accompanied by pickles, and meat is rarely affordable. Away from the main roads along the river, and those connecting the county-towns, transport to the villages remains primitive and none too safe – though accidents along the busy fast main roads are no less common.

---

[4]   Cited in Chau 2006: 47, 49. For some major temples, see Chau 2006: 49, Zhang Junyi 1993: 161–7.

Since the 1980s, daily buses to the towns have enabled some young villagers to seek work there, depleting the countryside of its labour force.[5]

1.3 Shaanbei in the twentieth century

Even after the overthrow of the imperial system in 1911, Shaanbei remained desperately poor, transport backward, infrastructure undeveloped, its population largely illiterate, and modern ideas slow to penetrate. Droughts led to frequent famines, most devastatingly in 1928–33; musicians were among those who migrated within Shaanbei to less disaster-struck parts in the hope of surviving.

Within the Yulin region, the Suide–Mizhi area was exceptional: though still poor, it was relatively densely populated (for Shaanbei) with high landlordism, dominated by the Ma clan, and was a trading centre with links to the distant cities of Taiyuan and Tianjin.[6] In a region otherwise devoid of modern education, the new Yulin and Suide middle schools were a base for emerging Communism; in the 1920s Communist luminaries like Liu Zhidan and Gao Gang were pupils at the former, and Li Zizhou a teacher at the latter.

Shaanbei was to remain free of Japanese occupation after the formal outbreak of war in 1937; as seat of the Shaan-Gan-Ning Border Government (occupying parts of Shaanxi, Gansu, and Ningxia provinces), it made a base for the early experiments in Communism that were to inform the policies of the People's Republic after the national 'Liberation' of 1949. The moulding of this 'Yan'an way' is a popular area for research.[7] But the various sub-regions had separate fortunes. Whereas the Yan'an region was firmly controlled by the Communists, much of the Yulin region remained in Nationalist hands right until 1949 – through the United Front against the Japanese and the civil war following the Japanese defeat in 1945. Communist power was always stronger nearer the centre of Yan'an and weaker in villages clinging to the more distant mountain gulleys.

The fortunes of Shaanbei through the following Maoist commune period from the 1950s to the 1970s have been less studied; as with my previous work, the precarious maintenance of tradition through this murky period is one major theme of this book. Shaanbei gained no privileges by virtue of its status as cradle of the revolution, and society remained locked in poverty. As throughout China, state control revolving around mass political campaigns comprised what has been seen as a new system of state ritual (Guo 2000), meant to replace the old 'feudal and superstitious' customs, based on family and local community, that were the

---

[5]   For useful background on the physical setting, see Fukao, Iguchi, and Kurishara 2007.

[6]   Selden 1995: 8–11.

[7]   For political background, see e.g. Selden 1995 (first published in 1971), Apter and Saich 1994, Keating 1997. For politically-moulded expressive culture around Yan'an, see Holm 1991.

contexts of most music-making. But my study suggests that such attempts enjoyed limited success, with tradition embattled yet resilient.

If Shaanbei was cripplingly poor before the arrival of the Communists in 1936, urban Chinese outsiders were still shocked by its poverty in the 1960s, after two decades of supposed progress under the Communist system. Shi Tiesheng (b.1951), later to become a challenging novelist, was one of many 'educated youth' rusticated to a village near Yan'an in 1969, during the Cultural Revolution. His first impressions reveal the shock of urbanites arriving in a chronically impoverished area:[8]

> In Beijing we had been told that socialism was like paradise. But as soon as we arrived in the countryside, we saw beggars. Throughout school we had been told that only lazy people would become beggars. In the beginning we really thought that the beggars were lazy people. But one year later, as it became very clear that this was not the case, I began to have doubts about the truthfulness of the propaganda. I also began to doubt the superiority of the commune system. I just did not see any superiority in it; in fact, it made things worse.
>
> [...] The peasants were on the brink of starvation. They ate almost anything. They were always on the verge of starving to death. [...]Their clothes were full of patches. In the daytime they put on what they had, and at night they slept naked on a mat on the *kang* [brick-bed]. All the children ranging from the ages of 2 to 15 or 16 lay naked together under one cover. The parents shared one cover – that was all. Those considered better off financially might have a table at home. [...] Some peasants were so poor that they couldn't afford to send their children to school. [...] The teachers were poor too. Some schools didn't even have money to buy desks. Students had to write on the floor.
>
> Because there was no electricity there, practically everything had to be done by hand. [...] There were no mechanical devices whatsoever. [...] There was a small coal mine in the area. At that time, casualties and injuries were daily occurrences. Even so, people badly wanted the job, because if one member could get a job in the coal mine, the whole family could survive.

Such observations are remote both from the propaganda about how the region had been transformed under Mao[9] – and from the hagiography of the Communists' model bard Han Qixiang, whom we meet in Part Two. Both film-maker Chen Kaige and novelist Shi Tiesheng, for all their more dominant magical realist instincts (for Shi's novella inspired by a blind bard in the region, see §5.3 below), homed in on a basic issue: the difficulty of imposing modern social change on a poor traditional rural society.

Since the 1980s, the liberalization of the economy, along with exploitation of the region's coal, oil, and gas resources, has allowed some to escape from the worst poverty. A sporadic supply of electricity came belatedly to most villages by

---

[8]   Leung 1994: 153–64; the following citations are from pp.153–4 and 158–60.

[9]   Including Jan Myrdal's rosy accounts (1967, 1973).

the mid-1980s, markets revived, and young people could seek work in the towns. Chau has nicely observed the social stratification of contemporary Shaanbei, based on a largely peasant population with rural registration, along with a minority of officials, state employees, and entrepreneurs; very few manage to escape peasant life by finding migrant labour or a state job in the larger towns. Meanwhile, traditions such as weddings and funerals, temple fairs and rain processions, were once again observed openly in traditional style.

Since the 1990s, the central government's 'Opening up the West' (*Xibu da kaifa*) campaign (involving the whole of inland northwest and southwest China, way beyond Shaanxi province) has aimed to redress the serious imbalance with the spectacular economic development of the eastern coastal regions. Though much trumpeted in the national and regional media, the campaign looks unlikely to deliver long-term alleviation of serious rural poverty.

Moreover, the new culture of individual enterprise and urban migration led many to perceive a loss of community. Peasants feel insecure under the reforms and nostalgic for Maoism; despite their own clear material progress, they feel left behind in the chase for wealth in the wider society that TV now frustratingly parades for them.[10] The traditional rituals that had revived were among the few remaining embodiments of community values.

The point is not to belittle the achievements of the revolution, nor of the reform period since the dismantling of the commune system in the 1980s. Under Maoism, some of the most serious diseases were controlled, and official statistics for one county[11] claim an increase of life expectancy from 35 in 1949 to 60 by 1989. Though reports still reveal an alarming lack of basic facilities in schools, just as Shi Tiesheng reported in the 1960s, literacy has improved, both under Maoism and since: whereas only a tiny minority attended school before the revolution, now most children, even girls, attend for a few years. By around 2000 considerable economic progress was visible in the main towns along the commercial arteries, but was still hard to credit in the thousands of remote villages. Indeed, superficial economic improvements may mask a regression, with many rural dwellers deprived of the basic access to healthcare and education they had enjoyed under Maoism.[12]

The point, rather, is that whatever the detailed ups and downs in social conditions in Shaanbei since the 1930s, they always lag far behind the cities, as in much of rural China: they were a shock to urban dwellers in the 1930s, in the

---

[10]   Among several well observed instances of this common point, see Chan, Madsen, and Unger 1992: 293–5; Liu Xin 2000: 12–16. For a fine list of the new problems, see Hinton 2006: 192–3. For social stratification, see Chau 2006: 26–43, and 2006b: 162–4; for Shaanbei history, Chau 2006: 20–25, and for the modern history of religion there, 45–8. For a vignette on youth culture in Shaanbei, see Chau 2006b. Liu Xin 2000 is an important study of the secular rural mindset, for a village just south of Shaanbei.

[11]   Mizhi 1993: 630, though such figures are unlikely to be rigorous.

[12]   For a salient defence of Maoist welfare efforts and a critique of the reforms, for a south Chinese village, see Gao 1999, esp. chs. 5–7.

1960s, and remain so today. Shaanbei peasants still describe themselves tellingly as 'people who endure suffering' (*shoukuren*) – a victim-like autonym, or the social awareness that might prompt revolutionary change? And material conditions, like the concern for the survival of children and the need for rainfall and good harvests, are among the main driving forces for ritual and musical events.

1.4 The film *Yellow Earth*

The official Communist version of the Yan'an period, which had already been challenged by Western sinologists, was undermined, with more poetic fantasy, by Chen Kaige's 1984 film *Yellow Earth* (*Huang tudi*).[13] In the film, an idealistic young cultural cadre treks through a barren mountainous landscape to collect folk-songs to use to arouse the peasants to fight for the revolution and their own emancipation. But he encounters their deep cultural conservatism. The film was the first big international success of the brilliant new wave of Chinese directors – though in China it was little known by ordinary people, and conservative critics were unable to accept its picture of continuing poverty and backwardness at the heart of the revolution.

Zhao Jiping, composer and music consultant for the film, spent time with director Chen Kaige's team in Yan'an and nearby Ansai county in January 1984. In Ansai they met the folk-singer He Yutang (b.1949), who impressed them deeply; director Chen Kaige described him as a 'poor and crazy folk genius'.[14] He Yutang sang the unaccompanied folk-songs in the opening wedding scene.

He Yutang's career illustrates an uneasy interplay between folk and state. Though he seems to have had some official connections at least by the end of the Cultural Revolution, spending time in the county opera troupe, until at least the early 1980s his style was largely unaffected by conservatory graces, and his songs in the film have a searing authenticity. After the filming, he spent a few months teaching at the Xi'an Conservatory in 1984, returning home to Ansai the following New Year. He sang for the 1986 TV documentary 'Yellow River' (*Huanghe*), and later that year won a prize in a national contest for music and dance. The *Guangming News* even held a solo concert for him, uniquely without any accompaniment. He went on to sing for over 30 Chinese films and TV programmes. He recorded a cassette just after undergoing a serious operation in 1990, but it is a kitsch affair with soupy accompaniment. His photo on the cassette, wearing a smart Western suit and tie, contrasts nicely with his traditional peasant image in the film and other publicity material. He also compiled a four-volume mimeograph of local songs. But by 2001 I heard that he was still making a meagre living as a cadre in the Hall of Culture of Ansai county.

---

[13]   The film has been the object of much appraisal in China and the West, e.g. Barmé and Minford 1986: 251–69, McDougall 1991, Yau 1991, Chow 1995; for comments on its music, see Zhao Jiping 1985, Tuohy 1999, Baronovich 2003: 21–3.

[14]   McDougall 1991: 31; see also Yu Peng 1996; He and Wang nd.

Apart from He Yutang, other singers are heard in the film, including the characters of the heroine Cui Qiao's father and young brother. The film also shows a large *yaogu* percussion ensemble, of the type for which Ansai county is renowned, again part of the Communist Party's image of Shaanbei; and a *chuishou* shawm band accompany a wedding procession – I could not find out who this band was, but it looks and sounds quite authentic. The film ends with a rain ceremony, which though romanticized, bears some resemblance to such rituals still performed in Shaanbei today (§1.6 below).

By contrast with such traditional sounds, romantic studio music is also used as a soundtrack, notably the romantic theme-tune 'Daughter's Song', composed by Zhao Jiping, With a full syrupy orchestral accompaniment, it is a most effective device, highlighting the young girl's longings to escape from the sufferings of peasant life.[15]

1.5 Shaanbei musics in change

The following sections give the skimpiest of outlines of performing genres in Shaanbei including folk-song, opera, and dance; contexts such as funerals and temple fairs; and practitioners like spirit mediums and beggars. Then in Parts Two and Three, two genres are discussed in greater detail: bards and shawm bands.

Apart from my limited fieldwork, the discussions below are largely based on Chinese sources. As *Yellow Earth* reminds us, Communist cultural cadres in Shaanbei were pioneers of folk music study from the 1930s. Their work, dominated by transcription rather than ethnography, was noble, but often led by politics. In Shaanbei, work concentrated on folk-song, *yangge* song-and-dance, and opera, all potentially mouldable for revolutionary purposes – as was the work of blind bard Han Qixiang, discussed in Part Two below.

Such early publications are often too prescriptive for our purposes. As throughout China, more systematic study on all aspects of the folk music heritage had to wait until after the end of the Cultural Revolution. In Suide county, an energetic local cultural cadre was Huo Xianggui (1938–2005), who had graduated in 1959 from the 'music special study class' of the Shaanxi Teachers' College in the provincial capital Xi'an. Even before the end of the Cultural Revolution, on 2nd April 1974, a meeting of music cadres in the whole region was held in Yulin by the Regional 'Hall of Arts for the Masses', in defiance of adherents of the Gang of Four, whose leftist agenda had held a stranglehold over the entire Cultural Revolution. At this meeting, led by Shang Airen (then head of the regional Bureau of Culture), the endangered state of folk music was lamented. Huo Xianggui was then acting head of the regional Cultural Education Department.[16] Over the next two decades he

---

[15]   It is the first track on the Hugo CD *Lady Lan Hua-hua*, sung by Feng Jianxue. This typically kitsch CD features several singers, all accompanied by the Chinese Orchestra of the Shaanxi Song-and-Dance Troupe, based in the distant provincial capital Xi'an. Cf. n.20 below.

[16]   Wenjiaoju: see Huo 1997b.

was to document folk-song, narrative-singing, opera, and instrumental music in Shaanbei – we will note his work below.

Our task in documenting local genres is made somewhat easier by the work of such local scholars, who, largely under the auspices of the huge national *Anthology* project since 1979, have done basic fieldwork on traditional genres in the area. The original local mimeographs, if you can find them locally, are far more detailed than the eventual edited provincial publications, and their authors are worth consulting. Of course, genres, here as elsewhere in China, overlap: folk-song, narrative-singing, and opera are a continuum, and instrumental and vocal music often accompany dance.

Folk-song[17]

Though the Communist myth of Shaanbei has ingeniously, or ingenuously, portrayed it as an archetypical paradise of industrious peasants, a rose-tinted homeland for both traditional and revolutionary folk-song, it is no simple task today to get a handle on the life of singing in society there. In view of the continuing vitality of social folk-song culture in Gansu and Qinghai provinces to the west,[18] the lack of local folk-song festivals in Shaanbei (either now or before Communism) is curious. And if the romantic depiction in the film *Yellow Earth* of a shepherd declaiming a song from a mountainside was once true to life, it appears to be rare now. Also largely absent from social life today are 'revolutionary songs';[19] even during the commune period, renditions were largely limited to (albeit frequent) political meetings. Change is hard to assess – if only one could eavesdrop on daily life in 1934, 1964, and 1994, for instance – but recollections of senior villagers suggest that singing is heard less often today than earlier in the twentieth century.

Since the 1990s, record shops, both locally and throughout China, have sold highly mediated CDs of 'Shaanbei folk-songs', including some revolutionary songs.[20] Shaanbei folk-song now has a rich virtual life in many Chinese websites. Indeed, peasants seem to be aware of the label 'Shaanbei folk songs' when talking

---

[17] AFS 37–621; Yang Cui 1995; Bai 2006. For some texts, including several ritual songs, see Zhang Junyi 2000. For comments on a selection of songs, see Qiao Jianzhong 2002: 1–30, with some exx. on the accompanying CD. Note also songs on the CD Fukao and Iguchi 1992, and on the CD with Fukao, Iguchi, and Kurishara 2007, as well as on the CDs Qiao Jianzhong 1996 – still the most useful overview on disc of Han Chinese folk-singing. A fine introduction to Chinese folk-song is Schimmelpenninck 1997: 1–24.

[18] While we await work from Antoinet Schimmelpenninck and Frank Kouwenhoven, see e.g. Yang Mu 1994a.

[19] As Yang Mu (1994b) observed; cf. Jones 2003: 306–9. For 'revolutionary songs', see Wong 1984.

[20] Among a plethora of such recordings, still more distant from the soil than the CD cited in n.15 above is a 1996 CD from China Record Company, *Shandandan kaihua hong yanyan* [Eng. title Folksongs collection of northern Shaanxi], featuring the female singer

to outsiders, even if their own terms for the songs they sing in daily contexts are more nuanced. The gulf between such mediated, commodified versions, with their polished singing style and smoochy or disco accompaniment, and singing in social life, sung in a rougher voice and usually without accompaniment, is easily heard.

'Famous singers' highlighted by Chinese scholars often come from strong family and village traditions, but tend to tailor their style to the demands of the state troupes to which they graduated.[21] However close such singers remained to the folk style, or however far they departed from it, their stage performances accompanied by new-style 'folk ensembles' have remained the tip of the iceberg. All music is worthy of study, but it is a less mediated style that dominates singing in daily life in the poor countryside of Shaanbei.

Thus under the broad umbrella of 'folk-song' are singers performing for drinking parties, the consecration of a new cave-dwelling, calendrical and life-cycle ceremonies, rain processions, and shamanistic exorcisms. Beggars doing the rounds of weddings and funerals now appear to be among the most common exponents of song (☉**D2, D4**).

Otherwise the nearest I got to hearing singing in context was when I visited a villager at his cave-dwelling during a lunchtime drinking session with a group of his male friends (☉**C2**). The singers were perhaps mediocre even without the prodigious amounts of *baijiu* liquor they were knocking back; with empty bottles strewn about the floor, one of the singers passed out on the *kang* brick-bed. Even if I could stomach the liquor, I realized how hard it would be for me to participate meaningfully in their world. Where opportunities to hear impromptu singing are few, asking singers to perform their repertory is sometimes a necessary expedient. I have attempted to get a few song sessions going, but have never overcome the artificiality of the occasion.[22]

Scholars of Shaanbei song adopt the pan-Chinese classification of *haozi* work songs, *shan'ge* mountain songs, and *xiaodiao* little melodies, but such boundaries,

---

Yun Enfeng (b.1940), born in Xi'an, and not apparently related to Shaanbei, having entered professional troupes at the age of 11. Cf. Fukao, Iguchi, and Kurishara 2007: 20.

[21]   AFS 1465–6 gives several brief biographies. Li Youyuan (1903–55), whose version of the anthem 'The East is Red' was so influential; his nephew Li Zengzheng (1917–84) was a locally renowned *yangge* leader. Zhang Tian'en (1910–69), from Wubu county, taught in the Music department of Northwest Arts Academy in 1951. Li Zhiwen (b.1931; see also Yang Cui 1995: 28–33, 37–8) pursued a career as 'soloist' for the folk-song choir of the Central Song-and-Dance Troupe in Beijing, the Yan'an Song-and-Dance Troupe, and the Yulin Arts-Work Troupe; he provided songs for many films. Ma Ziqing (b.1935), the only female singer listed, was selected for the Central Song-and-Dance Troupe in 1953; from 1958 she was in troupes in Yan'an and Xi'an; she has also featured on many records and films, including the CD *Lady Lan Hua-hua* (n.15 above) and the Qiao 1996 set. He Yutang was introduced above; for Wang Xiangrong, perhaps the biggest folk-song star in Shaanbei today, see §12.3 below.

[22]   Most Chinese song-collecting, done by this means, compares unfavourably with Schimmelpenninck's (1997) work on a largely defunct tradition in Jiangsu.

often porous, await detailed exegesis. Further, it is unclear how many of the songs collected are still sung in daily life. For instance, work songs were perhaps rare (here as in most parts of China) by the 1960s, though several were 'salvaged' by fieldworkers, including those performed by boatmen and coal-workers, and for earth-pounding.

Most renowned of Shaanbei folk-songs are 'mountain songs' (*shan'ge*) or 'mountain pieces' (*shanqu*), including a genre called *xintianyou*.[23] Though associated with outdoor rendition, they are sung indoors too for drinking parties. Themes (ostensibly, at least, referring to earlier history) are often the tribulations of love (a lover marrying another, forced marriage, or separation), of hired labour (*langong*) and migration. Final cadences descending to *so*, and a framework of two leaps of a 4th (such as low *so* to *do* and *re* to *so*) are common in Shaanbei vocal genres.

Some so-called 'little melodies' (*xiaodiao*) are in a more strict metre, though they may be hard to distinguish from 'mountain songs'. They tend to be less dependent on contexts such as ceremonial activity. This category includes some songs long ago assimilated from other parts of China, notably southern Jiangsu in east-central China; and some that were immortalized as 'revolutionary songs', including 'The East is Red' (*Dongfang hong*) and '30-mile Inn' (*Sanshilipu*). Under several sub-headings are the popular 'leaving by the western pass' (*zou xikou*) songs,[24] liquor songs (*jiuqu*), and 'guessing fists' (*caiquan*) or 'swinging fists' (*huaquan*) songs, sung at banquets for weddings, longevity celebrations, and funerals – as well as less structured male drinking sessions.[25] The 'little melodies' heading may also include some accompanied genres considered as narrative-singing, such as *errentai* in northeastern Shaanbei (n.31 below) and the 'little pieces' of Yulin city (§12.2).

However we classify songs, we need practical surveys based on ethnographic observation, ideally with historical depth; even recordings are dominated by commodified arrangements rather than field recordings.

Opera[26]

Though state-funded opera troupes are perhaps most visible on the opera scene today, they are outnumbered by privately-run folk opera bands (*geti minjian*

---

[23] The term *shanqu*, said to be used in the northeastern area of Shenmu and Fugu, may be more common in north China generally. Apart from AFS, for a more extensive published collection from an *Anthology* collector, see Yang Cui 1995, with 415 *xintianyou* songs arranged by mode, without dates of collection.

[24] AFS 191–203. Note also Hequ 1956, with data from Shanxi just east across the Yellow River, exceptionally strong on context.

[25] AFS 570–1, 573–96; Jin 1986: 97–103. Liquor songs in Shenmu and Fugu are said to be particularly strict in form. For good descriptions of this context, see Chau 2006: 151–3; Chau 2006b: 169–70. See also Tian 2005: 143–4, 186.

[26] See AO, and the more detailed regional volume AO Yulin. See also Chau 2006: 53, 138–42.

xiban) – in 2001 in the 12 counties and municipalities of Yulin region there were only 14 state-supported opera troupes in all, whereas there were said to be around 15 folk troupes in each county. Troupes are also invited from further afield, from further south in Shaanxi and from Shanxi just east. But today even the state troupes once again perform mainly for temple fairs, summer rain ceremonies, and other ceremonial occasions; performances in urban opera theatres are a very minor part of their activity.

Dilapidated old opera stages (typically before a temple) dot the landscape, if less impressively than in neighbouring Shanxi province; many stages were also rebuilt in the 1950s. Coarsely-scrawled graffiti backstage commemorate visits by troupes.[27] Most evocative is perhaps the 17th-century stage before the main temple in the White Cloud Mountain temple complex, where Mao Zedong himself enjoyed an opera in 1947 as Communist victory was nigh. However, with many small temples situated on remote hilltops, temporary opera stages are also commonly set up in the village for temple fairs.

Chinese sources document old-style troupes before Communism – in Shaanbei evidence before 1862 is sparse – but inevitably highlight the forming of state-funded troupes from the 1930s to the 1950s, during the Yan'an period and soon after Liberation, when they were named first 'arts-work troupes' (*wengongtuan*) and later 'county opera troupes' (*xian jutuan*).[28] Modernizing influences spread from the Communist base at Yan'an; typically troupes would perform not only fully-fledged opera but items such as *mihu* (a vocal genre originating from central Shaanxi), *yangge* song-and-dance, and the local *daoqing*.

Though the state troupes in Yulin, Hengshan, and Mizhi counties (as well as the Three Borders area to the west) mainly perform *Qinqiang* (the dominant genre of the distant Guanzhong plain around the provincial capital Xi'an), the most popular genre in the six southern counties of Yulin on which I focus, as well as in Shenmu and Fugu to the northeast, is the style from Shanxi province just east. Shanxi opera, now commonly known as *Jinju*, has been popular in Shaanbei since the late nineteenth century.[29] Opera companies – as yet still privately run – were formed for *Jinju* in Shaanbei after 1937 as Shanxi actors took refuge there.

'Little operas' (*xiaoxi*), often not fully staged and without costumes, are also popular, mainly *daoqing*, performed in the southern area around Qingjian,[30] and

---

[27]　For old stages, see AO 588–90, 591–2, 595–6, 602; AO Yulin 179–90.

[28]　For Shaanbei opera troupes, see AO Yulin 164–78; AO 532–4, 536–7, 541–2, 563, 570, 602–3.

[29]　AO 131–2, AO Yulin 58.

[30]　AO 104–5, 292–304. See also Zhou 1946: 66–73; Liang 1953; Holm 1991: 184–5. Regional forms of *daoqing* are common throughout north China; they are popular in Shanxi, whence the Shaanbei version may have derived. In Shaanbei a star of *daoqing* was Liu Hanzhu (1915–85), based in Hengshan (AO 764).

errentai, popular in the northeastern area of Shenmu and Fugu.[31] These too were adapted by the local state opera troupes, but rural activity appears to have remained more faithful to the old style. Puppet operas (*wanwanqiang*, also commonly known as 'little operas') were common until the 1960s but have been rare since.[32]

We got an impression of the current life of opera troupes from a chat in April 2001 with 40-year-old Li Wenyi, head of the official Jiaxian county *Jinju* troupe. Along with my Beijing colleagues Zhang Zhentao and Tian Yaonong, I had caught the bus from Mizhi, climbing its way up a winding but unusually well-repaired road east towards the Yellow River. Jiaxian county-town is perched on a hill above the river, which would make a romantic view but for the dilapidated tower-blocks and a startling sense of poverty. Though traders line the streets, and signs outside funeral shops advertise Daoist and Buddhist priests available for hire, the sullen greyness of the place still calls to mind the commune period.

The Jiaxian county *Jinju* troupe[33] was founded in Mutouyu village in winter 1940, soon performing modern politically-inspired items as well as traditional opera. In 1947 they accompanied Mao Zedong and Zhou Enlai on a month-long propaganda tour of Jiaxian villages; it was they who performed for Mao at the White Cloud Mountain temple fair.

The Jiaxian troupe now has over 60 members, giving over 400 performances a year, two a day. They are in competition with 15 privately-run folk opera troupes in Jiaxian county alone – and troupes from Shanxi across the river are also in demand. The county Hall of Culture has mounted a spirited attempt to protect the state troupe against such folk bands by issuing 'performance permits' for a hefty fee. Though the state gives retired performers a pension, the wages of the people still working (as well as costumes, props and so on) are all paid out of the troupe's actual income on the market. They seem to be doing all right: the best performers can make over 10,000 *yuan* a year, and by contrast with the decrepit troupe buildings in Suide, this troupe has just moved into a new building, with posh apartments, contrasting with the general squalor of the town.

The Jiaxian troupe takes work all over the southern Yulin region. Sometimes (mainly in the winter) opera troupes are invited for weddings and funerals, costing around 1,000 *yuan*. But the main context is temple fairs from the 1st to the 8th moons,

---

[31]   See e.g. AFS 421, 423–64; ANS 761–66, 959–60, exx. 766–958; AO 125–6, 388–92; Hu Jingfang 1954; Yu Huiyong 1957 (for another edition of which, cf. AO 659). For material on folk *errentai* groups in Hequ in Shanxi nearby, see Yang Hong 2005. Ironically, *errentai* gained a national reputation mainly through Ding Xicai (1920–89), who graduated to the distant Shanghai Conservatory: see Hu Jingfang 1954: 3–4; see also ANS 959 (which gives his death date as 1994), AFS 1465; for recordings, see Zhongguo 1994: 279–80.

[32]   Shadow puppetry has survived marginally in western Shaanbei, leading into eastern Gansu, where Frank Kouwenhoven tells me around 40 groups were active in the single county of Huanxian in 2007: see the DVD film CHIME 2008. Shadow puppetry is also performed east of Xi'an.

[33]   AO 536, also 132, 570; AO Yulin 169, 172–3.

mainly in the six southern counties of the Yulin region – without temple fairs, as Li said, they would be out of business. He reckoned they perform for over 30 temple fairs, large and small – most such contexts demand that they perform a series of items over three days. They also perform 'three or five times a year' for villages holding rain prayers, from the 5th to the 7th moons. Over the New Year period in Jiaxian county, groups of several villages often combine to hold the community *jiao* Offering ritual – for large-scale *jiao* an opera troupe is always invited. Li Wenyi had recently visited a temple fair to make a vow and a donation of 300 *yuan*, to guarantee the income of the troupe. He seemed to regard it as a kind of divine tip: 'Since we eat off the gods (*chi shenshen*), we should hand over a bit to them!'

But Li was not alone in being concerned for the future of traditional opera. The organizers and audiences are all over 50, so what future is there for opera? Supposing the authorities decide to campaign against feudal superstition again – an unlikely scenario, I thought, now the genie is out of the bottle, but he voiced the fear – then there will be no temple-fair operas, and hence no more opera troupes.

The majority of the troupe's work is playing traditional operas for the rural temple fairs, but while back at their urban base, performing for 'evening gatherings' (*wanhui*) for work-unit events or ticket-buying punters, they have to incorporate modern (not local) items including 'song-and-dance' and *xiangsheng* comic mimicry skits. The troupe is planning to start up a commercial song-and-dance hall (*gewuting*) and even a hotel, 'using commerce to support art', as Li says.

The following week, dropping in at the decrepit apartments of the *Jinju* troupe in Suide county-town, we got together with several distinguished retired performers for a poignant chat. The female performer Wang Yuqing (b. *c*1936) joined the troupe at the age of 7. Like the Jiaxian troupe, they are in competition with over 20 opera bands in Suide county alone, most privately run; and again, the troupe mainly performs for the gods, doing about 70 three-day 'sets' (*tai*) per year in temple fairs all over the area, each fair earning the troupe around 2,000 *yuan*.

The fortunes of rural opera under Maoism have been little studied. In general, Chinese sources hint at more activity for temple fairs even in the 1950s than institutional material might suggest. A 1963 provincial document announcing the banning of 55 'ghost operas' (with plots now deemed 'superstitious', mostly from the *Qinqiang* and *wanwanqiang* genres) admits: 'The last few years, there has been a certain increase among the people in towns and villages of superstitious activities like burning incense and worshipping the Buddha, even building temples and god statues. Some cadres and masses in villages in several areas are inviting opera troupes to perform "ghost operas" in order to receive the gods and fulfil vows.'[34]

The old Suide performers told us that the troupe was very lively in the 1950s and early 60s. 'There were temple fairs then too, but because we were an official state troupe, we had the mission to eliminate superstition, so we didn't perform for temple fairs. If we did, we only performed in the village itself, not before the temple. The troupe's wages were entirely provided by the state. Then they started

---

[34]   AO 899. Cf. material for Hunan, Jones 2003: 329–30.

forbidding old operas in 1964, so we started to perform new ones. From 1976 to 1979 the restoration was rapid – after that it declined rapidly too.'

Though opera in China is mostly performed for the gods, the content of the dramas is not always specifically liturgical; in some parts of south China, however, such 'ritual opera' is a lively scene.[35] In Shaanbei the main trace of 'ritual opera' is the *saisai* or *saixi*,[36] performed in the southern counties of the Yulin region for temple fairs and rain ceremonies until outlawed by the Communists in 1945. It used a small company of around a dozen, wearing masks of the regional deity Heihulingguan. It was recited, not sung, with shawm and percussion accompaniment. I have found no material suggesting any revival since the 1980s.

Our talks with members of the state troupes reminded us that opera in Shaanbei today, as in rural China generally, still revolves firmly around the ritual calendar: even an official source estimates that 70% of the income of state opera troupes in the whole Yulin region comes from temple fairs (⊙**A1**).[37]

Dance

Group dancing for communal festivities (known as *shehuo*, 'parish bands') was and is an intrinsic part of folk ceremonial in Shaanbei, but under Maoism it was again adapted and secularized by cultural cadres: dance was an influential aspect of the Communist campaign, in army units, schools, work units, factories, and so on. Though Chinese sources make the obligatory claim that 'the superstitious colouring' of such dances was abolished after Liberation, the *Anthology* contains some rather detached descriptions revealing persistent ritual connections.[38] The New Year period is the main occasion for communal celebration, and the main element in various song-and-dance items performed for the New Year's 'parish band' celebrations is *yangge*. Other related festive genres include mass drumming (*yaogu*, *naogu* etc.) and skittish small-scale forms such as 'three-talents blocks' (*sancai ban*), 'tyrant's whip' (*bawangbian*), 'boat on water' (*shuichuan*, ironic

---

[35] See the vast collection of material in the series Wang 1997–, including much on *nuoxi* exorcistic opera.

[36] AO 130, 632, 771–2 and AO Yulin 50, 61–2, 223, material derived largely from the last senior performer, Wang Jisheng (1921–65); Zhang Junyi 1993: 145–7. The *saisai* in Shaanbei appears to have been derived from that of neighbouring Shanxi, which has been more extensively studied: see e.g. Zhongguo 1990: 139–41; Johnson 1994; Qiao Jian 2002: 206–49. Cf. Hebei, e.g. Zhongguo 1993: 105–7, 399, 555; Overmyer and Fan 2006–7, Handan vol., pp.3–91. See also Dong and Arkush 1995: 65–72.

[37] AO Yulin 167. As Adam Chau reminds me, county governments still sometimes order the townships to hire the state troupes to perform in a secular context; but even these troupes now perform mainly for calendrical occasions.

[38] Apart from AD, note the pioneering study Holm 1991. For the parish, see Holm 1991: 157–8, and Zhao Shiyu 2002: 231–51.

Shaanbei term for the more common 'boat on dry land', *hanchuan*), and 'driving the donkey' (*pao lü*).[39]

Yangge, a festive and semi-dramatic group dance form with singing, is accompanied by percussion and often also by shawm music. It is common throughout north China, even in the towns; in Shaanxi, Shaanbei is perhaps the most celebrated area for *yangge*, but just to the south, Luochuan and Hancheng counties also have renowned forms.[40] Despite its pervasive reputation, *yangge* is largely performed at New Year, and its ritual base remains paramount.[41]

Still, like opera, *yangge* was taken up avidly by the Yan'an reformers in the 1940s, and it has long been used for parades for secular state festival days in the towns. From 1943 Communist ideologues in Yan'an further developed it into 'yangge operas', adopting elements from the vocal genres *mihu*, *daoqing*, and *Qinqiang*.[42] Today, amalgamation of old and new elements from pre-Communist, Maoist, and reform periods is likely, but again we need detailed case-studies of how *yangge* adapted under Maoism and in recent years.

One revelation of the ritual aspects of *yangge* is the 'turning the nine bends' (*zhuan jiuqu*) or 'formation of the nine bends of the Yellow River' (*Huanghe jiuqu zhen*). This cosmic representation through a maze of 361 lanterns is the climactic ritual of the New Year period.[43] It is sometimes led by Daoist priests, followed by all the 'parish band' performers and ordinary villagers. This ritual was largely a casualty under Maoism, but revived to some extent in the 1980s.

1.6 Contexts

I now outline some of the main contexts for musical performance in Shaanbei. By now it should go without saying that 'concerts' on stage are virtually unknown in rural China. Though some music-making may be considered 'secular' – such as the shop openings of shawm bands, or the work-unit parades of *yangge* song-and-dance troupes – it is ceremonial life that is the motor for most music-making: the common term is *banshi*, 'doing things', 'performing ceremonies', or what

---

[39]   AD 48–236, 549–66, 567–80, 777–92, 832–45. Note also Holm 1991: 287–315 and passim.

[40]   AD 48–138; AFS 482–92, 494–565; AO 122–5; AI vol.2, under the heading *guchui yue*, contains many shawm pieces for *yangge*. See also Holm 1991, esp. 141–213; Cecchinato 2002; Tian 2005: 126–36. For Luochuan and Hancheng, see AD 53–75; for the songs, see also AFS 482–569. For *yangge* groups in Beijing, see Graezer 2004, Hung 2005.

[41]   Apart from Holm (1991: 186–201), Chinese scholars (AD 48–53, 124–36) also admit frankly the ritual connections of yangge.

[42]   Holm 1991: 175–85 etc.

[43]   Holm 1994, and refs. in Holm 1991. See also AD 7, 50, 129–30; AFS 484–5, 499–503; Yuan, Li, and Shen 1999: 113–16; Jin 1986: 37–41; Zhang Junyi 1993: 184–90; and n.50 below.

Chau calls 'event production'.[44] Thus, with the revival of expressive culture to accompany that of popular religious practice in Shaanbei since the 1980s, the great majority of performance takes place for life-cycle and calendrical ceremonies.

Ceremonies marking the major occasions of the life-cycle are held by households. A *chuishou* shawm band, or a bard, are sometimes hired for the first-moon celebrations (*guo manyue*) for a baby,[45] as well as rituals for protecting children, including 'Crossing the Passes' (*guoguan*, §2.3 below, ☉**A3**), and longevity celebrations (*zuoshou*) for 60th, 70th, and 80th birthdays.

The most common events at which live music is heard are weddings and funerals. Known widely as 'red rituals' (*hongshi*), in Shaanbei weddings are often referred to as 'fetching the bride' (*qu xifu*) or 'leading the bride' (*yin xiuzi*).[46] Funerals, apart from the standard term 'white rituals' (*baishi*), are called 'old people's' (*laorende*) or 'burying an old person' (*mai laoren*).[47] *Chuishou* are among several types of specialist, including 'general managers' (*zongguan* or *zongling*), *lizhang* gift recorders, geomancers, and coffin-bearers – in this area since the 1950s few bands of 'ritual specialists' (in the narrower sense of groups reciting Buddhist or Daoist scriptures, either temple or lay) attend for funerals (see Preface, and §1.7). In Chapter 11 below, I describe the role of *chuishou* at funerals and a wedding I have observed. In addition, commemorative rituals are held after the burial: the 'seven sevens', the 100th day after the death, and first and third anniversaries, for some of which the use of *chuishou* has become optional.

Occasional rituals are also held, such as for the blessing of a family (§5.7 below), or to fulfil a vow. For the rituals of consecrating a new cave-dwelling (*helongkou*) and house-warming (*nuanyao*),[48] after the geomancer has fixed the auspicious day (*kan rizi*), guests come for a large breakfast including *gao* cake, with much toasting. The placing of the highest stone in the cave archway occurs at midday, when *chuishou* play, the *hao* trumpet is sounded, and firecrackers are let off. The master-mason throws candies and peanuts down for people to try and

---

[44]   Chau 2004, Chau 2006, ch.7; Jones 2007.

[45]   See Zhang Junyi 1993: 60–61, Cao 1999: 91–2.

[46]   Cf. Zhang Junyi 1993: 64–79; Tian 2005: 79–94; Fukao, Iguchi, and Kurishara 2007: 113–19. We need more data on the rituals and music of weddings in China both before and since Communism.

[47]   Cf. Zhang Junyi 1993: 80–92, Tian 2005: 95–106. For funerals and temple fairs in Shaanbei, note Chau 2004, Chau 2006, ch.7. For pre-Communist funerary practice in north China, see Naquin 1988; for Shaanbei and nearby western Shanxi, see Guo 1992: 198–217, with useful sections on geomancers, costumes, ritual equipment etc. For the Yan'an area, see Jin 1986: 113–18. For shawm bands in funeral music in Shanxi, see Jones 2007. For many case-studies on funeral practice from elsewhere in China, see the Wang 1997– series.

[48]   Cf. Zhang Junyi 1993: 30–31; Cao 1999: 87, 98; Zhang Junyi 2000: 122–3; Zhang Jianzhong 2000: 232–3 (for Yanchang county); Tian 2005: 138–40; Fukao, Iguchi, and Kurishara 2007: 58–71, 111–12. Contrast the nice but entirely secular account of cave-building in Myrdal 1973: 19–23.

catch, while the *chuishou* play to one side. Villager Zhihui described further: 'The foreman hangs a red cloth and throws the five grains (*wugu*) while shouting [singing], "Five grains for the host, five grains for the artisans, *helong zhengwei* facing directly the *ziwei* star, to the left throw gold, to the right throw silver".' *Chuishou* also play while the family is 'receiving guests' (*daike*, always signifying hosting a meal), with traditional 'rules' about the number and type of dishes served. Songs are sung while men drink liquor and play 'guessing fists' games.

Zhihui again: 'For house warming, you must Settle the Earth God (*antushen*). Usually the geomancer chooses the day, then you put the *changqing* streamers in a bowl of grain, the geomancer shakes his bell, burns paper, lights incense, and sprinkles liquor, the host kowtows to the earth spirit as the geomancer recites the scriptures. The host prepares three or four dishes, and friends bring liquor. Sometimes they also invite *chuishou* to play for 'receiving guests'. Everyone [meaning men, I believe] drinks, guesses fists, and sings liquor songs.'

As to calendrical ceremonies, most villages have temples that hold several temple fairs annually.[49] Some take place over two days, some for a week; three-day fairs are most common. The season lasts from the 3rd to the 9th moons. Most are quite small in scale, such as that of the Chenghuangmiao fair in Yuhe town, or the little Longwangmiao fair in Hezhuang village, but opera troupes, shawm bands, and bards are likely to be invited.

By far the largest temple fairs in the Yulin region are those of the Black Dragon temple (in Mizhi) and the White Cloud Mountain temple (in Jiaxian), which are major factors in the local economy. The Black Dragon temple, subject of Chau's thorough 2006 study, holds its main fair in the 6th moon, the White Cloud Mountain temple in the 4th moon, but both are a focus of ritual activity throughout the year. For the White Cloud Mountain, while we have material on the Daoists' ritual music (n.56 below), and I will sketch the activities of bards and *chuishou* there (§5.8 and §11.5), a still more wide-ranging ethnography is much needed.

A large-scale occasional ritual held in the Jiaxian area, mostly around the New Year period, is the Offering (*jiao*), sponsored by a group of many villages in a 'parish' clubbing together, rotating the host village over many years.[50] Another occasional ritual is the rain ceremony (*qiyu*). Rain is desperately needed in north China, and the modern state has not been able to protect the population from the vagaries of the elements. The film *Yellow Earth*, evoking the 1930s, ends with an imposing rain procession, with barefoot males stripped to the waist, adorned with head-dresses of willow leaves. Kneeling in the dust, they pray hoarsely to the Dragon Kings, deities presiding over rain. Of course this is a romantic view, whereas the reality today may seem more prosaic. Described diplomatically in

---

[49]   See Zhang Junyi 1993: 161–7; Chau 2006: 51–4. Cf. my notes on Shanxi temple fairs, Jones 2007: 71–84.

[50]   See Holm 1994: 814–20, Yuan, Li, and Shen 2001: 102–20. For an impressive 2004 *jiao*, including the 'turning the nine bends', see http://www.sbctyyw.com/html/shanbeiminsu/xinyangminsu/20070424/228.html.

the *Anthology* as a thing of the past, rain processions, after severe restrictions under Maoism, may not have openly revived much by the early 1980s when the *Anthology* work was done, but were again common in the 1990s throughout north China, if still less common than before the 1950s. Rain processions remain a lively context for expressive culture today, not only in Shaanbei but in other parts of Shaanxi, as well as Gansu, Ningxia, Shanxi, and Hebei.[51]

Rain processions in Shaanbei are commonly referred to as 'shouldering the god sedan' (*tai shenlou*) or 'shouldering the Dragon Kings' (*tai Longwang*). They mostly take place in the searing heat of the 6th moon. They are organized by a committee of senior male villagers, with all households contributing – only the women are not allowed to observe. The route is thought to be determined by the gods: in one village they had to stop because the gods were leading them over a cliff. Musically, male villagers sing (or 'shout', as they say) in solo and choral response, the 'rain master' playing gong, another villager playing drum, while shawm bands may play on arrival at ritual sites. Since many Dragon King temples are on remote hillsides, opera stages are often in the village; on return to the village an opera troupe is commonly invited to perform to thank the gods.

1.7 Performers

With Parts Two and Three devoted to bards and shawm bands, I now list some of the other main performers in Shaanbei, apart from the singers, opera troupes, and dancers mentioned above. Both in context and sound, these performers overlap: shawm bands maintain close contacts with members of opera troupes, and all take part in basic activities like temple fairs; folk-song is heard in the bards' repertory, in *yangge* melodies, and in instrumental versions played by shawm bands.

We unpacked the cluster of 'ritual specialists' in the Preface. In Shaanbei the main religious practitioners are geomancers and spirit mediums, working individually. Geomancers are locally called *pingshi* ('problem solvers'? 'masters

---

[51] For Shaanbei, note Xiao 2003, and excerpts from two rain rituals on the accompanying DVD. See also AFS 572, 606–8, with three rain songs from Dingbian, Jiaxian, and Fugu; Zhang Junyi 2000: 135–7; Zhang Zhentao 2002b: 191–3; Tian 2005: 107–15, 186–7. For Yangjiagou, see Iguchi 1998; Fukao, Iguchi, and Kurishara 2007: 34–8, 74–88; Guo 2000: 338–9. For elsewhere in north China, see Dong and Arkush 1995: 72–5, 77, 106–13; Yuan 2001; for Hebei, see Zhang Zhentao 2002c: 354–61; Overmyer and Fan 2006–7, Handan vol., pp.92–102, 124, 255–61; Baoding vol., pp.385–6; 513–14; 648, 663, 667–8, 681–3. For Shanxi, see Wen and Xue 1991: 399–400, Jones 2007: 72–3, 74; Wu Fan 2007: 129–75. Provincial vols. of the *Anthology* may give slim leads, e.g. impressive photos of the Lianhuashan 'water assembly' procession in Tongxin county of Ningxia (not far west of Shaanbei) in the Ningxia instrumental vol.

for well-being'?) or *yinyang*.[52] They are consulted for many major decisions in life, such as choosing auspicious dates for weddings and funerals, and suitable sites for moving the earth for dwellings in this world and the next, including checking the orientation of the grave with the aid of a *luopan* compass. They are male, and often have hereditary traditions going back several generations. Under Maoism they maintained activity more or less in secret. They have (usually hand-copied) manuals to advise the correct alignment with the elements, and containing the texts of incantations, which they chant *sotto voce* within a narrow pitch range while shaking a handbell. Though few might consider this as 'music', their activities at ritual events deserve our attention (⊙**B5, B6**).

Several kinds of healers whom we might call spirit mediums or shamans are active in Shaanbei,[53] though I have not yet managed to observe them in action. They often sing songs during their rituals, and some beat drums. In Shaanbei, the standard (and derogatory) Chinese terms *shenhan* (male) and *shenpo* (female) are less common than the local terms *matong*, *wushen*, *shenguan*, and *zouyin*, along with *tiaoshen* 'dancing the gods' and dialectal variants of the term *dietan* 'going into trance'; the term *sanshandao*, referring to their magic trident, is also used.[54]

> *One day in Yangjiagou we are chatting with a former village cadre, who also happens to be a spirit medium, while his wife prepares lunch for us, when in walks a young policeman from the township nearby, in search of a signature from our host for some bureaucratic trifle. I'm a bit alarmed, not so much as we're talking about some sensitive stuff here, but because my documents aren't scrupulously complete, as we reckoned we could probably economize on the full laborious rounds of local permits. Sure enough, the cop eyes me somewhat ferociously and goes, 'What's this wog doing here?' When our host explains that I'm from England, even before we have to launch into some spiel about collecting the fine local folk music heritage, blah-blah, international cultural exchange, whatever, he is open-mouthed. 'Do you like Manchester United?' he asks, spellbound. Relieved, I launch into my Beckham routine, we exchange cigarettes, and he leaves contented.*

---

[52]   For Shaanbei geomancers, see e.g. Guo 1992: 214–17; Chau 2006: 56–7; Chau 2006a: 170–72; Zhang Zhentao 2002a: 63–5, 75–6, 99–100. In Shaanbei, as in north Shanxi (Jones 2007: 5) and Inner Mongolia, the term *yinyang* is more commonly applied to lay Daoists.

[53]   Chau 2006: 54–6; Chau 2006a: 167–70; Kang 2002. Though Manchu shamans and mediums in Taiwan have been studied, Han Chinese mediums on the mainland are little known; see 'Shamanism, spirit mediums' on website http://web.missouri.edu/~clartp/bibliography_CPR.html; also http://website.leidenuniv.nl/~haarbjter/shamanism.htm. For Hebei, see e.g. Fan 2003, Dubois 2005: ch.4.

[54]   AD 497–506 has a fine description of a sanshandao ritual performed by a male medium in Hengshan county. The folk-song volumes (AFS 571, 596–606) contain 10 mediums' songs, some recalled by professional singer Wang Xiangrong (see §12.3). A few mediums' dances and songs have been adapted by the state troupes and performed for secular purposes at arts festivals. For such professional arrangements, see §12.3, and biography of Feng Chenjun (b.1934), AD 506.

As elsewhere in China, beggars (*jiaohuazi*) are a common repository of much folk music-making, doing the rounds of life-cycle ceremonies.[55] Though they of all performers should be concerned to move with the times, they also tend to preserve local styles.

In the Preface I noted the sparseness of the more 'classical' groups of ritual specialists in Shaanbei. The most celebrated are the Daoist priests of the White Cloud Mountain temple complex in Jiaxian county, now an isolated outpost of institutional Daoism in the region. Though lay Daoists seem rare, we did hear of several groups commonly known as 'fake priests' (*jia heshang*) operating in the vicinity, such as one based at Jinmingsi ('Jinming temple') village. Apart from their vocal liturgy and ritual percussion, both temple and lay groups also use *sheng-guan* melodic instrumental ensemble.[56]

> *We had a promising exploratory chat with a nice group of ritual specialists in a rather picturesque township in Jiaxian county. They hinted that they were in considerable demand for exorcistic rituals to pray to the gods for an end to the alarming number of unnatural deaths in the area.*
>
> *Checking in at the only hostel in town that anyone could think of, this warning didn't recede in our minds. We were led to an underground room adorned with a not-quite-hardcore American pin-up, and were soon offered '15-year old girls, as many as you want' by a salacious madame. Videos labelled with the classic euphemism 'Birth-control policy instruction' were on display behind the counter. We weren't offered a key to the room. The clientele gambling in the lobby looked distinctly seedy, and the hints of crime came all too easily to mind: as outsiders – we were surely not businessmen, but did they have such discrimination? – we might make tempting targets.*
>
> *So, in a fine display of fieldworkers' camaraderie, we looked at each other with a unanimous thought and set off for lunch as innocently as we could with all our bags, hopping on the next bus as soon as we were round the corner, leaving our 'fake priests' to take care of the spiritual needs of a community that appeared to need them badly.*

---

[55] For Anhui, see Li Mei 2001; and for Shanxi cf. Liu Hongqing 2004. Cf. §11.2 below.

[56] For such ritual specialists in Shaanbei, apart from the White Cloud temple (§1.6 above, Yuan, Li and Shen 1999, Zhang Zhentao 2002a: 144–62), see Liu Jie 1988: 10; Zhang Zhentao 2002a: 72–4, 150, 160–61; Tian 2005: 117–20, 145 n.18; and notes from the 'western route' in the 2006 CHIME fieldwork, in the website cited in p.xxvi n.17 above. For *sheng-guan* music across north China, see e.g. Jones 1998, chs.11 and 12; for Hebei, see also Jones 1999, 2004, and Zhang Zhentao 2002c.

* * *

So much for a fleeting overview of expressive culture in Shaanbei. I will describe my encounters with some Shaanbei musicians below. Part Two introduces solo itinerant blind bards, Part Three bands of shawm-and-percussion players – both types are mainly poor peasants paid to perform for ceremonial, outside the state institutional system. Part Four outlines traditional and official forms of music-making in the regional capital Yulin, acclimatizing us for a partial return to modernity.

Apart from observing music-making at the turn of the twenty-first century, I attempt to outline conditions under Maoism through the recollections of musicians, as I have begun to do in Hebei and Shanxi (Jones 2004, 2007). The more I do this, the more elusive is my picture of musical life under the commune system, but the more convinced I am that it is essential to our understanding of the 1980s' revival and Chinese cultural life today.

PART TWO

Turning a blind ear: bards of Shaanbei

Illustration 2   A story for well-being: Li Wenjin invokes the gods before the altar on the stove, beneficiary kneeling behind, Hongliutan 1999

Prelude

In Shaanbei, as in much of rural China, blind men often serve as protectors of children, acting as godfathers, telling fortunes, and healing, as well as singing stories for healing rituals. Such bards are discussed in Chinese musicology – and I can't find much discussion of them elsewhere – under the heading of 'narrative-singing', though this is only one aspect of their activities.

In China, narrative-singing[1] occupies a broad band in the middle of a continuum (outlined in §1.5 above) from folk-song to fully-staged opera. As ever, a few entertainment genres in the urban centres of Beijing and Tianjin, Suzhou and Shanghai, are far better known than the hundreds of genres (both entertainment and ceremonial) performed in villages and towns throughout China, now tentatively documented in the provincial volumes of the massive *Anthology*.[2]

Genres in Shaanbei subsumed by Chinese scholars under narrative-singing include the 'little pieces' of Yulin city (see §12.2) and the *dazuoqiang* (known as *errentai*, n.31 on p.17 above) of the desolate northeastern area of Fugu and Shenmu – both forms accompanied by instrumental ensemble. The genre known – not very well – to Chinese academics as *Shaanbei shuoshu* is largely a solo form, common throughout the villages of both the Yan'an and Yulin regions. One male blind bard sings stories while accompanying himself on a plucked lute and clappers; this aspect of his livelihood is subsidiary to healing and protecting children (see §2.3).

This story makes a sequel to a fine article on Han Qixiang, the Communist Party's model blind bard in Shaanbei during the Yan'an period (Hung 1993). My emphasis below on the maintenance of tradition contrasts with Chinese scholars' hagiographic accounts of Han Qixiang's work in popularizing new political stories. Whereas Han Qixiang appears to have been a model 'folk artist' propounding Party policies with conviction, most bards in Shaanbei have continued to eke out a living from their traditional exorcistic 'stories for well-being', both under Maoism and since the reforms.

---

[1]   Also known in English as story-telling or balladry, and in Chinese as *quyi*, *shuochang*, or *shuoshu* – the latter ('story-telling') is the common term in Shaanbei.

[2]   See the relevant articles in the 'China' sections of Grove 2000, Garland 2002, and their bibliographies. The CDs Qiao and Ruan 1998 make a succinct national overview. Relevant volumes of the *Anthology*, for each of the 30 provinces, are *Zhongguo quyi yinyue jicheng* [Anthology of narrative-singing music of the Chinese peoples] and, where available, *Zhongguo quyi zhi* [Monograph on Chinese narrative-singing]; see Jones 2003, esp. 326–30.

Though in decline since the 1960s, the bards appear to have adapted rather little in context or sound. Under the commune system, some spent brief periods being taught new stories in the county-town 'propaganda teams', but this hardly affected their repertory or contexts. Scholars, both in the West and in China, tend to be interested in the new, and in the political, which have remained marginal to local performers and their audiences. As with many other genres in rural China, the ability of such performers to adapt to modernity (whether Communist or capitalist) is as limited as the economic conditions of the villages where they earn their living. Still, the popularity of the genre has been threatened firstly by Communism and then by the media of TV and pop music.

I am painfully aware of the limitations of this study, both since performance contexts of these itinerant bards remain quite elusive to the outsider, and since the genre depends on verbal dexterity which I cannot hope to follow. Until someone manages to follow a bard around for a year, I offer this survey as a mere introduction.[3] Arranged diachronically, it is based on quite a small sample of bards, with material mainly from Mizhi, Suide, and Zizhou counties. A 1941 survey claimed that Suide county had 90 bards.[4] In Zizhou county in the 1950s, the state-run group (only occasionally assembled) was said to have around 60 members, and there were other bards not on its books; I was told that by the 1960s and 1970s the county probably had about 70 or 80 bards. Some bards introduced in the text below are listed here to help the reader identify them conveniently:

Han Qixiang (1915–89)	Li Huaiqiang (1922–2000)
Shi Weijun (b. *c*1924)	Wang Jinkao (b. *c*1930)
He Guangwu (b. *c*1932)	Tian Zhizi (b. *c*1933)
Zhang Jungong (b. *c*1933)	Li Wenjin (b. *c*1943)
Xu Wengong (b. *c*1948)	Guo Xingyu (b. *c*1951)

---

[3] Zhang Zhentao's notes from our 2001 trip are written up in Zhang 2002a: 214–21; Tian 2005 also contains notes from this trip. I have also consulted written sources (notably ANS, and material on folk customs and on Han Qixiang), cited in the notes below. For the cassette series of Zhang Jungong, see §5.4 below. For a brief taste, see Jones 2002; for a succinct version of this section, see Jones 2007a. For background, with some video clips mainly of official groups, see http://www.zgya.com/zgya/sbss.htm, and entries under http://www.snwh.gov.cn/feiwuzhi. For some fine photos, see http://www.798photogallery. cn/EN/photographer/photographer_17.html.

[4] Lin 1945: 46, cf. Hung 1993: 402.

Chapter 2

The tradition

In this chapter I give a rather timeless description based on traditional practice, to be refined – significantly, not much – in later chapters by outlining the careers of some individual bards in the second half of the twentieth century.

2.1 Social background

An itinerant man, usually blind or visually impaired, travels by foot over quite a wide area 'going from door to door'[1] to perform narrative-singing, mainly to help people fulfil vows and bring good fortune to families, accompanying himself on *sanxian* banjo (or *pipa* lute) and a pair of clappers. The performer is commonly known as *shujiang* 'story craftsman', the more honorific *xiansheng* 'master', or just as *shuoshude* 'story-teller'. I use the term 'bard' for convenience, and to evoke his broader ritual duties.[2]

As Communist ideologue Lin Shan saw clearly in the 1940s, the main purpose of such narrative-singing was to 'worship the gods'; despite the Communist Party's efforts, this has hardly changed since then. In the intervals between calendrical and life-cycle festivities, the bards provide a major source of entertainment, historical knowledge, and moral education for villagers, along with their 'practical' function of bringing good fortune.

Narrative-singing is one of a related set of livelihoods for blind men in Shaanbei, including fortune-telling, curing illness, and caring for godchildren. Until very recently, blind men had a kind of monopoly on these arts: sighted people couldn't 'steal their food-bowl' (cf. §4.6), and it was thought that they would go blind if they did so. Visually-impaired boys usually begin learning these arts when in their mid-teens. The pupil's family pays the master, who often teaches several boys at once. Though training is for a nominal three-year period, adversity generally makes pupils go out on the road sooner. Since the bard is either blind

---

[1] *Xingmenhu, huanmenhu. Xingmenhu*, referring generally to participation in a family ceremonial such as a wedding or funeral, is often used to describe bards' performance contexts. See Cao 1999: 89–90.

[2] Some sources use the more formal term 'narrative-singing artists', *shuoshu yiren*. For *shuoshu*, I use the terms 'narrative-singing' or 'story-telling'.

or semi-blind, in his early years on the road he may be accompanied by a sighted companion.[3]

Disabilities have long been common in Shaanbei; it is hard for disabled men to find a wife, not least because they are often unable to make a livelihood – hence the saying 'people won't follow [marry] you if your five organs aren't complete' (*wuguan buquan, renjia bugen*). However, most blind bards we met had been able to find wives – some such couples were 'introduced', either by village go-betweens or by the local government.

Actually, a match with a blind man was not the worst fate that could befall a poor village girl. The bards could make a living, at least; they were not dependent on agriculture and the caprices of the heavens (in a sense they actually profited from peasants' misfortunes, though no-one articulated this thought), they were considered auspicious and had a certain 'culture' (hence the name 'master'); they were often away from home, and when home were perhaps less able to use violence effectively on their wives than were sighted husbands.

In imperial times, Confucian ideology largely barred women from public roles; visually-impaired girls did not take up narrative-singing, and the Communist Party made no attempt to change this. Guo Xingyu knew of no female bards in the whole of Suide county in the 1960s, though Li Huaiqiang and He Guangwu recalled a few blind female bards from Shanxi province across the river. Today some female beggars (both blind and sighted) at temple fairs sing short songs, and play *erhu* fiddle or electronic keyboard, but they are not bards.

Villagers explained the male monopoly by 'feudal thinking': 'People would ridicule.' Bard He Guangwu also revealed traditional values: 'Women don't offer respects to the gods (*jingshen*), so they're not allowed to tell stories.' Here *jingshen* means not just offering respects to the gods (in their individual offering of incense at temple fairs, women manifestly outnumber men), but representing others in forging communications with the gods – though even here, since spirit mediums are often female, there is a further conflict deserving study.

2.2 Contexts

While narrative-singing is a popular, and (to locals) intelligible, form to entertain people, it is performed in ritual contexts to appease or reward the gods, called 'stories for vows'. Bards mainly perform for three contexts: 'stories for well-being' to bring a family good fortune; for temple fairs; and for a community at

---

[3]   For blind musicians in China, note Liu Hongqing 2004, a harrowing tale of blind singers' lives in Shanxi, just east of Shaanbei. The *Anthology* contains many biographies of blind musicians, notably in the narrative-singing volumes such as those for Henan and Anhui. Cf. my remarks on blind shawm players in Shanxi, Jones 2007: 17–21, 46–7.

New Year.[4] In a broad sense, these are all 'stories for well-being', intended to secure divine blessing.

Table 2   Occupations for blind men and contexts for narrative-singing

---

Occupations
begging (*yaofan*)
telling fortunes (*suangua*)
exorcism / healing (*antushen/zhibing*)
hanging the locket (*guasuo*), opening the locket (*kaisuo*)
narrative-singing (*shuoshu*)

Contexts for narrative-singing
stories for vows (*yuanshu*), to fulfil a verbal vow (*huan kouyuan*)
        household (*jiashu*) = for well-being (*ping'an shu*)
        temple fairs (*huishu; miaohui*)
        parish (*sheshu*)

   less common
        weddings (*hongshi*)
        funerals (*baishi*)
        moving into a new cave-dwelling (*nuanyao*)
        going off to the army (*canjun*)
        official meetings (*jiguan*)

News of the arrival of a blind bard in a quiet village soon spreads. A family may then choose to invite him to their cave-dwelling for a narrative-singing session, with the general goal of 'guaranteeing well-being' (*bao ping'an*). This may be requested both as a vow to the gods ('vow story') when one is suffering misfortune, and in fulfilment after it has passed ('fulfilling a verbal vow'). Vows may be made for childbirth, the safety of a weak child or of a migrant breadwinner, recovery from illness, the longevity of elderly relatives, and (often) the recovery of sick livestock ('feeding livestock' *wei shengling*). In this chronically poor region, perceived misfortunes or anxieties may be both specific (such as a journey) and of a general long-term kind. Li Huaiqiang was clear that stories for well-being are no use for serious physical illnesses. Tian Zhizi: 'For stories for well-being, we just tell one story lasting a couple of hours, getting 20 *yuan*, or [a set of] three stories for 60 *yuan* – in the 1950s we only got 1.5 *yuan*.' For a story for well-being, see §5.7 and ⊙**C4**.

Bards also make the rounds of the network of temple fairs, both large and small. For larger fairs an opera troupe is invited too, for smaller ones just the bards. The bards' most popular venues are temple fairs for the 'three emperors' (*sanhuang*), their patron deities. Local scholars mention the Qingliangshan temple fair just east of Yan'an, and fairs in Hengshan, Zizhou, and Suide, where 20 or 30 bards are still invited for three days and three nights of stories for well-being. They

---

4   ANS 963–4.

are given their own cave to stay in together, fed, and given money. Tian Zhizi: 'I told stories at temple fairs quite a lot – there are a lot more fairs now than in the 1950s – a large-scale fair can invite three bards, or one if it's a smaller fair. We get paid a lot – I'd get 150–200 *yuan* for telling nine stories over the three days.' Below we see that some bards themselves come to fulfil vows. For a story at a temple fair, see §5.8 and ⊙**A4**.

I have little information on 'stories for the parish', performed for the New Year's rituals in a temple or the courtyard of the organizer.[5] As with the occasional *jiao* Offering performed by ritual specialists in Jiaxian county (§1.6 above), Tian Zhizi implied that the 'parish' referred to a group of villages clubbing together for rituals lasting several days: 'Every village [in the parish] gives around 20 *yuan*, then a group of four or five blindmen together go all round the villages to perform.' Guo Xingyu: 'For stories for the parish we have to perform for a long time – sometimes till three or four in the morning. The fee is a bit more too.' This period just before and after the 1st moon is the busiest season for the bards, when people fulfil vows and have free time, seeking to guarantee well-being for the coming year. As a Suide villager told us in 2001: 'We always invite a bard to tell stories for well-being for New Year, so that our livestock will be healthy, because only bards can invite the gods.'

It seems that bards rarely perform their stories for weddings and funerals. Tian Zhizi: 'Here in Zizhou, people sometimes invite a bard for their wedding when they've made a vow to do so, but that's becoming rarer.' Guo Xingyu is sometimes invited for weddings to tell a 'celebratory story for well-being' (*ping'an xiqing shu*). I haven't seen this context, though beggars – not necessarily visually impaired – queue up to sing short auspicious texts (*shuoxi, nianxi*), accompanying themselves on a plucked lute or clappers, in return for payment (⊙**D2**).[6] Such short songs resemble folk-songs rather than narrative-singing. This is not another potential source of income for bards: it seems they are generally considered superior to this.

Some bards mentioned performing for 'official meetings'. Before the arrival of the Communists, Nationalist officials liked to invite bards to perform a story, and doubtless bards had narrated also for imperial officials; but there was generally a ritual element to such performances, whereas the official meetings characteristic of Maoism were secular. Since the dismantling of the commune system we heard of few current occasions, although recently small groups may perform on temporary stages set up in urban areas. By the way, while story-tellers elsewhere in China often perform in tea-houses, there appear to be none in Shaanbei.

---

[5] ANS 964, 1012–13. For the 'parish' in Shaanbei, see p.19 n.38 above.

[6] See also Cao 1999: 94; for a text, see Zhang Junyi 2000: 109.

2.3 Rituals for healing and protecting children

Bards also tell fortunes, cure illness, and act as godfathers – occasions when they do not necessarily perform stories. Fortune-telling, or advice for prudent action in conjunction with heavenly forces, remains a pervasive factor in villagers' behaviour, for which they may have recourse not only to blindmen but also to geomancers and mediums, as well as casting divination sticks in temples. My experience of these activities is limited, but in order to understand the bards' lives it is worth introducing such customs, even if they are less related to music.

Like geomancers (§11.1, ⊙**B6**) and mediums, the blindman performs healing in a ritual called Settling the Earth or Settling the Earth God (*antu, antushen*).[7] For this he recites incantations and depicts talismans, but does not perform stories. Guo Xingyu often performs these ceremonies: 'Families that are always having problems invite someone to Settle the Earth God, so that their hearts will be at peace. Sometimes I use folk remedies (*pianfang*); if it's a psychological abnormality then I have to depict talismans (*hua fu*), deploy my spiritual power (*fagong*), and recite incantations (*zhouyu*). Talismans are drawn with cinnabar (*zhusha*) or coal dust (*meizhi*) on yellow paper – you use incantations to make the talisman work, then you burn it and get the patient to drink the ashes.'

Blind bards often act as godfathers, performing ceremonies protecting children.[8] For the first full moon of a new baby, and for the ceremonies for hanging and opening the locket, a shawm band is sometimes invited to play during the feast (called 'receiving guests', *daike*) for family and friends, but the bard performs less often. Customs vary somewhat even within Shaanbei. Ceremonies to protect children include hanging the locket, the annual 'Crossing the Passes' ceremony at temple fairs, and opening the locket. These ceremonies have doubtless become rather less common since the 1950s, though neither campaigns against superstition nor any gradual improvement in healthcare entirely explain this. Although the only event in this complex that I have witnessed is the 'Crossing the Passes' (see below), villagers described to us contexts as they were still observed.

Parents may hang the locket (*baosuo, daisuo*) for their children to protect them from supernatural diseases (*guaibing*). Li Huaiqiang: 'Children are vulnerable to particular illnesses depending on their time of birth and which noxious influences (*guansha*) they have offended (*fan*). As long as you destroy the noxious influences they can't get ill. You hang the locket like if a child is obstructing a parent – once you've hung the locket it turns towards other people, and won't harm the people themselves. They'll be OK after the age of 12.'

'It's different for a bard to hang the locket from a family doing it themselves. We artists (I mean geomancers and bards) know how – people have to come and invite

---

[7]   For the text of a song sung for this ritual, see Zhang Junyi 2000: 119–20. Cf. Tian 2005: 121–2.

[8]   See also Zhang Junyi 1993: 60–63; Zhang Junyi 2000: 115–18; Cao 1999: 91–3, 95–6; Tian 2005: 123–5. For neighbouring Shanxi, cf. Wen and Xue 1991: 11–12 (*kaisuo*).

us, and we charge for it. When families do it, they just have a feast, no money changes hands. When they hang the locket, they just decide whose fate is good (lucky, *fuli*), then they make out their child as his, so he can grow up safe. "Lucky" means if your own children have grown to maturity, or someone in your family has become an official, has got authority (*quan*) and an official qualification (*gongming*).'

'You can hang the locket at any age. In the old days a family would give one *sheng* of grain (*xiaomi*) for hanging the locket, but these days they give money, according to their means.' A fellow villager observed: 'You don't hang the locket for all children: just if they cry a lot, or don't feed properly – then you invite a blindman to cure the illness, recite incantations, and hang the locket. On the red thread are hung a couple of coins – a couple of *mao* or a couple of *kuai*. The locket isn't necessarily hung first on the child's birthday, but from the next time then it is on the birthday, though it can be a bit before or after. When hanging the locket you only get a bard to perform if you've made a vow.'

Guo Xingyu: 'Some babies get a defect, like fever or always crying, so on the basis of their eight characters (*bazi*), if they need hanging the locket then we do it – you don't have to wait until their birthday. As soon as we hang the locket for them, they get better. Hanging the locket means guaranteeing (*lanhale*) the family's living.' Guo said it can be done for boys and girls alike, though I am dubious, given the far lesser value still accorded to girls.

Magic is part of the blindman's routine for hanging the locket, just like healing. Li Huaiqiang: 'While hanging the locket you burn incense and paper. You have to expound the magic (*shuofa*).[9] There are long and short magics, of several tens of phrases or just a few phrases. We talk of "long magic, short mantra" (*changfa duanzhou*), "the magic of the Zhou dynasty and the scripture of the Tang dynasty", and there's a "scripture of the ancient Buddha of Western Heaven" (*Xitian gufo jing*).'

Guo Xingyu: 'The yellow paper memorial serves as a tool to eradicate evil, transferring the magic power (*fali*) into it, you wipe the child's body with it, then burn it in a little bowl. Then you place a red thread (*hong sixian*, that is the "locket" – it's not a real locket) round the child's neck and recite a few incantations.' Local scholar Zhang Junyi reports that a spirit medium also sometimes recites incantations. In Yangjiagou, when landlord's child Ma Peiyun was given the locket in the 1920s, apart from a local bard and a Chinese-medicine doctor from Shanxi, a medium and a Buddhist priest attended.

Guo Xingyu: 'Then every year we hang another red thread till the child is 12. Every New Year the family must give the godfather a gift, but usually not after the child is 12, though some still go and pay a visit then. And when the godchild gets married they definitely invite the godfather.' Li Huaiqiang: 'When the child reaches 3, 6, 9 [and 12] the family has shoes made [for us] or gives us some cloth, and sometimes we get gifts of money – it depends on people's status (*menmen*), if they have no money then we don't ask for it.' Gifts of money have become more

---

[9]   Much could be written about *fa*; apart from the Buddhist dharma, it denotes skills, techniques, often with a supernatural agency.

common: in 2001 a villager told us, 'When the child reaches 3, 6, and 9, the family gives the master around 100 *yuan*, other years they give him around 20 *yuan*, for hanging and opening the locket they give around 200 *yuan*.' Li Huaiqiang, in his 70s, had hung the locket for three or four hundred children; Guo Xingyu, in his 50s, for 'over 290'.

Apart from giving annual gifts to the godfather, many families take their children to their local temple fair for the 'Crossing the Passes' (*guoguan*) ritual,[10] denoting the overcoming of various life crises for children below the age of 12. They don't have to cross the passes every year, only if they are thought to be at risk from a noxious influence – again consulting with a geomancer or blindman. If they need the ritual but can't attend for some reason, their parents do the same ritual with an item of clothing, shoes, or a hat. A bard does not preside, though what upright scholar Zhang Junyi calls a 'superstitious practitioner' may recite a brief auspicious text.

We saw a Crossing the Passes ritual in 2001 at the 4th-moon temple fair at Sishilipu township (☉**A3**).[11] The main entertainment at the fair is an opera on the stage down the hill from the temple; the temple itself is busy with people making offerings to the gods. Crossing the Passes is considered efficacious when performed soon after midday. On a table before the temple are a *dou* bowl and an incense bowl, with streamers and pennants stuck inside, the latter inscribed with slogans like 'great felicity in Crossing the Passes' (*guoguan daji*) and 'may Our Lady protect' (*niangniang baoyou*). At the far end of the table is a red paper hoop; at the near end, a chopper attached to a metal base.

As the three-cartridge cracker-firer is let off, the shawm band begins to play (cf. §11.4). The temple association chief (*huizhang*) throws a chopstick through the hoop, breaking the red paper, then throws a live rooster through, which is then kept near the chopper as an offering to the gods. Sixteen children queue up at the 'pass', wearing auspicious red headscarves, with thick ropes, tied around their waists, trailing behind them. As the parents offer incense, the children crawl one by one through the red paper hoop, under the table, and through the gap between the base and the chopper, as the officiant brings the chopper down to cut the rope behind them, indicating the elimination of calamity. The children are met at the other end by their family, and given a stick of lit incense, a small pennant, and a *yanyan* dough figure, as the association chief sprinkles rice on them. The atmosphere is jovial.

When the child reaches the age of 12, the opening the locket ceremony is performed. Again, until the 1950s a medium might also be called; a shawm band is still occasionally invited for the feast to 'receive guests', but the bard rarely

---

[10] The *guan* also equates with the *guansha* noxious influences. Ten are listed by Zhang Junyi (1993: 62–3). See also Chau 2006: 56–7. For similar rituals elsewhere in China, see Baptandier-Berthé 1994 (esp. 535–52), Bender 2001: 114. The DVD film CHIME 2008, filmed in Gansu not far west of Shaanbei, also includes excerpts from a Crossing the Passes ritual.

[11] Cf. Tian 2005: 124–5.

performs. The parents used to give the blindman a *dou* of grain, but now they give a bag of flour, or often cash. He puts a metal chain with 12 locks on it round the child's neck, reciting an incantation as he opens each lock.

Both hanging and opening the locket should be done on the correct day foretold, but in Yangjiagou the timing of the ceremonies was standardized in the 1980s, when lockets were often hung at the Pusamiao temple fair on the 8th of the 4th moon, and opened at the Heihulingguanmiao temple fair on the 15th of the 7th moon.[12]

2.4 Ritual equipment, stories, and music

For all the narrative-singing contexts, the bard performs before a small temporary altar. Inscriptions for the gods and family (*paiwei* or *shenweizi*), rectangular pieces of paper with a triangular head, mounted on *gaoliang* stalks, as well as *changqing* yellow paper streamers, are inserted into one or two rectangular bowls (*dou*), filled with grains of millet or corn. Before the altar are placed a lit candle, small bowls to hold incense and burn paper offerings, and offerings such as dough shapes, biscuits, dates, fruit, peanuts, cigarettes, and cups of liquor.

The altar is placed on the family stove or on a table; for the rituals to invite the gods and escort them away at the beginning and end of stories for well-being, it is placed on a table in the courtyard outside. Li Huaiqiang, though blind, prepared the *changqing* streamers himself; someone sighted and literate has to be found to write the inscriptions. Incense and paper are burnt before the altar periodically throughout the performance.[13]

The bard's own most common permanent ritual artefact is a red cloth with the titles of a pantheon of gods written on it; most bards we met had such a cloth (Illustration 3). When not in use it is rolled up and kept in the bard's bag. The cloth is unfurled and placed upright behind the altar, supported by two sticks inserted into a sleeve at either end of the cloth.

An invocation to the gods is chanted for the opening 'Inviting the Gods' (*qingshen*) and concluding 'Escorting the Gods Away' (*songshen*) rituals.[14] The pantheon is said to contain 72 gods, though the cloths we saw do not appear to contain all their names. The gods' names are handed down from master to disciple. Which deities are invited depends on the context – for curing livestock you invite the Horse King Elder (Mawangye), for instance, whereas the deity Zhenniantaisui oversees the building of new cave-dwellings. The powers of the gods are taken seriously, and bards will not recite incantations or chants to invite the gods out of context. Bards often have auspicious red paper slogans pasted onto their instruments.

---

[12]   Guo 2000: 346.

[13]   Cf. Cao 1999: 113–14. For photo and diagram, see Fukao, Iguchi, and Kurishara 2007: 15.

[14]   Ex. in ANS 1013. Zhang Junyi 2000: 137–8 also has the text of a 'song for Inviting the Gods'.

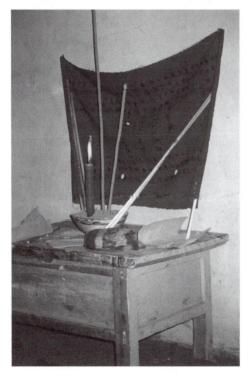

Illustration 3　　　Cloth pantheons listing the gods
(a) Li Huaiqiang, 1999; (b) Xu Wengong, 2001

On He Guangwu's *sanxian* is an inscription 'On going out may you see happiness, may noble people support you' (*chumen jianxi, guiren fuchi*).

Stories overlap with opera plots, relating historical tales of love, official success, solving of crimes, famous battles, and righteous protest, all familiar in Chinese fiction since the Ming dynasty, and often referring to still earlier times. While regional genres are stylistically distinct, such stories are quite widespread nationally. Bards' stories are like a cheaper, more portable version of opera that can be brought into the home to bring good fortune to the family. Like opera (and indeed TV soap opera), stories may be performed in sections at successive sittings. And like opera, they have long been a dominant form for poor people to learn of history, legend, and morality, only being challenged by schooling since the 1950s; while schooling even now is quite elementary, TV is doubtless replacing the bards' stories as entertainment. Stories are usually recited in the third person, with some sections acted in the first person.

The solo performer accompanies himself on a plucked lute and usually two percussion instruments attached to his left leg and right hand. He may rest his right foot on a low stool, and drapes a towel over his shoulder to wipe sweat from his face. The plucked lute is either the unfretted *sanxian* (*xianzi*) or the fretted *pipa*; the *sanxian* is most common, the use of *pipa* declining drastically in this area since the 1980s (§4.6 below).

The following chapters suggest that the contexts, stories, and music have remained quite constant through many decades of social change. Stories and music are discussed briefly in §4.6 below, but my focus here is the bards' activities in society over time.

2.5 Origin legends and early history

Origin legends current in the 1980s were collected by local scholars,[15] and are evidently widely known. They mostly explain the monopoly of blind men as bards. In one story, in ancient times an imperial prince was banished to the mountain forests after he lost his sight. One day he found a dead scorpion that had been struck by lightning. The prince stretched its entrails over its shell, and when he plucked it, it sounded resonant, as he accompanied himself in stories of the court, attracting large audiences. He then taught many disciples.[16] Wang Jinkao reminded us that *pipa* makers imitate the shape of the scorpion.

Another legend describes two brothers surnamed Huang (Yellow),[17] servants for a landlord. They committed an offence; one had a leg amputated, the other had

---

[15]   ANS 961–2; see also Han 1985: 1–4.

[16]   Cf. a version in Han Qixiang's *Fanshen ji*, Hu 1989: 172–4.

[17]   Some legends involve a third brother. Han Qixiang stated that bards associate their patron deities, the *sanhuang* legendary emperors of antiquity, with three brothers surnamed Huang (Han 1985: 2).

his eyes put out, and they were expelled. As they were begging, the older brother told a story while striking a wooden box, the younger brother put four strings on it, and that is the origin of the *pipa*. Later they picked out a round wicker basket, covered it with a piece of wood, put a pole on it, added three strings, and that is the origin of the *sanxian*.

In yet another legend, the Huang brothers met a savage tiger on the road and got separated. The older Huang ended up with his *sanxian* in the northern part of Shaanbei and taught eighteen pieces (*diao*) to eighteen pupils. The younger Huang ended up with his *pipa* in the southern part of Shaanbei and taught nine melodies (*qiang*) to nine pupils. Hence the tradition of 'nine *qiang* and eighteen *diao*' (*jiuqiang shiba diao*), a common phrase in Shaanbei and other Chinese musics, used loosely to mean the complete melodic repertory.

Though many other genres of Chinese narrative-singing from a more literate urban background supply considerable data from the nineteenth century and earlier, more concrete material on the early history of this tradition is virtually absent. Local scholars offer two very tenuous clues. They claim links with the Tang dynasty (618–906) by citing the rare form of *pipa* played by Shaanbei bards: in its shape, in its (nearly) horizontal performing posture, and in the use of a plectrum, it is said to resemble representations of the *pipa* in local iconography from the Tang. This line is inconclusive, as is a brief passage from 1670 in the Yulin prefecture gazetteer.[18] In general the stories themselves seem to be in a tradition consistent with Ming-Qing drama, though I wonder if a literature specialist could derive any firmer clues.

---

[18] ANS 961–2. The latter passage describes a performance of *quanqi* fables by a local narrative singer called Liu Di, 'melodious and full of character', on a par with an admired singer from the Jiangnan region, but it is also cited, I think more convincingly, as evidence by scholars seeking ancestry for the urban genre *Yulin xiaoqu*: Chen 1994: 126, ANS 607–8. Cf. §12.2 below.

Chapter 3

The Yan'an period

Having briefly surveyed the traditional contexts of the Shaanbei bards, let us now place them in a firmer temporal frame. Apart from written accounts, I rely on oral history, looking at the bards' fortunes under various phases of Communism – since some of the region was a Communist base-area from 1936, by the late 1990s there were few who could remember an earlier period. The Party's cultural programme in the 1940s certainly affected narrative-singing, and at first it may look as if new contexts and repertories simply replaced old ones, but we will soon see how misleading this impression would be. Put simply, the risk is to assume that if one new thing happens, then all the old things stop happening. The commune system only imposed severe restrictions from 1956, and even then there was some local latitude until 1965; bards seem to have been more independent of political control than some other more public musicians such as shawm bands (discussed in Part Three).

What little is known outside Shaanbei about its narrative-singing rests on the reputation of Han Qixiang, dubbed 'China's Homer'[1] but redder than red. We have detailed propaganda accounts of Han Qixiang's life, but our talks with less renowned bards reveal a complex story.

3.1 A village bard

Let us begin with a village performer virtually (but not atypically) untouched by new political agendas. As we saw in the Preface, Yangjiagou, in the hills east of Mizhi county-town, is a rather famous village. The late lamented Li Huaiqiang (1922–2000, known in the village as 'Immortal Li', Li *xian*: Illustration 4, ⊙**C3**) was a poor blind bard based there. He was among the great majority of narrative singers (and audiences) not amenable to the new stories encouraged by the Communist Party. Under Maoism, though he gained a house and a family, his livelihood was reduced; since the reforms of the 1980s he suffered from both the decline in popularity of the art and his own dwindling skills. He assessed his life dispassionately for us in 1999.[2]

---

[1]   Hung 1993: 400, citing Chen Ming.

[2]   Thanks to Guo Yuhua for her interview skills, and for providing me with notes from her 1998 talks with Li. For a photo and a brief note on Li, see Fukao, Iguchi, and Kurishara 2007: 14–15.

Illustration 4   Blind bard Li Huaiqiang, 1999 – note clappers on leg

Li Huaiqiang was born to a family of hired labourers working for the village landlords. Such poor families couldn't afford to send their children to school, and he attended 'winter school' for a mere few days. He could still see until he was about 8, but lost his sight completely by the age of 10. When 15 or 16 (*c*1936–7) his father took him to a blind bard to 'learn up the arts' of narrative-singing, 'history' (*lishi*), fortune telling, and healing illness. At the time there were no bards based in Yangjiagou; any that performed there came from outside. Li Huaiqiang's teacher was based in Taozhen town, and taught three or four pupils at once, including one still active as a bard in nearby Houjiagou village in 1999. Learning long stories phrase by phrase was time-consuming and expensive – his father had to scrape the fees together. Li contrasts that ruefully with the ease of young upstarts today who can learn just by listening to tapes.

Li began 'going out of the door' to earn a living before he was 18 – the traditional three-year training period was not strictly observed when people were desperate. He practised both healing and narrative-singing. He was often in demand to cure illness. When someone's child was ill, Li would give Chinese medicine, and if adults had some irregular illness (*xiebing*), some bad karma, for which orthodox medicine was no use, he would find them some special herbs.

Since Yangjiagou was still a landlord stronghold (Illustration 5), in the early days Li often performed stories all four seasons of the year for the landlords in the village itself. Such occasions – like longevity celebrations, or for the first full moon of new-born children – often lasted seven or eight days. The landlords had a shrine (*kan*) in their houses to the god of wealth, before which bards would tell their stories, and Buddhist priests would recite their scriptures.

Ritual has always remained paramount for bards like Li. 'Poor people (*shoukuren*) worship the Dragon King Elder (Longwangye), stockbreeders worship Horse King Elder (Mawangye), people in business worship God of Wealth Elder (Caishenye). When people make vows they invite us to tell stories, that's how we make our living.' Since vows are often fulfilled in the 1st and 2nd moons, bards are most busy then.

By the 1940s, Li's itinerant business was taking him on foot over a wide area, to the counties of Xichuan, Yinchuan, Hengshan, Bao'an (Zhidan), and Yulin. Recalling the old temple fairs, he mentioned the two most famous in the area, still very active now: 'I used to go to the White Cloud Mountain for over 20 years, I even went once after the end of the Cultural Revolution. I used to go every year, there were kids there that I'd hung the locket for.' But the Black Dragon Temple fair was not part of his circuit: he only visited it once when he was in his twenties. Li performed for the small temple fairs in his home village too, notably the 4th-moon fair at the Pusamiao temple. The temple fairs in the adjacent hamlet of Sigou were planned best, and were popular; people liked listening to narrative-singing there.

3.2 Han Qixiang's early life

So far the tradition of blind bards appears intact, but with the founding of the Communist base at Yan'an in 1936, political modernization began to be in the air. The most famous case of a blind bard creating new stories to support Party policies was to be Han Qixiang. Before we assess his later career, his earlier life is of a piece with that of other bards.

As with many other genres in China, the national reputation of narrative-singing in Shaanbei rests largely on one performer who came to the attention of cultural cadres and was cultivated by them.[3] A poor blind bard, Han took advantage of the opportunities offered by the Communist Party's programme at Yan'an of using

---

[3] For another example in Shaanbei, Ding Xicai, tip of the iceberg of the local *errentai*, see p.17 n.31 above.

Illustration 5   Remnants of landlord architecture, Yangjiagou 1999

the arts to reform society. Hung (1993) has begun to read between the lines of hagiographic Chinese accounts, including Han's own.

Han Qixiang (1915–89)[4] was the eighth of nine children in a family of poor hired labourers from a village in Hengshan county, going blind at the age of 3 from complications brought on by smallpox. After his father died when Han Qixiang was aged 6, his mother took him begging to avoid starvation; later they took temporary work for landlords. By this time they were already hoping he could learn to tell stories to survive; after he made himself a toy *sanxian*, a passing beggar sold him a real one.

In 1928 his mother sold off part of the meagre family landholding to send him to study narrative-singing and fortune-telling under the blind Du Weixin, from a village in Mizhi, studying for a month at a time over a nominal three-year period. Initial fees were 120 strings of cash plus six silver dollars. Han Qixiang was one of ten blind boys studying with Du.[5] He began going on the road to earn money after only a year, but by 1929 the terrible famine left him without business – the family split up, and Han Qixiang attempted suicide, being saved by a 17-*sui*-old passer-by called Su Xiangcheng, with whom he set off to Shanxi to flee the famine. In 1932, after returning to Hengshan, Han managed to find a female partner, a topic on which Chinese sources are laconic.[6]

So far this is a fairly typical story. But in the early 1930s a chance encounter with local guerrilla hero Liu Zhidan (Holm 1992) is said to have inspired him to begin singing in praise of the Red Army. We can hardly assess this, but it is not unlikely that he began inserting at least phrases reflecting the new political energy into his traditional repertory. His sworn brother Su Xiangcheng had also joined Liu Zhidan's army. Once Han was interrogated by a Nationalist general. In 1936 he is said to have formed a secret 'blind men's propaganda troupe' with four other performers. One, already a Communist Party member, was murdered by the Nationalists later that year; another had his tongue cut out. So the troupe was short-lived.

Han Qixiang continued performing – and telling fortunes. Later, inevitably, he would ridicule fortune-telling; but we cannot assume that he was so politically correct at this stage. His biography claims that he used fortune-telling as a pretext for philanthropic purposes on behalf of the Communists. Around 1939, when Wu Ziyou, a relative and protegé of He Shaonan (then Nationalist governor of

---

[4] Sources disagree about his birthdate. Some say 1908, Luo 1963 gives 1914; here I follow Hu Mengxiang 1989. Major sources for Han Qixiang are Hu 1989 (I am most grateful to William Hung for copying this major source for me) and Hung 1993, including good bibliographies; for brief notices, see Zhongguo 1983: 106, ANS 1148–9. See also Luo 1963, and commemorative articles and photos in *Quyi* 1989/10. For recordings, see Zhongguo 1994: 270. I have not seen *Han Qixiang chuantong shumu xuanbian*.

[5] For their names, see Hu 1989: 32; cf. Hung 1993: 402.

[6] See chronology, Hu 1989: 274–5.

the Suide region) was said to be exacting a crippling tax on bards, Han led 15 performers in exposing him.

In November 1940 Han moved with his partner and children to a village in the 'Red Area', 20 *li* north of Yan'an city.[7] Sources admit that he yet had little idea of the revolution. Educated patriotic urbanites, thronging from afar to Yan'an to join the resistance against the Japanese, might be idealistic, but for many peasants moving towards the booming area from the poorer northern counties nearby, the choice was economic rather than political: work, and indeed land, might be more readily available in the Red Area – though one might expect bards to be able to make a better living in a less revolutionary climate, as one bard indeed told us (§3.5 below).[8]

We are told little of Han Qixiang's next few years in the Red Area. His life may have been improving, but cannot have been as ideal as he and his biographers depict. Though he may have heard the new Party-sponsored versions of *yangge* song-and-dance, any innovations he made in this period would have been tentative and opportunistic. His activities were still sufficiently traditional that the Yan'an government once confiscated his *sanxian* and smashed his fortune-telling sticks.[9]

3.3 The Yan'an reforms

In the Yan'an base area, other performing arts like *yangge* group dancing, *mihu* vocal-dramatic music, and folk-song were being actively recruited to the Communist cause from at least 1942; a call went out in November 1942 to recruit still more widely.[10] Han Qixiang's first exposure to Communist cadres was when he performed a traditional story at a meeting in Yan'an to discuss narrative-singing on 2nd August 1944.[11] Party activist poet He Jingzhi, impressed, then asked him to perform at the renowned Lu Xun Academy for the Arts, and 'the rest is history' – or would be, if the following period were any easier to interpret.

So how far and how deep did the Communist reform movement extend? First we should credit the early reformers with a degree of genuine idealism. Confronting conditions of chronic poverty, expressive culture was naturally one

---

[7]   Luo 1963: 48–9 gives 1939.

[8]   For a fine instance of the limited goals of peasants in taking work in Yan'an, see Guo 2000: 359–60.

[9]   Hu 1989: 66.

[10]   A useful collection of Yan'an documents, many from Liberation Daily (*Jiefang ribao*) in the 1940s, is Yan'an 1988. For narrative-singing, see vol.14: 135–363; apart from the local genre, there was also energy in reforming migrant genres from the big cities, such as Suzhou *tanci* and the northern *jingyun dagu* (309–48) – genres that had no long-term impact on Shaanbei. Meanwhile in Zuoquan county of Shanxi province further east, bards had been organized into propaganda teams as early as 1938: Liu Hongqing 2004: 71–2.

[11]   For the discovery of Han Qixiang, see Hu 1989: 65–6.

weapon in the fight on behalf of the exploited peasantry. There were and are idealists: Han Qixiang appears to have been one, and even today, one cultural cadre I meet writes well about custom but supports Party ideology unwaveringly. A more subtle accommodation can be seen in blind bard Guo Xingyu, marrying old and new ideologies; several bards speak blithely of 'superstition' while practising it earnestly for their living, and refer to 'superstitious stories' (*mixin shu*) while performing them with gusto. Indeed, the term now carries negative connotations only for the educated urban elite (Chau 2006: 48).

Hung (1993: 396–7) takes an important step in revealing the conflicts involved in the Party's espousal of narrative-singing and its championing of Han Qixiang, showing a more questioning attitude than in most mainland Chinese studies:

> Did Communist intellectuals really 'learn from the masses' [...]? Was the story-telling campaign an example of folk-elite cooperation as claimed by the Party? Or did intellectuals continue to practise their traditionally perceived role as custodians of culture and tutors to the peasants? [...] The relations between Chinese folk artists and Communist intellectuals were by no means harmonious. The intellectuals played the role of tutor and their traditional condescending attitude towards folk artists remained strong.

The next step will be to assess the long-term influence of such a campaign at the village level where the bards were mainly active.

A 1945 article written by Lin Shan (b.1910), leading Communist Party innovator in Shaanbei narrative-singing, sets the tone for the sanitized and prescriptive picture of narrative-singing under Maoism. Typically, Lin admired popular oral literature, but deplored its links with superstition, both in plots and contexts – links that Party ideologues sought unsuccessfully to break.

Reforming narrative-singing was on the agenda of ideologues by the early 1940s, but as Lin admitted, the initiative had still had only piecemeal influence by 1946. He warned against banning the bards completely. His mission was brave, since some of his colleagues might regard the performers as irredeemably tainted by superstition. Lin describes two attitudes among local cadres: some had negative attitudes towards the bards, while others felt that they could neither ban them nor reform them, so they could only be allowed to continue as before.

In a 1944 campaign against 'witches' (*wushen*), some bards had been 'struggled', and their equipment confiscated – though spirit mediums were the main objects, the definition was vague, and bards also performed exorcisms, chanting incantations and making magic potions. The climate was changing: as the power of campaigns against superstition sunk into people's consciousness, they would have been increasingly nervous of inviting bards openly.

A further element in Lin Shan's reluctance to ban narrative-singing entirely was its effect on otherwise unemployable blind men. Lin pointed out that if the context was superstitious, the actual content of stories, apart from their opening and closing invocations, was not necessarily religious. He lists several new stories, apparently composed unprompted. In Yanchang county, one Gao Yongzhang had performed 'Liu Zhidan attacks Yanchang' and a story about land revolution. In Yanchuan a story had been performed about the Red Army attacking Qingjian town; in Qingjian the stories 'The Southern Anhui incident' and 'Chasing off He Shaonan'; in Jiaxian the story 'Working hero Li Lanying'. Bards from Suide and Mizhi had performed stories about the land revolution, fighting the Japanese, and free marriage.[12]

Lin described these bards as 'progressive elements' who should be cultivated. However, they remained in a small minority, and even their allegiance to Party policy was fragile. Lin mentions a famous blind bard called Yang [Shengfu] in his 40s from Yanchang, 'quite backward in his thinking', who nonetheless – under the guidance of the progressive Minzhong opera troupe and music cadre Anbo – composed a new story called 'Five brave soldiers of Langyashan'.[13] Yang was said to be keen for the cadres to write it down for him so people could read it out to help him remember it; indeed, it was published in 1946. Yang accompanied himself on *pipa* rather than *sanxian*, by the way – and below we see that his 'backward thinking' persisted.

In 1944 the Yan'an authorities began to promulgate the telling of new stories and to reform Han Qixiang. Within a year the whole district had three bards (Han Qixiang, Yang Shengfu, and Gao Yongzhang) able to perform new stories, and 16 such stories had been composed. Lin Shan mentioned two other bards who performed new stories despite having virtually no contact with officialdom – he was unclear if they had received any official encouragement to perform new stories or had been influenced by Han Qixiang.

Lin stressed the need for written compilations of new stories – not just those already performed by the bards, but by 'cultural workers'. He said that the bards were requesting them, though this may be a gloss: the conversation might have gone, 'If you want me to sing new stuff, you'll have to give me a libretto'. Five volumes of new stories were published in 1946, but their influence seems to have been minimal. Lin even sanctioned the documenting of old stories as the basis for new arrangements.

3.4 The training bands

Lin Shan estimated that each county might have two or three bards prepared to learn new material – a revealingly low figure. The Communist Party needed to accelerate the reform. In 1945 Party cadres, including Lin Shan, Anbo, and later Ke Lan, set up a 'Shaan-Gan-Ning Border Region literary association narrative-singing group'

---

[12]   *Pinyin* titles: *Liu Zhidan da Yanchang, Wannan shibian, Ganzou He Shaonan, Laodong yingxiong Li Lanying* (Li Ziying *apud* Hu 1989: 85–8). For new stories performed by bards in Zuoquan county of Shanxi, see Liu Hongqing 2004: 71–2.

[13]   *Langyashanshang wushenbing*: Yan'an 1988, vol.14: 183; see also Hu 1989: 121–3.

(*Shaan-Gan-Ning bianqu wenxie shuoshuzu*). Han Qixiang was soon recruited to the group, and a narrative-singing training band (*shuoshu xunlianban*) was set up. Lin Shan then accompanied Han to other counties to set up similar training classes. Lin Shan himself, by the way, was Cantonese, a cultural world away from Han Qixiang; I wonder how easily they adapted to each other's dialect.

Han began going on tours of the countryside, closely supervised by cadres. Newspapers promoted his performances – not that many locals could read them. In August 1946 Han was invited to perform for both Chairman Mao and General Zhu De. He was the object of an intensive campaign to utilize his talents for the revolution, though Hung reveals personal conflicts between Han and cadres, based on Han's lowly social status.

In Yanchang, as we saw above, Yang Shengfu had already impressed cadres with his version of 'Five brave soldiers of Langyashan'. Han Qixiang shared a room with him in Yanchang, but when Yang protested at Han's gratuitous modernizations, they held a contest. Local bard Yang performed his favourite traditional story 'The Yang family generals' (*Yangjiajiang*), while Han performed his new 'The reunion of Liu Qiaor' (*Liu Qiaor tuanyuan*). Guess who won.[14] Apart from Han, others who were cajoled into performing the occasional new item were not necessarily easy to reform.

At first glance the reform looks quite far-reaching. 'Within two years, 273 out of 483 known storytellers in Shaanbei went through the re-training process, including Yang Shengfu of Yanchang and Shi Weijun of Suide'; 'the class was launched in seven or eight localities'. 'At least 20 reformed storytellers composed new stories, with over 50 pieces as the result. Han Qixiang had half the total.'[15]

In fact, as our talks with several bards showed, the training sessions hardly added up to a 'process'. Bards were lodged together, sometimes for a few months but often for just a few days (see §4.1 below), and even if they could remember the new stories, they remained reluctant to perform them once they went on the road. For how long were they 'reformed'? What did they do after the official groups disbanded and they went back on the road alone? One crux is whether political performances were replacing the traditional contexts. Even those who did take part in the official teams to learn new stories, for a longer or shorter time, continued to earn their living from more or less 'feudal superstitious' contexts. You couldn't perform new items for hanging the locket, or as stories for well-being.

Lin Shan admitted, or claimed, that 'the quality of Han's work deteriorated' after the activities of the Storytelling Group were put on hold in early 1947, when Nationalist troops occupied Yan'an.[16] That was the end of Han's brief but seminal association with the group. According to cultural cadre Luo Yang, after Hu Zongnan's troops took over Yan'an, Han moved with his family to the Mudanchuan-Fengfuchuan area, continuing to perform for wounded soldiers.

---

[14]   Hu 1989: 121–4.
[15]   Hung 1993: 409, 422, after Lin 1949: 152.
[16]   Hung 1993: 420.

When the Nationalists reached Fengfuchuan and the Communists retreated, he changed his name and, Luo claims, was active singing propaganda pieces secretly in the evenings. Just as likely, this might have been a welcome interlude when he could perform the traditional items that his audiences liked as much as he. We may never know – Han would have no interest in making the propaganda about him any less virtuous or more truthful. Han performed his new story 'Great victory at Yichuan'[17] in the liberated areas around Yan'an before its recapture. He entered Yan'an the day after its liberation, performing enthusiastically for troops.

After the hiatus of 1947, the new story movement recommenced by 1948, though the narrative-singing group never revived as such. Lin Shan admits that Han Qixiang and Shi Weijun were less 'productive' since they could not find suitable cadres with whom to 'collaborate'.[18] Moreover, their scripts were no longer being edited and published. The golden age for the new stories was that very brief period from 1944 to 1947, just before the national 'Liberation'.

Han Qixiang was by far the most prolific author, 'creating' over 500 new stories, mostly in this early period. Such stories were often based on new novellas or opera scripts, and composed with the 'guidance' of cadres. As Hung points out, it was hardly a collaboration between peasants and intellectuals – it was never in doubt who was in charge. Still, Lin Shan claims, credibly, that cadres and ordinary people alike were full of praise for Han's new stories. What is harder to assess is how they were received in the 1950s and later.

Han Qixiang's most celebrated new story was perhaps 'The reunion of Liu Qiaor', adapted in 1945.[19] With superstition a major target of the 1940s, topics attacking such customs as shamanism and prayers for rain were common. But such practices – including some of those performed by the bards themselves – were proscribed with limited effect under Maoism, and were to revive openly under the 1980s reforms.

Still, propaganda like this could make a useful weapon, the bards having frequent opportunities to perform throughout the villages. Though Han Qixiang performed his new 'Zhangjiazhuang prays for rain' over ten times within a month, seven of these performances were in Yan'an itself, which may be significant – such stories must have been less welcome outside the revolutionary headquarters. Han himself admitted that this was not his most popular story: we can peep through the cracks here.

As we saw, many of the new scripts were published. But such efforts to popularize new repertory failed: they barely penetrated to the villages, where literacy was low (90% of the population was said to be illiterate in 1937) and

---

[17]   *Yichuan da shengli*, aka *Wazijie dazhan*, Yan'an 1988. vol.14: 274.

[18]   For the initial collaborators, see Hung 1993: 403, 406–7.

[19]   See Hu 1989: 93–102; Hung 1993: 410–14. For text, see Yan'an 1992: 361–400; for mus.exx., see ANS 1098–113 and index. Han adapted it from a *Qinqiang* version performed at Yan'an in 1943; the story became nationally famous in a *Ping* opera version in 1950.

money to spend on books nonexistent, nor did the bards who had briefly learnt the new stories introduce them into the common repertory.

The main object of cadres' attention was the plots. 'Improving' the music was deemed still less important, or less possible, than that of opera, and the melodic structure and use of the voice, lute, and percussion seem to have remained quite stable. Though Han Qixiang is said to have incorporated elements of various folk vocal genres such as *xintianyou*, *daoqing*, *wanwanqiang*, *Qinqiang*, and *mihu* into his style, this was surely commonplace among bards. Even when he performed new stories, he would naturally vary them every time, like bards worldwide, and he retained the colourful local vocabulary of bards throughout the area.[20] We are not told how often he now performed the many traditional items in his repertory. And one cannot merely assess his stories from the page, without being able to witness his performances and those of other bards of the day. Bards I met were less impressed by his technique or creativity than by his good fortune in meeting the right people at the right time and getting onto the government payroll.

3.5 Li Huaiqiang in the Yan'an period

We know less of other bards in the 1940s, either fellow-travellers on the revolutionary road or more conservative ones.[21] Returning to Li Huaiqiang's own account of the period will make a suitable contrast. His own early visits south to the Yan'an region, in 1938 or 1939, were part of his routine itinerant business. He went around Hengshan and Bao'an (Zhidan) counties too. 'No-one controlled what stories you told then, you could narrate what you liked.'

In 1943, after the Suide-Mizhi area was taken over by the Communists, Li found himself unable to make a living there, and went off to Yinchuan in Ningxia and nearby Xichuan. Li recalled that the Nationalist officials loved listening to stories – bards were invited to their quarters. They could travel freely then – only later, when the Communist-Nationalist collaboration ended, did the roads become impassable.

Still, his assessment of the Red and White areas was ingenuous. 'It was just the same under the Communists and the Nationalists. Under the Nationalists it was easy to earn money, people liked to listen to stories. After the Communists took control over people, not allowing superstition, at least there was provision for us disabled people, there was relief. So things were the same.' But he did remark, 'In the end the Communists came along and broke all the temple fairs up, so there was nothing left.'

I wonder how many bards chose to seek a living in either the Red or White Areas. Evidently old stories did not suddenly vanish throughout the Yan'an countryside. The Yulin region was a seesaw area between the two sides, and most

---

[20]   Hung 1993: 412.

[21]   For some more names, see ANS 962; Zhongguo 1983: 339.

local leaders would, as yet, be broad-minded about traditional forms. We cannot judge, but it is worth challenging the propaganda. And having blithely equated 'new stories' with items supporting the Communists, I wonder if bards in the Nationalist areas performed new stories *opposing* the Communists.

Li Huaiqiang dismissed our queries about the officially-organized groups – he had only the vaguest recollection of this experience. It might have remained an exciting moment in his life distinguished by its uniqueness – but apparently hadn't. Li went on: 'From 1945 they summoned all the blind bards to meetings – they weren't allowed to sing old stories any more, they had to sing new ones. I studied them and then forgot them all – well, I basically didn't study them! When you go out [on business], the common people don't listen to that stuff! New stories aren't good to listen to – people don't like listening to new stories, they like old ones! I could never forget the old stories I learnt when I was young, though. I can tell 20 or 30 stories. When you went out in the old days there was business, you could count on it – who'd have thought it would all come to an end?'

He knew of Han Qixiang but didn't hear him perform or meet him. 'That Han Qixiang, he got onto the official payroll. Oh yes, people in our business all know about Han Qixiang. In the Yan'an period people reformed it into new stories, but they didn't control us lot who narrated old stories, we just went off round the countryside narrating on our own.' He knew that some performers sang for political meetings, but didn't admit to doing so himself. No-one in Yangjiagou recalled Han Qixiang visiting the village, or even any new stories being told for meetings. Of local performers associated with the official troupes, Li had vaguely heard of Shi Weijun, but not of Guo Xingyu.

Li Huaiqiang was lucky to find a wife. 'I was 24 when I got married [*c*1946]. They came to take conscripts – people stuck to their old habits, no-one wanted to go off, but they forced them. But us blind people, we couldn't go off to the army, no-one wanted us – that's how I got a wife. People were afraid of joining the army, both sides were taking people off, no-one dared go, as soon as you went off you'd get killed. If it was today I couldn't get married – now it's hard enough for sighted men to find a wife.' Despite his privations under Maoism, he warmed to the theme: 'Society's different now, people have "turned over a new leaf", reforms and all that – too much reform, it's all gone too far.' But first, let us assess the bards' fortunes under Maoism.

Chapter 4
The bards after Liberation

4.1 The new troupes

After the national Liberation of 1949, every county government throughout China set up an arts-work troupe (*wengongtuan*), which soon metamorphosed into an opera troupe (*jutuan*). Some county authorities further set up a narrative-singing artists' propaganda team (*shuoshu yiren xuanchuandui*), which – in theory – not only performed but also collected items, revising them, composing new pieces, and training new performers, under the leadership of the county Hall of Culture (*Wenhuaguan*).[1] These narrative-singing teams were less permanent (and much less costly) than the opera troupes; they held training sessions (*peixunban*) for around a month or even a few days, and then divided into smaller teams to go off on tour round the villages. The tensions within such teams would make an interesting topic, but again, it is hard to assess their activities.

The official image, typically, is deceptive. A rosy official account (Jia 1992: 83) claims: 'If the mid-1940s were a thriving period for narrative-singing in Shaanbei, then in the War of Liberation after the victory in the War against Japan it didn't cease its onward march, but following the successive victories in the war, constantly expanded its influence. Especially after the establishment of New China, narrative-singing in Shaanbei attained the second climax in its history.' Even the candid local scholar Meng Haiping recalls this period up to the Cultural Revolution as a golden age for the blind bards, with county Halls of Culture organizing them into teams and issuing permits, so that district and village leaders had to receive them, hosting and feeding them – an unprecedented and welcome way to guarantee their 'food-bowl'.

Conversely, if the state now acted as the bards' patron, their richer patrons had disappeared, and their poorer patrons were becoming wary of inviting them; temple fairs and 'superstition' were under threat. Many bards were not recruited to the teams or were unwilling to join, and even those who did join took part only intermittently. Although those not registered in the teams were not given permits, they still managed to perform. From our interviews it is clear that they still relied on the old contexts such as 'stories for well-being' and godfather duties.

---

[1]   ANS 962. For new stories performed by a team in Zuoquan, Shanxi, in the 1950s, see Liu Hongqing 2004: 130.

4.2 The folk–state standoff continues

Apart from Han Qixiang, another performer mentioned in the 1940s as creator of new stories is Shi Weijun, whom we did not meet.[2] Born in 1924 in a village south of Suide town, he was semi-blind in his first year. In 1939 he studied for two months with the blind bard Yang Chenggong from a nearby village, starting to make a living the next year.

As we saw above, Shi Weijun was already credited with several new stories in the Yan'an period. In 1946 he was recruited to the Suide county Cultural Association. As retired members of the Suide opera troupe recalled, in 1952–53 the troupe organized a training session for blind bards, led by Shang Airen, deputy chair of the county Cultural Association, getting together a dozen or so blind men to 'reform their thinking' as they learnt and exchanged new stories.

According to the *Anthology*, from 1946 to 1960 Shi Weijun organized over 20 training sessions for bards throughout the area, teaching over 180 performers, but he returned to his village in 1956 to make a living independently. Blind bard Guo Xingyu, himself no simple official mouthpiece, hinted that Shi Weijun found it hard to adapt to official demands after Liberation. 'He was the old chief of the Suide propaganda team. Later he was with Han Qixiang, and served as chair of the county Cultural Association. But then he gave up – he didn't even want his wages, he lost his standing [*gongling*, length of service], and went off on his own to tell stories. The regional arts-work troupe wanted him to join, but he wouldn't.' Again according to the *Anthology*, after 1968 Shi Weijun was once more connected to the Suide county blind peoples' propaganda troupe. But it is clear that he was ever reluctant to take part in official events.

In 2001 blind bard Guo Xingyu (§4.5 below) took us to see his blind master Wang Jinkao in his village south of Suide (Illustration 6).[3] Wang (known as Niur, b. *c*1930) married a sighted girl in 1947; they have three sons and a daughter, all peasants in the village. Wang accompanied himself on *pipa* (§4.6 below). When Guo Xingyu studied with him in about 1962 he was running a kind of blind school in Qingjian. Guo learnt in a group of five or six blind boys, whose parents had to pay fees.

Wang Jinkao appears to have had minimal contact with the new ethos: he could tell new stories like 'Wang Gui and Li Xiangxiang', but if he had ever taken part in training sessions or belonged to the county team, no-one cared to remember. Guo Xingyu told us more about the Suide team. 'In 1955 Han Qixiang came to lead a session lasting around two months, mainly teaching new stories. There were around 30 people in the team, dividing up into four or five small teams, chasing all over the county. But some artists weren't willing to learn new stories, in their way of thinking they couldn't accept it – they weren't issued with permits.'

---

[2]   Material here comes from ANS 1150, as well as our 2001 interviews with his colleague Guo Xingyu and members of the Suide *Jinju* troupe.

[3]   He is mentioned in the *Shaanbei shuoshu* article in Zhongguo 1983: 339.

Illustration 6   Guo Xingyu with his master Wang Jinkao, 2001

We gleaned more data on the training sessions from He Guangwu (b. *c*1932), a semi-blind bard from a village west of the river, south of Mizhi town. 'I began to lose my sight when 15 (*c*1946) and couldn't work in the fields any more. My father was dead, so my mother and older sister got me to learn narrative-singing, otherwise I couldn't have survived. I began learning the arts (*xueyi*) when I was 17 (*c*1948), with a master from Zizhou county. I studied for three years – the first story I learnt was "Returning home" (*Huanxiang ji*).' He went on to list a dozen other traditional stories. Although this was supposedly a climactic period for the new stories, the old stories were being transmitted as if nothing had changed.

He Guangwu married when 21. Their families arranged the match; his betrothed lived in a village only two *li* away, but they wouldn't let her see him, and she only discovered his disability at their wedding. Now she jokes about it and is evidently happy that the family is relatively prosperous with many great-grandchildren; we didn't like to press her on how it seemed then.

He Guangwu went on: 'In 1955 I took part in a blind artists' training session organized by Suide district – our village was part of Suide then. There were 35 of us, studying for two months in Suide town. In 1964 I also studied for 45 days in the Mizhi county Hall of Culture with Master Han Qixiang – we called him Elder Han (Han *ye*) or Chairman Han (Han *zhuren*). In Suide we learnt new items like "Wang Gui and Li Xiangxiang", "Li Shuangshuang", "Opposing the USA and supporting Korea", and "Opposing shamans". Suide county issued us with a graduation certificate, and Mizhi county issued a "propaganda certificate" with the date of our study, the name of the head of the Department of Propaganda, and the name of our master Han Qixiang all written on it. With this certificate, every village received us, helped us find somewhere to stay, got people together to listen to our stories, and gave us grain coupons and a salary. At the beginning, we got 8 *jin* of grain for every story we told; later it was 2 *yuan* per story, nowadays it's 20 *yuan* for a two-hour story.' But despite his sojourns with the state groups, his concept of his livelihood barely took official contexts into account.

In 2001 we also visited Tian Zhizi (b. *c*1933) at his son's home in Miaojiaping, a little town south of Zizhou on the road to Suide. He had belonged to the Zizhou team, and also studied in the Suide team. 'My eyes were no good from young – I began studying narrative-singing in 1944. My master was Wang Jialai from Zizhou county. When I learnt I lived at his house – his fee was 3 *dan* of grain per year, and I learnt for three years.' Through the War of Resistance and the War of Liberation – again precisely the period when the new stories were supposedly in the ascendant – Tian supported himself by curing illness, reciting incantations, and depicting talismans. He instinctively gave us a jaundiced, if sound, justification for such activities: 'They're all things to kid people (*hongren*).'

'I began telling stories in 1951, and in 1952 became chief of the Zizhou blind people's propaganda team, which had been formed the previous year. I was chief of the team for three years; it had over 60 members. Between 1952 to 1956 I studied new stories at the Jiuzhenguan hall in Suide.' Their boss was Shang Airen, an influential cultural official in Shaanbei. Despite my suspicions, Tian recalled, 'In the 1950s the peasants loved hearing new stories. The main ones I learnt were "The outstanding troupe member", "Zhang Yulan takes part in the election", "Opposing shamans", "The tobacco pouch", "Mother Gui makes shoes for the army", and "Wang Piqin takes the southern road".'[4]

Through the 1950s and 60s, although the bards from the team sometimes went on tour in small groups, Tian usually went round on his own. When he was 28 (*c*1960), Tian married a girl from the same town, which he claimed was 'free love', not arranged. In 1962 he spent a period working in Yan'an with none other than Han Qixiang, earning 36 *yuan* a month. Later he resigned and returned home, still making a living as an itinerant bard, also telling fortunes, hanging and opening lockets – by 2001 he had over 200 godchildren.

---

[4]   In *pinyin*: *Youxiu tuanyuan, Zhang Yulan canjia xuanjuhui, Fan wushen, Yankoudai, Gui muqin zuo junxie*, and *Wang Piqin zou nanlu*.

4.3 Li Huaiqiang under Maoism

Let us return again to Li Huaiqiang in Yangjiagou. 'During land reform there were meetings all the time. The Communist Party controlled people, eliminating superstition. When they wanted to hold a meeting they first summoned a bard to narrate a [new] section, so everyone turned up – then the bard sang the old stories that people liked.'

This was a common theme, of great significance for our understanding of the Maoist period. The bard would attract people to turn up for tedious political meetings, and satisfy the demands of political expediency by performing a brief political item first, before the fun began. Scholar Meng Haiping recalled: 'Both old and new stories were heard then. Until 1956, they began with a short section with new content, then moved onto the old stories like "The story of five women reviving the Tang" (*Wunü xing Tang zhuan*).' This common ruse is nicely captured in Wu Tianming's 1987 film *The Old Well*, set in neighbouring Shanxi.

Li Huaiqiang originally lived in a miserable cave-dwelling made of earth, but after land reform, he was helped to 'buy' a comfortable cave-dwelling right at the top of the village from the former landlords, which had been servants' quarters. The landlords also had to 'sell' him their precious *sanxian* banjo, which he bought for one *dan* of grain.

If in that sense Li was able to profit from the overthrow of the landlords, he soon suffered from their demise. 'We were allowed to narrate stories in the early days after Liberation, but people's consciousness was raised, people had studied a lot of books.' I didn't care to argue with him there, so he went on, 'They said narrative-singing was boring, so there was a lot less of it – it got less all of a sudden with the collectives (*nongye hezuo* – from the mid-1950s). People like us just tilled the fields, told fortunes, we could just about get by, the state gave us relief. We couldn't just die off – some people were given relief, some were put in old people's homes, some with skills (*jishu*) could go out and heal illness and tell fortunes.' And he was still taking large numbers of godchildren, whose parents' regular little gifts always presented a lifeline.

If Li Huaiqiang was unaware of it, the Mizhi county authorities were attempting to organize bards. Gao Zhiqiang, former chief of the county Hall of Culture, recalled, 'The county first set up a narrative-singing team in the early 1950s, organizing over 20 blind bards, training them all together to sing new stories. The Hall of Culture issued them with performance permits, which meant that the district and village authorities had to host them – that resolved blind men's problem of livelihood.' But, as we have already seen, the teams never controlled blindmen for long.

4.4 Han Qixiang after Liberation

Meanwhile Han Qixiang's efforts on behalf of the revolution continued unabated.[5] He continued to perform and organize training groups throughout the counties of Shaanbei. He took part keenly in the Korean War propaganda, organizing a group of over 30 blind bards. He was chosen as a delegate to the Great Assembly of Cultural Representatives (*Wendai dahui*). In 1950 he was chosen as chairman of the Northwest Storytelling Society (*Xibei quxie*), and spent periods in the provincial capital Xi'an.

But his absorption into the new urban élite began causing problems. He encountered antipathy from two cadres 'whose bourgeois ideology was very severe', and who wanted him to look more respectable in an expensive pair of dark glasses. Another tried to get him to abandon his partner and find an intellectual woman. But he reported their thinking and stuck to his old ways, and partner; we are not told what happened to the cadres. Again, such stories give a glimpse of conflicts.

He also insisted on sticking with his meagre official salary, despite comments from friends that he could now make a much better living by going out on his own – again, an interesting conflict, the truth of which will remain obscure. He may have retained some idealism, or he may have been given no choice; perhaps he felt that the official route gave him better prospects – though he does seem to have chosen a poor rural life in preference to that of a typical cadre.

He wrote new stories to support the 'Three and Five Antis' campaigns in the early 1950s, and was given several awards. But he was uncomfortable, and claimed that his creativity was being stifled by the new vocabulary he was learning as he lost contact with the masses. Again, this is significant: he had (or voiced) no complaints about the new subjects themselves, but bemoaned the difficulty of bringing them to life in vocabulary that could communicate to poor villagers. But of course language itself was a major tool by which the Party was inculcating conformity.

After attending a conference in Beijing in 1953, he requested permission to move to a poor village called Yanglaozhuang, back in Yan'an. His claim was that this would enable him to experience life and create new works. Though always in demand to attend meetings and perform in Beijing and elsewhere, he continued his tours of Shaanbei villages, and spent considerable periods in Yanglaozhuang over the next dozen years. Heroic as this may have been, his experiences remained utterly atypical.

Yanglaozhuang was a very poor village with only 15 households. Even by Shaanbei standards, health was appalling; it had only two children, both brought from other villages; children born in the village were invariably born dead or disabled. That Han chose it suggests genuine revolutionary zeal – unlike his 'intellectual' minder, who was apparently horrified and soon left him alone there. Still, the villagers reportedly treated him like 'Chairman Han' until he made a point of wearing the same clothes and eating the same food as them. He was one of the

---

[5]   This section is based on Hu 1989: 149–51.

first co-op members in the village. Though still receiving his salary, he took part in production and commune affairs. He even gave some of his savings (deposited, impressively, in a bank) to the new commune – in 1955 he gave 100 *yuan*. Indeed, he did not take any payment from the peasants, or the village leadership, for his performances. A 1963 report by Luo Yang describes his saintlike behaviour while exposing a black market arising during 'temporary' adversity in the village after a natural disaster.

So impossible was it in the village for children to survive that 'superstition' was rife, with villagers seeking exorcisms – cadres feared negative effects on production and the setting up of communes. Han discovered the real cause was the polluted water from the well and the appalling sanitary conditions, and took action. Two children were born next winter, whom Han regarded as treasures. He also took responsibility for the village's health problems. Here we may see elements of the blindman's traditional arts: bards also trained in medicine, and made a living by adopting godchildren. Some parents in the village began giving their children names with the element 'Han'. Did he even perform stories for well-being, or take on godchildren, one wonders? Anyway, his fame and wider contacts must have helped the village; if he was popular, it would have been because he – like the gods – could benefit the inhabitants. He also acted as cultural cadre, setting up a 'club' (*julebu*) and a *yangge* song-and-dance troupe. He was admitted to the Communist Party in 1955, his third year in Yanglaozhuang.

During this period Han continued composing new stories, including 'We can't withdraw from the communes' (*Buneng tuishe*) (how very true!), reportedly converting peasants who were opposed to collectivism. Having heard that in some Zichang villages women were reluctant to work in the fields, and men reluctant to tolerate them doing so, he composed pieces exhorting them and praising female labour heroes. More revealing admissions here.

In 1957 Han spent a period in hospital in Beijing having treatment for his eyes. It was then that he heard of Braille and began learning it. This was of course itself a rare luxury, only obtainable through his superior status and contacts. He was right to thank Mao and the Party for having the chance to learn Braille, but how many other blind people in rural China had such a chance? It was indeed possible even for blind singers to own librettos, copied for them by a literate sighted person. In the 1940s a blind singer in Yanchang who composed a new story wanted someone to write it down for him so he could ask people to read it out to remind him.[6] Even for those few blindmen who had access to Braille, it was tough. Tian Zhizi told us: 'I studied Braille for a bit while I was at Baoji, but I couldn't learn it properly.'

The period from 1957 to 1960 was considered as the second climax of Han Qixiang's compositional career. His autobiographical story 'Turning over a new leaf' (*Fanshen ji*) was composed for the anti-rightist movement in 1957, and was lengthened by 1959, a cadre called Wang Zongyuan setting up with him in a

---

[6]   Lin 1946: 50.

new cave-dwelling in Yanglaozhuang to adapt it.[7] In 1957 Han was named vice-president of the Chinese narrative-singing workers association (*Zhongguo quyi gongzuozhe xiehui*), a post which he again held in the 1980s. He was to hold many other official cultural posts.

In 1958 he answered the Party's call to reform the mountain areas, going on another tour as the Great Leap Forward got under way, accompanying labour projects. He composed a 'Story of the Leap Forward' (*Yuejin ji*). The items he performed on such tours were often semi-improvised according to the events unfolding in the village.[8] By summer 1958 he was part of a distinguished troupe of narrative singers from many Chinese genres, busy performing in urban festivals all over China, in Beijing, Henan, Hubei, Gansu, and Sichuan.

During the natural disasters of 1959–60 he also roused villagers. He performed 'Turning over a new leaf' for peasants disgruntled with the paltry goods available on New Year's Eve, supposedly enlightening them to how much their lives had improved since the bad old society – if only we could know their true reaction to this!

His 1960 'Returning home' (*Huixiang ji*), composed on returning with his second son to his old home village for the first time since 1940, is a companion piece to 'Turning over a new leaf'. He was also composing poems and 'street narrative-singing' (*jietou shuochang*). Such stories continued to be published in national magazines such as *Quyi* [Narrative-singing]. Though illness again forced him to spend periods in hospital in the early 1960s, he still went on the road to perform in villages. While in hospital he learnt of the new legend of Lei Feng – the quintessential revolutionary goodie-goodie – and naively, or astutely, composed a story in praise of him.

Another revealing passage: though Han was said to encourage other singers to perform new stories, some singers not only disliked the new repertory but wanted to compete with him with their old repertory. In spring 1963 they competed at the market at Yan'an – at a time when traditional culture was indeed making a brief comeback. Inevitably, Han Qixiang is said to have won over the audiences so that few remained to hear the old items.

By 1964 he was touring with others from the Yan'an narrative-singing group to publicize the Socialist Education movement, prelude to the Cultural Revolution (Zhang Qian 1965). In the summer of 1965, on a visit to a production-team outside Zichang county-town, cadre Zhang Qian witnessed his flexibility in improvising stories about local events and people. There, and in another nearby village, Han found out about local women who had contributed to labour projects, and praised them in his stories. In another village he arrived in time to use his art to struggle a 'landlord element who was organizing bad activities'. Then too he was taking medicine with him and explaining sanitary precautions. Zhang Qian also went with him on a visit to the Zichang narrative-singers training band. Apart from his selfless identification with the bards and his constant exhortations, Han also

---

[7]   Hu 1989: 163–74.

[8]   Hu 1989: 188–90.

criticized some of them who were more concerned about earning money than the effects of their propaganda. Again, this suggests discontent in the ranks. By this time he was performing national revolutionary pieces like 'Stealing the seal' (*Duo yin*).

On a trip to Beijing Han was able to buy Mao's *Selected Works* in Braille. Apart from frankly political writings, he also read new fiction. On tour he often took a battery-operated radio to allow him to keep up with events. By the early 1960s he was able to commit his scripts to the page with a blind typewriter.[9] By 1965 he was taking the Braille edition of Mao's *Selected Works* with him on tour – no easy feat, surely.

Through the unremitting hagiography, such official material also unwittingly gives a glimpse of constant conflict and difficulties. What did Han Qixiang think of old and new stories, and his later life? Obviously his circumstances improved immeasurably under Communist patronage. He stood to gain, but must have been aware of what he was losing too. By the eve of the Cultural Revolution he appeared to have maintained thoroughly revolutionary credentials; his selfless work for Communism was constantly praised in public, and there appeared to be nothing to criticize.

4.5 The Cultural Revolution, and Guo Xingyu

Unusually, the Cultural Revolution was a significant period of activity for blind bards, who continued to perform both in their traditional contexts and in the state groups. The latter now had a new lease of life as 'Blind artists Mao Zedong Thought propaganda teams'. In Mizhi, the county Hall of Culture organized a dozen bards into one such team, touring villages, mines, and schools[10] – villages without electricity, mines where accidents were routine, and schools with few tables or chairs, if you will forgive me for reminding you.

Tian Zhizi was still taking part in the propaganda teams. 'In 1972 I was mainly taking disciples at Wubu county – that was because the Wubu Hall of Culture invited me to come to train members for their propaganda team.' Though it was ever harder for bards to perform without the sanction of the teams, popular taste still appeared to require an escape from the relentless revolutionary diet. Tian Zhizi had claimed the new stories were popular in the 1950s, but 'from 1967 [traditional] narrative-singing was forbidden – by that time people preferred old stories, or at least they didn't like new ones, so we bards told some old ones in the villages on the quiet.'

Xu Wengong, sighted bard: 'During the Cultural Revolution I still performed in secret in the villages – the people liked to listen and protected me. I still hung lockets on the quiet too.' Guo Xingyu: 'In the Cultural Revolution one couldn't

---

9   Photo, Luo 1963: 57.
10   Mizhi 1993: 542.

hang the locket openly, but for those who needed it we still did it.' Geomancers were also still furtively active.

Back in Yangjiagou, Li Huaiqiang, who had never belonged to a team or performed in a group, still relied on a minimal handout from the village government to survive; with his wife and five children, times were desperate. 'In the Cultural Revolution they didn't invite us bards any more, it just stopped. But people like us still went out – mostly to tell fortunes, not so much to narrate stories.' And he sometimes sneaked out to hang the locket for children in exchange for 'a couple of little coins.' Li was soon branded an 'ox demon and snake spirit' (*niuguisheshen*), accused of feudal superstition. They took his manual off and burnt it. They took his *sanxian* banjo away too, but he got it back after half a year. 'Monkey kids, coming to our houses to get us to hand things over – if you did, then you were let off, if you didn't then they paraded you through the streets.' Li was only paraded once. The only time he could recall when the authorities regulated narrative-singing was in the year of rebellion (*zaofan*) of the Cultural Revolution, when all the brigades had to organize blind bards into narrative-singing teams to go round and make propaganda, the county Hall of Culture taking a cut.

A younger blind bard more able than many to move with the times is Guo Xingyu (b.1951),[11] with whom I spent some time in 2001. His case is quite exceptional among bards I have met; at the same time, his traditional ('superstitious') livelihood has remained constant. Brought up in a Suide village, he was blind from young. He studied narrative-singing and fortune-telling for ten moons with Wang Jinkao from the age of 12 (*c*1962) – the *Anthology* claims that he first studied with Shi Weijun for two moons. He started going out on business when about 16, on the eve of the Cultural Revolution. 'When I was young I enjoyed learning everything from my master, curing illness, depicting talismans and chanting mantras' – which he was quick to point out are all 'rational' (*youdaolide*).

'I often studied informally and briefly with other artists, asking people to read me out old books, and I composed lyrics myself – if someone read me out a story I could memorize it at once. When I was just starting out we mainly told old stories, though in public contexts we told bits of new stories. New ones I liked telling, before and during the Cultural Revolution, were "Fuss over an abortion", "Eliminating transactional marriages", "The great immortal who eats ghosts", "Eliminating superstition", and "The tale of the city youth returning to the countryside".' Another bard recalled, 'In 1964 we told "Birth control" and "The three main rules of discipline and the eight points for attention".'[12]

In 1968 Guo Xingyu joined the Suide county blind peoples' propaganda team, which had several dozen bards, divided into three or four sub-groups. 'In the 1960s we were issued with narrative-singing permits; we had to hand over part of our

---

[11]   See ANS 1149–50, and our talks in 2001. He told us he was born in the 12th moon of 1951; Huo Xianggui gives 1948.

[12]   In *pinyin*: *Jueyu fengbo*, *Pochu maimai hunyin*, *Chigui*, *Pochu mixin*, *Zhishi qingnian huixiang ji*, *Jihua shengyu*, and *Sanda jilü baxiang zhuyi*.

income to the Hall of Culture as "public assets" (*gonggong jilei*) – the state also took a certain amount of training expenses (*peixunfei*), but later that stopped. In the 1960s and 1970s the whole county probably had about 70 or 80 bards – about 40 or 50 didn't enter the training bands, they had to tell stories on the quiet.'

Guo became a versatile instrumentalist too, teaching himself *guanzi* oboe, *erhu* fiddle, and *dizi* flute for fun. Sometimes he would 'mess in for a laugh' on shawm with the *chuishou* bands, but he never did jobs with them. He has even composed new pieces (including a song 'Chairman Mao has stayed in our village'), taking part in official festivals in Suide, Yulin, and Xi'an, and winning second prize in a provincial festival for his 1976 *erhu* fiddle solo 'Meeting the bride' (*Yingqin*).[13] He was praised by the venerable Han Qixiang. He appeared a model bard in the new mould – little would one think he was still performing stories for well-being and healing all the while.

Ironically, perhaps the worst case of penalization was revolutionary Han Qixiang himself, inactive and subject to public criticism throughout the period. As late as 1976, just as the Gang of Four was about to be arrested, he was summoned to perform in Xi'an and criticized, though by late 1977 he was well back on the road to rehabilitation, taking part again in meetings.

As we saw, bards mostly worked solo; even when they assembled for temple fairs and New Year's festivities, they performed in sequence, not together. But under Communism, bards were sometimes organized into small groups to perform for non-ritual contexts. The *Anthology* states that after Liberation, bards sometimes grouped together in threes or fives to perform in towns in work units or on the streets, performing standing or on procession. Though bards did not mention this to us, it may have been one part of the picture. It is a common feature of state troupes that they added instruments. A solo bard usually plays *shuaban* clappers on his leg and *mazhazi* clappers on his hand, and sometimes a *xingmu* woodblock too; now a few bards were credited with playing several percussion instruments at once. Han Qixiang is said sometimes to have added small cymbals; in Jiaxian the blind bard Ma Ruizeng played overtures on *sanxian* and 12 percussion instruments at once, imitating the percussion overture of Shanxi opera.[14] Though the teams might add extra melodic instruments, even the 1980s' cassettes by Zhang Jungong's state-funded team (§5.4 below) feature such extra instruments only sparingly.

But both new contexts and musical innovations remained a minor feature even through the years of Maoism, and after the commune system was dismantled, tradition became yet more dominant.

---

[13]   This is an intriguing (and rare) illustration of the 'conservatory style' as mastered by a folk musician. He didn't tell us that it was composed with help from cadre Huo Xianggui. Inspired by the style of local shawm bands, it uses high positions, unlike local fiddle technique – though he heard of Abing only later in the 1980s.

[14]   ANS 14.

4.6 Themes and music

The social context and modern history of the Shaanbei bards, main topics of this essay, are valid themes in themselves, about which I have merely scratched the surface. A whole book could and should further be written about the stories and the music – though I am still less qualified to write it, having little grasp of the local language or fictional world. So this section will merely outline some basic aspects to show how much more there is to study.

The material so far should illustrate the validity of taking the traditional contexts, stories, and music as a constant, appearing similar in the 1930s and 1990s despite government attempts to reform them. In this section I will not consider the new stories; though their texts are new, musically they are similar to the traditional ones – only they are much shorter, in single episodes rather than the serialized long plots of stories from imperial times.

The music is subsidiary to the plot; none of the bards I have heard take as much pride in their *sanxian* intonation as in their story-telling. But audiences enjoy the performance, and analysis in terms of text or literary features alone fails to evoke the effect when matched with vocal melody and the accompaniment of lute and clappers. Indeed, He Guangwu summarized the indispensable quality of the *sanxian* accompaniment: 'As long as I've got my *sanxian* the words are all there – if I don't have the *sanxian* I forget them!'

Musical instruments

The bard accompanies himself on a plucked lute and usually two kinds of clappers attached respectively to his left leg and right hand. He rests his right foot on a low stool, and often drapes a towel over his shoulder to wipe sweat from his face.

The *shuaban* (commonly called just *ban*), three or four strips of datewood tied together at one end, tied to the bard's left knee, maintains a regular beat throughout both vocal and instrumental sections. The *mazhazi*, five strips of bamboo separated by four small pieces of bamboo tied to the right wrist and bound in a leather loop, sounds automatically whenever the lute is plucked, making a faint rustling sound. Some bards also punctuate their spoken dialogue with a *zhutou* (or *zhunao*, 'pig's head'), local term for the *xingmu* woodblock that is a common tool of story-tellers elsewhere in China, rapped down periodically on a hard surface. The plucked lute is either the unfretted three-stringed *sanxian* (known as *xianzi*) or the fretted four-stringed *pipa*. The *sanxian* is most common, the use of *pipa* having declined drastically since the 1980s. Both are still commonly made by local carpenters, though *pipa* are harder to make, more costly, and harder to play.[15]

---

[15]   For the Shaanbei *pipa*, see Li Jianzheng 1984, Li Shibin 1988, Ai 1996, ANS 969–72 and transcriptions; a section in AI has an introduction (857–8) and four 'solo' pieces from Zizhou bards (872–5). For a video clip of *pipa* bard Feng Shusheng, apparently from the Yan'an region, see http://www.zgya.com/mggl/ONEWS.asp?id=197.

According to Han Qixiang, *pipa* accompaniment was common in the 1940s in the Yan'an region (in Ganquan, Qingjian, Yanchang, and Wuqi), and it was familiar to cultural cadre Anbo.[16] Li Huaiqiang recalled from his early years on the road in the 1940s that the *sanxian* was common in the central Shaanbei area, the *pipa* further north and west around Yinchuan in Ningxia and in Inner Mongolia; when he toured there, he had to take up the *pipa*, which was more popular there than the *sanxian*.

Fieldwork during the 1980s showed that the *pipa* was still widely used. Scholar Li Shibin met over ten active *pipa* players, claiming that it was played in Zizhou, Suide, Mizhi, and Qingjian, as well as in Zichang, Yanchang, Yan'an, and Ansai further south; and that Zichang and Zizhou alone had over 80 players.[17] This rare form of *pipa* (Illustration 7, ☉**C3**), held less vertically than the 'modern' *pipa*, and played with a plectrum, was a major discovery, reminding scholars of the Tang dynasty *pipa*. Like other Chinese scholars of the 1980s, they were keen to conjure up 'living fossils' and evoke the glories of ancient dynasties, but they mustered less publicity for this supposed relic of the Tang *pipa* than did scholars of *Nanyin* music in southeastern China.

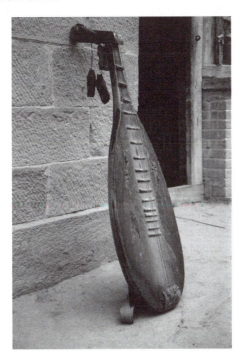

Illustration 7   Wang Jinkao's *pipa*, 2001

----

[16]   Han 1985: 4; Yan'an 1988, vol.14: 162.
[17]   Li Shibin 1988: 42.

Guo Xingyu: 'In the 1950s and 1960s, the *pipa* was played in the villages, the *sanxian* in the towns.' But even in the 1950s Tian Zhizi's propaganda team in Suide had only one *pipa* player (Ma Shande, now dead) among over 60 members. 'The *sanxian* sounds high, the *pipa* sounds low, so people prefer the *sanxian*' – he glossed 'high' as bright, loud, and clear. Xu Wengong, from a village in Qingjian county, learnt on *pipa* when 17 (*c*1964), but later felt that with its small sound it was less popular, so he changed to *sanxian*.

By the 1990s the *pipa* was rare in the Yulin counties. He Guangwu told us there were more *pipa* bards in Yanchang and Zhidan, but we heard of none in the Zhenchuan–Mizhi area in 1999; one alert Mizhi villager hadn't seen any since he was young in the 1940s. By 2001 well-travelled Guo Xingyu thought that the *pipa* was basically obsolete. He took us to see his master, Wang Jinkao (72), no longer active as a bard (⊙**C3**). The first *pipa* he learnt on when 12 was bought for him by his parents, but later he gave it to a disciple; the *pipa* he played for us was over 60 years old – he had bought it from another old bard over 40 years previously.

Bards formerly used sheep-gut strings for the *sanxian*, but metal or nylon have been common since the 1970s; for the *pipa* they persisted with sheep-gut. Bards commonly have a lovely embroidered purse for spare strings hanging from one of the pegs. Both *sanxian* and *pipa* are traditionally sounded with a small plectrum of ox-horn, though I saw no bards using one. The use of the plectrum for the *pipa* is now rare in modern China, though it was indeed common in the Tang dynasty. The bridge is made of black *gelan* wood.

Bards tune by ear, with no fixed pitch standard. Several *sanxian* tunings are reported. Perhaps most common are 'old blackbean' (*lao heidou*), or 'individual string tuning' (*danyin diao*) tuning (*do-so*-high *do*), and 'paired string tuning' (*shuangyin diao, do-so-so*) with the two upper strings tuned to the same pitch. Li Huaiqiang tuned to low *so-do-so*, which Guo Xingyu described as the main tuning, though he said 'paired string tuning' sounds more robust (*zhuang*). Tuning in two 4ths (*re-so*-high *do*) has been recorded in parts of Jingbian and Shenmu. Though the number and disposition of frets on the *pipa* is not standard, the 'orthodox tradition' (*zhengzong*) is four lower *xiang* frets and thirteen upper *pin* frets, all of bamboo. Its strings are tuned in pairs of 4ths or 5ths. It is held at an angle slightly above horizontal, but played entirely in high positions. The melody is played mainly on the upper string of the *sanxian* and the top two strings of the *pipa*, the lower strings being sounded as a drone.

Stories, language, music

Stories overlap with opera plots. Like opera – indeed like soap opera – they are performed in sections, commonly three episodes (*huihui*). Like opera, these stories have long been a dominant form for poor people to learn of history, legend, and morality, only being challenged by schooling since the 1950s. Schooling even now is quite elementary, though TV and pop music are doubtless replacing traditional stories for entertainment.

Local scholars impressively list 289 stories, all but 27 apparently traditional.[18] Li Huaiqiang said he knew about 20 or 30 stories. Bards distinguish categories such as civil and martial stories, and 'immortal stories' or 'god stories';[19] relating tales of love, official success, solving of crimes, or famous battles, all known from popular fiction and opera since the Ming dynasty. They are chosen partly according to the context. Li Huaiqiang: 'For temple fairs we narrate god stories – superstitious stories like "The lantern of the precious lotus" (*Baolian deng*) and "The Match of the immortal woman" (*Xiannü pei*). At people's houses we narrate stories for well-being about the official [imperial] exams.'

Though the currency of such plots appears to have been unaffected by the whole seemingly dramatic course of twentieth-century history, below we will note Li Huaiqiang's assessment of the coarsening of the bards' language over his lifetime. Without judging it, such a colloquial form could not help absorbing elements from a changing language, which is partly what keeps it relevant. Bards improvise phrases on the basis of a well-known story – as He Guangwu observed: 'We respond to the changes on the spur of the moment (*suiji yingbian*), the lyrics aren't fixed and dead (*dingsi*).' Scholars have described a rhyme pattern consisting of 13 sounds, but it seems to be used loosely. Stories are mainly told in the third person, the bard sometimes impersonating the characters in the first person for spoken sections.

As to musical features, here I can only summarize the analysis of local scholars; note that they may have articulated a more systematic vocabulary than the bards themselves, derived partly from study with Han Qixiang.[20] Singing dominates the story, but some sections of dialogue are spoken. The story is sung in symmetrical sequences of two phrases, reflected in the melody. Tempo is generally rather fast, but there are subtle changes to match the drama. Melodic sections are mainly in pairs of lines of seven or ten words; bards sometimes sing triplets over the duple beat of leg-clappers, enabling them to sing lines of ten words to the same tune as that for lines of seven words. The basic duple metre is often alleviated by extra beats in the *sanxian* cadential phrases; bards often play a 5-beat cadence on *so* as interlude, and they sometimes punctuate a recited section with a single clap on *sanxian* or woodblock.

Melodic features have much in common with other Shaanbei vocal genres. Indeed, bards incorporate material from other genres, such as *xintianyou, yangge, daoqing*, and *mihu*. Leaps of a fourth are common, and two main scales are used, both based on a pentatonic scale, with two further degrees used as passing notes:

---

[18] ANS 1688–90. This list may derive largely from Han Qixiang's own list of traditional items, listed in Bibliography as Han Qixiang (?), and from those mentioned in his autobiographical stories. In ANS, coverage of Han Qixiang's modern stories, most influential and innovative of the genre, is prominently featured, but most of the fieldwork reflects the traditional style, including some ritual pieces.

[19] In *pinyin*: *wenshu, wushu, xianjia shu, shenshen shu*.

[20] See e.g. Han 1985: 4–6. The exx. in ANS (973–1147) seem to complement their analysis (966–72) rather well.

huanyin ('happy notes') with a natural *ti* descending to a low *so*, and the more plaintive *kuyin* ('wailing notes') using a lower *ti*. Two main singing forms are distinguished: *pingdiao* and *kudiao*, both of which may use *huanyin* and *kuyin* scales. Local scholars illustrate typical forms but also variations, which is what makes them interesting. *Pingdiao* progresses in two couplets, the first phrase in each cadencing on *do*, the second descending to low *so*. *Kudiao*, said to be derived from local vocal genres such as *daoqing*, is used for sad scenes. Its melodic line is mainly conjunct, with a narrow range, and without leaps or *guomen* interludes on lute; scholars distinguish several types according to mood and tempo. A third style, *wudiao* ('martial tune') is fast, mainly for battles or agitated scenes, with phrases often asymmetrical, and few breaths or *guomen* interludes.

The bard does not play the lute while singing: the story is told only to the accompaniment of the *shuaban* leg clappers, maintaining a regular beat. The lute only punctuates the story with an overture (*qiban*), brief cadential ostinatos between phrases, and longer *guomen* melodic interludes between sections of the story, always accompanied by the regular beat on the clappers. Scholars distinguish large, small, and martial (*wudiao*) overtures.[21] For the instrumental interludes, bards may play pieces adapted from other traditions, such as shawm pieces or versions of folk-songs; as in opera, they have suitable melodies (*paizi*) for every stock dramatic situation. Types of tune (*diaokou*) include 'walking', 'warrior', and 'princely'.[22]

4.7 New stories fail to catch on

Such is an outline of the themes and music of the Shaanbei bards, still largely traditional around 2000. Despite the propaganda surrounding Han Qixiang, not only does no-one value new stories now, but few recall them being popular even under Maoism. He Guangwu gave the rough outline: 'Before the Cultural Revolution we mostly told old stories, during the Cultural Revolution mostly new ones, now it's mainly old ones again.' But he too recalled, 'In those days, usually we'd tell a section of a new story first and then tell an old one.' Other bards like Li Huaiqiang had no time for new stories at all. He had heard 'Smashing superstition' on tape at a villager's house, but 'people don't like it, it's not good to listen to – you can't sing stories like that for families, only for big meetings where tickets are on sale!' He Guangwu had learnt 'Opposing shamans' in the training session in the 1950s, but he too commented wryly, 'You can't tell that story nowadays – that'd be blasphemy!'

So why didn't the new stories become popular? Sure, villagers might be conservative and escapist in their tastes, being more excited by stories of emperors and concubines, scholars and maids, generals and outlaws. But the new stories might have been entertaining and meaningful in the contexts of the 1940s too. The irony was that the whole purpose of the new stories since the 1940s was to address

---

[21] ANS 1027–48.

[22] In *pinyin*: *zoulu diao, zhanshi diao, weiwang diao*.

current issues of great importance to the peasantry: namely tackling endemic social problems inherited from the old society.

But problems that might be arising under the new society were not now to be publicly aired. I would surmise that villagers might have been open to new stories, but were disillusioned by their glib political correctness, their failure to reflect complex new realities. The new stories were surely rarely heard in the villages apart from at mass meetings by which people were anyway alienated. If villagers were able to host a performer to sing to invite the gods to heal their livestock, the new stories were inappropriate. In the early period of the 1940s, they may have had considerable novelty, and even helped people confront genuine problems, like forced marriages, opium, landlord exploitation. But maybe the themes didn't keep pace with the problems: by the 1950s their perceived problems included campaigns, communes, irrational directives, and thus the new items seemed false, like the propaganda itself.

Still, as we saw, the items performed on Han Qixiang's tours in the late 1950s were often semi-improvised according to the events unfolding in the village. That is, problems such as reactionary thinking among the peasants could be ridiculed; perhaps even bourgeois thinking of local leaders; but central policy could hardly be questioned. The spectrum of opinion expressed has not been recorded, but He Guangwu appeared to marry the traditional concept of bards' auspicious role in society and the political correctness of Maoism: 'We shouldn't tell stories satirizing society, with bad effects, or words of opposition. When you begin telling a story, it's all auspicious phrases (*jiqinghua*).' Thus for rain ceremonies he recites an auspicious phrase to encourage rain to fall. Or he may sing a typical passage like:

Plucking the *sanxian*, I tune the notes,	弹起三弦定起音,
audience of men and women, pure of body;	男女观众一身清;
Men and women, young and old, all sit down,	男女老少都坐下,
if I tell the story badly, please criticize;	说的不好请批评;
The mouth of the bard is an infinite receptacle,	书匠的口开量的斗,
whatever I want to tell, it's all there in my belly.	要说多少肚都有.

As to issues current since the reforms of the 1980s, several performers mentioned stories about the birth-control policy – that is, supporting it; given its massive unpopularity, has anyone dared sing stories opposing it? If no stories have arisen dedicated to sensitive issues such as official corruption, they are doubtless subtly aired in passing, if not as flagrantly as the fictional balladeer in Mo Yan's visceral 1988 novel *The Garlic Ballads*:[23]

A prefecture head who exterminates clans,
A county administrator who wipes out families;

---

[23] Mo 1996: 73. For stories about corruption sung in Zuoquan, Shanxi, see Liu Hongqing 2004: 59, 191.

No lighthearted banter from the mouths of power:
You tell us to plant garlic, and that's what we do –
So what right have you not to buy our harvest?

Since the government mounts regular poster campaigns warning of sexually transmitted diseases, even if it has been slow to admit to the appalling danger of AIDS, I wonder if the bards could now be enlisted to tell stories warning of such perils. It seems unlikely.

At any rate, one cannot help be impressed by the adaptability and creativity of story-tellers, and whatever the constraints on public speaking both under the communes and since the reforms, they must always rely to some extent on keeping their audience entertained with topical remarks which will strike a chord. As Tian Zhizi reminded us, 'Narrative-singing artists can all improvise texts.' One trifling instance: while I was present for a bard's story, they always included a phrase or two about me. He Guangwu sang:

For turning over a new leaf we depended on Mao Zedong
For our freedom we relied on Deng Xiaoping;
With the reform and open policy our times are good
For our good times we don't forget Jiang Zemin.
For narrating stories we like to tell about the Great Peace;
Even an English friend comes to have a listen.

Little did I expect to find myself in such exalted company.

All agreed that new stories weren't popular, but even if the subjects remained traditional, Li Huaiqiang pointed out that the bards' language had been evolving along with the language in society generally. A certain change of style, reflecting the times, had evidently left him behind. 'In the old days you sang of "Lady" or "Mistress" (*furen, xiaojie*), now it's "missus" (*poyi*); in the old days it was "setting up as a family" (*chengjia*), now it's "the couple have got together", "they held hands as they walked", "they kissed" – it's so lacking in culture! Old people won't listen to that stuff, in the old days it was real cultured, now it just ain't the same. But you have to adapt yer language to the times, eh?'

So why should people apparently prefer stories about events many centuries earlier to ones about their society now? That is an issue too broad to attempt here, but local scholar Meng Haiping explained the ability of the old stories to survive under Communism: 'Traditional stories propound truth, goodness, beauty, and filial piety (*zhenshanmeixiao*) – that is China's traditional morality, the Party doesn't oppose that, and doesn't suppress it.' Though there is ample evidence to show that they *did* oppose it, deliberately, regarding it under headings such as 'bourgeois morality', Meng is still making a good point, because the Party he refers to is that on the ground, where continuity is more evident in local practice than the rupture often advocated by central theory.

Chapter 5
The reform era

In Shaanbei, as elsewhere in China, as the commune system began to be dismantled from the early 1980s, traditional culture revived more openly. We saw above that bards were active throughout the commune period, both in and out of the new teams; if the old contexts and stories had never died out, after the end of the Cultural Revolution there was no longer such need for collusion or duplicity. Li Huaiqiang recalled, 'As soon as Mao Zedong died, they stopped controlling us bards.' But like other traditional performers, they were soon competing with new economic pressures, TV and pop music taking their toll: where Communism had failed to marginalize tradition, capitalism looked like succeeding.

Ebullient local pundit Meng Haiping again had a perceptive comment: 'In those days [under the communes] they tried to destroy traditional culture, but couldn't; now they don't control it any more, but it gradually declines anyway. 1984 to 1990 was the best period. Ever since the great wave of economics started, culture has been dying out.'

In this chapter I discuss four main themes: the collapse of the teams, the encroachment of sighted performers, local fieldwork, and a major cassette series. Finally we revisit some bards, and observe performances of stories for well-being and for a temple fair.

5.1 The teams decline

I have shown that official initiatives always played a minor role, but let us first look at the teams. At first there was no obvious change in official policy, and some county authorities continued their efforts to organize blind performers. In Mizhi county,[1] 'from 1973 to 1982 the Hall of Culture held one or two training sessions annually for blind bards to learn new stories advertising the policies of the Party and the nation. In 1978, 17 performers were registered, including Gao Qingwang, Li Yongfa, and Yang Junshan. From September 1984 the narrative-singing hall was opened as a venue; within two months there were over 50 performances, with [total] audiences of over 5,000.'

But entry by ticket was a short-lived experiment: by about 1986, as prices rose and more modern entertainments became popular, the hall had to close down. The cultural authorities soon came up against economic reality, having to resort

---

[1]   Mizhi 1993: 542.

to more viable money-making ventures like setting up halls for video games, or classes teaching electronic keyboards.

In Jiaxian county, poorer still, the head of the Bureau of Culture observed, 'In 1982 the Bureau of Culture held a blind men's narrative-singing training session for over 30 bards; from 1983 to 1989 over 20 men took part each year. Each session lasted three days. They stayed in the main hall of the Hall of Culture, bringing their own bedding. The Hall of Culture taught them some new lyrics – the bards' memory is so good, they learnt them very quickly. The new lyrics were of all sorts: birth-control policy, the reform and open-door policy, the private enterprise system, keeping up with the times. The Bureau of Culture gave them performance permits and issued a document to the district governments telling them to host the bards if they came to perform. From the host they earnt a dozen *yuan* plus their food for each story.' But by the 1990s the Jiaxian cultural budgets were much reduced, and even regular employees were lucky to receive their salaries, so they were rarely able to organize sessions for the bards. 'Now the Disabled People's Union (set up by the county government in the 1990s) gives blind people benefit anyway, so they make no effort – their skills aren't as good as the older generation.'

In general, as one cultural cadre told us: 'Later the bards didn't want people to control them, and we didn't have enough money anyway, so we gave up.' For the cultural authorities, their purpose was hardly different from the commune period, even if state policy would never again be so 'hard': they still sought to teach the bards new stories to spread education about party policies, and they still aspired to both 'controlling' and 'looking after' the bards – ambivalent meanings of the term *guan*. The organization of teams was still partly an attempt to control the bards and exact a tax. Meng Haiping lamented the declining powers of the cultural authorities; 'Hengshan county used to organize the teams really well; now the Hall of Culture doesn't organize them, it's all gone private (*dan'gan*).'

But from the bards' point of view, if they had managed to circumvent the system even under Maoism, they could now do much better on their own without government interference, and they were more free to act on that calculation. They were used to going on the road to tell stories for well-being, and their audiences didn't need new stories.

By the 1990s the propaganda teams were virtually defunct, existing mainly in name. In 2001 Guo Xingyu was still nominal head, and 'political instructor' (*zhidaoyuan*), of a team in Suide with several dozen bards on its books, but as he admitted affably, 'Now the group's ideology is in a bit of a mess!' Tian Zhizi succinctly described the Zizhou blind artists' propaganda team: 'Now, though it hasn't been disbanded, no-one looks after it – it's becoming a "beggars' team" (*yaofan dui*).' Bards depended more than ever on their traditional livelihood and repertory.[2]

---

[2]   Contrast again Zuoquan in Shanxi, where a blindmen's propaganda team has persisted since 1938 (Liu Hongqing 2004), and Zhangzi in south Shanxi (Zhang Yanqin 2006).

5.2 Han Qixiang experiments

Meanwhile Han Qixiang was back in high esteem again, after his tribulations in the Cultural Revolution.[3] His attempts to revive official narrative-singing in Yan'an seem to have been no more successful than those elsewhere in the area.

A Yan'an Region Hall of Narrative-singing (*quyiguan*), formed in 1975 or 1976 and headed by a younger official called Guo Zhiwen, was said to be the first state-run professional performance organization for the bards – the propaganda teams, presumably, having always been temporary, and their bards not directly funded long-term by the county but paid *ad hoc* by local governments when they arrived to perform.[4]

In a revolutionary but typically inconsequential move, Han Qixiang and other leaders now trained five young performers, who broke all the taboos: they were not only sighted but female, as well as being senior secondary graduates. One of the recruits was Han's only daughter Yinglian, whom, as he admits, he had to persuade to learn. In line with the official ethos of such an enterprise, they were given some training in modern official music education such as reading music in cipher notation. They were touring the villages within a year; sources recount further idealized stories of their performances educating the villagers into better behaviour.

One account offers propaganda for the reforms alongside a portrayal of Han's selflessness. In one village peasants offered food to Han and his students, but Han had trained his students to sing the classic revolutionary song 'The three main rules of discipline and the eight points for attention' as a way of declining hospitality. This only made the villagers indignant – they protested that their lives were better now, and they offered their food gladly. In the end Han had to accept. In all, Han's undimmed idealism looks all the more sad in the reform period.

In the 1980s Han Qixiang was based in Yan'an city, while continuing to sit on many national committees. In 1981 he did a tour. A second batch of 11 students was recruited to the Hall of Narrative-singing in 1985, but their village registration permits made it difficult for them to remain in Yan'an, as Han complained. A 1985 photo shows six young female students.[5] Han was ever keen on 'new stories', but was teaching them 'The reunion of Liu Qiaor', a classic of his 1940s' repertory, hardly in tune with the requirements of the reform period. Modifications were made to the format, with a group of performers acting out the story and several accompanying instruments. By 1986 they had incorporated aspects from song-and-dance and opera. A belated attempt was being made to make the music as modern and respectable as the texts.

Han Qixiang died in 1989, glowing paeans in the national media soon recalling his tireless efforts for the revolution. According to Guo Xingyu, Han's

---

[3] Hu 1989: 212–17.

[4] ANS 962–3. Hu 1989: 285 says it was formed in 1976. But ANS 1148 gives 1957, and Zhang Qian 1965 uses the term, so there is more to this than meets the eye.

[5] ANS, at front of vol. 1.

Hall of Narrative-singing has since become a dance hall (*wuting*) – an inevitable development utterly symbolic of Chinese society today. But in the countryside, if the old contexts are declining, they have lived on.

Female performers became a bit more common in the 1980s: we heard of one in Dingbian, and one in Yulin. They were usually part of the small groups which formed since the 1980s. In Zizhou county, groups of three to five people have become more common, with *sanxian* banjo and *mei* flute, sometimes including one woman. If the influence of Han's attempt to train female bards was limited, sighted performers did soon become common, as we see shortly.

5.3 New research and images

Lin Shan had encouraged the writing down of traditional stories, but under Maoism, despite the theoretical brief of cultural officials to document local folk music, Han Qixiang seems to have been the sole object of research on Shaanbei bards.

We saw (§1.5) how Huo Xianggui and others had begun researching the folk musical heritage in Shaanbei as early as 1974. Bards were one of Huo's main interests. He began recording excerpts from bards such as Wang Xueshi in Hengshan.[6] As traditional culture was rehabilitated, in 1982 a provincial survey team did some work, making audio recordings.[7] The *Anthology* narrative-singing project for Shaanxi was initiated from 1986, with Huo Xianggui co-authoring the *Anthology* section on Shaanbei narrative-singing. Several other local scholars were now also documenting the bards in counties throughout Shaanbei. The *pipa* attracted attention from provincial scholars, as well as local cadre Ai Keqi (see §4.6 above).

Though most of their work was done by contacting the bards through the urban teams, rather than accompanying them on tour, local scholars were now concerned to document ritual aspects of the performance. People's mind-sets had become much more free than under Maoism – one local scholar who recorded bards for the *Anthology* was not going to be hoodwinked into toeing the Party line by recording new stories: 'When I recorded them, I chose anything about Heaven, Earth and Man, and rejected everything about the Party, Chairman Mao, and Socialism!' One might see this as a political bias in itself, but I would see it as a shrewd correction of any tendency the bards might have to play safe by performing a politically-correct piece for a government representative.[8] All these fieldwork recordings remain in private hands, and are likely to remain so (cf. §8.2 below).

An aside on outsiders' images of Shaanbei bards perhaps belongs here. Nationally, little if anything is known of the Shaanbei bards apart from revolutionary Han Qixiang – and even his recordings are hard to find. Blind bards,

---

[6]   E.g. ANS 1004, 1006, 1011, 1032, 1034, 1038, etc.

[7]   ANS 1037.

[8]   As I observed in Jones 2003: 309.

of course, are still commonplace today throughout China. Abing, the most famous blind musician in modern China, did not quite count as a narrative-singer, I think; in Shaanbei, though his image is known in educated circles, there are too many instances nearer home.

Since Shaanbei is often featured romantically in the national media as a revolutionary base, brief sanitized glimpses of Shaanbei folk culture are occasionally broadcast. The standard images are *yangge* dancing or a cheesey folk-singer, but in 2001 I saw a young sighted man do a passable imitation of a Shaanbei bard on a national CCTV chat show featuring the cult Shaanxi novelist Jia Pingwa.

Avant-garde Chinese artists have presented a less revolutionary image of Shaanbei. One fine antidote to Han Qixiang is the blind bard in the novella *Life on a string* (*Ming ruo qinxian*) by Shi Tiesheng (b.1951), one of many 'educated youth' rusticated to a village near Yan'an in 1969 – we saw his bleak impressions of Shaanbei in Part One. This 1985 story mystically evokes the life of an itinerant blind bard and his young blind disciple.[9] 'The old man believes that when he has broken one thousand strings, he can open up his *sanxian* and find a prescription inside which will restore his sight. When he finally does so, the piece of paper inside is blank.' The story was made into a film by Chen Kaige (1991), director of the brilliant *Yellow Earth*, also showing the gulf between the harsh realities of Shaanbei life and the Party's ideals. Qu Xiaosong, *avant-garde* composer of the music for the soundtrack, later wrote an opera on the theme, premiered in Brussels in 1998.[10] Though Qu Xiaosong has long been much interested in folk music, he used no original music from local bards.

Such *avant-garde* creations, with their mystical minimalism, are more popular outside than inside China. While far from ethnography, they at least offer an imaginative alternative to the revolutionary idealism of official sources.

5.1 Cassette culture 1

Though it looks unlikely that the field recordings will become available, a major initiative of the 1980s was an extensive cassette series, widely available in shops in Shaanbei towns since the 1990s, featuring but one bard, Zhang Jungong.[11]

In Shaanbei, shops selling cassettes, CDs, and VCDs became common in the larger towns in the 1990s. The selection is dominated by pop music; most traditional music on sale is local opera (mainly *Jinju* and *Qinqiang*) or grossly conservatory-modulated 'folk-song'. There are also a few tapes of Shaanbei shawm bands (§9.4 below).

---

[9] For translation, see Tai 1989: 171–205. For further comments on images of Shaanbei in modern fiction and film, see Fukao, Iguchi, and Kurishara 2007: 146–8.

[10] Kouwenhoven 1997: 112–15.

[11] See Jia 1992, Yan 1996.

The influence of such tapes is hard to assess. Houses we have visited, both in villages and towns, are more or less bare of either books or tapes – indeed, there is precious little furniture. Few cassette players are to be found; when they are, trying to hear tapes can be frustrating, as the quality of both tape and machine is poor. Electricity is sporadic and expensive, and batteries aren't cheap either. I suspect that even if people have cassette machines and tapes, the latter break after a couple of times, certainly the narrative-singing tapes. Such tapes sell for about 2 *yuan*, which is a lot more for a Shaanbei villager than for us. Though most households now own a TV, many villagers say they can't afford to watch it; reception of the one or two channels (one local, one national) is poor.

Despite what looked to me like a small market, even the first print of 120,000 tapes of Zhang Jungong's stories is said to have yielded over 200,000 *yuan* profit by 1992, and they were still selling well in 2001. With my experience of Shaanbei villages, and of urban record shops, I was incredulous: where were all these buyers?

Enquiries in 2001 yielded clues. In the bustling market town of Zhenchuan, one tape shop was selling over 100 copies a month of the Zhang Jungong series, and another claimed to sell around 1,000 a month. Most were pirated, partly inaudible, and liable to break, but never mind that. A shawm player in Sishilipu town, on the road between Mizhi and Suide, told us that 80–90% of families there had cassette recorders, and about half of those had tapes of local shawm bands or Zhang Jungong.

In the poor village of Yangjiagou, I was told that about half of the 300 households in the village have a cassette recorder, and have bought tapes of local music. I made a quick survey. Shawm player Chouxiao is familiar with the commercial tape of Li Qishan's shawm band, and has a couple of mimeographed scores of shawm music, apparently his only books, in his very poor house. Semi-blind Older Brother can't read, and hasn't heard any tapes. Old blind narrative-singer Li Huaiqiang had heard some of the famous tapes of Zhang Jungong, but couldn't afford to buy a tape-machine or tapes, and regarded them as alien. One family had played a tape of *chuishou* for the *helongkou* ceremony consecrating their new cave-dwelling. Nearby in the affluent Black Dragon temple, the temple-keeper had a decrepit radio cassette player, and had borrowed the Zichang shawm tape, which Chouxiao knows and likes. An old guy selling incense was listening to it, and also a tape of *Qinqiang* opera. I still couldn't really imagine this market.

So who is Zhang Jungong? Again, I haven't met him, so this account is based on official sources. Zhang Jungong (b. *c*1933)[12] came from a village near the county-town of Hengshan, but fled famine to Ganquan (south of Yan'an) when 10. Blind in one eye, he first became a versatile singer, only formally studying narrative-singing with one Zhang Jinfu from the age of 25 (*c*1956/7). He went to Yan'an in 1960 or 1961, working with Han Qixiang and others. He returned to Ganquan in 1962 to make a living, touring with his younger brother as far afield as Gansu, Inner Mongolia, Ningxia, and Shanxi. For the Cultural Revolution,

---

[12]   *Apud* ANS 1149; he was born in 1931 *apud* Yan 1996.

though as we saw bards were far from inactive, Zhang's official biography has a typical lacuna.

As Maoism began to collapse, in 1978 Zhang toured Shaanbei, Inner Mongolia, Ningxia, and Gansu with the Ganquan narrative-singing (*quyi*) propaganda team, which he had formed. In 1979 he recorded the soundtrack of the series 'The Big Dipper' (*Beidou*) for Changchun TV. He won several prizes: in 1985 in Yan'an commemorating Mao's seminal 1942 *Talks at the Yan'an Forum on Literature and the Arts*, in 1986 at a provincial festival, in 1987 in festivals for the disabled of the Five Northwestern Provinces and at national level. Since 1985 he has been secretary of the Yan'an region narrative-singing society. If this litany of institutional exposure looks impressive, he was still said to be doing itinerant village performances in the early 1990s; as ever, it is easier to document isolated instances of official exposure than a lifetime serving rural ceremony.[13]

Zhang has over 20 disciples, notably his son Zhang Heping (several of whose *sanxian* pieces are included in the *Anthology*) and two nephews. According to the sources, he has been influenced by *mihu* vocal style, experimenting with solo-choral effects, and has composed or re-arranged several dozen new stories.

So from 1986 a major series of commercial cassettes called *Shaanbei shuoshu* was issued by the Shaanxi Audio Publishing Company. This could have been a fine series, using the experience of local scholars to record singers throughout the region; instead, it features only Zhang Jungong's group, based in a county well to the south of the area where most fieldwork has been done. The series was masterminded by Dang Yinzhi, credited, along with one Chang Yuhong, as 'composer' on the project. Dang was a cultural cadre in the Yan'an song-and-dance ensemble who had mainly studied Han Qixiang's music. The other main performer on the series is Zhang's son Heping.

The cassettes were released in the late 1980s and voraciously pirated. The series featured both old and new stories. Best known (and most popular) of the 'new stories' since the 1940s is 'Wang Gui and Li Xiangxiang'. Several stories occupied two cassettes, though their total length was less than 90 minutes. Like 'concert' performances given by professional troupes, versions are likely to be shorter than those performed over a whole evening or more in village households. The tapes present a more arranged, operatic effect than the solo bards. Spoken dialogue is used more often, often including a female voice, and a small ensemble including *zhudi* flute, *erhu* and *banhu* fiddles, small drum, *bangu* drum, and small gong.[14] Such larger groups were always on the agenda in the troupes under Maoism, but were still a minor part of the overall picture offered by people we met in 2001. It is hard to tell if the groups performing at the 2006 CHIME conference in Shaanbei,

---

[13]   Cf. Jones 2003: 311.

[14]   ANS 1030–31.

and on a recent Chinese website, reflect a more recent trend, or the tendency to present an official image.[15]

Apart from anything else, the availability of cassettes (and indeed, websites) now made it possible to learn without a teacher. In the regional capital, Yulin city, Bian Ziya and his four brothers have formed a group, having apparently learnt from the Zhang Jungong tapes. Li Huaiqiang realized how much easier it was to learn now: 'Now they have tapes, all they have to do is listen.' In Yuhe town, the bards invited for the Chenghuangmiao temple fairs (15th of the 1st moon and 2nd of the 8th) are mostly disciples of Zhang Jungong, as he is famous for his tapes.

5.5 Blind bards

Meanwhile, bards were still making a living from itinerant stories for well-being in the twenty-first century. Let us now survey the recent fortunes of some of the bards we met above.

Guo Xingyu is an impressive example of someone who can 'ride two horses at once', following political trends astutely while continuing to take godchildren and cure illness. 'From 1972 I was head of the blind men's propaganda team organized by the Suide Hall of Culture. I entered the Party in 1975, and from 1978 I was political instructor of the team. In the 1980s I composed some new propaganda-type stories on the basis of the political needs of the time, mainly things like advertising the spirit of the Party's 12th and 14th Plenary, and birth control, like "Fuss over an abortion" and "Marrying Late" (*Wanhun ji*).[16] I composed some new operas too, in *daoqing*, *mihu*, and modern opera (*geju*) style.' By 2001, as we saw, the team was moribund. Guo and his (sighted) wife divide their time between his home village and an apartment in the suburbs of Suide town. He has rarely performed as a bard since getting heart disease around 1991; now his main livelihood is curing illness by depicting talismans and chanting incantations, and hanging and opening lockets. Relying on his traditional magic, he legitimizes it with a fashionably scientific-sounding defence: 'magic power is rational (*fali you daoli*)'.

Li Huaiqiang, quite frail in his old age, was also less active as bard by the late 1990s. Lucky enough to have found a wife during times of war, Li has two sons and three daughters; but the family has remained poor, and the sons have been unable to find wives. In 1999 Li performed for the 4th-moon temple fair in his

---

[15]   The CD Fukao and Iguchi 1992, track 7, contains a section from the traditional story *Jinchai yuhuan ji* performed by six musicians (three men and three women) from the Ansai People's Opera Troupe on tour in a village in 1990. Cf. the only other commercial cassette of *Shaanbei shuoshu* I have found, *Wang Gui yu Li Xiangxiang*, also from Shaanxi sheng yinxiang chubanshe, and also in a polished style, with six singers and ensemble from the Ansai narrative-singing troupe (*quyituan*). The website http://www.zgya.com/zgya/sbss.htm, from Yan'an, mainly features groups, notably that of Zhang Jungong.

[16]   These were already known before, so he must mean that he revived them.

village, and he still did the occasional story for well-being for families fulfilling vows. But he told us: 'I'm almost without business these days, 80% of my work is gone. Most temple fairs don't have narrative-singing any more. These days people read books a lot' – surely he overestimates this! – 'and don't want to waste time away from work. The state doesn't control it any more, people just don't want to be away from work. They've got TV and recordings too now.' He used to perform for audiences of 80 or 90 people, but now it's only for around 20 or 30, mostly elderly. 'I can't keep up.' This didn't apply generally to narrative-singing in the area, but to Li in particular – elderly, frail, and no longer a gifted performer.

In the exceptional conditions of Yangjiagou, the occasional visit from Japanese tourist groups, Chinese and foreign scholars, and visitors to the memorial hall to Chairman Mao's 1947 sojourn, had allowed Li to supplement his meagre income – 'They always get me to perform when someone comes.' But his main income still came from his godchildren, as it had done under Maoism. While we were in the village, one of his godchildren's children was getting married, and when he paid a visit he was given 20 *yuan*; when he left they gave him *mantou* steamed buns, and later they gave him some clothing.

Having complained about the coarsening of the bards' language, Li went on to lament the changing times. 'In the old days bards used to wear a robe, and a hat with a pigtail. Nowadays it's all simplified. Then it was *wagai* hats, sitting at a high table; now you don't get changed, and just sit on a stool, it's much simpler. And the gods used to be more efficacious, they were dead efficacious – if you didn't follow them you could die. Once someone's son died, and the parents made a vow to beg him to come back to life, so I obeyed the gods, and he really did come back to life.'

Li Huaiqiang died in July 2000, falling from a narrow mountain path while on his way to another village to hang a locket. Since his death, other itinerant bards occasionally stop off to perform in the village.

Meanwhile Tian Zhizi was also winding down his activities. When we go to look for him at his son's general store where he now lives, he is sleeping off a drinking session, but he comes round. It was Guo Xingyu who recommended we visit him, and despite his reputation as a tough cookie, he is most affable. He has four children – the oldest son, 38, runs the store, the second son, 36, graduated from Xi'an Arts College and now works at the *Yulin Daily*; the two daughters are married. Tian stopped performing in about 1996 – 'the kids were filial, they didn't want me to go out any more'. He went on, 'I have 28 disciples in all, eight in Wubu, four in Yulin, two in Shenmu, also in Yan'an, Ansai, and Bao'an [Zhidan]. I took some disciples while I was at Yan'an in 1962, others stayed at my house to learn. In 1972 I was mainly taking disciples in Wubu, when the Wubu Hall of Culture invited me to come to train members for their propaganda team.'

We find He Guangwu at a small temple fair at Jijiashigou, near his home village. He has agreed to tell fortunes for a family there to help them overcome adversity, and hasn't brought his *sanxian*. He agrees to tell a story for us back at his home if we take him back to the temple fair later. The new railtrack runs through these villages south towards Xi'an, and some villages are now dissected

by it: blindman He Guangwu is literally on the wrong side of the track. His family
has done well. He is active over a small area, proudly claiming to be well known
within a radius of 20 *li* (10 kilometres), and he hasn't taken any disciples. But he
is busy. 'People still invite me, and I still go. For temple fairs, or if a donkey isn't
eating its fodder, or if a family member is on a long journey, you must invite a
'story for well-being'; and I tell stories for opening the locket, weddings, moving
into a new cave-dwelling, and sons going off to the army.' Like most blind bards,
he is also busy telling fortunes and healing.

5.6 Sighted bards

Though Han Qixiang (1985: 3–4) mentioned competition between blind and
sighted bards when he was learning in the 1930s, narrative-singing in Shaanbei was
largely a monopoly of blindmen, and only since the eve of the Cultural Revolution
has the taboo against sighted people performing been challenged. Now it is a *fait
accompli* for sighted men to muscle in on the trade: there are fewer blind people
anyway, as both cadre Gao Wanfei and poor villager Li Huaiqiang pointed out,
since health has improved (though still appalling); nor do sighted men fear going
blind any longer if they take it up. Half of Tian Zhizi's 28 disciples are sighted –
presumably those he taught since the 1970s. Despite the comment above that their
new disabled allowance makes them lazy, blind performers who are still active
rather resent the encroachment on their 'food-bowl'. 'Originally sighted people
weren't allowed to tell stories – if you're sighted you can do anything [else].' Now
not only can sighted people learn, but they can even learn from the tapes, saving
them money but depriving senior blind bards of teaching fees.

Scholar Meng Haiping pointed out: 'In the old days, bards' social status was
low; now for everyone all that counts is money, social status no longer comes into
it.' This was certainly true for trendy young *chuishou* shawm-band musicians in
the towns, but less obvious for the bards. Unlike the *chuishou*, bards have not
spruced up their image so ambitiously, and remain quite modestly paid; nor have
they yet availed themselves of the mobile-phone revolution that has occurred since
about 1998. Whereas *chuishou* often ride motor-bikes, bards (even sighted ones)
mostly go on foot.

Guo Xingyu: 'Now there are sighted bards everywhere – many senior-secondary
graduates, not wanting a hard life, go and tell stories. In Zizhou, Hengshan, and
Yulin there are a lot of sighted bards, and there are some in Mizhi and Jiaxian too.
Now there are fewer than 30 blind bards in Suide, but there are more sighted ones.
They began appearing in the 1980s or 1990s, they drove the blind ones away;
the blind ones were very angry about it – but they had permits too." He went on
darkly, "Now how did that come about? Perhaps by bribery. Now blind artists are
in great difficulties. There are more of them west of the river, but quite a few of the
old artists have died; east of the river their skills aren't quite so good.'

We met a sighted bard at the White Cloud Mountain temple fair in 2001 (§5.8 below). Xu Wengong (b. *c*1948) from a village in Qingjian county, began learning at 17 [*c*1964] from an uncle, so the taboo was perhaps being broken down even then. He has never taken part in any county-organized teams, or learnt new stories. As we saw, during the Cultural Revolution he was protected by villagers as he went round performing and hanging lockets on the quiet. He learnt on *pipa*, but later felt that its sound was too small and it was less popular, so he changed to *sanxian*.

We met sighted bard Li Wenjin (b. *c*1943) in 1999 when he performed informally for staff at the Black Dragon temple office, as a kind of advertisement for his arrival in the area. He comes from a village in Zizhou county. Soon after Liberation, in the early 1950s, he studied for three winters in the evenings in the 'school for sweeping away illiteracy'. His parents died early. But he only began studying narrative-singing in the early 1980s, with the old blind bard in his village. His master could never find a wife: 'people won't follow you if your five organs aren't complete' – though most of our blind mentors were exceptions. Despite the economic imperative, Li stressed that both he and his master liked the music. There was a libretto (*benben*) that he could follow – as we saw, even blind performers sometimes owned a libretto. Li Wenjin is active as far afield as Shenmu, Fugu, Yinchuan, and Dingbian. He usually sings with his eyes closed – in imitation of blind bards?

A couple of days after meeting him at the temple where we are staying, we bump into him on our way back there, and he tells us he will be doing a story for well-being that evening for a family in the nearby village, so he invites us along.

5.7 A story for well-being

After supper, Li Wenjin performs a 'story for well-being' (⊙**C4**) to help a family with an epileptic son. The family is to give the bard 7 or 8 *kuai* plus food and lodging for the night. The audience of a dozen people, family and neighbours, mostly older women, listens informally. The structure of the 'story for well-being' performance is:

- Inviting the Gods (*qingshen*)
- Settling the Gods (*anshen*)
- Audience with the Gods (*canshen*)
- The story proper (*zhengben shu*)
- Escorting the Gods Away (*songshen*).

Before the session begins, two *dou* bowl altars have been filled with ears of corn, in which are stuck *changqing* yellow paper streamers and *shenweizi* god placards, prepared for the occasion. Anyone can do this, though since bards are usually blind, the god placards are written by a sighted literate person. During the story, the bard sometimes directs the son to burn paper before the altar.

For Inviting the Gods outside in the courtyard, the bard kneels before the altar of streamers and god placards placed on a bench. His fast mantric chant for inviting the gods is an isorhythmic vocal melody revolving around *re*, *do* and low *so*, accompanied by an ostinato on the *sanxian* alternating *so* and *do*.[17] While he chants, the son kneels behind him, and a male family member lets off firecrackers and burns incense and paper.

As the family member takes the altar inside and places it on the stove, the bard plays a short interlude as they re-enter the cave-dwelling, and he and the son again kneel before the altar for 'Settling the Gods' (Illustration 2 above). The bard continues to chant in a similar style to the previous section, and more paper is burnt before the altar.

There is a pause as the bard straps the *shuaban* clappers onto his left leg and attaches the *mazhazi* clappers to his right (plucking) hand. Then, after playing the instrumental prelude (*qiban*) of the 'opening scene' (*kaichang*), he begins to sing. Guo Xingyu: 'The opening narrative (*kaichang bai*) of the story is "Audience with the Gods" (*canshen*). After the gods are settled down, we first recite auspicious phrases for well-being like "May you enjoy wealth all four seasons, and your livelihood prosper" (*Siji facai, shengyi xinglong*)'.

Only now does 'the story proper' begin. Not related to the ritual sections, it is ordered (*dian*) by the host from those in the bard's repertory. Tonight Li Wenjin performs the martial story 'The Tale of the Bandits' (*Xiangma zhuan*) about righteous uprisings against the Sui dynasty, over 1400 years earlier.

Finally, for 'Escorting the Gods Away', they go outside to the courtyard again to kneel before the altar; as the bard recites, firecrackers are let off, and the streamers and inscriptions burnt.[18]

5.8 A story for a temple fair

As we saw in §1.6, temple fairs are of various sizes, lasting from two days to a week. Even small fairs, like the one where we found He Guangwu, or the fair at Guo Xingyu's home village, generally manage to invite an opera troupe. Guo Xingyu: 'Sometimes you have to tell stories for all three days, and can earn 200–400 *yuan*. Temple fairs revived gradually – like our Xuejiamao fair restored in 1985, at first it was just singing an opera, later they [re-]built the temple, and only later did they [re-]make the god sculptures.' The temple fair at Sishilipu township (cf. §2.3, §11.4) is rather larger – as Wang Shifa commented: 'Our temple fair has invited bards, and they come to do stories for well-being too. Some bards are blind, some sighted.'

---

[17]   For texts and musical transcriptions from other bards, see ANS 1012–15, and for the following sections inside the house, 1145–7.

[18]   For sound comments on the balance between ritual and entertainment in puppetry in distant Fujian, cf. Ruizendaal 2006: 331–8, 345–8.

As we saw, the largest temple fairs in this part of Shaanbei are those of the White Cloud Mountain and the Black Dragon temple. Of several fairs at the White Cloud Mountain temple complex in Jiaxian county throughout the year, dominating the county's economy, the week-long fair from the 1st to the 8th of the 4th moon is the most important. A visit in 2001 gave us perspectives (⊙A4, cf. §11.5).[19] The largely mountainous counties of Jiaxian and Wubu, in the eastern Yulin region, on the western side of the Yellow River, are the poorest areas of a poor region. We had little time in Jiaxian, and I suspect further fieldwork would reveal a lot more tradition – and adversity – than my descriptions of the situation around Mizhi and Suide suggest. Pilgrims, and musicians, come from quite far afield, notably from Shanxi just east across the Yellow River. Hence one might wish to use the mountain as a springboard to subsume the western counties of Shanxi within our map of ritual and musical culture.

The most prestigious rituals at the temple fair are those of the resident Daoist priests, but all kinds of musical activities accompany the pilgrims. A dire array of beggars and cripples has assembled around the temples; one woman begs with her young handicapped son chained to a rock. Of the beggars (some blind, some female, most disabled in some way, sometimes solo, sometimes in pairs), many perform short songs, sometimes accompanying themselves on *erhu* fiddle – one picks out a tune on a battery-powered electronic keyboard. They do not count as bards. In the main square we hear a young blind man from Linxian in Shanxi tell a short story with *sanxian*, with an older man helping him collect money. He is learning his trade, but is presently more like a beggar.

Many pilgrims attend the temple fair under the auspices of a dozen or so regional associations (*hui*, traditionally called 'associations for dispensing tea', *shicha hui*). Each association has raised funds to build its own caves in the temple complex. Some of the bedding and mats is left there from year to year, some is brought by individuals. Gruel kitchens are also regional, with a small fee (3 or 4 *mao*) paid at the entrance; there are also many 'tent restaurants' for individual pilgrims. Most of the pilgrim associations are named after their county, or a group of counties; some are named after a township.[20] Each association has particular allegiances among the many temple gods: thus the refurbishment of the Wulonggong temple was paid for with donations from the 'First association'. Individuals may make offerings too, but the most substantial donations are organized by the regional associations. They also sponsor different daily rituals: e.g. the Wubu association pays for the one on the 5th, the First and Yulin associations pay for those on the 8th.

Apart from the daily performances of opera, bards perform in a less public and commercial arrangement that is also typical of Shaanbei temple fairs. One evening we visit the cave of the 'Zizhou, Qingjian, and Ansai association' (*Zizhou-Qing-An hui*, known as 'First association', *touhui*) to hear the sighted bard Xu Wengong

---

[19]   Cf. Zhang Zhentao 2002a: 146–64, and for the bard, 215–18.

[20]   Our list of the associations (Zhang Zhentao 2002a: 151–2) differs somewhat from that of Chau (2006: 258 n.25), and the situation seems to be fluid.

perform. He comes to this fair every year as part of this pilgrim association, in order to fulfil a vow. 'My father was a model labourer, and was head of this association' – note this typically casual link between Communist and traditional authority (cf. §7.3 below). 'He came here to take part in the rituals and made a vow, because I'd had stomach disease for 12 years, and sure enough I got better. So I've been coming here to fulfil the vow every year since the temple restored, to revere the great god (*dashen*) Zhenwu; I come here to avert calamity (*tuozai miannan*).' The association leader (over 60) tells us that some other bards come to the temple fair not to make money but to fulfil vows.

There is no need to 'invite the gods', since they are already present, but on the left of the cave, as you stoop to enter, is an altar behind which the bard's red cloth pantheon is displayed (Illustration 3(b) above); individual pilgrims periodically burn paper and kowtow before it. Opposite the altar, Xu Wengong is performing an episode of the story *Wagangzhai* – another martial story about righteous uprisings against the Sui dynasty.

The pilgrims sit on mats at the rear of the cave, listening to the bard intently but informally. They consist mostly of men over 50, but even those over 60 were brought up largely under Communism. Yet such senior men entirely represent tradition; associations like this surely represent a kind of passive alternative to government control.

> *Back in the county-town, returning to our hostel one evening, we switch on the TV to find a documentary about coal-mining accidents, which are reported nightly. There are some rather fine investigative programmes on TV these days, and the main theme of this one is how the response of the village Communist Party leadership to the disaster, rather than considering improving safety measures, has been to give funds to construct a new village temple in the hope of divine protection. OK, in this case the programme happens to fit into an agenda of rationalism against superstition, a view we sometimes feel inclined to challenge, but tonight I can only go along with the presenter's lament.*
>
> *Only later did I put together further pieces of a grisly jigsaw. Under the tradition of posthumous marriage (minghun), revived in northwest China,[21] within five years after the death of an unmarried male over the age of 15 sui, a suitable dead unmarried female is found. Indeed, shawm bands often perform, and a Daoist may officiate. The unnatural deaths of many men in unregulated mines were bad enough, but newspaper reports in 2007 revealed that women (often disabled, or from poorer provinces) were being murdered to cater for this market.*

---

[21]   Cf. Zhang Junyi 1993: 81; Jones 2007: 58, for Shanxi.

Conclusion: narrative-singing and healing

Despite the substantial material published on Communist reforms of narrative-singing, and ethnomusicologists' eager search for change and modernization, it was hard while observing daily life in Shaanbei around 2000 to credit such reforms with much long-term – or even short-term – influence. My point is not to discredit official efforts, either in the cultural or political spheres. But rather than basing our assessments either on the new stories of Han Qixiang or on a revival or reinvention since around 1980, it appears that the Maoist period rarely succeeded in eradicating 'superstition' and transforming culture: the 'problems' that Lin Shan clearly saw in the 1940s have not changed significantly. This is clear both from the context and content of narrative-singing today, and from local people's recollections of the Maoist era. People remained loyal to their traditional concept of local village culture rather than to the state.[22] Though state-funded troupes are undoubtedly an aspect of overall musical activity, this point appears to be of wide relevance for many of the performing arts in the Chinese countryside today, and for our understanding of modern China.

If the bards are now threatened by the recent spread of TV and pop music, they are still in demand for their 'stories for well-being' as well as for their healing skills. While they did assemble for public rituals like temple fairs and New Year, they mostly performed solo. Since the 1940s, there has been a disjuncture between the secular, political performances of the official teams and the rituals of the solo bards. Narrative-singing has perhaps become a lesser aspect of the blindmen's activities than their godfather and healing duties.[23] Indeed, since sighted bards do not necessarily learn the healing arts of blind men, a potential divorce also looms between narrative-singing and healing – all the more since people can now learn stories by listening to commercial tapes. Part Three will further explore the resilience of tradition and the limited impact of politics with reference to the shawm bands.

---

[22]   Guo 2000: 350–52 and *passim*.

[23]   Again, contrast Zuoquan in Shanxi, where a team has remained active, performing for largely secular occasions, and for whose members telling fortunes seem to have become a lesser part of activities, though they continue to serve as godfathers (Liu Hongqing 2004: 62, 122–4, 194). Zhang Yanqin (2006) describes teams of bards in Zhangzi, still further south in Shanxi, performing mainly for life-cycle and calendrical contexts.

PART THREE

Lives of Shaanbei blowers

Illustration 8   *Chuishou* playing for funeral at side of soul hall, Yangjiagou 1999

Prelude

Having surveyed the solo bards, let us now introduce the musicians of shawm-and-percussion bands, known as *chuishou*, 'blowers'.

Shawm-and-percussion bands are common throughout the Islamic world, including north Africa and Eastern Europe (Poché 2000), and were common until the 17th century in Western Europe. The shawm-and-percussion band is surely by far the most common form of instrumental music-making among the Han Chinese,[1] as can be seen from the provincial volumes of the *Anthology*. The Shaanbei bands and those of north Shanxi (Jones 2007) are but two dots on the vast Chinese shawm map; in social background and musical aspects, we can at least begin to note common themes and intriguing variations.

The *bili*, ancestor of the *guanzi* oboe still widely played in north China, is clearly documented as taking root in Chinese ensembles by the sixth century CE. But the shawm (historically, and officially, called *suona*: see below) – a wooden pipe with a small double-reed enclosed in the mouth, with a pirouette and a flared metal bell – appears to be a much later arrival. Like the *bili*, the shawm came to China by way of Central Asia, but despite several claims based on early murals (apparently as far back as the Han dynasty, 206 BCE–220 CE), evidence before the Ming dynasty (1368–1644) is isolated and dubious.[2] While wind-and-percussion ensembles are documented in early Chinese courts and armies, the first reliable literary and iconographic evidence for bands with shawms and percussion is from the Ming.

If early evidence is piecemeal, we can trace some living Chinese shawm traditions back to around the eighteenth century. Though the musicians were always low class, even outcasts, the vast imperial apparatus required their services for ceremonies both at the local courts, for the armies, and for the life-cycle ceremonies of officialdom; shawm bands soon also took root among the common people for life-cycle and calendrical ceremonies. This imperial heritage is the background of living traditions.

Chinese scholars did some fieldwork on local shawm-band traditions in the 1950s, and more from the 1980s – most provincial volumes of the *Anthology* for instrumental music are dominated by their repertory. Despite Communist rhetoric, however, the genre has suffered by its continuing low-class status. Until the 1950s the musicians often smoked opium; still today, many are poor, some with visual

---

[1]   Jones 1998, ch. 10; Liu Yong 2006.

[2]   See Liu Yong 2006: 16–37. For folk wind-and-percussion bands, see also Qiao and Xue 1999 (for early sources, note Zhang Zhentao's list on pp.478–503). Note also work on *yuehu* 'musical households', p.96 n.3 below.

or other disabilities. However, under the commune system everyone was in the same boat, and since the 1980s the ability of the *chuishou* to earn good money has helped to ease practical discrimination.[3]

Doubtless *chuishou* music saw changes from empire to republic, and through the troubled first half of the twentieth century. Under Maoism, though some 'new songs' were added, the old contexts and repertory were impoverished; it became even harder to make a living from being a *chuishou*. The revival from the 1980s was a boon for them. Though in Shaanbei the *chuishou* remained more or less traditional until 1995, since then the 'big band' format, with its repertory based on pan-Chinese pop heard on TV, looks set to replace the old repertory; this change was prepared by the secular ethos and even the melodic style of communism.

Overview of *chuishou* in the Yulin region

Shawm bands are common throughout Shaanbei,[4] constituting the main melodic instrumental music there for life-cycle and calendrical ceremonies. Here a traditional band consists of five musicians: two shawms with drum, small cymbals, and gong. As to other instrumental music, percussion ensembles are common for calendrical festivities such as New Year, and until the 1940s *sheng-guan* ritual music was played by Buddhist and Daoist priests. Melodic and percussion instruments also accompany opera, narrative-singing, and dance.

This survey is again based on Mizhi and Suide counties, most renowned throughout the Yulin region for *chuishou*, with further samples from Zizhou, Jiaxian, and Wubu. Just west of Suide, away from the main transport artery, Zizhou (also said to have good village *chuishou*) is noticeably poorer. From there south towards Yan'an, the bonds of tradition are said to be stronger, with shawm players still virtual outcasts. Shawm bands are also common in the poor eastern area of Jiaxian and Wubu, similar in style to those in counties of the Linxian-Lüliang region in Shanxi just across the Yellow River.

As in other parts of China, it seems that outstanding *chuishou* in Shaanbei remain common today both in the vicinity of major military outposts from imperial times – like the Yulin region[5] – and in areas where more affluent households could afford to hire them – like the towns, or the landlord stronghold of Yangjiagou. But since Communism gained ground in the 1940s, there has been a widening gulf between the few shawm-playing professionals in the state troupes and the host of

---

[3] For nice perspectives on the common world phenomenon of low-status musicians, see Merriam 1964: 134–44.

[4] Apart from sources cited in Part One, note research by Chinese fieldworkers, mainly since 1974: Huo and Ai 1979; Gao Wanfei 2000; cf. AI. For more notes from our 2001 visit, see Zhang Zhentao 2002a: 51–173, 193–4; Tian 2005, notably 148–82 (for his estimates of numbers, see p.157).

[5] Cf. Yanggao in Shanxi: Jones 2007.

freelance folk semi-professionals playing for weddings and funerals. While some shawm bands in China have lengthy hereditary traditions and artefacts from the 19th century, in Shaanbei it is rare to find musicians with a family tradition of more than three generations, and early evidence is slight, so my account is again based almost entirely on oral recollection.

It is not simple to estimate numbers, since some groups are far more active than others. Some bands based in a town work virtually full-time, while *chuishou* in remote villages may be hired only occasionally, their small income supplementing their livelihood very modestly. Moreover, for concurrent bookings, one extended family may be able to get together several bands on demand.

Local scholar Gao Wanfei told us that the counties of Mizhi, Suide, and Zizhou are the most active for *chuishou*. In 1989 an official source estimated that there were over 60 bands in the 396 villages and 15 townships of Mizhi county.[6] But in 2001 we were told, more reliably, that there were 120 or 130 bands in Mizhi able to go out on business – about one for every three villages. Less good *chuishou* are employed less often and earn less money. One young fixer told us: 'In the 14 districts of Mizhi county there are 138 *chuishou* bands – they all turn out at New Year, but most of the year they till the fields. There are only four or five professional [full-time] bands, all in the county-town – they haven't got any land any more.'

As to nearby Suide, *chuishou* Wang Shifa told us: 'Now in the whole of Suide county there are over 200 *chuishou* – they can organize over 100 *guyue* bands.' Here he was talking of the shawm players, treating the percussionists as a less skilled group who can be recruited *ad hoc*. 'The situation in Zizhou is more or less the same as in Mizhi and Suide, elsewhere there aren't quite so many. In the 37 production brigades [villages] of our township, before the Cultural Revolution there were seven or eight bands, now there are at least 15, over 30 *chuishou*' – again he was reckoning the numbers of shawm players. In 1995 the single town of Matigou (population 20,212) in Zizhou was said to have 16 professional *chuishou* bands; for Zichang county, an official source describes an increase from 100 to 800 *chuishou* since the reforms around 1980.[7] The demand for *chuishou* may also be judged from the fact that recently Chang Wenzhou has been making and selling around 1,000 shawms in the Shaanbei region each year.

Gao Wanfei again: 'There are too many *chuishou* in this area, especially around Mizhi and Zhenchuan.' This explained their migration to counties further west, and to Yulin city north (§12.1 below). Still, this study refers only to one part of the Yulin region – time spent with bands further to the margins of Shaanbei would doubtless also be fruitful.

Before studying the fortunes of the *chuishou*, we can make some basic comparisons with the bards. Both are an important part of social, ceremonial, life in Shaanbei; both are paid by the host, though they are considerably cheaper than opera, the most prestigious ceremonial performance. The bards mostly work on

---

[6] Mizhi 1993: 539–40.

[7] Sources: Tian Yaonong 1999 fieldnotes; Zhang Jianzhong 2000: 237.

their own, whereas *chuishou* form groups of five or so; there have always been far more *chuishou* than bards. Of course, like opera troupes, the bards perform programmatic music, whereas the purely instrumental music of the *chuishou* is abstract. The bards tell stories to entertain within the context of ritual healing; the shawm bands, by their sheer volume, announce that a public event is being staged, but unlike the bards, do not act as intermediaries with the gods.

If the Party's attempts to register and reform bards in Shaanbei were less than successful, they made no such attempts for the *chuishou*. While they had a firm agenda for the bards, it proved impotent, even under Maoism; for the *chuishou*, conversely, whose music had a less explicit message, the Party had no particular modernizing agenda. We saw how Han Qixiang was far from typical of bards, but the *chuishou* did not even have a Han Qixiang. Still, their performing contexts (also life-cycle and calendrical) suffered similarly under the Communist social revolution. Since the reforms, the *chuishou* have adapted more – but again we find contexts and music remaining quite resistant to political change.

Chapter 6
Chuishou before Maoism

In China, the period before the national 'Liberation' of 1949 or the Japanese invasion in 1937 – or in Shaanbei before the establishment of the Communist base area in 1936 – was far from the stable 'golden age' often portrayed even in Chinese sources. However, it will serve to describe the status and functions of the *chuishou* before the radical extension of state control with the commune system in the 1950s. Though we will observe limited change in context and sound into the twenty-first century, many of these comments also apply more or less to the present.

6.1 Terminology

The most commonly used name for all the musicians, both collectively and individually, is *chuishou* ('blowers', viz. wind players), which I adopt below to refer both to shawm and percussion players in a band; the terms *gushou* ('drummers') and *chuigushou* ('drummers and blowers') are also heard, but *chuishou* is more common, as in the expression 'learning [to be a] *chuishou*' (*xue chuishou*). As in Shanxi, the term *xiangshou* ('resounders', meaning 'people who make a noise' (as in the Shanxi term *xiangda*, 'resonant percussionists') is also heard. The standard term for the music and the band (here and elsewhere in north China) is *guyue* ('drum music'), or *guyue ban* (or *banzi*, 'drum music band'), though today some more ambitious groups call themselves *guyue dui*, *dui* being a more modern term for band. As throughout north China, the most commonly heard term for their performance is *banshi*, performing a public ritual, literally 'doing things',[1] or (a term I shall use below) 'doing business'.

The traditional band comprises five musicians: two shawm players, with drum, small cymbals, and gong. As in many parts of China, musicians and their audiences rarely use the word *suona* for their shawms. If they mention the instrument at all, they call it *wazi*, *nazi*, or *wawa*, 'kid'.[2] Still, the term *suona* is commonly known. The influence of official culture has been quite pervasive since the 1930s; the term was doubtless announced in the regional festivals of the 1950s, and there have been sporadic '*suona* contests' since the 1980s; a few cassettes entitled *Shaanbei suona* are on sale, and the term now features on Chinese websites. Thus *chuishou* are bilingual enough to call it *suona* when talking to cultural cadres or visiting scholars. In a flawed attempt at neutrality, I mainly use the English term 'shawm'.

---

[1]   Hence the title 'Doing things' for the DVD with my 2007 book on Shanxi.

[2]   Cf. *weirwa* in northern Shanxi: Jones 2007: 90.

The instruments are collectively called *jiashi*, a term sometimes used to refer to the percussion, which are 'struck' (*sao* or *saosao*). Further musical terms will be introduced in §8.4 below.

Not only are terms for instruments and contexts obscure to the outsider, but proper names – not just for musicians, of course – are a minefield. People are never known by their formal name, whether they have a family nickname ('small name' *xiaoming*) or an 'art name' (*yiming*). Often they are simply known by surname and ordinal rank in the family, such as Li the Fourth or Chang the Fifth.

6.2 Caste, opium, and disability

Shawm players throughout China are traditionally of low social status, almost a caste. In Shanxi and some other parts of Shaanxi, outcast 'musical households' (*yuehu*) were common in imperial times, and their descendants are still *chuishou* today.[3] In Shaanbei the pejorative term *guizi* (*guizhe*, or *guijia*), like the widely-used insult *wangba*, denoted a low-class person. Such old taboos are rumoured to be more persistent in the Yan'an region of southern Shaanbei. The term *guizi* is known but little used today: it is understood as 'not good'. Though few know how to write it (even *chuishou* with a modicum of education, itself rare), the *gui* might be associated with pejorative terms like 'kneeling' or 'ghost', but scholars usually write it with the character for 'turtle'.[4]

Former puppeteer Zhu Guomin told us: 'Barbers (*titoude*), foot-washers, *chuishou* – none of them could enter the examination arena, or eat with other people.' Chang Wenjin: 'The *chuishou* weren't allowed to enter the examination arena and were *guizhe*. *Guizhe* means not being allowed to enter the examination arena: opera performers (*xizi*), geomancers, spirit mediums (*wushen*), and barbers were all *guizhe*.' *Chuishou* attached to a *gufangzi* agency (§6.5 below) were sent out begging when there was no work for them.

A well-known local saying expressing the ostracism of being a *chuishou* is 'marching before people, eating after them' (*zou zai renqian, chi zai renhou*). As one *chuishou* observed, 'In the past [*sic*], people despised *chuishou*. At a job, even if a table wasn't full, they still wouldn't let the *chuishou* come and sit with them

---

[3]   See the works of Xiang Yang (including 2000, in English), Qiao Jian et al. 2002, Hansson 1996: 55–75, 163–70, and Jones 2007: 23–30. We have little information on the *yuehu* in Shaanbei, only further south and east.

[4]   I would like to see an etymologist get to grips with this term. *Guizi* is often written with the characters for Qiuci, the medieval Central Asian kingdom of Kucha, and indeed there was a 'county of Kucha' just north of Yulin in the Han dynasty (Ma 1995). Cf. Xiang 2000: 10. Chinese scholars have seized on it rather too readily, but fail to establish a connection with the *chuishou*, who surfaced about a millenium after the end of the Kucha county: Gao Wanfei 2000: 2, Zhang Zhentao 2002a: 54–5; Tian 2005: 150–54, 199–200. For the term in southeastern Shanxi, see Qiao Jian 2002: 138, 345–6, Xiang 2001: 45.

to eat.' The *chuishou* still play outside in the courtyard, huddling around a fire in winter, exposed to the heat in summer; they are fed there too.

Despite the caste stigma, in poor villages where *chuishou* were only needed occasionally, they were effectively not very different from ordinary peasants. Before the 1950s, when Yangjiagou village had more *chuishou* serving the landlords more often, *chuishou* might have been considered rather separately – though even then they mostly 'bore suffering' by tilling the fields like other villagers. But today, with fewer *chuishou* and fewer ceremonies in the village, it is hard to see any clear class difference, and village *chuishou* provide a service that is part of the *xianghuo* 'mutual aid' bonds of small communities.[5]

Opium smoking was common throughout China before Liberation, and even the Communist-controlled area of Shaanbei remained a major opium production centre through the 1940s. Until the 1950s, *chuishou* (unlike bards, for instance) were routinely linked to opium – a common estimate was that eight out of ten smoked it. But dismissing facile stereotypes about addiction, opium was a social drug for rich and poor alike, and small doses did not necessarily lead to addiction or serious health problems. I find we know little about the details, and it is getting late to collect detailed oral history. Some richer funeral hosts used to supply opium to *chuishou* (perhaps not the higher quality they smoked themselves, but 'dross', and surely not sharing it but supplying it in a separate room), to help them stay awake and play with more energy, and opium was widely available at temple fairs. Thus busy bands might take it frequently, though not necessarily in large quantities. Was it thus part of their payment? Only in some cases did it lead to debilitation, poverty, and early death. The link with opium, though widely acknowledged, is part of the general disparagement of *chuishou*. Opium might help the *chuishou* overcome fatigue, forget their social rejection, deaden physical pain, kill hunger, even enhance their performance – like heroin for jazz musicians, it became part of their lifestyle.[6]

Typically, almost all the *chuishou* we met denied that their own fathers smoked it. Zhao Suotong: 'Most *chuishou* used to smoke opium, like Li Daniu, Li Zhonghong, Li Sanzhao, and Shen Fulin. But Du Chengzhang and my father didn't smoke it! When *chuishou* arrived on a job, sometimes the host would give them a pipe to raise their spirits, to make them play with more energy, but once they were hooked, they felt terrible if they didn't have any.'

Li Daniu smoked opium, and had problems with the upright atmosphere at the Communist Party arts school in Yan'an. Holm describes similar problems there for famed opera performer Li Bu – whose lowly status was also evident from the fact that he married a woman from a *chuishou* family.[7] Chang Wenzhou recalls playing late into the night for weddings and funerals on the eve of Liberation, when the

---

[5]   For this principle in Yangjiagou, see Fukao, Iguchi, and Kurishara 2007: 89–100.

[6]   For an exposé of opium myths, see Dikötter 2004. For opium's capacity to help people stay awake, see his p.69.

[7]   For Li Bu, see Holm 1991: 131–2; for his wife, see Zhou 1946: 11.

host might bring out some opium to smoke, but he was too young to acquire a habit. And the Changs again denied a problem in the family. In Yangjiagou, people couldn't agree whether Feng Guanglin smoked; they didn't think Chang Xinhua or Chang Bingyou smoked; but the Zhou family of *chuishou* were notorious addicts.

Another crucial factor was that families were reluctant to give their daughters to marry *chuishou*. If *chuishou* could find a wife at all, they often married late – limiting hereditary transmission. Although in some parts of north China shawm bands pride themselves on long hereditary traditions, here we rarely heard of more than three generations, and we met many *chuishou* whose fathers were the first in their family to learn, during the 1920s or 1930s. Communism cannot be entirely blamed for any break in transmission.

Their difficulties in finding a wife were partly attributable to the caste system, but *chuishou* were not the only men unable to find wives: rather, men with disabilities were likely to be poor, and taking part in a shawm band was one route to alleviating their desperate circumstances. No-one said specifically that *chuishou* were disabled: they were just low in status, often opium smokers, and therefore married late, if ever; poor able-bodied peasants were more likely to find a wife sooner.

I have met, or know of, several visually-impaired *chuishou*: the great Hao Yongfa was blind, and in Yangjiagou, Feng Guanglin was blind, and Older Brother and Ma Zhenyin are partially sighted.[8] But as we saw in Part Two, blind teenage boys often took up narrative-singing and fortune-telling as a living; indeed, we met several blind bards who had prosperous families. Even sighted *chuishou* often found it hard to get a wife. In Yangjiagou again, blind Feng Guanglin, semi-blind Older Brother, and his Fourth Uncle were unmarried; Yunwenr and semi-blind Ma Zhenyin are divorced. Elsewhere, famous *chuishou* like Li Daniu and blind Hao Yongfa were bachelors, while Jin Wenhua 'shared' a woman – polyandry was quite common among poor peasants (Sommer 2005).

As throughout north China, it was, and is, unthinkable for rural women to become instrumentalists performing in public, so there were never any female *chuishou*, not even percussion helpers. Their exclusion from public society is summarily expressed in the common phrase 'It wouldn't be convenient'. They have to stay at home, to sew and look after the children. But they go to the fields, and attend weddings, funerals, and temple fairs. Recently a few female *chuishou* have emerged, but they remain rare (§10.3). As to audiences, men are said to appreciate the music more, being more involved in the organization of the public events where the music is performed, and standing around outside to listen more than the women, who mostly remain indoors.

As elsewhere in China, the main network was family; 'hereditary transmission' (*zuchuan*) was admired. The shawm bands may be mainly familial (grandfather, uncle, father, son, brothers, cousins, nephews), but are often quite distant relatives. However, it was and is common for boys from poor families to apprentice themselves to a master from another lineage. Thus different surnames within a

---

[8]   Again cf. north Shanxi: Jones 2007: 17–21, 46–7.

band are common. And according to *chuishou* Older Brother, 'The members of a shawm band aren't very fixed – *chuishou* always play this year with one band, next year with another.'

6.3 Contexts

Here, just as I did for the bards, I will outline the 'traditional' contexts for *chuishou* until the 1940s. Most of these contexts remain the daily income of the *chuishou* today, although in later chapters I will show modifications, with radical impoverishments under Maoism from the 1950s to the 1970s.[9] So in some senses, this may just as well be read as a contemporary account; at least it indicates continuing consciousness of the 'old rules' governing ritual performance, given the requisite conditions such as money and time. Of course, there have been subtle changes in people's compulsion towards these old rules, but we can leave them for the later chapters, and also the few new contexts.

For ceremonial occasions the *chuishou* music is as indispensable as firecrackers. Such sounds fulfil a basic need that public ritual should be *honghuo*, 'fiery' or *re'nao*, exciting, party-like, lively.[10] Thus almost every life-cycle and calendrical ritual was, and is, likely to involve *chuishou* (see Table 3). There are two types of *chuishou* band: one is 'ordered' (*dingde*) or 'invited' (*qingde*), that is hired in advance, the host paying; the other is 'offered for free' (*songde*), the host just feeding them, not paying them. Good bands are usually 'ordered', while others come along mainly to get fed.

Contexts for music-making were introduced in §1.6 above, and are further described in Chapter 11. Funerals are the main context for *chuishou* to perform; sometimes two or more bands are invited. The ceremonial sequence for weddings is less complex than for funerals, and though *chuishou* often play, they are not so indispensable. Again, for temple fairs, one or more bands (usually a local band) may have a fixed invitation, others may come on spec. They accompany processions making offerings to the gods, both for the temple committee (as in the White Cloud Mountain *yinggong* ritual) and for individual donations (as in Sishilipu, §11.4, ⊙A2), and they also play informally in the courtyards outside temples (⊙A4). Now, as before the 1950s, *chuishou* may be hired for the rituals of consecrating a new cave-dwelling and house-warming. For hanging and opening the locket (§2.3 above), relatively well-off families may hire *chuishou* to accompany the feast.

As we saw in the Preface, we cannot assume simply that ceremonial life was richer before Communism. The majority of the population was desperately poor, limiting their abilities to hold impressive events. There was considerable variation: in the landlord stronghold of Yangjiagou village, for an exceptionally opulent

---

[9]   Cf. Jones 1998: 22, citing outstanding work by Li Runzhong in northeast China.

[10]   See Chau 2006: 147–68.

Table 3   Performing contexts for *chuishou*

•	weddings
•	funerals
•	commemorative rituals after death: (the 'seven sevens'); (100 days); first
(•)	anniversary; (third anniversary); (*qingming*); (*hanshi*)
(•)	first-moon and 100th-day celebrations for baby (rare)
(•)	hanging and opening the locket (rare)
(•)	longevity celebrations
(•)	placing the top stone of a new cave-dwelling, and moving into a new cave-dwelling
•	rain ceremonies: only after it rains, for 'Settling the Gods'
•	calendrical: temple fairs etc.
•	*yangge* song-and-dance festivities for New Year
	(secular:)
•	urban *yangge* parades
•	opening a business (*kaiye*)
•	sending off sons to the army
(•)	political campaigns under Maoism

funeral eight bands might be hired, while even for the three-day wedding of the son of a moderate landlord family there in 1938, only one band was hired.

However, villagers did commonly assert that ceremonial activity (both life-cycle and calendrical) was far richer before the Communists took over.[11] The landlords could afford to invite *chuishou*, and there were no ideological restraints. Older Brother pointed out the greater complexity of commemorative rituals involving *chuishou* before Liberation: 'The situation with the landlords was a bit different from now. When there was a death, they had to hire *chuishou* to go to the grave every seven days so the family could burn paper, and again for the first and third anniversaries. *Chuishou* were also hired for the *qingming* and *hanshi* festivals to go to the lineage graves to venerate the ancestors.' Only some of these occasions have revived.

6.4 The Chang family and the 'official blowers' story

Having outlined contexts, the rest of this chapter sketches the lives of some *chuishou* before Liberation. Though *chuishou* appear to have been hired by regional imperial *yamens* as well as for folk ceremonial, early historical material is lacking, and we can only sketch a history since the late nineteenth century from oral fieldwork.

---

[11]   See also e.g. Johnson 1994, for Shanxi.

Discussion of Shaanbei *chuishou* inevitably begins with the Chang lineage of Changshiban village, in Yindou district of northeastern Mizhi county.[12] A single surname often dominates the shawm players in any area: Chang in Mizhi, Kang in Jiaxian – surnames which are anyway common. Chang Wenjin (cousin of famous Chang Wenzhou, on whom see below) claimed eleven generations of *chuishou* down to his generation, though the *Mizhi county gazetteer* says eight. But he has no firm genealogical basis: 'My grandfather Chang Zhongyuan was a famous *chuishou*, but that's as far back as I know. My father was one of seven sons, who were all good *chuishou* in the old home of Changshiban.'

Chang Wenjin plausibly claimed that the Chang *chuishou* of Changshiban were exceptional: 'The Chang *chuishou* all had wives. When we had no work we would go home and till the fields, we never went begging; and the Changs basically never smoked opium.'

In support, Chang Wenjin evoked a widely-known story. A common version goes that in the Qing dynasty, one Chang Jucai[13] led a *chuishou* band to Sishilipu town to escort the important *Xuetai daren* official all the way into Mizhi town, playing 'in one breath' for the whole 40 Chinese *li* (20 kilometres). The official was so impressed that he abolished the rule preventing *chuishou* from taking official exams, visiting their ancestors' graves, and marrying outside their lineage. He gave the band the title of 'official blowers' (*guanchui*). Chang Wenjin went on: 'Because our old ancestors earned themselves a name for blowing, they set great store by this honorific title. In the old days *chuishou* were *guizhe*, but after the Mizhi *chuishou* were awarded the name of 'official blowers' (I don't know when this was), they weren't *guizhe* any more, and could enter the examination arena.'

The local myth is that not just the Changs, but *chuishou* in the Mizhi-Suide area generally, gained higher status thanks to this official favour. Local scholar Gao Wanfei (2000: 3) claims that *chuishou* as far afield as Zizhou and Wubu use the term 'official blowers'. This story is widely known, and has now been legitimized by the *Anthology* collectors: it is found in the biography of the Chang band there (AI 965). It has been cited as a long pedigree for the betterment of the social status of the *chuishou* in this area, contrasting with areas of southern Shaanbei, though it seems dubious that they were ever integrated fully into respectable society.

The story's attribution to the Chang *chuishou* has been contested. Gao Wanfei's version features a *chuishou* named Gao Zengxiang from Yuhe town, north of Mizhi. Gao Wanfei is not on good terms with Chang Wenzhou, and it is interesting that *chuishou* from his own lineage should have claimed this story for themselves. Gao Zengxiang later moved to Mizhi town and took many apprentices, including the Zhao and Du families, as well as Gao Wanfei's own forebear Gao Jianxi.

The *Anthology* dates this incident in the early Qing (late seventeenth century); but Gao Wanfei and the *Mizhi county gazetteer* give the late Qing, the late nineteenth century. The later the date, the less glaring the impasse between their

---

[12] AI 965–6, 973–4.

[13] The *Mizhi county gazetteer* (Mizhi 1993: 539–40) also names his brother Yicai.

supposed social betterment and the stark reality of their continuing lowly status. A nice *chuishou* called Wang Shushan (b. *c*1944) revealed this confusion: 'When my grandfather was a *chuishou* they were still called *guizi* and despised. Later [*sic*!] a *chuishou* made a name by playing to receive *Xuetai daren*, so the Suide and Mizhi *chuishou* were no longer *guizi*.'

The term 'official blowers' did not necessarily mean that the Chang or the Gao *chuishou* were regularly employed by imperial *yamens* for official functions in Mizhi or other county-towns – though shawm bands would indeed have been thus employed, all over China. The only band we heard of in Shaanbei that was said to have served as 'official blowers' for the county *yamen* was the Wang band in Jiaxian county (§11.5 below). And if the 'official blowers' story explains why their status is somewhat higher than in yet poorer counties further south towards Yan'an, even today it still doesn't butter any parsnips for poor village *chuishou* in the ravine-villages further from the main road. The main catalyst to improving status has only come since the 1980s: money – and that only for a few well-placed bands.

Most respected senior master of the Chang *chuishou* in modern times was Chang Wenqing (1909–82), known as Chang Mao. His first public success was around 1925 in winning a challenge at a big ceremony for a rich family, at which five or six shawm bands were hired.

According to the *Mizhi county gazetteer*, in the spring of 1942, Communist cultural cadres Liu Zhi and Zhang Lu visited Chang Mao while on an official visit to Mizhi, where he played several pieces for them.[14] The mournful quality of the piece *Fenhonglian* made such an impression on them that they arranged it into a funeral piece (*aiyue*) for mixed Chinese instrumentation for the 1943 ceremonies to receive the soul tablet of Genghis Khan and the reception of the coffin of local resistance hero Liu Zhidan. According to the *Anthology*, Chang actually played the piece *Fengfeng ling* for the reburial of Liu Zhidan in 1943, whereafter Shaanbei cultural workers Guan Hetong, Zhang Lu, and Liu Zhi arranged it into a piece later commonly used for official funerals. The *Mizhi county gazetteer* specifies that in 1956 Liu Zhi arranged it for woodwind band and large gong as a memorial piece (*zhuidao yinyue*) for the film *Shangganling*, whereafter it was commonly used for the secular funerals of Party cadres throughout China.

Meanwhile Chang Mao and his extended family of *chuishou* were still in constant demand for traditional ceremonial throughout Shaanbei. Chang Mao's brush with the new Communist officialdom did little to better his life. Despite his fame, he was not yet recruited to urban state troupes. After losing his wife in 1944, Chang Mao became itinerant with his 5-*sui* year old son. After the famine of 1947, he set up as a *chuishou* in Zhidan county further west. His younger brothers Wenqian and Wen'gang, and his son Xingfa, were also active as *chuishou* there.

---

[14]   Mizhi 1993: 539. For Chang Mao, see AI 973–4, Zhidan 1985.

6.5 Drum shops

The Chang lineage was typical in Shaanbei in that senior *chuishou* often set up a 'drum shop' (*gufangzi*) away from their home, teaching many apprentices, who stayed at the house while they were learning and went out on business with the boss. Chang Wenjin again: 'My father's generation were always going out on business. Before Liberation they set up drum shops in Zhidan and Ansai counties.'

A drum shop was like an agency, where people came to hire *chuishou*. According to Zhao Suotong, 'Only *chuishou* with a reputation could run a drum shop', and scholar Gao Wanfei observed, 'The old term drum shop denoted authentic professional *chuishou*, a bit like opera performers in a *keban* troupe.' Older Brother: 'Drum shop means a group of *chuishou* who leave their native home and go to another place to rent a cave-dwelling and do business professionally.' But some operated from their home village, and were considered to run drum shops. Chang Wenjin: 'In the past the artists in the drum shops were all men without wives; they came together when there was a job to do, and when there was no work they split up and went off begging.'

The high season for *chuishou* was winter, when most funerals and weddings took place; in the summer, the low season from the 3rd to 9th moons, many *chuishou* joined the opera bands (*xibanzi*), doing the rounds of the temple fairs which took place then. But some drum shop bosses appear to have kept their shop all year round; though there were fewer weddings and funerals in the summer, their services were still required.[15] After the 13th of the 9th moon there were no more operas, so the opera bands disbanded – some used the winter to rehearse.

Zhao Suotong on his grandfather's times: 'In those days there weren't so many *chuishou*, and not many people entered the drum shops.' A large town might have two or three recognized drum shops. Zhu Guomin: 'Mizhi town had two families of *chuishou*, Qingjian town had three.' Still, often there were enough *chuishou* attached to a single drum shop to form several bands; even today the success of a leading *chuishou* continues to be measured partly in how many bands he can send out, and thus how extensive is his family and apprentice network. Chang Wenjin: 'While we were in Changshiban our family alone could send out over a dozen bands, up to 20.' Zhang Hulin: 'Chang Mao's drum shop could organize 11 bands.'

Despite primitive transport conditions, *chuishou* were mobile, and also in economic competition, so they knew each other. Before the commune system they could set up drum shops, mostly away from their homes; under the communes they were highly restricted; since the reforms, with migration again easier and transport improving, *chuishou* have again travelled quite widely within Shaanbei – though, as we see below, the concept of drum shops later died out.

---

[15]   See e.g. the biographies of Feng Guanglin and Chang Wenqing, AI 970, 974.

6.6 Other celebrated *chuishou*

We can illustrate the lives of the thousands of *chuishou* active in Shaanbei by the stories of a few of those who achieved limited fame. Apart from the Chang *chuishou* in Changshiban village, Mizhi town had some famous *chuishou*. Our main source for this early period in Mizhi town is Zhao Suotong (b. *c*1932); though he has not played since the 1980s when he became ill from liver disease, he is very affable.

Zhao Suotong's grandfather Zhao Fuying (known as Zhao the Fifth, Zhao Wu; to Zhao Suotong he was 'Fifth granddad', *Wuyeye*) had moved from Zhaoshiban to set up a drum shop in Dingjiagou west of the river in Longzhen district.[16] Zhu Guomin recalled: 'Zhao the Fifth could play for 30 *li* without taking a breath. He was the best *chuishou* I've ever seen.' As usual, he doubled in the summer with the 'little opera' bands, playing *huhu* fiddle.

Zhao Suotong went on to tell us of his father. Zhao Jinrang (*c*1905–85) was a *chuishou* all his life, selling cold noodles in the summer low season. He made his base in Mizhi town. In the 1930s and 1940s there were only two or three recognized bands in the town. Zhao Suotong recalled the Mizhi scene in the old days. 'My father and the old fellow Gao Jianxi [descendant of the Gao from Yuhe town cited as first 'official blower' above] ran a drum shop in Mizhi county town. Ai Jiacai (uncle of Li Daniu and Li Erniu) also had one, running several bands. Shen Fulin and his brothers were good *chuishou* too.'

In the 1950s Zhao Jinrang took part in official festivals in Yulin and Xi'an, and was a major source for Huo and Ai's monograph in the 1970s (§8.2 below). He could play for six hours at a stretch, and for a meal of 60 or 70 guests, a lengthy occasion requiring several sittings. He also played *guanzi* oboe and *meidi* flute for the 'fine blowing' context (§6.8 below). He had many apprentices. In his 80th year in 1985, he played for the 'turning the nine bends' New Year's ritual procession in the town. Even proud Chang Wenzhou recognized the Zhao style in the county town as 'rather good'. Zhao Suotong began learning the shawm with his father when 16, around 1947. 'The Chang band used to say "Only Master Zhao [his father Jinrang] can compare with Zhao Suotong".'

Still in Mizhi town, the Du family was also renowned. Du Chengzhang (*c*1911–early 1980s?) was a good player. The Du *chuishou* worked often with the Zhaos. Zhao Suotong called Du Chengzhang 'godfather' (*ganda*); he claimed that his father used to lead on the top part, Du playing the lower part (for heterophony, see §8.5 below). But Du's sons became labourers.

Zhao Suotong recalled his early days learning the shawm: 'I saw several drum shops then, but later they set up shop at Yan'an and Ansai, and ours was the only one left in Mizhi town. Our drum shop only ran one single band for jobs – the apprentices we took stayed at our house.' Gao Wanfei: 'The Zhao band couldn't monopolize all the business in town, bands from outside also came in to

---

[16]   Mizhi 1993: 539, and our interviews with him in 2001.

play. For funerals, the town band played first, leading the *yingzhang* procession.' When Zhao Suotong was 17 [*c*1948] he spent a period in Du Chengzhang's older brother's drum shop in Yan'an.

In Suide county, the fortunes of Li Daniu (formal name Li Changchun; milk name Niu, and the oldest son, so Daniu; 1909–82 *apud* Huo 1997a) reveal the friction between tradition and innovation.[17] When young, Li Daniu lived in the Huayansiwan quarter of Mizhi town, like Zhao Jinrang. In 1942 at the Communist Party's new base at Yan'an, cultural cadre Zhou Yang at the Lu Xun Arts Academy (*Luyi*) sought a 'politically reliable' and talented young *chuishou* to educate, and to teach the school's own pupils. It was about this time that Communist cadres had come across Chang Mao. But the Suide district committee eventually chose Li Daniu, so in the early winter he set off for Yan'an, walking for four days to get there.

At the Lu Xun Arts Academy, Li often played for cultural cadres like Ma Ke and Zhang Lu, several of them notating his pieces; Li Huanzhi's 1956 'Spring Festival Overture' (*Chunjie xuqu*)[18] is said to have been inspired by Li Daniu playing popular traditional pieces. Since he was illiterate, they tried to teach him to read, and made him attend political study sessions. He was also an opium smoker; he didn't take to reading, couldn't stand the regulated life, and after two months there he set off on the long walk back home.

In 1947 Li Daniu moved to Suide town. In the 5th moon he was sent on a secret mission with an underground Communist Party member to Yulin city, where the Nationalist 22nd army had just conscripted new recruits. Li was to lend credence to the agent's guise as a *chuishou*. In a single night the agent persuaded the new army brigade to disband, but next morning they were both thrown in prison as they were leaving by the south gate. The following day they were taken off for execution, but Li was reprieved when they learnt that he was really a *chuishou*, not a Communist. He later went on a mission to Shanxi for them, but never took the career path that his brush with Communism might have suggested. As he observed, 'Eating state food is never so free as being a *chuishou*.' In the 1950s he spent some time as odd-job man at the hall of commerce and the Mizhi secondary school, and as a roving livestock-selling intermediary (*yahe*). He can't have been getting much work as a *chuishou*.

Li Daniu could never find a wife; scholar Huo Xianggui characterizes him genuinely with the Communist (and indeed international) cliché of 'poor but honest'. Huo tells a story that reveals *chuishous*' own sense of inferiority. One morning in 1974 Huo invited Li Daniu to his room, and wanted to take Li out for breakfast, but Li wouldn't go. As Huo was about to go off to get food to bring back, Li wanted to sit outside to wait for him, with the room locked; only half-joking, he said, 'How am I supposed to explain if something in your room goes missing?'

---

[17] Huo 1997a, and my 2001 interviews with Huo Xianggui. Tian 2005: 197 gives 1911–87, based on an earlier essay by Huo.

[18] Zhongguo 1992: 26.

If the Communists could claim some successes in recruiting poor artists, as we saw with the blind bard Han Qixiang, Li Daniu's career shows that it was not easy. After his early recruitment led to nothing, he could barely survive as a *chuishou* under the commune system.

Blind *chuishou* Hao Yongfa (1918–83) came from a Suide village.[19] He lost his sight when 5, and learnt shawm from 12 with his father. Later he went on to learn *wanwanqiang* local puppet operas with one Hu Yanhua, and from 1933 he worked for Yang Hongyou's celebrated 'little opera' [local term for shadow-puppetry] band,[20] playing *banhu* fiddle and shawm for *wanwanqiang* and *Jinju* puppet operas. From 1939 he worked as an itinerant *chuishou* and opera accompanist through Shanxi further east across the Yellow River. He came back to the Yang puppet band in 1941, singing and playing percussion too; he was attached to this band for almost 30 years. The Yang band did some work as 'propaganda team' for the Communists from 1946, and in 1956 was invited to become the 'Suide folk shadow-puppet team'. Hao Yongfa took part in a provincial arts festival in 1955, and is credited with innovations in *wanwanqiang*.

Hao was another blind *chuishou* who could never find a wife. After the puppet band had to disband in 1964, he settled in a village in Yihe township, supporting himself by playing shawm and performing *daoqing* vocal music, though he was apparently not a bard or fortune-teller. *Chuishou* Liu Deyi recalled him with respect. 'When he went out on business he walked at the back, with the *chuishou* in front leading him with a small stick.' Scholar Huo Xianggui admired Hao Yongfa a lot too. Like other *chuishou* we met who had brushes with Communist cultural cadres, his art remained largely uninfluenced by the official style.

Another outstanding player was Jin Wenhua. He came from Suide, but fled west of the Wuding river to Jingbian county in 1947 to escape the civil war, and stayed there. Again, he 'shared a woman' with another poor man; he was apparently not an opium smoker. Huo Xianggui began visiting him in 1974, and he was another important source for Huo's transcriptions. Huo took him to perform in Xi'an too in 1979, but his desperate poverty limited his ability to engage with officialdom.

Two brothers who apprenticed themselves to the Chang style were He Zengtong (b. *c*1925) and his older brother He Zengrong, from a hillside hamlet not far from Zhenchuan town, with a population of only 100 or so. He Zengtong has a slight stammer. 'My master was Chang Wenzhang from Changshiban. My older brother Zengrong learnt from him, and I learnt by listening a lot. I started doing business when I was 13 (*c*1937). I know Chang Wenzhou, he plays well, I used to make up a band (*daban*) with him. I've got six or seven apprentices – two in Dingbian.' He appears to have had no contact with state-supported troupes.

---

[19]   This account is based on AO Yulin 221–2, and my 2001 chats with Huo Xianggui.
[20]   See AO Yulin 218–19.

6.7 Yangjiagou under the landlords

So far we have mainly introduced *chuishou* with a reputation who were able to set up in business from an urban base. While communication between village and town may have improved, mainly since the 1980s (roads, still terrible, and TV), the cultural gap has widened. Despite migration to the towns in search of work, most of the population is still stuck in the poor villages, and most work for *chuishou* is there.

We introduced the former landlord village of Yangjiagou in the Preface, and its bard Li Huaiqiang in Part Two. Just as Li was busy performing for the landlords, their ceremonies also kept several bands of *chuishou* busy. By 1999 Yangjiagou's shawm players were not distinguished, but before Liberation, under the landlords, there were several excellent bands – one might compare it to its fine architecture of which pale shadows remain (Illustration 5 above). The village can boast at least two famous shawm players, Feng Guanglin and Gao Maomao – from different generations, they are also poles apart stylistically. Both left the village for wider fame; but the musicians who were left behind also have a revealing story. My material here comes mainly from the unassuming *chuishou* colleagues Older Brother and Chouxiao.

Though Yangjiagou was a landlord base by the late nineteenth century, it only seems to have become a magnet for *chuishou* from the 1920s. Many migrated from other villages to serve the landlords in Yangjiagou, including the Chang and Gao families, and Feng Guanglin. By the 1930s, on the eve of the Communist arrival in the region, there were over ten bands serving the landlords, though for most village *chuishou*, then as now, music was a subsidiary income; they relied mainly on tilling the fields and manual labour for the landlords.

Chang Xinhua

Chang Xinhua (*c*1881–late 1950s), grandfather of our friend Chouxiao, was the most celebrated shawm player and 'fixer' for the landlords in Yangjiagou. Chouxiao heard that Xinhua was the third generation of *chuishou* in his family. The family is distantly related to the Changs of Changshiban. 'Our family moved from Changshiban to Yangjiagou 79 years ago [1922]. With 72 landlord families here, there were jobs [*shi*, ceremonial business] almost every day.' Older Brother: 'Chang Xinhua was the first *chuishou* in Yangjiagou. When he was just beginning to do business here he had to invite helpers from Changshiban; later when he had his own apprentices in the village he didn't need to any more.'

Chang Xinhua was the landlords' trusted 'fixer' (*huzi*, or *lanshi*). As another elderly villager recalled, 'All you had to do was say the word, and he would have a band ready. If his own band had enough players then fine, if not then he could find others from outside.' As fixer, he took a share of the fee; so did the supplier of the instruments (*jiashi*); often this would be the same person.[21] Musically, Chang Xinhua was a natural 'second fiddle': though not good at the upper part, he was unrivalled on the lower part. Chang Xinhua's son Chang Wenbiao (*c*1916–*c*1992) also played well; the *wen* character in his name placed him in the same generation as Chang Wenzhou. Below we meet his own son, Chouxiao.

Though Chang Xinhua had to pay *chuishou* coming from outside on the spot, the deal for the village *chuishou* was more complex: their earnings were calculated over a long period. Every year on the 30th of the last moon, Chang Xinhua would take his band around all the houses to play, then again next morning, when people would make gifts, whether of cash or of food (like *huangmo* or *gao* cake), loading it into his sack. For really poor people unable to make any gift, he would still go and play a short piece, expecting no reward – this is a common folk conceit, independent of Communist hagiography.

For ceremonial events there was a spatial hierarchy between bands from the village and outside. Chang Xinhua's own band generally occupied the main courtyard, while a band from elsewhere would play outside the gate. When Ma Xingmin's daughter got married, the family specifically asked Chang Xinhua to book two shawm players from Changshiban. And even the home team was not as prestigious as any priests invited to perform their liturgy.

Feng Guanglin

Another celebrated *chuishou* in Yangjiagou was a semi-blind man who settled here to find employment with the landlords. Feng Guanglin (1899–1972) was born to a poor family in a village just further east.[22] His family were not musicians, but he began playing percussion in shawm bands from an early age. One of his female relatives had married to Yangjiagou, so he went there to work for the landlords, where good business was to be found. He may have moved to Yangjiagou as early as 1915; he took up as a *chuishou* only after coming to the village, first playing percussion and then learning shawm with Chang Xinhua. He was certainly a junior to Chang Xinhua in his early years in Yangjiagou, but soon outshone him.

Feng Guanglin was almost blind, and never found a wife. It is unclear if he smoked opium. He was active over a wide area, including Shanxi province across the Yellow River, working not only for shawm bands through the winter but in the summer with itinerant opera, puppet, and *daoqing* groups. He was still based in Yangjiagou when the Chang brothers (see below) learnt with him from around 1933. Older Brother thought he returned to his old home of Fengjiagou at some point, where he taught two nephews.

Villager Ma Zhongyi (b.1923) recalled Feng as a versatile musician, playing many instruments, including the stringed instruments of the landlords' children

---

[21] For shawm band fixers, cf. Liu Yong 2006: 128. For fees, see §10.4 below.

[22] AI 970–1; Feng 1984. He came from Fengjiagou village in Jizhen district, and was known as Jiur, local pronunciation for *che* 'cart'.

– he was glad to have more musical company when they came back for the school holidays, and despite his low class he was welcome. After the Japanese invasion of 1937, still more students returned from Beijing and Tianjin, and Feng took part in frequent musical gatherings.

In 1944 Feng Guanglin was recruited to the Suide District Arts-Work Troupe of the Shaan-Gan-Ning Border Region, through a chance contact of his pupil Chang Bingyou, one of whose brothers was working as a cook for the Suide district committee. Later Feng moved to a job with the Shaanxi Provincial Song-and-Dance Opera Theatre in Xi'an, mainly performing revolutionary songs and new operas until his death in 1972. In Xi'an his experience was appreciated by the scholar Liang Wenda, author of a substantial 1956 mimeograph of transcriptions of his varied repertory of shawm and opera pieces[23] – pieces for which he can have had little use in his state job.

Though Feng had no heirs, Yangjiagou villagers had heard a bit of his later life. Ma Zhenyin: 'Feng Guanglin was the best shawm player. I saw him when I was young, but I never heard him play, I was only 12 [*c*1944]. He went to Xi'an during the War of Liberation, and later he "entered the state" – took part in revolutionary work – and never came back.' It was a life of two halves; how he adjusted to the salaried urban life might make an interesting story, but he was almost the only *chuishou* in Shaanbei who did remain there for a long period.

Chang Bingyou

Our *chuishou* friend Older Brother (§7.3 below) is a wonderful source of local history. Like Chouxiao's forebears, his grandfather's generation had moved from Changshiban. They moved first to Qingyangchuan village, and from there on to Yangjiagou to do temporary work (*langong*) for the landlords – Older Brother thinks around 1915. Though their old home was the base of the celebrated Chang family band, to whom they are distantly related, it was not a family of *chuishou*; his grandfather was a noodle maker.

Older Brother's father Chang Bingyou (1916–98, sign Dragon; Illustration 9), known as Chang *daye* 'Elder Chang', was the youngest of five brothers, and hence was also called Chang the Fifth. The brothers all worked as servants and noodle makers for the landlords. Three of the brothers learnt shawm with Feng Guanglin: Bingyou was first in the family to take it up, in about 1933; the oldest brother Bingren and fourth brother Bingwen also learnt. The study period was three years. Feng Guanglin (the master, *shifu*) lived and ate at their home for the whole training period, during which time he also claimed his pupils' share of payment for jobs. Bingwen played the best; he would often play second shawm to Feng Guanglin. He died unmarried in 1951, aged 40. Bingren died in the 1950s, earlier than Chang Xinhua.

In 1936, when he was 20, Chang Bingyou was married to a 15-*sui*-old girl from Jiaxian county; *chuishou* performed for the wedding. In his career as a *chuishou*

---

23   Feng 1984, alas hard to find. Some of his pieces are included in AI.

Illustration 9   Elder Chang (1916–98), *chuishou* in Yangjiagou. The cloth tied
   around the head, an archetypal image of the peasant revolution in north China,
   is now rarely worn.

he travelled to Suide and Zizhou as well as elsewhere in Mizhi. Business was best
in the winter, but working as a *chuishou* was always a supplementary income: he
tilled the fields all his life.

Other chuishou

By 2001, Ma Siwang (b. *c*1917) was the oldest (former) *chuishou* in the village.
'My family was very poor. My father Ma Shouliang could play *suona* too, but
he didn't join a band; my grandfather couldn't play. First I learnt the percussion,
then I became a *chuishou* on *suona* when I was 17 or 18 (*c*1933). I joined the
band of Li Wenhai from Xiaojiata village in Suide – he was my master. I played
with Feng Guanglin, he was the best at the time, he always got the highest fee.
In those days Yangjiagou village could send out a dozen or so bands: four bands

from Chang Wenbiao, two from the Ma family, two from the Zhou family, and two more put together *ad hoc*. All these bands had moved to Yangjiagou to work for the landlords.'

Another *chuishou* in Sigou, a satellite hamlet of Yangjiagou, was Ma Qiantang (b. *c*1940). His family has also lived in Sigou for under 100 years. His grandfather had a small amount of land, but just before Liberation he bought more. They later moved to Hougou hamlet nearby. 'I learnt *chuishou* from young with my father Ma Rusheng. I was going out on business playing percussion when I was 8 (*c*1947), and played the shawm from 17. My father had two *chuishou* bands, the other was run by his younger cousin Ma Ruzheng. Before the Cultural Revolution our family band mainly did business outside [the village], around Sanjiaping district in Suide, and Sishilipu, Houjiagou, Baijiagou, Guanjiazui – now we don't go to Sanjiaping any more, it's too far. In Yangjiagou it was mainly the Chang band, they were the old fixers – when there was business you sought them.'

As to other lineages, the Zhou band had no musical descendants. Older Brother: 'The Zhous learnt from the Changs, and did business along with the Chang band.' Ma Qiantang: 'My father learnt from Zhou Fuqi.' They left, or were driven out of, Yangjiagou around the 1940s. Ma Qiantang: 'I guess they moved to Yanchuan because there were fewer *chuishou* there, so there were jobs to be had.' Older Brother suggested a further factor: 'The Zhou *chuishou* were opium smokers. In those days the landlords would choose people to work for them who were good labourers and were trustworthy, so no-one was hiring the Zhou family, and they moved to Yanchuan.'

There was also a band in the Kang family. Chang Xinhua had an apprentice called Kang Wenzhi, now dead. The sole descendant is his nephew Kang Shezhang (Wuwa, 'Fifth kid'), whose father also played. The Kang lineage is substantial in Jiaxian county, where it is a major provider of musicians, including Daoists in the White Cloud Mountain temple and shawm bands. As to the Yang band, Yang Zhongming (1913–81) was the first in his family to learn, also with Chang Xinhua. His cousin Yang Zhongyin (Yang Zhen) sometimes ran a drum shop in Suide town. Both were considered good *chuishou*.

6.8 Instrumentations and priests

To conclude this chapter, a note on instrumentation. Though the main line-up is the two large shawms with three percussion, *chuishou* also used a subsidiary instrumentation for certain parts of ceremonies.

Until the 1940s the *chuishou* performed for funerals at which Buddhist or Daoist priests (or both) were also often invited. Indeed, one *chuishou* observed that before the 1950s *chuishou* were less common than now since they were in competition with the priests – though I don't feel this works as a causal explanation, since the two serve different functions. Whereas such groups of lay ritual specialists are common in areas of Hebei and Shanxi that I have studied (Jones 2004, 2007), in Shaanbei they are now quite rare (see p.xxii n.8, and p.25 n.56).

Apart from their main duties of singing the vocal liturgy accompanied by ritual percussion, the priests also punctuated their rituals by playing a local version of *sheng-guan* ensemble music, with *guanzi* oboe (commonly known here as *mimi*, and made of tin), *sheng* free-reed mouth-organ, a small shawm called *haidi* (or *haidir*, *haidizi*) and a frame of gongs, with percussion accompaniment – an instrumentation best known in Shaanbei in the White Cloud Mountain temples (§1.6, §1.7 above).

More accomplished *chuishou* bands also used a version of this subsidiary instrumentation for accompanying ritual feasts. Chang Wenzhou and Zhao Suotong were familiar with it. The Yangjiagou *chuishou* also used it – Ma Siwang recalled: 'In those days we had two sets of bands, one for "coarse blowing" (*cuchui*) or "large blowing" (*dachui*), one for "fine blowing" (*xichui*) or "small blowing" (*xiaochui*).' The coarse blowing, the standard line-up of two large shawms and three percussion, was played on procession, and for the seated suites at the ritual site. The fine blowing, using *guanzi*, *haidi*, small gongs, small cymbals, and drum, but no *sheng*, was used mainly for 'receiving guests' (*daike*) at feasts (*zhengxi*); a *meidi* flute was added for the *kaiji* ritual. Ma Qiantang recalled, 'In my father's day they played *haidi* with *guanzi*, but not with the large shawm; there was no *sheng*, that was played only by priests.' His father played *haidi*, his uncle *guanzi*. Chouxiao's grandfather and father also played *guanzi*. He still keeps a tin *guanzi* handed down from them, and learnt to play it from his father; he would love to play it again, but now has no-one to play with. He says shawm bands played some of the same pieces on the *guanzi* as the priests, like the mournful funerary pieces *Ku lingding* or *Lingqian ku*.

Of the gongs, one was the *dangdang* (possibly the same as a frame of two gongs called *erpingzi*),[24] one the smaller *shouwa*. Zhao Suotong has kept a small *erpingzi*. Some equated it with the *yunluo* frame of ten pitched gongs played by ritual specialists elsewhere in north China.

Incidentally, scholar Huo Xianggui claims that he coined the terms 'greater blowing' and 'lesser blowing' in the 1970s, and the musicians went along with it, as it fitted with their own concepts. Musicians seem to deny official involvement in their art, while officials may be too quick to claim it.

* * *

In the first half of the twentieth century, neither the town bands nor those of landlord-stronghold Yangjiagou were typical; many village bands performed only occasionally when required, as still today. But so far, before the consolidation of Communist power, despite disturbed social conditions and extreme poverty, the varied programme of life-cycle and calendrical ceremonies offered many *chuishou* a lifeline, both in the towns and the villages.

---

[24]   As on the White Cloud Mountain: Yuan, Li, and Shen 1999: 66.

Chapter 7

Chuishou under Mao

It is a hoary Communist cliché that in the 'old society', folk musicians, such as the lowly shawm bands, were despised and rejected, whereas after Liberation they were esteemed and their lives improved radically. In fact, for the *chuishou*, as we found with the bards, any notional improvement in status after Liberation might seem to have been cancelled out by the collapse of their patrons and contexts. Nonetheless, *chuishou* kept active, after a fashion; most senior *chuishou* active since the 1990s learnt their trade in the first 15 years after Liberation, roughly from 1949 to 1964.

Unlike ritual specialists (Daoists, mediums, geomancers), they weren't singled out for persecution; they too might be hired for 'superstitious' contexts, but weren't themselves 'superstitious practitioners'. One *chuishou* commented astutely: 'Chairman Mao didn't tell anyone to overthrow the *chuishou*, they were pitiable enough already – they only got to take home the leftovers from the feast'. Of course, their ability to continue practising varied. Politically this period was complex, like the preceding one: parts of the region had been under Communist control since the late 1930s, and after the commune system began to be enforced most rigidly from the mid-1950s, there was a temporary lull in political control in the early 1960s. If the overall picture was increasingly bleak, local conditions varied from month to month and from village to village.

7.1 The 1950s

As we saw, a steady stream of fine *chuishou* emerged from the Chang lineage of Changshiban village. By the 1990s, Chang Wenzhou (b.1936, ⊙**B1, D3**) was perhaps the most widely respected shawm player in the whole of Shaanbei. He has made a good career from the shawm, graduating from his remote village to official success under Maoism and then a thriving business in Mizhi county-town under the reforms.

Chang Wenzhou began playing percussion in the band of his father Chang Jiazhong there from the age of 8 (*c*1943), and later recalled his father's playing with admiration. He himself could play the upper part by the age of 15 – in 1950, soon after Liberation. Amazingly, he claims to have graduated from Mizhi town Senior Secondary: it was very rare for a village *chuishou* to advance so far in formal education, seeming to vindicate the Chang family's emancipation with the title of 'official blowers' – though I remain incredulous. Still in Changshiban, his cousin Chang Wenjin (b.1937) also learnt *chuishou* from his early teens, but 'didn't study many books'. The two cousins did a bit of metalwork, and began making shawms – unusually, not just the wooden bodies, but the metal bells and throats too, as we see below.

As to ceremonial activity, no-one made a clear distinction between the early 1950s and the period from the mid-50s when the commune system was implemented; people recalled the whole period as one of cultural impoverishment, contrasting funerals in the 1940s. The most lavish funeral Chang Wenzhou remembers was a five-day event in Fengjiagou village when he was only 8 or 9 (*c*1944), for the father of a Nationalist commander. Three bands of *chuishou* were invited, besides 30 Buddhist priests, who performed a full sequence of rituals, including *sheng-guan* music. Zhao Suotong recalled an exceptional funeral in the 1940s, of a merchant family in Zizhou county. 40 pigs were slaughtered for the funeral feast, and eight *chuishou* bands were invited, including two from Suide and several from Zizhou and Mizhi.

Chang Wenzhou recalls that under the commune system (when he was in his twenties, after about 1956), they weren't allowed to play, but they would still do occasional business on the quiet. As several *chuishou* recalled, if they did go out on business they had to hand over a percentage of their fee to the production-team, who would give them work-points in return. Though the production-team did well out of this, the *chuishou* were still left with enough to make it worthwhile: a day's individual work-points varied from 5 to 2.6 *mao*, while total earnings for a five-man band before the production-team 'tax' (of around 40%) varied from 10 to 5 *yuan*. Li Qishan: 'Just before the Cultural Revolution, we were paid 3 *mao* each for a day's labour [in the fields]; to go out and play for a day we [the whole band] got 10 *yuan* – we gave 4 *yuan* to the production-team, and kept 6 *yuan*.'

In Sishilipu town just south, Wang Shifa learnt *chuishou* from the age of 12 (*c*1960). 'I liked playing the shawm when I was young. Our family situation was very bad, so my father agreed to let me go off and be a *chuishou*. In those days the payment for accompanying *yangge* was quite high, the two shawm players could earn 5 *yuan* between them a day.' With the daily rate for labour here fixed at 5 *mao*, being a *chuishou* as a 'supplementary occupation' would have been attractive.

Chang Wenzhou elaborated on the commune period: 'That was a dead tough time – you were lucky to get *gao* cake or noodles even at a funeral, and people weren't supposed to invite *chuishou*. You couldn't put on any satisfactory ceremonies in the period between Liberation and the communes either, the landlords had been overthrown, their property had been divided up into nothing, and poor people couldn't put on a proper do. There were no proper events in the Chairman Mao era.' From this it appears academic to periodize the post-Liberation period: people considered it one long cultural desert.

Soon after the national Liberation, apart from any changes in context, there was one severe jolt – for the 80% of *chuishou* who smoked opium. Liu Deyi: 'After Liberation the government collected everyone together and prohibited it. People my age, still teenagers, didn't smoke it. But once the government prohibited it strictly in the 1950s, no-one could go back to it.'

7.2 Drum shops in Suide

In bustling Suide county-town we chatted with Liu Deyi (b. *c*1935), a charming *chuishou*, illiterate but cultured. His house is clean, his children successful – and not *chuishou*. 'I was the first *chuishou* in my family, not from a hereditary tradition. Our old home was in Liujiawan village, but we moved to Suide town when I was 1 *sui* old. I played percussion from 14, and shawm from 16 [*c*1948–1950]. We were so poor that I had no choice but to become a *chuishou*.' The business still seemed to offer desperate families a way to survive.

Liu described the drum shop scene in Suide county-town when he was learning just around Liberation. 'My teacher was Yang Zhongyin from Yangjiagou, who had moved to Suide town, he ran a drum shop here – that was what it was called while I was learning, no-one uses that expression any more now! In those days there were three drum shops in Suide town, those of Yang Zhongyin, Ma Shengxiang (also called Ma Shuan), and Bi Shenghua. The *chuishou* all lived at the boss's house, but ate their own food. Ma Shengxiang and Bi Shenghua also ran itinerant "little opera" [shadow-puppet] bands in the summer season.'

He was clear about some of the other Suide *chuishou* that we had heard of. 'Li Daniu and Li Erniu were based here, but they didn't run drum shops. Nor did Wang En, he just had one at his old home of Yan'goucha village in Nanshan district, but his two sons didn't learn.' Wang Shifa said Wang En died in the mid-1990s.

According to Wang Shifa, 'Drum shops in Suide were like my band now: now the head of the drum music group (*guyuedui*) is called band boss (*banzhu*), then it was called So-and-so's drum shop. Only people with good technique could set up a drum shop. Like, supposing Yanchang county-town hadn't got any *chuishou*, we'd go and set up a drum shop there.' Wang went on, 'Before the Cultural Revolution in my district of Sishilipu, there were seven or eight bands, now there are at least fifteen.'

As we saw, Wang Shifa began learning when 12 in about 1960. On a visit in 2001 to a temple fair in his home township of Sishilipu, he introduced us to two other *chuishou* who had learnt just before him. The affable Wang Shushan (b. *c*1944) is known as Mao Xiao. First he described the scene in Sishilipu before Liberation. 'My grandfather played percussion, but there were no *chuishou* in our family the generation before that.' Wang Shushan's father was called Wang Weifang (1915–99). 'His master was Li Wenhai [the same as Ma Siwang's master, §6.7 above], who was living at Fengdianmao. In those days my dad could send out nine bands from his home. There was also a band boss called Yan Hanshan, who could send out eight bands. Later there was only our one band in Sishilipu.' Wang Shushan went on, 'I started going out on business with my father when I was 13 [*c*1956], and I tilled the fields a bit too. I'm a famous *chuishou* in this township, I went to play last year for the closing ceremony of a festival in Xi'an [the provincial capital].' Blithely ignoring the dominance of Chang Wenzhou, he went on, 'I'm the only one around here who can make shawms.'

In Sishilipu we also met Wang Shushan's stepbrother Cao Laiqian (b. *c*1943). He came over with his mother when she remarried into the Wang family, and started learning with his stepfather from the age of 16 (*c*1958). Though one might expect the campaigns that heralded the Cultural Revolution to have stamped out activity, Cao told us, 'My master ran a drum shop in Shiwan village. I ran one too in 1965–66 when I was 24. When I was just learning, a lot of *chuishou* were going out to run drum shops. But there are a lot more "drum music groups" (*guyuedui*) now than there were drum shops then. When I and my master ran drum shops, it was just for *chuishou*, we weren't running an opera band too, so when work was little in the summer we came home and tilled the fields. I married when I was 21 [*c*1963] – my wife was introduced to me by someone. One band of *chuishou* was invited; the band boss was Liu the Third, he was a good *chuishou* round here – he's dead now.' Was this the famous *chuishou* Liu Zide, one of Huo and Ai's informants?

As Wang Shifa observed, most players round there were only first or second generation. Also learning from the mid-1950s was a famous player in Lijiagou village on the main road north towards Mizhi town, Li Qishan (b. *c*1949). 'My father Li Junfu was the first in my family to play; he learnt from my uncle in Zhangjiada village. I started playing percussion in my father's band when I was 7 [*c*1955], and learnt shawm with him when I was 15 [*c*1963]. In the past it was always poor fellows who learnt.'

7.3 Back in Yangjiagou

In Yangjiagou too, villagers tended to play down change. Of course, changes had been under way before Liberation, not just because of Communist campaigns but through a whole complex cycle of warfare, deprivation, and the wider economic picture. Older Brother (speaking from reliable hearsay): 'During the wars, especially in 1946 when Hu Zongnan invaded, people rarely held proper weddings and funerals or hired *chuishou*, no-one had time to perform proper rituals.' Thus several villagers said there was no change after the Communist Liberation, and even that they earned the same just after Liberation. Ma Qiantang: 'In the early period after Liberation, you could still hire several bands of *chuishou*.'

Even after collectivization they could still do business; they were still paid, though they gave a cut to the commune, gaining work-points in return. Ma Qiantang again: 'Under the people's communes, every day a band went out to do business we had to hand over 2 or 3 *yuan* – we earnt 5 or 6 *yuan* a day – then the production-team would give us a day's work-points, worth 2.6 *mao* each.'

But as the Party's power was consolidated, fewer bands were active: some left the village, many changed jobs, entering urban factories or just returning to full-time work on the land. Ma Qiantang had been taking part in his father's band since around 1947. 'After I graduated from primary school in 1958 [when 19!], they were recruiting workers in Xi'an, so I signed up as an apprentice gas welder. But I came running back in 1961 – the monthly wage for 1st-rank workers was only 36 *yuan*, and even potatoes cost 1 *yuan* a *jin*.' This return to the villages in the early

1960s after the mass lay-offs caused by the economic disasters following the Great Leap Forward is a common feature among villagers I have met in north China.[1]

Ma Siwang also sought a new livelihood. His wife recalled: 'When I was married at the age of 15 [c1939], we hired one band of *chuishou* for the wedding. The activities of the *chuishou* were more or less the same before and after Liberation. But when my old man was about 30 [c1946] he gave up being a *chuishou* and became a stone-mason. He didn't like the *chuishou* life-style, "marching before people and eating after them", and you couldn't earn as much as from being a mason, so he stopped playing the shawm.' Ma Siwang reminded us: 'Before Liberation, going out to do business wasn't the main thing for the Yangjiagou bands anyway, they only went out in the winter, not like the drum shops in the towns who relied on doing business all the time. I didn't take part in an opera band either before or after Liberation. Even before Liberation, weddings usually only lasted a single day – now they sometimes last three days, though.'

Older Brother considered that by the late 1950s the village could still raise four or five *chuishou* bands. Ma Zhenyin gave the same figure for the eve of the Cultural Revolution. Again, the definition of a band is elusive. Older Brother reckoned: 'There were still a dozen or so bands in Yangjiagou just after Liberation, but now there are only a few.' I might only detect two bands now (his rather occasional band with Chouxiao, and that of Hu's family: see §10.9 below), but both can muster enough shawm players and percussion deputies to constitute separate bands on demand. Apart from the various Chang and Ma families, several *chuishou* were still active in the Yang family. Yang Zhongming had a band, in which his son Anying (known as Yunwenr, b. c1945), played percussion when young, learning shawm when 20 [c1964]; his older brother also learnt, but later gave up.

Ma Zhenyin

Ma Zhenyin (b.1933; sign Rooster) sometimes plays drum in the band of Older Brother and Chouxiao. He has a reputation in the village as a versatile musician, but was left semi-blind after his eyes were injured by firecrackers in 1953 during a state festival. He was married to a disabled woman, but the marriage was soon a casualty of his time away from home and they divorced. He is very poor, surviving on a pitiful state disabled benefit; unlike our semi-blind bachelor friend Older Brother (see below), he has no family support network. He lives alone in a very poor and unkempt cave-dwelling; tatty old newspapers on the walls are blackened with grime.

Ma Zhenyin began taking part as percussionist with the band of Chouxiao's father Chang Wenbiao around 1949, taking to the drum, and played often with them until 1956. 'In the early period after Liberation I followed Chouxiao's father's band. Chouxiao's grandfather Chang Xinhua was very famous, but he didn't play as well as his son.'

---

[1]   Cf. Jones 2004: 131–45; Jones 2007: 15.

Ma Zhenyin also learnt to play *huhu* fiddle, singing and accompanying the ancient plays of the puppet opera, and taking part in *yangge* festivities. From 1952 to 1964 he 'chased round' with a dozen or so puppet troupes, such as the band of Ma Zongchang in Majiachuan, Ai Keying's band in Longzhen, and the band of Yang Hongxiong, younger brother of Yang Hongyou (§6.7 above) – the Yang family band had several generations of experience. Ma Zhenyin entered a state-funded puppet opera troupe (*mu'ou jutuan*) in 1956. 'For the Great Leap Forward in 1958 they told us to rehearse new operas – they wouldn't let us do old ones, but we couldn't sing the new ones! During the Socialist Education campaign in 1964 they wouldn't let us play any more – geomancers and *chuishou* were all down on their luck (*beileyun*).' He went on, 'There's no shadow-puppet opera any more, I guess it's been defunct since 1967 or 1968. Now, although the temple fairs have revived, the puppeteers have all scattered, and the equipment has disappeared, so it can't be revived.' But somehow the shawm bands have survived.

Older Brother

Under the commune system, *chuishou* Chang Bingyou (§6.7 above) served for a period as chief of one of the village's production-teams; he was also a leader of the village temple committee (*huizhang*). To hold such public leadership, either modern or traditional, was unusual for a lowly *chuishou*. Village pilgrims used to walk all the way to the White Cloud Mountain for the 4th-moon temple fair there, then still a major event despite Communist control. By the time shawm bands were reviving in the 1980s with the demise of the Maoist communes, Chang Bingyou was in his 60s, and hardly played.

He and his wife had two boys and five girls; they didn't 'hang the locket' for any of them, as they all seemed healthy. In fact the first-born son died when 4; the oldest daughter was born in 1939. The third child Chang Yanzhang (known as Shiyao or Dage [Older Brother], b.1945, sign Rooster) was left partially blind from young by smallpox. He was to be Chang Bingyou's only pupil on the shawm. He began playing cymbals in his father's band from the age of 12, around 1956, taking up the shawm when 17 or 18, in about 1962 – both quite late.

The Yangjiagou *chuishou* still managed to play through the 1950s, even after the Great Leap Forward. Older Brother: 'In the Great Leap Forward, people came from Zhenchuan to demand metal implements like woks, but there was no campaign as such in the village, and no furnaces. We gave up old woks, but didn't have to give up instruments.' Though Older Brother recalls no problems, others say that anti-extravagance campaigns (*puzhang langfei, dacao daban*) from 1958 influenced *chuishou*. One villager observed that when these campaigns were enforced, *chuishou* were effectively thrown out of work, having to rely entirely on their work-points from tilling the fields. Still, they kept going until 1965, though Older Brother regretted, 'It was a shame I had to stop so soon after learning.'

Accompanying *yangge* song-and-dance with short simple four-square melodies was now mentioned more often than weddings and funerals, with their more complex repertory of long suites. Older Brother recalled the main contexts under Maoism as *yangge* at New Year, other commune-led secular events like the Children's Festival, or sending men off to the army, also requiring *yangge*. There was an army brigade at the commune seat, so perhaps Yangjiagou was under closer supervision than some places. But other *chuishou* assured us that for funerals, they still observed the proper sequence more or less, on the quiet, except when cadres came from outside to implement campaigns.

But like Chang Wenzhou above, all agreed that whatever the niceties, there were no proper funerals under Maoism. Typical was just one perfunctory meal of *heguo*, a slab of *gao* cake, one solitary *chuishou* to lead the way on procession, and the burial team. All the villagers were poor, and food was basic, so they couldn't put on a proper show even if political conditions permitted. Older Brother: 'Families [today] whose economic conditions are a bit better may invite *chuishou* to receive guests for the first full moon and 100th-day celebrations after a birth. And now you can hire *chuishou* for moving into a new cave-dwelling, and for weddings and funerals; some people still hire them for longevity celebrations too. Before 1965, people's lives weren't so good as they are now, so it was rarer then.'

7.4 The official connection 1

We have already noted a few instances of ephemeral official recruitment for the *chuishou* in the 1940s: Chang Mao and Li Daniu, and the longer-term employment of Feng Guanglin. In Chapter 9 below, we also find Ma Hu and Wang Xinxi spending time in state work-units. These cases are interesting partly by virtue of their rarity, and did little to alter the general status or activities of the *chuishou*. They did not suddenly begin playing a new revolutionary repertory for staged performances; those in the countryside, supplementing their living by accompanying ceremonial, always vastly outnumbered those few recruited to state troupes.

The official festivals held throughout China in the 1950s, at regional, provincial, and national levels,[2] identified many outstanding musicians, giving them a certain prestige, and occasionally a new career path; one purpose of these festivals was to select musicians for the new state-supported troupes. As we saw, in every county throughout China an 'arts-work troupe' (*wengongtuan*) was set up; later they were renamed 'opera troupe' (*jutuan*). (I would also expect army troupes to have recruited shawm players, but no-one in Shaanbei offered any information on them.) In Shaanbei, though *chuishou* were often versatile as opera accompanists, they were less likely to adapt to the new instrumental repertories of the state troupes. Some *chuishou* took part in the occasional festivals in the regional capital Yulin or even the provincial capital Xi'an, and a few even spent a few years in the state troupes, but Feng Guanglin's lengthy stay was exceptional. We have several clues

---

[2]   See e.g. Zhongguo 1989: 884.

that even if invited, *chuishou* were wary of official salaried life, or felt insecure: the concept was simply alien.

As we saw, Chang Mao was a much-admired *chuishou* by the 1940s, who was known to Communist cadres in Yan'an but was not chosen to join them there. Having set up in Zhidan county, he won a prize in the Second Shaanxi Provincial Arts Festival in 1955, and was sought by the provincial circus troupe, but 'he felt his lack of Culture, and it was inconvenient to leave home, so he didn't go.'[3] Chang Wenjin recalled: 'Beijing wanted him to go once, just after Liberation, but he still didn't dare go. No-one else in our lineage went to arts-work troupes until Chang Wenzhou [in the late 1970s].' Chang Mao did go on to spend brief periods in the Northwest Arts Training School (*Xibei yishu zhuanke xuexiao*, predecessor of the Xi'an Conservatory) and the Yan'an Song-and-Dance Troupe (*gewutuan*). But he relied on local ceremonial business; apart from setting up a drum shop in Jingbian in 1960, he remained based in Zhidan.

It was one thing to identify good *chuishou* for the festivals, but it didn't necessarily lead to long-term employment; cadres were wary of *chuishou*, but even if they dared extend an invitation, *chuishou* themselves were diffident, aware of the cultural gulf or just afraid to leave their roots in the land.

Li Qishan's father took part in county and regional festivals in the 1950s, but it led to nothing. He Zengtong: 'I took part in festivals organized by the county Hall of Culture, but no arts-work troupe invited us to join. I have no Culture, the arts-work troupes wanted people who could read cipher notation, people with Culture.' Similarly, Zhao Suotong, who had learnt *chuishou* in 1947, and was proud of his playing, recalled, 'The Yan'an Arts-Work Troupe came to ask me to join, but I have no Culture, I didn't dare take part, afraid I might not fit in.' Later he mended sewing machines, still taking on folk business on shawm when asked. Even in a conveniently-situated town like Sishilipu, according to Wang Shushan, 'None of the *chuishou* round here have entered arts-work troupes, or took part in the festivals of the 1950s and 60s.'[4]

Scholar Guo Yuhua notes that Yangjiagou villagers who migrated in the 1940s to work as labourers for the Communists in Yan'an returned home, not regarding it as an opportunity for upward mobility.[5] And as we saw, for every Han Qixiang who espoused Communist arts policy, there were hundreds of blind narrative-singers still performing 'stories for well-being'.

In fact, under Maoism, bolstered by the populist rhetoric of the new ruling ideology, many peasants with a bare modicum of 'Culture' (say, minimal literacy) rose quickly to dangerous power; indeed at many periods under Maoism poor-peasant background was enough to guarantee employment. Yet here we see how

---

[3]   Zhidan 1985: 2. Further material in this paragraph comes from AI 973–4.

[4]   This may vary by region. As my colleague Zhang Zhentao tells me, in Shandong some fine village wind players were recruited to the state-funded troupe with the support of an enlightened troupe leader.

[5]   Guo 2000: 359–60.

the social stratification of 'having Culture' or 'not having Culture' remained deeply entrenched on both sides of the fence. A few poor village musicians might see an opportunity to 'eat off the state', but most had neither the will nor the self-belief to reinvent themselves. Though happy to migrate to set up an urban drum shop, they were reluctant to abandon the familiar soil and network of their poor village homes for a salaried and supervised life in an anonymous apartment-block. The vast majority of *chuishou* stayed behind in their villages, their livelihoods increasingly impoverished, as was the ceremonial culture on which they relied.

Though I never tire of challenging the Communist claim that the status of folk musicians improved significantly after Liberation, Older Brother and several others claimed that the status of *chuishou* did rise. Ma Siwang was among several who observed, 'No-one called *chuishou* "*guizi*" after Liberation.' I deduce that one major aspect of this was that after the overthrow of landlords and other more prestigious elements, everyone 'bore suffering' more or less equally. The most prestigious elements in society were now Party members, but their privileges amounted to little as social differences were levelled; no-one had much respect for anyone. If all were more or less equal under the new regime, the new equality of the *chuishou* with other poor peasants can have amounted to little: they didn't suddenly feel a new self-esteem. Partly, occasions to perform and make money were fewer; if their old occupation had always been subsidiary, it was becoming even more so.

In Mizhi and Suide counties, this issue is complicated by the widely-known 'official blowers' story, whereby their status had already, supposedly, been elevated some considerable time before Communism. Though they appear to believe it, whether this tradition was true in practice seems doubtful. They are also aware that while their nominal status rose (whether in the nineteenth century or in the 1950s), *chuishou* were still held in low esteem. As we will see, this continued to be so even after the economic liberalizations of the 1980s allowed them to challenge prejudice by gaining higher incomes. Society was changing throughout late imperial and republican China, and modern ideas were being taught in progressive schools in the region. However, such education barely penetrated the Yellow Earth, and the status of *chuishou* was not on the agenda for redefinition. Indeed, I learn that in parts of south Shaanbei it still isn't – and below we see that even in Mizhi, old ways die hard.

7.5 Loss-assessment

We have to see the shawm bands in the whole context of the decline of traditional culture under Maoism. As Guo Yuhua (2000) observes, inspired by Geertz, a new 'state ritual' system of political power, enacted through political campaigns, sought to replace the traditional ritual system of survival techniques. Below (§9.7) I will assess decline in musical capability, but here I list some other aspects of impoverishment.

The freedom of *chuishou* – and many other types of musician – to practise was increasingly limited. Before the arrival of the Communists there were many more occasions to perform and compete, maintaining standards. They still played for weddings and funerals, but such ceremonies were themselves observed more simply. Other mortuary ceremonies like the 'seven sevens', and commemorations after 100 days and the first anniversary, had mainly been observed by the former landlords; for the *qingming* ancestral festival *chuishou* were no longer used. Such impoverishment was already in evidence in the 1940s, with unsettled social conditions and the early control of the Communists. Few people could afford to be 'meticulous' (*jiangjiu*).[6]

As we saw, new contexts included secular festivals decreed by the state and sending off sons to the army – for which *chuishou* were hired by the district government.[7] These at least gave *chuishou* a chance to play 'small pieces' and *yangge* pieces, but the range of contexts, and the repertory, were shrinking.

We also saw how the *chuishou*, apart from their main repertory for two shawms and percussion, also sometimes played a subsidiary repertory with an instrumentation known as 'fine blowing', similar to that of the priests, with *guanzi* oboe and *haidi* small shawm but without *sheng* or gong-frame. As priests performing vocal liturgy and *sheng-guan* music disappeared in the 1950s, the *chuishou* might logically have taken over some of this repertory, but as ritual became simplified they too now played the 'fine blowing' style much less. It is not exactly that the *chuishou* have taken over from the priests. The two groups performed different roles for funerals before Communism, but the role of the priests has largely been erased, leaving only that of the *chuishou*, along with geomancers and funeral managers.

Some players from hereditary traditions still learnt *guanzi* in the 1950s, like Wang Shushan in Sishilipu township: 'I can play *guanzi* too, I learnt it from my father. The *guanzi* hasn't been extinct in this area for so long.' But most *chuishou* said it was rarely played since the 1950s. Chang Wenzhou keeps, and can still play, a *guanzi* made of tin. 'During meals *chuishou* should play the *guanzi*, but we gave up in the commune period, before the Cultural Revolution, no-one learnt, and it's hard to play – it's more tiring to play *guanzi* for ten minutes than shawm for an hour.' But being tiring wasn't the issue. If the context had demanded it, they would have kept going; but the whole impoverishment of ceremonial life was grinding their commitment down. 'Fine blowing' was prescribed for ceremonial feasts, called 'receiving guests'. Ma Siwang in Yangjiagou: 'The fine blowing style gradually stopped being used [he claimed even by the 1940s], because life was getting increasingly difficult, and for feasts people no longer prepared the 'eight dishes and eight plates' (*badie bawan*), just very simple food, so there was no need for fine blowing any more.'

Meanwhile the drum shop system, too, was dying out. We saw how drum shops were still active in Suide town in the early 1950s, and the term was still in use in

---

[6]   Cf. Hebei 'gone to the dogs', Jones 1999: 45.

[7]   Gao Wanfei 1999: 10.

Sishilipu township in the late 50s, but as the commune system hardened, privately-run enterprises were doomed; besides, it was hard to earn a living from rituals when people were so poor and constrained, and society was mobilizing people to till the fields, make steel, or work in factories. Chang Wenjin, then still based in Changshiban: 'Because they wanted to put collectivization into effect, you weren't allowed to run drum shops any more. They were abolished from 1960.' Liu Deyi: 'By 1964–65 there were no more drum shops.' This didn't mean that there were no more *chuishou*, rather that no fixer ran a visible shop in a town where they assembled any more. If you needed *chuishou*, you could still go to the band boss's house.

Chuishou have their own language, variously called 'trade talk' or 'black talk', or in more pan-Chinese language 'family talk', or 'outlaw talk'.[8] A common explanation for this secret language was that they often performed for ceremonial, and didn't want to 'offend people' (*dezui ren*). Zhang Hulin says they only use it now 'for some inconvenient situations'. Ironically, that very afternoon Tian Yaonong observed that he and I were doing the same thing when we used English to secretly discuss how to bargain down a cab driver – our own 'black talk'.

This once rich language is now much reduced. It was widely used by *chuishou* until the 1960s, and is still known to many senior players. Today the apprentices of senior *chuishou* often know phrases, but use it rather little – young Zhang Hulin recalls that his master knew the whole lot, and though he too knows many phrases, his band doesn't use them much. Other denizens of the underclasses spoke trade language too. That of opera performers seems to have been similar; barbers also had their own talk, but I don't know if it overlapped. Chang Wenjin: 'The *Gelaohui* [secret brotherhood] also used black talk, but it wasn't the same as ours.' In Yangjiagou, Older Brother didn't really know the language: 'None of us use trade talk in Yangjiagou, we didn't learn it, though I've heard some *chuishou* using it. The elders said, if you're going to learn trade talk you have to learn it properly, you can't just use it casually.' I surmise that largely village-bound *chuishou*, working mostly among neighbours, had less need for a private language than mercenary *chuishou* often performing among strangers. And perhaps the language has declined as the social stigma of being a *chuishou* has waned.

Vocabulary we elicited refers mainly to situations in daily life such as money and eating. Of course, their own terms for their instruments (§8.4 below) are a kind of trade talk. For haggling over money, there is also a more widely-known silent manual language conducted under the cover of someone's jacket, that we observed at the White Cloud Mountain temple fair.

---

[8]   In *pinyin*, *hanghua*, *heihua*, *jiahuhua*, *jianghuhua*. See Tian 2005: 177–80. For the secret language of *chuishou* elsewhere in north China, see e.g. Jones 2007: 43; Li Runzhong 1986: 103; Liu Yong 2006: 129; and note Wu Fan 2007: 119–25. For Fujian, see Ruizendaal 2006: 46–7.

7.6 The Cultural Revolution

While musicians recall a certain continuity until the mid-1960s, evidently for some periods their music was vastly impoverished. If worse was now to come, the Cultural Revolution was not a period of complete silence for traditional music (cf. Jones 2004, for Hebei, and Jones 2007, for Shanxi). Anyway, by 1966 the ceremonial life of Shaanbei had been more or less circumscribed for over 20 years.

Wang Shifa, who as we saw had been learning from around 1960, started leading jobs on shawm when 18, exactly as the Cultural Revolution broke out. His main activity on the shawm for many years now was to be accompanying *yangge* song-and-dance for secular parades – one component of the traditional repertory which consisted of short vocal-related pieces, not exactly political but quite distinct from the traditional long suites.

Cao Laiqian, in the same township: 'During the Smash the Four Olds campaign [prelude to the Cultural Revolution from 1964] *chuishou* weren't allowed to do business – *chuishou* don't practise superstition, but they reckoned it was the old customs of "extravagance and waste". We were still allowed to play for *yangge*, though.' Villagers in Baijiayan recalled that through the Cultural Revolution they didn't dare put on traditional ceremonies: 'extravagance and waste is the greatest crime', as they had learnt to parrot from Mao's *Sayings*. Village *chuishou* He Zengtong pointed out that even if families dared invite *chuishou* to play, they had no money, so they couldn't afford to put on a proper ceremony.

Li Qishan: 'Our business was interrupted for over ten years during Socialist Education and the Cultural Revolution. In 1966 a cadre called Meng from the political committee of the Armed Forces Department (*Wuzhuangbu*) confiscated our instruments, and my dad said, "I'm fed up with this, I'm not doing it any more".' Only *yangge*, organized by the local authorities, was immune. Chang Wenzhou: 'During the Cultural Revolution shawm music was only used for *yangge* for the production-teams. We played for the odd funeral too, on the quiet and perfunctorily, as best we could, but it was so much more simplified. After Chairman Mao died no-one controlled it any more, and things got a bit better.'

When Wang Shifa married in 1974 they still weren't allowed to invite *chuishou* to play. Yet he stressed that in his area the traditional *laosangu* suite sequence wasn't interrupted even in the Cultural Revolution – 'You still had to use *laosangu* for weddings and funerals.' Cao Laiqian went on, 'There were people learning to be *chuishou* during the Cultural Revolution too, just not so many as now.' Feng Xiaoping, then a young boy in a nearby Suide village: '*Chuishou* played in the Cultural Revolution too, playing the old pieces as long as no-one came on an inspection tour, playing Mao songs when they came.' Zhao Suotong: 'During the Cultural Revolution you could play the shawm at New Year, but couldn't earn money from it. Still, I did business for people in secret, taking my shawm along in a hemp bag.'

In Yangjiagou, an elderly villager hated the Four Cleanups, but said it had no effect on the village's cultural life. Geomancers still practised their arcane arts discreetly for funerals even during the Cultural Revolution; they could perform on the quiet, even their incantations barely audible. But the whole point of shawm music was to attract people, to draw attention to a (now irredeemably 'feudal and superstitious') ceremony. Still, 'the mountains are high, the emperor is far away' – mountain villages are distant from the attentions of prying county cadres. Ma Qiantang recalled certain periods as being more severe: '1967–68 and 1973–75 were the worst.' It wasn't that the Communist Party didn't seek to control them – 'There was nothing they couldn't control (*meiyou guanbuliao*)', as one *chuishou* remarked caustically – it was just that they didn't always succeed. 'We did a bit on the quiet, it was just that if we were discovered, then they confiscated our instruments.' Older Brother: 'Yeah, our shawms were confiscated once, but they gave them back later.'

So he still played occasionally through most of the Cultural Revolution. 'Although we weren't allowed to play for weddings and funerals, we were still needed for *yangge* at New Year. Sometimes for a mass meeting, or if some new speech of Mao had been published, we would play for the celebration. *Yangge* is all in [the fast metre] *liushuiban*, you hardly play any *manban* [slow metre] pieces.'

But the New Year's *yangge* ceremonies still followed the old format: 'Our *chuishou* band still went round the houses to pay greetings with the *yangge* team, the hosts gave us liquor, cigarettes, or a few coins.' And when pressed, Older Brother pointed out that the old suites weren't entirely dormant: 'In the Cultural Revolution we still played the old standards, like *Da Kaimen* and *Xifeng zan*. In those days if you played the shawm, then those were the standards – if you didn't play them then what else was there to play?' While *chuishou* were clear that they were only free to take up the fuller traditional repertory again properly around 1979, no-one spoke of any problems in recalling it.

Chapter 8

The early reform era

Even before the official ending of the Cultural Revolution in 1976, an enterprising local cultural cadre began documenting shawm players' traditional repertory. Overt ceremonial activity only began again in about 1979. Society was still locked in poverty; it was to be several years before many villages acquired even a sporadic supply of electricity.

8.1 The commune system is dismantled

First step to the economic and cultural liberalizations throughout China was the dismantling of the commune system. Chang Wenjin told us his exceptional story. As most *chuishou* lack even a basic formal education, they rarely serve in positions of power in the village or town, being virtual outcasts, and unlikely to get involved in political activism. But Chang Wenjin now became a village cadre.

'The natural conditions in our village of Changshiban are very poor. Our production-team had a real tough time. I became team chief in 1977, and secretly divided the land up among the households. The authorities found out, and made me enter a study-team. But in less than half a year the whole country began implementing the responsibility system – I'd just done it a year too early! Later the provincial Party Secretary came to pay me a courtesy visit at my home!' Whereas some ritual musicians in other parts of China (Hebei amateur ritual specialists, and lay Daoists) preserved their village's ritual practices while becoming local cadres and applying their literacy to the revolution, this seems to be a rare instance of a *chuishou* becoming a cadre.

As to musical activity, in Yangjiagou a revival was still not possible during the Hua Guofeng interregnum from 1977; they still played mainly for New Year *yangge* and other official collective activities. Older Brother considers that he only took up the shawm again seriously when they began observing weddings and funerals properly again in 1979. The revival along with the reforms was as much to do with the greater availability of resources as with ideological constraints, as Older Brother pointed out with typical bluntness: 'If you had money you could spend it, if you didn't you couldn't!'

According to Zhihui, the authorities used to do propaganda about customary activities in the villages – they didn't exactly interfere in weddings and funerals, they just railed against extravagance and waste, and against feudal superstition. Since the reforms, as he observed, the authorities actually support temple fairs, like the major one at the Black Dragon temple. 'Superstitious thinking has deep roots in the villages, it's hard to eradicate it all in one fell swoop.' Campaigns against extravagance and superstition go back at least to the late imperial period, but even the more far-reaching campaigns of the last half-century haven't been enough.

The revival is said to have stimulated a significant increase in *chuishou*. In Zichang county, one source states that their numbers grew from 100 to 800.[1] Older Brother: 'Before Liberation there were no *chuishou* in Zizhou town, it developed after [the end of] collectivization – now there are a lot of *chuishou* there. No-one wants to learn in our village, though.'

8.2 Local research

Research on folk music had commenced even before the end of the Cultural Revolution. There was plenty of study (much of it albeit politically-motivated) of folk music in Shaanbei from the late 1930s, mainly on folk-song, *yangge*, and opera. Above we noted a certain limited interest in the music of the *chuishou* from Communist cultural cadres, but the only publications of which I am aware before the 1980s were a book of transcriptions of the repertory of Feng Guanglin, and 43 pieces transcribed by Xi'an scholars from a *chuishou* band in Yulin city in 1957, both mimeographed 'for internal use only' in the distant provincial capital Xi'an.

As we saw in §1.5 and §5.3 above, local cultural cadre Huo Xianggui began collecting folk music throughout the Yulin region in 1974, several years before most Chinese researchers were able to resume work,[2] co-authoring the *Anthology* section on Shaanbei bards, of whom he also collected a rich treasury of recordings. Huo began to visit senior *chuishou* and notate their repertory; his volume of transcriptions, with a cultural cadre in Suide called Ai Pu, was mimeographed locally in 1979. In those early days, testing the limits of freedom, the atmosphere was still tense, and fieldwork had to take place clandestinely. On 2nd October 1974 Huo tried to record shawm players in Suide town (Huo 1997a). With cadres from the Hall of Culture, he had to ask the county Armed Forces Department (*Wuzhuangbu*) to intervene to summon *chuishou* to play. They began playing in the courtyard of the Hall of Culture, but so many people came to look that recording became impossible. They moved to a smaller courtyard, but people still climbed onto the roofs. Eventually they were persuaded to be silent, and recording went more smoothly. Of over a hundred *chuishou* whom Huo and Ai visited in the counties of the Yulin region, they list as most accomplished (ages in about 1978): from Suide, Li Daniu (68), Hao Yongfa (63, blind), Liu Zide (68); from Mizhi, Zhao Jinrang (76), Du Chengzhang (70), Chang Wenzhou (42); from Wubu, Li Zhenchun, Wang Xinxi (both *c*50); from Jingbian, Jin Wenhua (over 70), Zhang Wancheng (70); from Jiaxian, Kang Mingde (76), Kang Runwu (over 50); from Yulin, Zhu Xinmin (70) (see p.198 n.2).

---

[1]   Zhang Jianzhong 2000: 237.

[2]   Huo and Ai 1979: 1–4.

▲ 陕北部分唢呐艺人集体照

Illustration 10   Assembled shawm players from Mizhi county, 1981. In this rare early photo, probably taken at a Yulin festival, the two women on the left are local cultural cadres; then front row, from left Chang Yinshan, Chang Wenzhou, Chang Wenjin, Chang Wenyi (still living in Changshiban in 2001), Li Bingcheng (from Houjiagou, Yangjiagou district), Li Jinfu (Li Qishan's father, from Lijiagou), Li Junying (Lijiagou), the singer Ma Yukuan (Yangjiagou district), and a cadre. Back row, from left: two cadres, Li Qishan (Lijiagou), Zhao Yingyao (Luozhen), Li Zishan, Li Runshan (both from Lijiagou), Feng Baolai (Yangjiagou district), Li Qianshan (Lijiagou), and the cadre Ma Xianzhong. These are only some of the *chuishou* from Mizhi county; the festival assembled players from all over the Yulin region.

In 1979 Huo wrote a script for Shaanxi provincial radio and they broadcast a 70-minute programme with his recordings of *chuishou* music. Huo later became a 'second-level composer', and by at least 1991 was deputy troupe leader of the official Yulin Folk Arts Troupe (§12.3 below). After retiring, Huo had been living in Beijing, and I met him briefly in Yulin in 2001 while he was packing to move to Xi'an, whither he had already sent all his precious tapes. He was hoping to get his recordings of unaccompanied folk-songs issued commercially. Given that there are precisely no such recordings released in mainland China, and that the market is flooded with CDs of kitsch bel-canto Shaanbei folk-song with cheesey accompaniment, his project was going against the tide, and remained unfulfilled.

This problem is multiplied nationally, with precious local recordings from all over China languishing inaccessibly in offices in regional capitals and Beijing. Huo's 1970s' notebooks should also be valuable, since several *chuishou* he was visiting were in their 70s. By 2001 it was quite rare to find elderly *chuishou* – apart from Ma Siwang (85), who had given up in the 1950s, He Zengtong and Zhao Suotong (77 and 72) were the most senior we found.

8.3 Chang Wenzhou eats off the state

Chang Wenzhou's early career was introduced above. His rise to success causes him pride, and leaves no place for modesty. But the more we talk to him, the less clear I am on the sequence of events in his life, so the following account is even more provisional than I would wish. In about 1973, aged 38, he won first prize in a regional festival.[3] From 1974 Huo Xianggui notated 104 of his pieces. A few years later, after a festival for which all the 12 counties of the Yulin region chose their best players, 'I was the only one who was kept on, I played best of all in the whole region! Then they organized a Yulin region *suona* study group (*xuexiban*), and summoned us to rehearse [new] pieces like "Happily greeting the spring" (*Xi ying chun*).' The latter was apparently arranged, and named, by Huo.

Such short secular pieces, of course, were already at some remove from the traditional repertory, as was the concept of 'rehearsing' (*pailian*). But the pieces were still played as a suite (*tao*) – as Chang observed, you could only bring out the 'flavour' of traditional pieces in the context of a suite. Even this is an important recognition, since *suona* music in the conservatories tends to consist of short individual pieces. The new repertory and style accompanied a new secular context: 'We took part in a conference and performed (*yanchu*) for ministers in the north building of the county hostel.' Still, such occasions were rare. 'That time they spotted me, and the chief of the Regional Arts-Work Troupe took me on, so I entered public life with a regular salary. My family still lived in the village then. I spent six or seven years in the troupe, earning 38 *kuai* a month.'

We saw above that state troupes might manifest a 'contradiction' between folk musicians and more educated modernizers – a theme deserving more research. Chang was one of several village recruits considered 'thick' (*erbaiwu*, '250')[4] by more literate urbanites in the troupe. While Chang was in the troupe, Huo Xianggui tried to teach him the modern system of cipher notation (*jianpu*) – with limited success. Li Shibin, another colleague in the troupe, later a fine fieldworker based in Xi'an, recalled that Chang was too independent to be able to learn new compositions. Chang didn't see the big deal about the new stuff, and claimed he could compose several hundred pieces in a day; when he produced some, they

---

[3]   Mizhi 1993: 539, though he told me it was when he was 35 or 36, which would be 1970–71.

[4]   Jones 2004: 55.

were all simple and repetitious pieces based on the traditional *guogu* ostinato interludes, unusable in the troupe.

This was a murky period: traditional arts were still not officially permitted, and such repertory as Chang Wenzhou performed for the troupe must have been stultifying for him. In 1984 he gained another first prize at a Yulin region *suona* contest, his cousin Chang Wenjin second prize. But the salary in the troupe was paltry. 'I got fed up, the pay was too little, I had a family of six, we couldn't get by.' That year, after breaking his leg in a road accident, Chang Wenzhou got himself sent back with his family to Mizhi county-town to be a teacher in the Second Junior Comprehensive there. 'I did that for four or five years – well actually, it was just a name, I didn't do any teaching at all, I was always going out to perform, going off to the provincial capital.' Huo Xianggui recalls taking Chang Wenzhou to Xi'an for official festivals twice, once in 1979, and that Chang felt uncomfortable with the context. He had been used to making a living independently even during the spartan 1950s and 60s, and was also making and selling shawms. His family still had land in his home village of Changshiban.

From the 1930s to the 1960s, the Zhao and Du families had been the most renowned *chuishou* in Mizhi town. By the 1980s, although Zhao Jinrang played till his last year in 1981, and his son Zhao Suotong was still active for a few more years, the Zhao and Du families were in decline, and Chang Wenzhou became the most renowned *chuishou* in the town. He was now to become a crucial influence on *chuishou* throughout the area, and his experience in the Yulin Arts-Work Troupe was a factor in his ideology. He is a bridge between tradition and modernity. But it was his instruments as much as his playing which confirmed his reputation (Illustration 11).

8.4 Instruments

The common traditional band has five musicians: two large shawms, drum, small cymbals, and gong, with one of them doubling on *hao* natural trumpet for liminal ritual moments. *Chuishou* call their instruments by local names:

Shaanbei term	meaning	instrument	official name
wazi	kid	large shawm	*da suona*
qiao pizi	beat skin	barrel drum	*gu*
tong (tonggu)	(onomatopoeic)	knobbed gong	*luo*
shandian	flash of lightning	small cymbals	*xiao cha*
shengtong	rising tube	natural trumpet	*hao*

Chang Wenzhou: 'For the shawm, people use cypress, or for good ones, sandalwood – the heavier the better.' Gao Wanfei: 'Li Daniu used to make shawms from the wood from old coffins. Because they have been oiled by human greases, they had an ideal mix of hardness and flexibility. Later, because they couldn't find

Illustration 11   Chang Wenzhou with some of his shawms, 1999

enough old coffins, they left red pine to soak in an oil barrel in an oil depot for three months, which became the best material.'

Until the 1980s, throughout the area, shawms were generally smaller than today, with a smaller bell, but there was no standard pitch. Pieces transcribed in the 1980s for the *Anthology* show considerable variety: b♭, b, c¹, c♯¹, d¹, f¹, even g♯¹. Shawms were not made by special makers, players just made the wooden bodies themselves by imitation; they had to ask smiths to make the metal bells (*wanwan*) and 'throats' (*houzi*) for them, then filing them down themselves.

The old shawm looked like a chicken leg (*jitui*), so it was known as chicken-leg *suona*. It was quite short, with a smaller, narrower bell and a thicker throat. Makers had experimented in modifying the early chicken-leg shawm before Chang

Wenzhou; Li Daniu is said to have 'invented' a larger bell (and perhaps body) for the shawm, perhaps even as early as 1928.[5]

Around Mizhi county, shawm pitch commonly ranged from d[1] to f[1], but a common length was 1.15 *chi*, with a lowest note of d[1]. A late-1980s cassette of Gao Haijun's band from Wubu county (see below) is in D. In Yangjiagou, Ma Siwang recalled: 'In those days we played small *suonas* of 1.05 or 1.1 *chi*. These large shawms of 1.2 and then 1.3 *chi*, with a big sound, were invented by Chang Wenzhou. In the old days it was very hard to make a long body.' Still, further west in Shaanbei the shawm was often longer, hence lower in pitch: in Hengshan it was 1.2 *chi*, in Jingbian and Dingbian 1.3 *chi*.

The chicken-leg shawm was still used in some areas for many years to come. In Suide, Liu Deyi: 'When I was learning [around 1948–50] there were two types of shawm, large and chicken-leg. I guess the chicken-leg shawm died out around 1958. Its body was 1.05 *chi*, with a wide neck and a small bell.' Cao Laiqian: 'I played the chicken-leg shawm until I was 30 (c1974). It's not easy to play, it isn't right – I haven't seen it for ages.' We saw *chuishou* from Shanxi using them at the White Cloud Mountain temple fair in 2001.

In Changshiban, many of the senior Chang *chuishou* (including Chang Mao and Chang Wenzhou's father Jiazhong) made the wooden bodies, but not the metal bells or throats. Now some young *chuishou* in Changshiban began experimenting. Chang Wenjin: 'Me and Chang Wenzhou began making shawms at the same time. I started making them when I was 14 (c1951) and began doing metalwork when I was 20 – gongs, cymbals, *hao* trumpets and stuff. We learnt to make the whole lot – we just made them by copying the old ones. We felt that longer bodies had a more robust (*zhuang*) sound. In 1958 I began making large shawms of 1.25 and 1.28 *chi*.' Note that 'robust' was also a desired quality for *sanxian* tuning (§4.6). Chang Wenzhou: 'The old generation used shawms in D; the change to C came when I was around 20 [c1955].' He gave precise measurements as 1.28 *chi* for C, 1.13 for D. So although he doesn't rate the shawms he made when he was young, they were already making large instruments in C by the late 1950s. However, they were based in remote Changshiban, and though the Changs went on jobs over quite a wide area, transport and information were still slow, so diversity persisted.

The standardization of the large shawm had to wait until after Chang Wenzhou's period in the Yulin Arts-Work Troupe and the reforms of the 1980s. Again, scholar Huo Xianggui told me he helped Chang Wenzhou standardize the large shawm in C. Li Qishan: 'In the early days we all used shawms of 1.1 *chi*. For the 1981 *suona* festival at Yulin (Illustration 10 above), when there were players from all 12 counties of Yulin region, me and Li Zishan were the two youngest *chuishou* playing. Chang Wenyi, a cousin of Chang Wenzhou, was using a large shawm of 1.3 *chi*. After I'd heard that shawm, with such a big sonorous sound, I made a special trip by bike to find Chang Wenyi, and bought a pair from him. That 1981 festival was the first time we'd seen shawms that big.'

---

[5] Gao 2000: 2; Tian 2005: 197–8.

When Zhang Hulin learnt in the 1980s near Suide, they were using shawms in F, but as the revival gained pace, and as *chuishou* needed to replace their old instruments, they realized the fashion for the larger shawm in C. In Yangjiagou, Yunwenr recalled: 'I reckon people gradually began using 1.3 *chi* shawms in about 1982 – there weren't many large shawms around before that.' Still, in poorer villages like Yangjiagou they continued to use the smaller shawms handed down in the family. The shawms my Yangjiagou friends used for our 1999 recording session were the smaller ones in D from the time of Chang Bingyou, dating from the 1930s. The bells came from elsewhere, the bodies they made themselves; they have a beautiful tone, and the worn finger-holes feel comfortable. But for a funeral earlier in the week they used newer shawms in C provided by Chouxiao.

By the way, as Wang Shifa observed, the holes on the large 1.3 *chi* shawm are a long way apart, so you can't get your fingers round it till you're 13 or 14. So on the smaller shawms before the 1980s they could begin learning a couple of years earlier.

I find this a rather unusual change. Pitch has tended to rise in Western art music, and has done so in modern times in Shanghai (from C to D); in most Chinese villages evidence suggests that it has stayed the same for many centuries. In Shaanbei it has recently been standardized at a rather low pitch, I would think in conflict with a general move towards brighter sounds emanating from the official ethos. At the same time, it inadvertently left space for the addition of those brighter sounds some years later.

Chang Wenzhou has not rested. 'The shawms I make now are perfect! I grope and I calculate, that's my invention and creativity.' He spent five years inventing a low D shawm of 1.6 *chi*, finally perfecting it in the 3rd moon of 1999, 'unique in all China'. 'Now I'm inventing a 1.8 *chi* shawm too, with a lowest note of C an octave below the 1.3 *chi* one. It needs keys, as the body's too long.' He is also sensitive to intonation, possibly adapting subconsciously to his time in the troupe. 'On Chang Mao's shawms the fourth hole was out of tune.' He uses his middle finger as a standard for the internal diameter, and then his ears, and now sometimes a pitch machine – mainly his ears, since he only got the machine quite recently.

There are other makers – we also heard of one in Jiaxian, one in Yangjiagou district in a village near Hecha, and one in Shanxi across the Yellow River – but Chang Wenzhou's shawms are universally recognized in Shaanbei as the best. Shawms are sold by the pair, players seeking compatible timbre between the two. Li Qishan in 2001: 'People from outside buy Chang Wenzhou's shawms for 200 or 300 *yuan* a pair, but we buy them for 150 *yuan*. Often after we take them away and play them for a while, we take them back and exchange them, only hanging onto them once we've made sure they're OK.' Yuanr: 'Sometimes we don't pay cash up front; like, he gets asked to do a funeral, and asks us to go instead of him, so we don't ask him for the fee, we exchange shawms for the money.'

Soft reeds (called *mianshao* or *budaishao*) have become more popular now. Li Qishan recalls that as soon as he bought his first pair of large shawms in 1982, he realized the reeds need changing. 'In those days the reeds for the large shawm weren't supple, so I improved them.' The best reed is found in Zizhou county, in Shuangmiaowan and Shanhuangbu. 'There is a lot of reed there, but only one area where it's specially good – unless you know it, even if you know there is good reed somewhere round there, you can't find it.' Here a good reed can last as long as five years (see Wang Laiwa's sad story in §10.8 below) – in north Shanxi, shawm players are lucky if a reed lasts a year. Chang Wenzhou gave me eight new reeds and one wonderful old one, all soon enthusiastically slobbered over by my *chuishou* friends in Yangjiagou. In 2001 *chuishou* bought nine reeds for 26 *kuai*. Reeds are kept in a specially-made small wooden casket – one of few attractive traditional pieces of craft still to be found in the area, available in 2001 for around 3 *kuai* in the two main music shops on Second street in Yulin city. Some players use an old plastic medicine container, but this does not store the reeds so well.

The traditional hand-made drum is disconcertingly like a Western toy drum, with straight sides. The Yangjiagou *chuishou* have a drum that they made in the late 1970s, whose skin (made from ox- or donkey-hide) gives a sadly dead sound. More successful urban bands now use a standard factory-made drum, more resonant. Makers like Chang Wenzhou and Chang Wenjin now only get occasional orders for *hao* trumpets. Though traditionally the *hao* should be sounded in pairs, since the 1980s most bands only use one; now many bands replace it altogether with the Western trumpet recently fashionable for pop music in the big band format. Thus many village bands will decide not to replace their old *hao*.

8.5 Music

This is a suitable place for a brief discussion of aspects of the traditional style that survived throughout Shaanbei villages and towns into the 21st century, merely hinting at its complexities.

The learning process

The basic and common reason for 'learning *chuishou*' (before Communism, under Maoism, and since the reforms) is because a family is helplessly poor: learning *chuishou* offers a way of surviving. Even under Maoism it offered a way of scraping a bit more income; and now, with money a major incentive, *chuishou* are catering to a busy market. Kids know they can escape from poverty thus – especially if they can take a leading role or become boss of a big band incorporating pop music.

Family members begin playing gong as early as 5 years old. Senior *chuishou* may also cultivate teenage apprentices, taking them on jobs with them and claiming their fee for the three-year training period. Starting on gong, then cymbals, apprentices learn the melodic material by long exposure, gradually absorbing the melodies and the patterns for the sequence of metres. Percussionists, less well paid and less familiar with the music, may not be very good, especially the gong player; but prospective drummers have to work out the 8/4 *manban* pattern on the drum, and where not to leave the main beat empty.

By their early teens, students are ready to take up the shawm, beginning with the lower shawm part. Wang Shifa: 'My apprentices have to play the lower part for three years, they can only play the upper part after that – they graduate (*chushi*) after five years.' From 11 to 14, Feng Xiaoping only played the lower part – he would have got a beating if he'd dared to play the upper octave within earshot of his master. Learning the shawm too seems to take place mainly by observation. *Chuishou* mentioned practising on their own, but I have not yet heard them, nor have I elicited any technical tuition. Still, teachers must say something. Liu Deyi: 'When I learnt there were no scores. First I learnt the percussion, then once I was familiar with the standards (*paizi*), my master played the upper part, I played the lower part, and I gradually learnt circular breathing and fingerings. All those techniques were taught by the master, like he'd say, "When you change breath, don't use it all up before you inhale – inhale when you've still got half a mouthful left".' Also basic to the style is the language of pitch glides and guttural sounds. But the main way of learning is by going out on jobs with the band.

Nor have I heard of masters teaching fingerings to students: mostly it seems to be done by observation and experimentation. Some are obvious; different shawms require different fingerings, and players have their own devices, particularly for the pivotal notes from c^1 to f^1. Most *chuishou* play with their left hand on top. Incidentally, sometimes players like to reverse hands to show off, or put both hands on the same side, playing with one hand backwards; but there is no 'fooling around' like the dismantling and reassembly of the shawm as in north Shanxi (Jones 2007: 84, 113).

The heterophony of the two shawms, the division of roles between upper (*shangshou*) and lower (*hashou*, Shaanbei rendition of the standard *xiashou*) parts, is a beautiful stylistic feature. The *hashou* sustains more, hence the common synonym *latongtong*, 'dragging out the lowest note', always using the lower hand to reach down towards the lowest note (*tongtong*). The upper player 'blows his own way' (*chui zidao*),[6] soaring off into the upper range, and taking more breaths. Within the basic octave division, the upper player sometimes returns to the low register at cadential points. The slower *duoban* section, where the drum drops out, is often less heterophonic, closer to unison.[7]

Though the upper player is paid more than the lower player, several musicians pointed out that it is easier to play the upper part. Zhao Suotong: 'The lower player can't just play inflexibly (*si*, 'dead'), if you play wrong you can't get the flow.' He added, 'If two players are about the same standard then they take it in turns to play upper and lower parts.' The lower player is often an apprentice of the upper:

---

[6]   Cf. early jazz: Ansermet attributed this very phrase to Sidney Bechet (Ward and Burns 2000: 73). Cf. 'walking shrill' (*zoujian*) in north Shanxi: Jones 2004a, Jones 2007: 95.

[7]   Chinese transcriptions of such music throughout China are mostly of one single composite line. For rare transcriptions of both parts in Shaanbei, see Huo and Ai 1979: 233–45; Gao 2000: 43–60; cf. Tian 2005: 227–32. Cf. my analysis of Shanxi shawm pieces, Jones forthcoming.

if the master is not satisfied with his apprentice during a piece, he glares at him. When the lower player wants to play the upper part and take a higher cut of the fee, he goes off and forms his own band. But like violinists in Western art music, some players prefer to play one or the other part, while others play both happily. In Yangjiagou now they all take turns, though Chouxiao sounds best on top.

Suite form and metre

On procession, or while standing, short pieces punctuating the ceremony are most common, but some longer sequences are also played, as we see in §11.1 below. While seated or squatting at the ritual site, the *chuishou* perform long suites in a prescribed sequence. The basic suite form is known as 'crossing the three drums' (*guo sangu*) or 'old three drums' (*laosangu*) – 'drum' here implying metres. The melodies from which they choose are more or less fixed, but between them they play repetitious but flexible modular *guogu* interludes. Players refer to a firm metre as *Taihangshan*, the tortuous and imposing mountain chain running through nearby Shanxi; this is most important in pieces with many syncops, such as *Xifeng zan* (see below).

The two shawm players warm up informally and briefly with a free-tempo *liangdiao* ('airing the scale', as in opera), which now sounds like just tuning up, rather than the often lengthy slow free-tempo sections which are a glorious feature of many instrumental suites in China. But Feng Xiaoping pointed out, 'You can tell a good band at once from their *liangdiao*.'

The suite proper (⊙**B3**) begins with a long slow piece, repeated several times, in 8/4 *manban* metre, with four cymbal clashes and one gong stroke per measure. A *guogu* formulaic interlude then leads into a short piece, repeated many times, in fast 2/4 *liushui* metre. Another, different, *guogu* interlude slows the tempo down, leading into a short piece, also repeated many times, in the slower 2/4 *duoban* metre, the drum dropping out. When the tempo picks up again with the entry of the drum, the suite concludes with long fast improvised sections in hectic *erliushui* (*jiaban*) metre, some with titles like *Yazhiyou* and *Hongqiqi*, and the final *Shachangwei*.

For the melodies within the three metrical components of this framework, the leading shawm player may choose any *manban* piece, any *liushui* piece, and any *duoban* piece. The long *manban* pieces and the shorter *liushui* and *duoban* pieces may all be repeated many times, both at the ritual site and on procession. Sometimes more than one *liushui* and *duoban* piece are played. No matter how many repeats they play, *liushui* and *duoban* sections are quite short; a considerable part of the overall time-scale of a suite is occupied by the *guogu* interludes and the fast final improvised sections, in which the shawm players play short ostinato-like patterns revolving around individual notes, often a 4th or a 5th apart.[8]

---

[8] Cf. the Shandong 'tassels', Jones 1998: 146–8; also Jones 2007: 97, Jones forthcoming.

Though this outline, as in many other genres in China and the world, may be considered as a gradual accelerando, it varies from the supposedly typical Chinese mould. There is no obvious free-tempo introductory section; after the opening slow piece the suite then accelerates at once to fast, not medium, tempo; it then slows up for the mid-tempo *duoban*, without drum, followed by a rapid accelerando.

Repertory and scales

In the late 1970s Huo and Ai made a rather thorough list of the Shaanbei shawm repertory under the following categories, showing titles of melodies and variants transcribed from many different *chuishou*:

style	titles	variants
'traditional melodies'	70	216
opera melodies	20	40
yangge and 'lesser melodies'	42	68
other	13	23
totals	**145**	**347**

Unlike the 'traditional melodies', the *yangge* and little melodies are often four-square, based on folk-songs and anticipating TV and film tunes. Of course, this is an aggregate of pieces throughout the region: even an experienced *chuishou* has a smaller repertory in practice.

Li Qishan: 'I used to take apprentices – if I didn't want to teach them, I didn't teach them good pieces. Artists are small-minded, afraid their stuff will be taken off. But if I wanted to teach someone, I wouldn't hold anything back, I'd teach them all the good standards.' Pupils learn short pieces first; Gao Jiu cites *Shang tiantai* as an easy-learning piece, while Zhang Hulin favours melodies like *Shang nanpo* (the *duoban* piece in ⊙**B3**, as well as for burning the paper house in ⊙**B5**), *Bulala*, and *Dieduanqiao*.

Some *chuishou* know vaguely of a core of 'eight great labelled pieces' (*bada paiqu*), perhaps pieces that can be played in different metres and scales, a criterion said to indicate hereditary transmission. But there was no agreement on the list. Some pieces are often played for a particular context, such as *Dabaidui*,[9] used for the return after fetching the bride, or *Baichang*, used for the entombment. But the repertory is not heavily contextual. Some pieces are played only in *manban* metre (notably *Da Kaimen*, by far the most common opening *manban* piece); some mainly in *liushui* or *duoban*; and some, like *Xifeng zan*, are common in both *manban* and *duoban*. But the traditional repertory has continued to dwindle.

---

[9]   Apart from Huo and Ai 1979: 79–85 and Gao 2000: 63–70, Chang Wenzhou's version of *Dabaidui* for *yangge* is transcribed in JCD 66–70.

Similarly, you can play any piece in any of the three main scales, 'as long as you can', but in practice some pieces are more common in some scales than others; for instance, popular *manban* pieces in the plaintive scale of *jiadiao* include *Xifeng zan* and *Huadaozi*. Scales are called *diaokou* (cf. *diaomen* in other areas of north China). Formerly the sequence of scales throughout a ceremony was a major device for variation, now much reduced. The three main scales are *bendiao* (tonic C), *fandiao* (F) and *jiadiao* (B♭). As elsewhere in China, senior *chuishou* still know of a theoretical cycle of seven scales, though they appear never to have been used equally, and now the other four appear to be obsolete.[10] *Bendiao* is used for the opening of rituals (*qishi*, 'starting the ritual'), and in the morning. *Fandiao*, traditionally played in the afternoon, is good for playing Shaanbei folk-songs, as the lowest note on the shawm becomes a *so*, cadential note of most Shaanbei songs; it is now the main scale used for pop pieces. The plaintive *jiadiao* (equivalent to *meihuadiao* in north Shanxi, and *jiazhidiao* in Beijing and Hebei) is prescribed for the evening of a funeral, but is now losing out to *fandiao*, although it clings on in villages like Yangjiagou where they don't play pop music much (⊙**B4**).

I mentioned the frequently-used melody *Xifeng zan*, with its many syncopations over its 23 measures. The DVD features several versions: in *bendiao* scale (rendered ambiguous by its frequent featuring of *ti* in a temporary *so* scale), versions in *manban* (⊙**B2**, to Invite the Soul, and ⊙**B5**, for Road Offerings) and *duoban* (the exhilaratingly zany version of Chang Wenzhou's band over the closing credits); and the *manban* version in *jiadiao* scale (⊙**B4**, after the return to the soul tent).

While we are listening to *Xifeng zan*, a brief note on the titles of melodies, merely to illustrate the complexity of the subject. The ancient titles of *qupai* ('labelled melodies') of Chinese folk instrumental ensembles rarely carry programmatic significance, serving mainly for identification, rather like jazz standards. In the Shaanbei shawm repertory, apart from titles obviously derived from folk-song or opera, titles have much in common with those of instrumental ensembles throughout China, particularly northern wind bands. Though pieces with the same title in different regions are not necessarily related, the overlapping of titles between regional repertories should constitute one clue in assessing regional styles. We do now have a substantial volume of transcriptions in the *Anthology*, if they are reliable, but trying to compare regional variants would be a Herculean task, certainly with little access to recordings.[11]

And so to *Xifeng zan*: the title is quite rare among shawm bands, and not exactly a classic 'labelled melody'. It appears to mean 'Hymn to the West Wind', though this is evidently a corruption of 'Hymn to the Western Quarter' (*Xifang zan*), a title used, for instance, in Wutaishan in Shanxi further east. Instrumental versions of hymns are more commonly played by Buddhist and Daoist ritual

---

[10]   For a basic introduction to scales in Chinese instrumental music, see Jones 1998: 111–19; cf. Jones 2007: 91–4.

[11]   For the 'labelled melody' system in Chinese instrumental music, see Jones 1998, ch.8. For instances, cf. Jones 2004: 257–8, Jones 2007: 102–13.

specialists, though here any relation to instrumental or vocal versions played by such specialists remains to be explored.[12]

Language and aesthetics

Criteria for a good band are not easily elicited. As with the bards' tuning of the *sanxian*, we found the concept of *zhuang*, 'macho', to tally with the sound ideal of the *chuishou*, although this is now being diluted by the recent preference for smaller, higher-pitched instruments. Whereas people gather round to hear a good band, an inferior shawm player may be compared to a donkey braying (*lüjiao*), or just called 'blowing a drag' (*chuide mafan*). People's negative assessments of *chuishou* revolve around the concept of 'chaos' (*luan*). Some can assess a band on grounds of timbre, tuning, and rhythm. I doubt if audiences recognize *Liu Qing niang* or *Xifeng zan* or most of the other main melodies, though they will recognize more popular *yangge* and *xiaodiao* pieces based on folk-song, as well as some melodies in *duoban* metre, which are slower and played more in unison. Some listeners may follow the sequence of metres within a suite, or the use of different scales. But the main onus for the maintenance of the repertory seems to come from the performers themselves – who are not so obstinate as to complain if audiences now prefer to hear pop music.

---

[12] For shawm versions in the three main scales, see Huo and Ai 1979: 33–7, Gao 2000: 79–83. The White Cloud Mountain Daoists have a *sheng-guan* instrumental version (Yuan, Li and Shen 2000: 263–71, AI 1689–90) but apparently not a vocal one. In Shanxi, Wutaishan Buddhist ritual has both vocal (Zhongguo 2000: 1588–90, 1608–9) and *sheng-guan* (1697–1704, apparently a suite of melodies) versions of *Xifang zan*. To illustrate the problems of trying to compare transcriptions, AI 1082–6 gives several shawm versions of '*Xifang zan*' from Shaanbei and central Shaanxi, but I doubt that any of them are actually *Xifang zan* at all; AI vols. for Gansu and Ningxia also have arcane listings for this title. I detect no relation between our shawm piece and any of these versions.

Illustration 12   The 'big band' accompanies Receiving Offerings procession,
   Baijiayan funeral 2001

Chapter 9
Modernization and the 'big band'

So far we have found impoverishment, resulting from official initiatives to secularize society, more significant than any 'development' from any official cultural support. What I will now try to document is the limited respects in which the complex of modernity has been interacting with traditional ways since the 1990s.

We saw that under Maoism, *chuishou* were more immune from the concern of cultural cadres than bards, in that their music was non-programmatic; the *chuishou* had no Han Qixiang, no state-organized training sessions for new pieces. Officialdom is not entirely separate from the life of the common people: the chain reaches right into village life, and political vocabulary and thinking pervade people's consciousness. Still, as we saw with the bards, villagers themselves often see their traditional ways as separate, and state interference remains unwelcome.[1]

If we could, we might seek to trace official contacts back to the *chuishou* who played for the imperial *yamens*. Then, there was no gulf between officialdom and folk culture: all subscribed to a common pool of tradition. *Chuishou* continued to play for officials in the republican period – by the 1940s, for both Nationalist and Communist officials. Under Maoism, state-supported troupes were formed, mainly for opera; *chuishou* played a very minor part. Official, secular, festivals were also held, both in towns and villages; *yangge* festivities were partially secularized and 'revolutionary' songs promoted. Since the end of the communes, we may list '*suona* contests', training sessions, cassettes, and TV, as well as the continuing state troupes.

As ever, state influence under Maoism and since has to be put in perspective. Compared to the vast amount of material for operatic institutions, I find rather little evidence that shawm bands have been much affected by state initiatives. While documenting these modern influences, I must stress that they were overall very marginal right until the late 1990s – when TV, pop music, and the 'big band' looked likely to transform the scene substantially.

9.1 The official connection 2

As we saw in §7.4, under Maoism very few *chuishou* spent much time in the state-supported troupes. Only Feng Guanglin seems to have stayed; Li Daniu spent two months in Yan'an; and in this chapter we meet a couple more *chuishou* who spent periods in official troupes. Of the famous Chang lineage, though Chang

---

[1] Cf. Guo 2000: 350–53.

Mao and later Chang Wenzhou were recruited to the troupes for a time, the only other Chang *chuishou* to have done so are Chang Zilin and Chang Liancheng, who joined the Yulin Folk Arts Troupe right at the end of the twentieth century.

In fact, the situation of salaried urban musicians is now different. Under Maoism a job in a state troupe provided a meagre salary that might be a tempting option in a society where private enterprise was dangerous and ceremonial life limited. Now an official job only provides a work-unit, housing, a small salary, and a certain reputation; most members (notably those of the opera troupes) rely on folk ceremonial (life-cycle and calendrical) for their main income.

In a revealing sign of the times, the festivals (*diaoyan*, *huiyan*) of the 1950s showcasing outstanding folk genres and musicians gave way in the 1980s to contests (*bisai*, *dasai*). A packaged image of Shaanbei culture was also sometimes presented at regional or national events, such as the 1990 Asian Games in Beijing. Training sessions (*peixunban*, *xunlianban*) have been held locally since the 1980s. Sometimes these encouraged the traditional style – at the Jiaxian Bureau of Culture we were told that around 1982 they organized a training session for senior *chuishou* to teach new apprentices old pieces. But later such sessions were more often for the small *suona*, and then for brass bands (see below). Such initiatives were influential. Coming from the (albeit increasingly impotent) local cultural authorities, they lent prestige to musicians favoured, and encouraged a fashion for new instruments (small *suona*, brass bands) and styles (pop, and 'national' repertory).

I have no evidence that urban '*suona* associations' (*suona xiehui*) founded since the 1980s are common or influential, but further data would be interesting. In the Yan'an region, the Zichang county *suona* association was founded in 1984, and training bands and contests were held; the leading players recorded for films and TV,[2] and the association is represented on cassette (see below). Just south of Shaanbei, Hancheng county also formed a *suona* association.[3] However, though contests and training sessions have been held in Mizhi, Suide, and Zizhou counties, I have heard of no *suona* associations as such there. Village *chuishou* Chouxiao hoped I would start one in London, which was prophetic of him (§10.6 below).

9.2 Conservatory style

The twentieth-century arrangements of the national 'conservatory style' are best known for solo instruments such as *erhu* fiddle and *dizi* flute, but the *suona* shawm was also recruited to the conservatories and state-funded troupes, including army troupes. Shawm players, mainly from north China, gained exposure since the 1950s, like Zhao Chunting, Zhao Chunfeng, and Ren Qirui from Hebei, and several players from Shandong, the Northeast, and Henan (Jones 1998: ch.10). One might assume that such soloists had distilled folk traditions that were already

---

[2]   Zhang Jianzhong 2000: 237–8.

[3]   AI 975.

defunct, but the *Anthology* fieldwork of the 1980s reveals the rich variety of living local traditions. While my material suggests that we downplay the importance of the conservatory style in Shaanbei, its limited influence is worth describing.

I have found the mediated Shaanbei shawm style at two levels, considerably removed from the local scene. In the capitals of Shaanbei's two regions, Yulin city has its Folk Arts Troupe (to which, in its previous incarnation, Chang Wenzhou belonged; see §12.3), and Yan'an city has a regional Song-and-Dance Troupe, in which Ma Hu became '*suona* soloist'. In the Xi'an Conservatory in the provincial capital, Gao Maomao claims a background in the style of his old home in Shaanbei.

Ma Hu (proper name Ma Shengwu) is billed on the cover of his cassette (§9.3 below) as 'famous Shaanbei *suona* player'. Son of the famous Suide *chuishou* Ma Shuan, he entered the state-funded Yan'an Song-and-Dance Troupe when 16, becoming '*suona* soloist' there. He was part of the band accompanying *yangge* for the central government leaders in their Zhongnanhai headquarters in Beijing in 1957. In the 1970s he was composer and player of 'A *yangge* troupe has come to Zaoyuan' (*Zaoyuan laile yanggedui*, first piece on the B side of the cassette), canonized as 'an outstanding piece composed in Shaanxi since Liberation'. He holds titles such as 2nd-level national player, and is a member of the Chinese Musicians' Association. He has made several foreign tours since 1985 with the provincial Shaanxi Folk Arts Troupe and so on, marketing an all-singing all-dancing image of Shaanbei culture on stage (cf. §12.3).

Gao Maomao (Gao Xiaopeng)[4] was born in Yangjiagou in 1968, at the height of factional fighting. Like most of the other *chuishou* in the village, the Gao family had come from elsewhere (in this case Gaojiaping) to work for the landlords. Maomao's grandfather was admired as a drummer, and his father Yunming learnt shawm with the father of our friend Chouxiao (§6.7 above). But when Yunming found himself on the wrong side in the Cultural Revolution, the family moved south to Yichuan county in the early 1970s.

In Yichuan, Gao Yunming eventually did well from cultivating hillside orchards. The young Maomao went to school there, and from 1977 learnt the shawm with his father, who made him a small instrument to practise on. By the age of 16 he had a reputation in the area for performing weddings and funerals. In 1987 he published a cassette tape locally, and in 1988 he was admitted to the Xi'an conservatory. There he adopted the typical eclecticism of the conservatory professional. His teacher came from Hebei province, so he learnt the Hebei style. After five years in Xi'an, he visited the Central Conservatory in Beijing, and also sought out senior shawm players in the Shanghai Conservatory, as well as in Henan, Anhui, Shandong, and the Northeast. He claims to have studied with many 'old artists' from Shaanbei and Shanxi, but in the Xi'an Conservatory he mainly teaches his students the Hebei style. He has played for many film soundtracks, including *Red Sorghum* (*Hong gaoliang*, set in Shandong).

---

[4]　For data on Gao, I thank Iguchi Junko, as well as Yangjiagou villagers.

Gao Maomao could not remember Yangjiagou from his infancy, but returned there with the Japanese ethnomusicologist Iguchi Junko in 1995. He performed for a wedding with the village *chuishou*, and as a successful emigrant he was treated with some deference, but the gulf between their musical worlds made the experience difficult for the home team. Chouxiao gave (or was persuaded to sell?) his father's old instruments to him. Through Maomao's contacts with the Japanese scholars, he was part of a group invited to perform in Japan in 1996.

As we saw, the large shawm was tending to move from a small body and narrow bell with a coarse reed, to a larger body and wider bell with a finer reed and a more mellow sound, more comfortably able to play decorations in the higher register. We also saw how until the 1950s a small shawm called *haidi* was used by priests, and by the *chuishou* for the 'fine blowing' format. From the mid-1980s another type of shawm, slightly larger than the *haidi*, began to be added by urban *chuishou*, playing along with the two large shawms. It is known as *erwawa*, 'second kid' (the standard large shawm being known as *wazi*, 'kid'), or in official parlance 'small *suona*'. This instrument, though long a component of traditional bands in provinces further east like Hebei and Shandong, is the one mainly promoted in the conservatories, but had not yet formed part of the main instrumentation of the Shaanbei *chuishou*.

According to Chang Wenzhou and Zhang Hulin, since the 1990s both audiences and *chuishou* began to feel that just hearing two large shawms all the time was a bit monotonous. Though the small *suona* was already used a bit in the 1980s, many *chuishou* bands took it up from 1995, when Gao Maomao was first invited by the Mizhi county cultural authorities to teach a training session for the national style of small *suona*. This became an annual event. Though scholar Gao Wanfei, concerned for the maintenance of tradition, doesn't much like the small *suona*, young *chuishou* Zhang Hulin admires Maomao's technique, and shows us a VCD (called 'Highlights of Mizhi *suona*', *Mizhi suona jingxuan*) of the 1996 contest.

Also since the 1990s, urban *chuishou* sometimes add *sheng* free-reed mouth-organ, originally played in Shaanbei only by priests with *guanzi* oboe, but now included under the influence of modern conservatory style. The addition of the small *suona* and *sheng* was in line with the gradual but partial movement since the 1980s towards a more 'scientific' national style. But senior *chuishou* like Chang Wenzhou can see the risks of the dilution of the local style, as we see in §10.7 below.

9.3 Cassette culture 2

From the mid-1980s several Chinese films and TV programmes featured the Shaanbei *suona*. Internationally the most celebrated of such films was *Yellow Earth* (see §1.4), though the film was not a success in China. It shows a traditional shawm band playing for wedding processions; it is said to be from Mizhi or Jiaxian counties, but I have not been able to find out who they are.

Such films, naturally, showed the bands only briefly as local colour. Rather more significant are commercially-released audio cassettes, of which I have found several available locally – though a small selection, it is rather more varied than the single bard commercially recorded (§5.4 above). Many recordings of Chinese folk instrumental music were published on vinyl before the Cultural Revolution, even some of shawm players, but as far as I know none from Shaanbei.

Commercial cassettes of Shaanbei shawm bands were first on sale locally by the late 1980s: Li Qishan released a tape in 1986, and Gao Maomao (not himself a player of the local style) in 1987. As we saw in §5.4, such tapes are a very small part of the selection available in urban music shops, and seeking them out there is no easy task. But by contrast with folk-song or even the narrative-singing tapes, the few shawm tapes are basically unmodified in style. Some feature pieces recorded as continuous suites, while others just have single pieces. By the end of the twentieth century, while TV and VCDs had recently become common, the influence of cassette culture in Shaanbei seemed minimal. More recently, one might add websites, though they tend to present a sanitized image at some remove from local realities.

I sweated blood to get hold of some of these cassettes. Few shops stock more than a couple of them, and I finally tracked down a selection on an expedition by foot to a dingy general store in the sleepy township near Yangjiagou. As I eyed the cassettes up over the counter, the dour assistant, who apparently hadn't ever sold any of them, and certainly not to a foreigner, spotted a business opportunity. She ingenuously asked 5 yuan each for them – I had enough experience to realize they sold at around 2 yuan. My Beijing companion Guo Yuhua was indignant, and we launched into some increasingly impolite haggling. But the assistant wouldn't budge. I generally get angry when people try to overcharge me in China, but having been searching for these tapes for years, in this case I was inclined to allow myself to be ripped off – the three tapes I had set my heart on would still cost less than a half-pint of London beer. But for Guo Yuhua the principle was clear, and she dragged me out of the shop, refusing to let me part with my money. After some spirited exchanges as we set off back to Yangjiagou along the filthy main track, debating the balance between adhering to principle and yielding to corruption, I dashed back to the shop and bought them at the inflated price, flinging the money at the assistant with a vain display of sarcasm that went clear over her head.

Cassette tapes of Shaanbei shawm bands

Shizi ling ['Command of the lion', title of a piece], China Record Co., Shanghai branch, nd [1986 *apud* Mizhi 1993: 540 and Gao 1996: 150].
Named shawm players Li Qishan and Chang Jing, but there are no sleeve notes. Recorded in Xi'an. The pieces (recorded individually, not in suite form) are at the popular end of the spectrum.

Shaanbei suona: Xiqing taoqu ['suites for joyous celebration'], Gansu yinxiang chubanshe GY 035, 1988.
Jointly produced by the Yan'an diqu guangbo shiyeju, Yan'an diqu wenhua wenwuju, Zichang xian wenhua wenwuju, and Gansu yinxiang chubanshe, this cassette features various members of the Zichang county *suona* association. Five shawm players are named, and one drummer. Chouxiao likes this tape.

Shaanbei suona dachui ['large blowing'], Beijing yinxiang gongsi YY9025, nd, *c*1988.
Features Wang Xinxi's band from Wubu county. Wang learnt from the age of 15 from Feng Maochang. In middle age, apparently before the Cultural Revolution (he was 60 in the late 1980s), he spent five years as a shawm teacher in the Northwest Arts School, predecessor of the Xi'an Conservatory, where Chang Mao also spent time. He was among those visited by scholars Huo Xianggui and Ai Pu in the 1970s – Huo Xianggui recalled that Wang knew all the scales. Side B comprises a continuous suite lasting nearly 23 minutes.

Shaanbei suona qu jingxuan [Highlights of Shaanbei *suona* pieces], *vol. 1*, Zhongguo wenlian chuban gongsi, nd [1988 apud Gao 1996: 150].
Features the brothers Li Qishan and Li Zishan. After this 'vol. 1', I haven't heard of a second cassette. Indeed, the brothers now have their own bands and rarely play together.

Shaanbei suona, Shaanxi sheng Xibu yinxiang chubanshe [Xi'an], 1989, 2 cassettes.
Features the band of Gao Haijun and Gao Shuhong, also from Wubu county. Gao Haijun is grandson of the famed Gao Yuzhi, known as Mao the Fourth.

Nao honghuo ['festive bustle']: *Shaanbei suona*, Xi'an: Shaanxi yinxiang chubanshe, XL-9718, nd [late 1990s?].
Featuring Ma Hu (see above), this is the furthest from the traditional style. The items are mostly short popular pieces, and are heavily arranged with *sheng*, *dizi*, and extra percussion. The *guogu* interludes sound false, four-square and inflexible, far from those *in situ*. The timbre of the *suona* itself is far more mellifluous than that of the traditional instrument. The sleeve-notes are full of clichéd patriotic propaganda.

9.4 Following fashion: the Shaanbei big band

Chuishou bands in Shaanbei remained rather constant through most of the twentieth century. I have described change under Maoism mainly in terms of impoverishment: apart from losing the 'fine blowing' format, their basic instrumentation was unchanged, and the traditional repertory was only partly supplemented by vocal-derived pieces, so with few new elements in context or repertory, *chuishou* mainly experienced a decline in both.

Since the fall of the commune system, against the general picture of the restoration of traditional practices, we have already seen several musical changes taking place gradually – now hinting at a less insular tradition, following a more pan-Chinese, outward-looking fashion. First the standardization of the C shawm around 1980, then the addition of the small *suona*, followed by the *sheng* mouth-organ. All of these may be seen as leading to a major change, which happened only around 1995: the formation of the 'big band' (or 'brass band') incorporating Western brass instruments and playing pop music – around a decade after similar innovation in some other parts of north China.[5]

Brass bands have caught on in many parts of the world, often through colonialism, through soldiers, traders, and missionaries. They often play local tunes, adding some local instruments.[6] Brass bands were first introduced to China by Western armies and missionaries in the late nineteenth century.[7] But they appear to have been rare in the countryside through the Republican period into the 1950s, and brass instruments only became popular through the model operas in the Cultural Revolution. I came across several brass bands on my travels since 1986 in Hebei and Fujian. Many were separate brass bands with no connection to the *chuishou*, but *chuishou* bands were beginning to incorporate the style too.[8]

Though early missionaries established bases in Shaanbei and many other parts of rural China, I have heard of no brass bands in Shaanbei under their influence. By the Republican period, the few progressive schools in Yulin were teaching a semi-Westernized musical curriculum, and Western orchestral instruments were played at the Communist base at Yan'an from the 1930s, but in such a poor area it seems that they never spread from Yan'an.

So in backward Shaanbei, *chuishou* only began adopting brass band instruments around 1995. As with the small *suona*, the Shaanbei big band seems to have been started off through official encouragement, through the modernizing agendas of schools, county Halls of Culture, and the opera troupes. The earliest mention of

---

[5]   Cf. the pop music revolution in northern Shanxi shawm bands, Jones 2007: 30–38. *Pinyin* terms: *dabanzi, tongguan yuedui, xiyang tongguan yueqi*. For the varied pop scene in China, see Baronovich 2003, notably 10–52, 190–272.

[6]   Note the fine CDs *Frozen Brass*. For urban wedding bands in India, see Booth 1990; for Nepal, Tingey 1994.

[7]   Han Kuo-huang 2001: 231–3.

[8]   E.g. Jones 1998: 59–60, citing a 1989 report from Hejin further south in Shanxi.

brass instruments I heard was from a nice euphonium player with Wang Shifa's shawm band in Suide, who learnt at school in 1963. In the Cultural Revolution the Mizhi county *Qinqiang* opera troupe bought a few brass instruments to use in the revolutionary model operas. Gao Zhiqiang (b. *c*1941), then a *huhu* fiddle player in the troupe, remembers how they picked them up, but never used them much. Since the 1980s they have used them in schools for events like raising the national flag. Since the mid-1990s Gao, who had gone on to head the county Hall of Culture, has organized occasional brass band training sessions. First the head of the vocational secondary school agreed to lend him a classroom; later Gao left the school and set up a 'Brass instruments and electronic keyboard training band' at his home, with 20 students at a time. Though with this step he doesn't appear to have been seeking a revolution in the *chuishou* band, he does approve of the combination of trumpet and *suona*. I have heard of no separate brass bands performing for ceremonial here before the *chuishou* added brass instruments.

In Mizhi, Suide, and Zizhou counties, Western brass instruments were only added around 1995, but the style soon became common in the main towns. By 2000 all the professional bands in Mizhi town were busy providing this line-up – those of Chang Wenzhou, Chang Zilin, Chang Liancheng, Gao Jiu, Zhang Hulin, and Zhao Laixi, as well as Li Qishan nearby. All three bands of *chuishou* in the town of Miaojiaping south of Zizhou county-town have added brass instruments. However, though Hu's band in Yangjiagou village uses them, few of the part-time bands in the villages will be able to afford the investment. Wang Shifa in 2001: 'Seven or eight of the fifteen bands in Sishilipu district haven't added Western brass instruments.'

Li Qishan: 'People nowadays like to hear the trumpet with dancing, twisting, and singing (*tiaoniuchang*), with a sound-system – they only care about being 'red and fiery' (*honghuo*), not about art (*yishu*). Now even we've bought a drum-kit and trumpet and all that – without that stuff no-one would get invited!' Wang Laiwa: 'Now people care about putting on a big show (*paichang*, extravagance) – when an old person dies and there's a funeral, people [viz. the host family] try and make a name for themselves (*yangming*).'

Li Qishan described three formats, depending on the taste and budget of the host:

small band ('old three drum', *laosangu*)	5 musicians	2 large shawms drum, gong, cymbals
medium band	7 musicians	adds 1 small *suona*, trumpet
big band	11 musicians	further adds sax, trombone, drum-kit, singer

As we see in §11.2, since some parts of rituals still require the traditional line-up and repertory, band bosses have developed a modified agenda in which the traditional band alternates with the big band. In fact the big band may include the following components as available:

large shawm (1 or 2)	traditional drum
small *suona*	small cymbals
sheng free-reed mouth-organ	knobbed gong
	(other gongs from opera)
sax	(large cymbals)
trumpet (1 or 2)	
trombone	drum-kit
euphonium	electronic keyboard
	singer (usually female)

The addition of these instruments is a further reason why the large shawms will continue to be made in C. As Chang Wenjin said, they now mainly make shawms in C and D, to match the *sheng* and the trumpet. In Yanggao in north Shanxi, where the traditional large shawm, and indeed the *sheng*, is in E, they now use a shawm in F (traditionally used for popular 'small pieces'), to suit trumpet and keyboard (Jones 2007).

The small *suona* is the main soloist in this outfit, not just the Western brass. Feng Xiaoping: 'In today's society, the small *suona* sounds good, better than the large *suona*' – we might compare the bards' recent preference for *sanxian* over *pipa*. The drum-kit is also fashionable, and the sound system important. The small *suona*, trumpet, and sax engage in histrionics. The drum-kit and traditional drum, and traditional and modern melodic instruments, all play together. Even the two-note fanfares for liminal moments at rituals, played on the traditional *hao* trumpet, are now often played on the Western trumpet instead.

Zhao Laixi: 'Singing in the drum music bands is very well received now – they don't get invited unless they've got a singer.' Though cool young male *chuishou* Gao Jiu sings, female singers are the norm. When Li Qishan books a female singer, she comes from outside his home village (for fees, see §10.4). Now a shawm player also sometimes does a turn with his bag of tricks, imitating opera (*kaxi*) on various wind instruments, in a borrowing from Hebei or Shandong provinces.[9]

The new bands are conscious of presenting a smart new image in keeping with the times. They often wear suits and ties, and large shades are *de rigueur*; many ride motor-bikes. With the mobile-phone revolution in the towns since around 1998, successful urban *chuishou* all use them to enhance their availability for work, and many have name-cards too, giving their address and phone number, listing the kind of work they accept, and their expanded instrumentation, all in thoroughly modern language. Chang Wenzhou's name-card has a brief biography.[10]

---

[9]   See Jones 1998: 36–7.
[10] See Zhang Zhentao 2002a: 126–7.

9.5 New and old repertories

The new big band repertory consists mainly of pan-Chinese pop, TV, and film themes, as heard on TV, CD, and VCD, and in karaoke bars. Such music is largely centripetal in that it somehow conforms to central Party policy, rather than the more rebellious rock-and-roll, popular with Beijing and other university students and a relatively urbane audience in the big cities. On our way back to town after a village session, I am happy when a town driver plays a tape of the Beijing rock band Black Panther, but this is rare; few people in Shaanbei have heard of rock-and-roll, either in towns or villages.

The pop pieces are mostly short and four-square, often with question-and-answer phrases in dialogue, the small *suona* usually taking the solo.[11] Whereas the two shawms of the traditional band play in a heterophony based around octave doubling, with a range of two octaves, the big band can provide around four octaves, from small *suona* to trombone. However, the heterophony of the traditional style is largely absent, as they all basically play in octave unison, ignoring even the basic harmonies of their pop models. A sequence of pieces, each repeated many times, is played, without the traditional *guogu* interludes.

The traditional repertory seems largely unknown to the audience, and anyway consists of pieces whose titles have no obvious significance; the system of scales, and the metrical sequence, were the main respects in which *chuishou* conformed to the 'old rules'. As that system declines, some bands choose well-known pop themes appropriate to the context, as we see in §11.2 below.[12]

Senior *chuishou* pride themselves on being able to play for several hours at a time – or recall the days when they did. Li Qishan: 'Originally [*sic*] we could play for five hours in one breath, till our fingers went numb.' Chang Wenjin: 'In the old days you had to play the *laosangu* suite for two hours, now it's all over in 20 minutes. That only began changing about ten years ago.' He warmed to the theme: 'Now the *chuishou* are a complete mess, they play slow or fast if they feel like it, there's no rules any more. Now they don't even necessarily play *Dabaidui* when the bride comes to the new home. The most sonorous (*hongliang*) standards are about to become obsolete!' Other subtleties too are declining: *qiangban* tempo, using the same proportions as *manban* only faster, used to be much appreciated for its drumming, but is becoming rare.

Chuishou today play fewer traditional pieces in fewer scales for a shorter time than their grandfathers. This is partly to do with the gradual simplification of the ceremonial practices that they accompany – even if those practices still maintain remarkable continuity from imperial times. More generally, locals perceive a breakdown of social order, the general 'chaos' of post-reform society. In Yangjiagou, Feng Guanglin was said to know even more shawm melodies than the famous Chang Mao. Chang Xinhua and Feng Guanglin played in more scales,

[11]   Cf. India, Booth 1990: 248.
[12]   Again, cf. Booth 1990: 256.

because they still needed them then. Even Chang Bingyou's generation already didn't need them – 'there was no time' for them any more in weddings and funerals. Short, more popular, *yangge*-type melodies may have become more common than the longer pieces like the 'eight great pieces' mentioned by Chouxiao.

The repertory is now being supplemented constantly by pop and TV themes. These are likely to be more short-lived than the traditional repertory that has been handed down for many generations. Those players with few old tunes and many new ones have no problems with this, since they earn good money, and will do better business than the more traditional village *chuishou*. The new repertory is easy to remember and easy to understand. It is considered more 'fancy' (*hua*, decorated), even if players presently use a simple (and to me tedious) unison compared to the richer heterophonic ornamentation of the traditional style. Though many village bands had not adopted the new instruments by the late 1990s, I guess most could play a few pop or TV themes on demand.

As I noted in discussing the pop revolution among shawm bands in Shanxi (Jones 2007: 30–38), whereas other world traditions have continued to flourish while allowing space for the brass band, I tend to be concerned for the *chuishou* traditions as they are faced by the incursion of the pop style. My colleague Zhang Zhentao provocatively defends the choices of the *chuishou* in forging this combination of traditional Chinese and modern Western instruments.[13] Apart from the fact that the assimilation of music of the 'Western barbarians' (including the shawm itself) has around 2000 years of history in China, *chuishou* have a perfect right to experiment, and it is not the place of urban scholars to pontificate whether the sounds of the two types of outdoor instruments can blend appropriately in the contexts of rural music-making; nor is it exactly our business if people prefer new tunes to old. The big band is doubtless an important theme for our studies of change. If personally I am underwhelmed by it, I would be only too happy if I could see it catching on in the world music scene *à la* Buena Vista or Bollywood Brass Band, but for the time being I suspect its main audience will remain people in Shaanbei, for whom it is designed.

While local community events, like temple fairs and funerals, reassert local values, pop music seems to enable Shaanbei audiences to espouse, and share in, the trappings of modern national 'progress' even as their condition in a backward area denies them a fair share of its economic gains. Chang Wenzhou's pop repertory is doubtless very popular; indeed, one might see his practice today as a perfect combination of traditional and modern elements, good for local people seeking to espouse modernity while clinging onto local tastes. The big band style was spreading rapidly by 2001, but, as we see in chapter 10, the traditional line-up and repertory, that (like the ceremonies they accompanied) had remained rather constant through the twentieth century, had as yet retained their niche in the market.

---

[13]   Zhang Zhentao 2002a: 93–5.

Chapter 10
Chuishou around 2000

Having surveyed the reviving *chuishou* scene in the early reform era, and having noted the more recent addition of the big band, we can now assess the condition of bands in towns and villages around 2000.

10.1 Mizhi town

Since the 1980s, *chuishou* and aficionados have talked of three main styles (*pai*) of *chuishou* in Mizhi town: Zhao, Chang, and Li. Though the Zhao style is now considered defunct, and there is no love lost between Chang Wenzhou and Li Qishan, they accept the classification. But with traditional repertory now taking a back seat to pop music, it is unclear how such styles will be redrawn in future.

Chang Wenzhou has consolidated his reputation as the most senior *chuishou* and shawm maker in Shaanbei. Apart from his official performances since the 1970s in Yulin and Xi'an, his crowning glory was playing for the Asian Games in Beijing in 1990, where he was one of many shawm players from Shaanbei accompanying *yaogu* group drumming from Ansai, another packaged image of the Communist revolution in Shaanbei. He made ten pairs of shawms and *hao* trumpets for the festival.

'When I came back from Beijing, people came to see me, someone from Shanghai too, wanting to produce a tape. But it fell through – they wanted to offer me a buy-out, but I wanted royalties. Then later they found Li Qishan through the Bureau of Culture instead, and recorded him.' He claimed 'No-one listens to those tapes at all now', but such tapes do appear to sell, as we saw. Anyway, Li Qishan had already released a tape in 1986.

Chang Wenzhou maintains his contacts with the official style, deploying his nephews and apprentices keenly, aware of doing good business by keeping up with the times. People call him Master Chang (Changshi); on his name card (*c*2000) he calls himself *dashi* 'great master'. He and his wife work from their house, which is busy with his apprentices, and with *chuishou* coming to try out his instruments – just like the old 'drum shops'. On our initial visits in 1999 and 2001 he phones round his friends to get them to see how famous he is because we have come. He is obsessed with the idea of performing in Beijing – and now England, alas a vain dream. His main motivations may be fame and [hence] money, but also, typically, because he feels 'I've never been anywhere in my life'.

Now that he has got pulmonitis and is getting a bit frail to go out playing, much of his income comes from selling his instruments. He was preparing to demolish his old house in East Great Street and build a two-storey house, costing over 100,000 *yuan*, a vast amount, so he was doing good business. On our 2001 visit he is so busy preparing to sell at the White Cloud Mountain temple fair (§11.5 below) that scholar Gao Wanfei tells him he should look after his guests, not just think about earning money.

One of Chang Wenzhou's sons runs an instrument shop in Suide county-town, selling all kinds of instruments, opera costumes, and so on. When we enquire casually there, he outdoes his father in asking 300 *yuan* for one shawm – but then you don't expect to buy anything in China without a contact. Many shops in the area sell shawms claiming to be by Chang Wenzhou, and he is understandably disgruntled. 'Some makers say they're my pupils, though they haven't learnt with me even for a single day.' My colleague Tian Yaonong astutely suggests he puts a stamp on the shawm bodies. Another of Chang's sons is a teacher; not inclined to take up the shawm in the Cultural Revolution, now he has a good job it is too late.

One *chuishou* observed candidly: 'Chang Wenzhou may be famous, but he's getting old, he has liver disease, and the people in his band aren't so great technically, so now he's not getting invited so much.' But he is still invited to perform – either going himself or acting as a fixer. Though he is quite aware that the new pop style dilutes the local flavour, he can only go with the flow. He is a tough cookie. The slow responses of his movements and speech make his time as a teacher implausible, and we saw he was considered 'thick' during his time in the troupe, yet as my colleague Zhang Zhentao notes, all that vanishes when he plays; here all is intelligence.

Chang Wenzhou's band works like a folk conservatory. His star pupil Gao Jiu (b.1972) started playing percussion in a *chuishou* band when young, studying with Chang Wenzhou from the age of 16. Later he learnt the small *suona* with help from a manual. He now has his own band, a name-card, and a mobile phone. He also sings, and is dead cool in his huge shades. Chang Wenzhou's nephew Chang Zilin is now considered a bright star, his reputation confirmed by winning a local contest in 1999 and gaining a post in the Yulin Folk Arts Troupe; in 2000 another nephew, Chang Liancheng, won first prize.

Chang Wenzhou's *chuishou* cousin Chang Wenjin (see above) moved to Mizhi town in 1988. Though they only live a few minutes' walk away, they have little to do with each other, and we learnt of him by chance. He now makes his living from making shawms and percussion, and also makes fake antique money, antique teapots, and so on. He acted as one of the judges in the Mizhi *suona* contest in 1999. More amenable than Chang Wenzhou, he too gives me a casket of reeds, carefully chosen.

We can make the transition to Chang Wenzhou's rival Li Qishan by introducing local scholar Gao Wanfei (b.1952). Gao played gong in his father's band when young, but he was discouraged from pursuing the lowly *chuishou* life (§10.3 below), and ended up in the Mizhi Hall of Culture as an enthusiastic scholar of the

shawm bands.[1] Following in the footsteps of Huo Xianggui and Ai Pu, he compiled
a mimeograph of transcriptions as early as 1981 (revised in 1984), which he later
updated and managed to get formally published – no mean feat. In 2001 we arrived
soon after its publication, and soon found ourselves roped in to doing a plug on
local TV for it. The book consists largely of transcriptions, unfortunately lacking
any indication of who played all the versions, unlike the Huo and Ai mimeograph
and his own earlier volumes. It is easy to criticize such works. Their social material
is questionable and sanitized, their transcriptions too basic, making only a starting
point. Cultural cadres are also responsible for exhibitions, contests, and so on,
promoting calligraphy, painting, and photography. They tend to do fieldwork to
create myths, and their work is not detailed. But they live there, and in a sense they
speak the same language as the musicians, they bear the same suffering.

Gao Wanfei is on much better terms with Li Qishan than with Chang Wenzhou.[2]
As we saw in §7.2, Li Qishan (b. *c*1949, Illustration 13) learnt on the eve of the
Cultural Revolution. He has made at least two cassettes (§9.3 above); he featured
on the soundtrack for the popular 1985 film 'Life' (*Rensheng*) and in person in the
TV film *Lanhuahua*. His village of Lijiagou is conveniently situated on the main
road just south of Mizhi town on the way towards Suide. It has a population of over
600 – a chart at the family-planning office in the village primary school lists 513,

Illustration 13   Li Qishan with son Li Shengli and grandsons, Lijiagou 2001

---

[1]   Gao 2000: 290.

[2]   For Li, see also Gao 1996, a bland eulogy that would madden Chang Wenzhou.

in 117 households, of which all except three are surnamed Li. It is said to be the richest village in the vicinity – many men are in building, working as contractors further afield, and two or three are *yuan* millionaires. It is also a *chuishou* village. Li claims that there are enough *shangshou* (upper) players to organize a dozen or so bands – even his own family (with his father, his third uncle, as far as the nephews) can form nine bands, besides cousins, who can organize three bands. Li's own family has only five *mu* of land between six people, not enough to live off.

Li is considered something of an upstart. Chang Wenzhou is not alone in resenting his *guanxi* ('connections') with the Hall of Culture. More significantly, people criticize his small repertory. Even the meek Yangjiagou *chuishou* find his playing 'boring'. But he is affable and retains dignity. 'You can only set yourself up in society if you play well and behave well. It's no good not being a good person. At the New Year's festivities when we met another band, my reputation is big, but I still gave way to them, putting my shawm down. When we met them later, they came over to make friends, calling me 'Master Li' (*shifu*). If you flaunt your talent all over the place, people will curse you behind your back, it's still no good. Peasant consciousness, eh!'

Li Qishan now also maintains a big band. His son Li Shengli (b. *c*1973) learnt shawm with him; he went on to learn trumpet by himself, and studied cipher notation at the county Hall of Culture. Many of the other bands in their village incorporate the big band style.

A younger *chuishou* doing good business from Mizhi town is Zhang Hulin (b. *c*1969), who came from a village on the border with Zizhou county. His father had taught himself shawm from young; he had five sons, and when he was injured and disabled, the family was in great difficulty. 'I came home after I graduated from junior secondary when I was 17 (*c*1985). I lost my opportunity to continue studying in school, our life was terrible then – that was when I learnt *chuishou*.' He learnt for three years with Zhong Tianren (called Hou Si, Monkey the Fourth, b. *c*1944) from Zizhou, mainly by going round on jobs with him. Since Hou Si himself had learnt with Chang Mao, 'I guess my style is that of Changshiban, because my master learnt from Chang Mao who ran a drum shop.'

Zhang Hulin moved to Mizhi town around 1993; he has now bought a cave-dwelling on the hills above the town for 28,000 *yuan*. His four brothers have all got places of their own in Mizhi town, and are part of his band; if business is busy, they can split into several bands. 'My four brothers have apprentices, who don't earn money yet but don't pay anything either. First they learn cipher notation, then they study the instruments; they all live and eat at the house of the band boss, and study and practise in their free time.'

Now that Zhao Suotong is no longer active, the illustrious Zhao style is said to have become extinct. His son is a shawm player, but spent 15 years in prison on a suspended death sentence for his part in a gang rape – the leader, son of another *chuishou*, was executed. After his release from prison he organized a big band with nine members, including his son (19 in 2001), who had been learning shawm for two years; a 21-*sui* old on trumpet, *suona*, and *sheng*; and a sax player (20) and his wife, who sings pop songs and 'Shaanbei folk-songs' – after graduating from primary school in 1995 she joined the county *Qinqiang* opera troupe, but had just left to join this band full-time.

10.2 Little Hong Kong

Zhenchuan township (known locally as 'little Hong Kong'), on the busy main artery between Mizhi and Yulin, has long been a thriving commercial centre. He Zengtong told us there are now four *chuishou* bands in Zhenchuan, but no discernable styles. Next to a funeral shop in the town, we also saw a sign advertising 'Shanxi *suona* groups' (*Shanxi suona dui* – note the modern term), contactable through an agent. Bands from Shanxi (just across the Yellow River) were said to be in some demand since their style was novel.

Perhaps the most successful young *chuishou* in the Zhenchuan area is He Siwa ('Fourth kid': He Zhanyin, b. *c*1962), son of elderly *chuishou* He Zengtong (§6.6 above). Though based in a hamlet some distance from the town, the family is prospering. From their peaceful and spacious cave-dwelling, with its tiled floor, whitewashed walls, and cement courtyard, it is easy to see why they don't move to town. He Siwa followed his father on business from young, soon after the end of the Cultural Revolution, and learnt shawm from 17 with the same master in Changshiban with whom his father had studied. He learnt the old repertory, but is now most in demand for pop pieces. Like many young *chuishou*, he knows cipher notation.

Another busy band boss in Zhenchuan is the sincere young Yuanr (real name Li Yongzhang, b. *c*1967). His old home is Shushan village in Mizhi. He used to play percussion in the Mizhi *Qinqiang* opera troupe, and learnt the small *suona* by himself. He then managed to spend a year at the Xi'an conservatory studying the 'national' style of small *suona* with Gao Maomao (§9.3 above). He won a second prize in the 1996 Mizhi county *suona* contest. Yuanr also learnt the modern style of *sheng*, with 17 and 21 reeds. He also learnt to mend *sheng* with a professional *sheng* player from the Mizhi county opera troupe. 'There's a *sheng* mender in Hengshan county, but he charges 100 *yuan* a time – we're not prepared to spend that!' He doesn't play the large shawm, but he is familiar enough with the old repertory to accompany on drum, though much more comfortable with the more popular style. He sometimes plays *sheng* or percussion with Chang Wenzhou's band. His wife is in the Suide county *Jinju* opera troupe; they have a nice young son. Yuanr is also commonly known as 'The Stammerer' (*Jiekazi*) – both his colleagues and mine had a terrible time concealing their mirth when he and I got talking, since I also stammer. Imagine the number of tapes you'd need to record the interviews.

After a time working in He Siwa's band, Yuanr formed his own, working with Shi Weiren (b. *c*1948) from Suide. Shi graduated from senior secondary in 1968, having learnt *huhu* fiddle and *dizi* flute from his schoolteacher. He then worked as a teacher in Suide for over ten years, sometimes teaching music. He moved to

Zhenchuan in 1998, and began to study the large shawm (uniquely late, apart from me!) and *sheng*. In 2001 Yuanr's big band included around a dozen young musicians between the ages of 38 and 16, with little background in the *chuishou* tradition.

Yuanr is on good terms with Chang Wenzhou, and has the foresight to build a long-term career. 'We've just bought 12 shawms from him. We're afraid that after he dies, no-one will be able to make them, or at least they won't be so good.' Yuanr's band is regularly invited for the major Black Dragon temple fair, a public platform that keeps them in business year-round.

An eccentric character trying to set up as a band boss around Zhenchuan and Mizhi is Ai Guorui (b. *c*1966), from Shigou district in Mizhi. He learnt trumpet and sax on Gao Zhiqiang's music course in vocational secondary school, and has spent time in the army. He used to work with He Siwa and Yuanr, and moved to the county town in 2000. Ai Guorui has all the business enterprise of the new 'socialism with Chinese characteristics'. 'If I'm gonna do this, I gotta understand my own position, otherwise I won't have no food to eat, right? So I did a survey. In the 14 districts of Mizhi county there are 138 *chuishou* bands – they all turn out at New Year, but most of the year they till the fields. There are only four or five professional [full-time] bands, all in the county-town, they haven't got any land any more.' He has no scruples about following fashion. 'I often play new pieces. Though there are a load of similar *chuishou*, they can't do business, because they ain't got nothing new. You can only do business if you learn new scores (*xinpu*) and new instruments.' However dubious his credentials, he has a great turn of phrase. Looking at me, he exclaimed, 'To me, traditional pieces sound like this wog talking!'

The current position with apprentices studying while living with the band boss sounds not unlike the old drum shops – only now they don't smoke opium or go out begging, and they spend little time on traditional repertory, instead learning pop pieces on small *suona*, trumpet, and sax, with the aid of cipher notation.

10.3 Status since the reforms

As we saw, *chuishou* were considered outcasts before Liberation, a stigma that, if never erased, became less relevant under Maoism. Under the reforms since 1980 another modification of status has occurred. They began to earn good money, and as model capitalists under the new ethos, they could attract wives. Fixer Yan Xiangcheng (in Yulin): 'Now *chuishou* can sit up at table (*shangxi*), and for funerals they can eat under the awning.'

This may not always be so in the villages as one goes further south, but it's a tendency. While the pejorative term *guizi* is now little used around Mizhi, we learnt that it is still current in the southern area of Shaanbei, south of Yan'an, and perhaps even in parts of Suide and Qingjian. There, little change has occurred either under Maoism or the reforms, and *chuishou* are still outcasts; no-one will share a table with them, they can only intermarry, and a man who takes up the profession loses his old friends. Zhang Hulin: 'When I was young [in the 1980s!] *chuishou* were despised – when we did a job we were always put up in a bachelor's cave [bachelors themselves being despised]. They're still despised in Yan'an, around Ansai. I've done jobs in Ansai where if the *chuishou* don't finish their food, the host won't take it away, he gets them to take it with them, or chucks it away.'

Even around Mizhi, despite the 'official blowers' story, *chuishou* still seem to be at a certain social remove from other villagers. They serve funerals, like grave-diggers, playing while others are eating and getting fed separately at the end. They are a group of men often away from home. As we saw, scholar Gao Wanfei used to play gong in his father's band when he was young in the 1980s. But his father wouldn't let him become a *chuishou* or learn the shawm; sometimes he'd pick a shawm up while the band was resting, but his father would rush over and stop him. 'Being a *chuishou* is begging', he said. 'The sons of a *chuishou* can't find a wife, and no-one wants the daughter of a *chuishou*, they're the dregs (*xiajiuliu*).'

Wang Laiwa (b. *c*1965) learnt from 1979 with a 60-*sui*-old *chuishou*. Even then the old prejudices were accepted. 'My master didn't have any heirs. He used to say, "*Chuishou* and opera performers can't find a wife, no-one will let their daughter marry you, and you can't enter the examination arena". I wouldn't let my son become a *chuishou*, I still feel it's degrading.' So much for the special prestige of the Mizhi *chuishou*. As Wang's master observed, opera performers were still despised too. Gao Wanfei again: 'When I worked with the [state-funded] opera troupe, and we took our instruments and bedding to the villages to perform, one villager said, "Look, some people have come from the authorities", and another said, "They're not people, they're opera performers (*xizi*)"!'

Zhang Hulin: 'Now there's not so much discrimination. *Chuishou* can earn quite a lot of money these days, and they're mostly young men, including quite a few who've left state opera troupes to become *chuishou*', maybe meaning the subsidiary ones like singers and trumpet players. Most Shaanbei *chuishou* perform in their ordinary clothes, like seldom-washed Mao jackets and home-made cloth shoes; the media image, and major secular festivals, still often present them in a romantic faux-peasant costume of embroidered waistcoat or satin (well, nylon) jacket, as well as a white cloth wrapped around the head, that archetypal but long-outmoded image of the revolution in north China (cf. Illustration 9 above). But Zhang went on, 'And we're quite well turned out – when we go out on jobs we wear a suit and tie, and leather shoes. We're the ones who are raising the status of *chuishou*.' Indeed, this new generation of trendy urban *chuishou*, with their saxes and shades, riding their motor-bikes, seem to suffer little social handicap. Still, Zhang's wife points out ruefully: 'When our neighbours see my two sons they say, "Hey watch out, *chuishou* with sons eh?" – meaning that *chuishou* can't have good children, you have to keep an eye on them.'

If being a *chuishou* was already not much of a hereditary tradition by the 1950s, the system now actually seems to work against it. Now the sons of successful *chuishou* are quite unlikely to continue the tradition, since with money and family pretensions they may stay on in school, aspiring to get a proper job. Only boys from poorer families will drop out of school in the hope of making easy money. Few young *chuishou* have attended secondary school for long – many are junior secondary drop-outs.

We saw that tradition allows only male musicians. Throughout China since the 1980s, one can document a few female shawm players.[3] In Shaanbei, Liu Deyi told us of some female *chuishou* who had come from Henan province, and my colleague Tian Yaonong met a good female band from Zizhou. But such cases are very rare. As we saw, female pop singers were becoming a common part of the big band by around 2000.

10.4 Changing economics

Chuishou have always been considered 'semi-professional'. Though they till the land, some rely on its produce more than others. Many perform infrequently for ceremonies as required. Even 'full-time' *chuishou* working for fixers in drum shops before Liberation relied partly on begging, and joined opera troupes during the summer. Despite their calculations of monetary values, before Liberation, and indeed right into the 1980s, many *chuishou* were paid in kind, such as grain.

As we saw above, the network of ceremonial had dwindled during the Maoist era, depriving shawm players of a living; apart from the loss of their main patrons the landlords, there were also ideological constraints. They still did occasional business on the quiet, but they had to ask for leave of absence from their work-team, handing over half of their fee in exchange for work-points. Some said that *chuishou* were rather better off than most under the commune system. But whatever the benefits for ordinary peasants of the dismantling of the system in the 1980s, the free market was a boon for *chuishou*.

The size of fee depends on the hiring family's conditions, and on *guanxi* contacts, both familial and social. Sometimes *guanxi* may oblige *chuishou* to do a job for a rather small fee; where *guanxi* don't apply, they can choose to take only more lucrative jobs. In Shaanbei, *chuishou* bands divide the overall fee up unequally between members depending on responsibility, the percussionists earning least. This seems to be common in China, though in north Shanxi they all take equal portions apart from one extra for the fixer.[4] Anyway, the fixer, supplier of instruments, and band boss (*huzi/lanshi*, *jiashi*, *banzhu*, generally rolled into one) makes the most profit, even if he doesn't go on the gig. Li Qishan: 'The main time is New Year, when anyone who finds a job and does business can be band boss and take an extra share of the fee.' Both before Communism and since the reforms, one fixer may provide several different bands. During rituals the players are also fed, and receive gifts like liquor and cigarettes.

---

[3]   Liu Yong 2006: 122–4. For north Shanxi, see Jones 2007: 38–40.

[4]   Cf. Liu Yong 2006: 127–8. For more detail, see Tian 2005: 169–74. For north Shanxi, see Wu Fan 2007: 305–8, and Jones 2007, index refs. under 'earnings'.

The upper player takes the most, then the lower player, then the three percussionists.[5] Zhang Hulin told us that at his teacher's drum shop (*sic*) soon after the end of the Cultural Revolution, the proportions were:

upper player	3 shares
lower player	2 shares
3 percussionists	1 share each
band boss	2 shares

He explained, 'Because all the *chuishou* usually lived in the drum shop, and weddings and funerals were all arranged through the band boss, he still got his two shares even if he didn't go on the job; if he did go, then he got an extra share. When there was no work, the band boss would send the *chuishou* out begging.' Wang Laiwa, *chuishou* in a poor village: 'When I started as lower player around 1980, I earnt 3 *mao* a day, the upper player got 4 *mao*. Later I played the upper part, with my apprentice playing the lower part. Later for the three-day job I got 9, 17, 30, 60 *yuan*, as prices gradually went up.'

Fees for weddings and funerals are calculated for the total period, usually three days, arriving on the first afternoon and returning on the third afternoon. Chang Wenzhou: 'Payment is still based on tradition: e.g. taking a total fee of 100 *yuan*, 10 *yuan* goes to each of the three percussionists, the rest is split in various ways like 'thirds' (*sanfenzhang*: equal shares for the two shawm players and the fixer) or 'two-and-a-half' (*liangfenban*: a full share for both shawm players, a half share for the fixer).'

Revealingly, Older Brother in poor Yangjiagou village used 10 *yuan*, not 100, to illustrate the total. Again, the three percussionists get 10% each, the lower shawm player 20%, the rest (50%) going to the upper shawm player, who usually supplies the instruments. In this band, since they often share duties on upper and lower shawm and percussion, that tends to even up their incomes. For a small-scale funeral we attended in 1999, the five-man band received 280 *kuai*, of which Older Brother, as fixer, got 120. Ma Zhongyi, not a player but an expert on ceremonial propriety, called the division '10ths' (*shifenzhang*): two for the fixer, two each for the two shawm players, one each for the three percussionists, and one for the supplier of the instruments.

As to the big band, band bosses, who have invested in the new instruments, retain a proportion of the total fee and then divide the remainder, as shown in Table 4. Such fees also depend partly on age and experience. Young apprentices are not yet entitled to a fee. If Li Qishan books a female singer, she gets 70–80 *yuan*, not considered as a formal member.

---

[5] Scholar Huo Xianggui was alone in telling me that traditionally the leading shawm player and drummer got the most, then the lower shawm player and other percussionists got the same. Indeed, I wonder why the role of drummer, surely much more important than that of the other percussion, is now so poorly paid.

Fees are higher in the peak (winter) season, when there are more weddings and funerals, than in the summer season; food, and corpses, go off more quickly in the summer, and people don't hold such grand ceremonies. Yuanr told us in 2001 that for funerals his big band charged 1,200 *yuan* in winter, 1,000 *yuan* in summer; for weddings, 800 or 900 in winter, 500 or 600 in summer. Zhao Laixi's big band also charged over 1,000 *yuan* per event for the winter.

Shop openings are quite lucrative, being well paid for a short session, often in the home base or an accessible town. For the opening of a new mobile-phone shop in Mizhi town in 2001, the boss paid 400 *yuan* for *chuishou* to play for four hours; in Suide town, Wang Shifa's big band got 800 *yuan* for one three-hour session.

Despite the trend for the big band, below we see that the smaller, cheaper, band could still do business.

Table 4   Fee division of three big bands, 2001

(a) Li Qishan

band boss = upper player	40 shares
lower player	30 shares
small *suona*	20 shares
2 '*chuihao*' (trumpet, sax)	12 shares each, 'or 10 if they're not good!'
3 '*chuihao*' (plus trombone)	10 shares each
3 percussionists	10 shares each
retained by band boss	50 *yuan*

(b) Zhang Hulin (sample total 1,000 *yuan*)

upper player	250–300 *yuan*
lower player	120–130 *yuan*
trumpet, trombone etc.	100–120 *yuan* each
percussionists	50 – 70 *yuan* each
retained by band boss	?

(c) Yuanr

band boss	20 shares
lower player	13 shares
trumpet, sax	11 shares
percussion, according to importance	10, 8, 5 shares
retained to buy and repair instruments	10 shares

10.5 Rivalry and violence

Chuishou throughout China are renowned for their rivalry. Two or more bands often perform at a funeral, giving rise not only to competitive standards, but sometimes to violence. Apart from sheer technical quality, the main traditional criteria for excellence are quantitative: how large a repertory a band has, how long they can play for, and how many scales they can play in. Older Brother: 'If you meet a new band, and they're not too friendly, then you can have a bit of a competition to see which pieces they know.' Even under Maoism, *chuishou* found ways to undo their rivals. Zhao Suotong recalled, 'Once in a folk instrumental festival organized by the government, Du Chengzhang played percussion for all the bands, and deliberately put them off with his drumming, helping Chang Mao and my father win the prizes.'

Economic competition is even fiercer since the reforms. For more opulent funerals two or more bands are again invited, giving them a chance to compete directly. In about 1995 Chang Wenzhou and Li Qishan were among five bands invited for a big funeral near Zhenchuan for the parent of a local entrepreneur. He spent 50,000 *yuan* and hired an airplane; food, liquor, and cigarettes were all high class. The most lavish funeral Chouxiao has seen was in another village in the mid-1990s, when there were eight bands of *chuishou*.

Chang Wenzhou has been struggling to maintain his reputation. Zhao Suotong told us wryly: '20 days ago, Chang Wenzhou's band was doing a job in Guanzhuang village, and was going to run up against Zhang Hulin's band there. Chang Wenzhou thought this was a good chance to put Zhang's band down (*yaxiaqu*), so he went to Suide to invite the famous *chuishou* Liu Jun to join his band. Though they made a formidable combination, Zhang's band wasn't doing badly either, and after a time they were still level-pegging. Chang Wenzhou couldn't claim the upper hand, but Liu Jun, because of his reputation, wanted a lot of money from Chang Wenzhou, who couldn't satisfy his demands, so they parted on bad terms.'

This story shows how Chang realizes the need to offer something new to outdo his rivals; at the same time he is vulnerable. Unlike Li Qishan's claim to modesty, Chang Wenzhou is too senior or confident to feign generosity. Though his music can move with the times, his mentality remains largely traditional, inflexible; his financial toughness and lack of subtlety leave his relationships unsentimental and fragile.

Beyond rivalry, violence is associated with many musical traditions in the world, partly when they spring from a violent underworld, like jazz, tango, rebetika, gangsta rap, and so on. Violence may be peripheral to the music itself, as when performers and patrons are anyway involved in violence and use music as an outlet. The jazz world was violent, but 'cutting' contests were usually gentlemanly. Another situation is where the music encourages violence – either through the lyrics or ethos, or, as here, through rivalry. In China, a society where violence is routine and pervasive – from both imperial and modern regimes down to family and personal relationships[6] – rivalry may lead to insults, blows, or worse.

Li Qishan pointed out that taking turns to play makes a more 'fiery' atmosphere (*honghuo, re'nao*). 'But there are often conflicts – once, two bands couldn't agree (*tanbulai*) so while they were competing they started fighting.' One enterprising young band leader put it frankly. 'People in the same business are enemies (*yuanjia*). A host often invites two bands, playing alternately. If we play well, the other band comes over to start a fight (*qihong*). After I started my own band, my old boss made a fuss; at the temple fair, just as we got to the best bit, he turned up and played chaotically.' It got worse. In 2000 he was beaten up by a gang of thugs hired by his rivals. They broke two of his fingers, slashed his eyebrow, and he had to spend over a month in hospital. The culprits did a deal with the police and were not punished.

10.6 Changing learning processes

If oral-aural transmission remains dominant, other methods now serve subsidiary functions. The use of *gongche* written notation, or in the form of oral mnemonics, is standard for the *sheng-guan* music of ritual specialists, but was probably never common among shawm bands throughout China, and was rare by the 1950s.[7] In Shaanbei, local scholars have found no *gongche* scores for shawm melodies, and even elderly *chuishou* hardly heard their masters sing *gongche* mnemonics.

Few *chuishou* seem to have learnt the modern system of cipher notation (aptly called 'simplified notation' *jianpu*) at school, but several young *chuishou* picked it up later while in the army, and some in training classes organized by the county Hall of Culture. Chang Wenzhou learnt it while in the Yulin troupe but writes it with difficulty. Young *chuishou* read it with difficulty too, but sometimes use it to learn pop pieces more quickly. They listen to TV, and if they hear a good theme, they may write it down; sometimes they buy a published song book. Gao Wanfei's book (2000) of cipher-notation transcriptions of traditional repertory may have an influence: the pieces are now easily available, if *chuishou* can read them and then translate them into their idiom, and indeed if they are required to play them – three big ifs.

As to cassettes, He Zengtong said, 'When my son Siwa learnt – also with my master Chang Wenzhang – he used a tape recorder to record other players,

---

[6]   One might cite imperial and modern government punishment systems, and the birth control policy; domestic violence is endemic, and apprentices were commonly beaten in opera troupes and temples. See e.g. Lipman and Harrell 1990; Perry 1985; many reports from Amnesty International; Jing 1996; Liu Xin 2000: 122–5, 143–50; Pickowicz and Wang 2002; for shawm bands in Shanxi, see index refs. to 'violence' in Jones 2007. For a thorough list, see http://website.leidenuniv.nl/~haarbjter/violence.htm.

[7]   For *gongche*, see Jones 1998: 111–26. For its regional use among *chuishou*, see Liu Yong 2006: 62–7, Jones 1998: 172, Jones 2007: 92–4.

it was much easier than when we learnt.' But I haven't heard other players say this. Though several players have, or have heard, the few commercial cassettes available (see §9.4 above), their influence seems small.

As to my own learning process, my visits have been all too brief: though I have recordings, they cannot replace daily live practical exposure. I had heard tapes of Shaanbei shawm music since the early 1990s, but had my first 'lesson' on shawm with Chang Wenzhou on my first visit to Shaanbei in 1999. While staying with Older Brother at Yangjiagou I learnt a bit more with him, and Chouxiao also taught me quite formally, apparently conscious of my different needs from those of local recruits. With no ulterior motive, he also hoped I would start a 'suona association' in London, a concept which then held little appeal for me.

I took a pair of Chang Wenzhou's shawms home to London, but did little practice, and I was still a virtual beginner when I returned in 2001. Again I was preoccupied with interviewing players about their music-making in society, and though I went round with shawm bands hearing them perform ceremonies, I did virtually no playing until my final week, when I was alone in Yulin city without my trusty fieldwork companions, and thought that taking 'lessons' might be the most profitable way of using my time. Feng Xiaoping (§12.1 below), who my colleagues thought might be a promising teacher for me, turned out to be so. Having met many elderly chuishou, *I realized that if I was to undertake a short training period I might compromise and seek a teacher with whom I had some hope of communication. Xiaoping's* chuishou *father was also on hand, but now plays poorly and posed an even greater challenge to my limited communication skills. Xiaoping plays in a traditional style, but is young and adaptable, having spent some time at the Yulin School of Arts. He is aware that trying to teach a foreigner, one not in the first flush of youth to boot, is a special case. That week of daily sessions with him taught me enough to get a handle on the music to be able to imagine how to progress.*

This time Chouxiao helped me buy a whole set of instruments to take back to SOAS, and my friends there were happy to form a band. We met every week, I copied recordings for them, and we memorized simple versions of a few short suites, mainly from notation prepared by me. We even went on to play for a few conferences. Later we also began trying out the still more complex pieces from north Shanxi (Jones 2007). When we have time to meet regularly we make progress. For now I think we should settle for those two styles, rather than trying to master a smattering of regional styles like they teach in the conservatories. Local players learn by osmosis, by playing percussion as part of a band with at least some experienced members, for years before they take up the shawm. But we are all beginners, and our learning process is condensed into listening to recordings and studying scores, which to date has proved far inferior. Trying to run before we could walk, we were crawling along, but I still value the experience as a handle on understanding the music, and the challenge is a lot of fun.

10.7 Keeping up, dropping out

Several responses to the new big band style were in evidence by 2001. We have seen some bands taking it on readily, mainly in the towns but also in the villages. But since the style was still only a few years old, we met several senior *chuishou* who felt unable or unwilling to follow fashion, and were effectively driven out of business. In some other parts of China this had already been happening several years earlier.[8]

Some older players didn't mind going into semi-retirement. Chang Wenjin: 'Now I'm old, and not in good health, but my life is pretty good. Being a *chuishou* is a lowly life, and I can't keep up with the times. Today someone's just come to ask me to go and do a job, but I'm not doing it. It's just these last two or three years that I haven't been going out on jobs. I was a *chuishou* from Liberation right through to the Cultural Revolution; when there was nothing to do I tilled the fields at home. Now I've bought this house [in Mizhi town], and I still have two courtyards with ten caves at our old home [village].'

In Sishilipu town, Cao Laiqian (b. *c*1943) wasn't so well-off, but didn't mind taking a back seat: 'Now I'm old, and I can't play pop songs, I haven't played shawm since 1997. Since brass instruments were added four or five years ago, the older *chuishou* haven't been able to keep up with the times. There are a lot of old standards that are good to listen to, and there are some pop songs that aren't, but now it's felt that pop songs are good to listen to. So now I mainly till the fields – occasionally people invite me with a small band, and then I can earn a bit extra, but I rely on agriculture now.'

Whether or not they played pop songs, older *chuishou* invariably expressed dismay at the replacement of the old repertory by the new pieces. He Zengtong: '*Laoguban* [the traditional repertory] is good to listen to, pop songs aren't good.' His son He Siwa complacently reckons the old pieces 'can't be lost' (*shichuanbuliao*); trendy and versatile Gao Jiu also claims they'll keep playing them. Musicians pay lip-service to the concept of preserving the old – now an official, if empty, mantra in Chinese culture. But I suspect they are giving us the answers they think we want to hear. Wang Shifa told me, 'I'm only teaching my apprentices the old pieces,' but he only *needs* to teach them the old pieces: they can pick up pop on their own.

Older non-musicians, too, said they disliked the new repertory, but felt obliged to go along with it. This is a constant theme. Surely, I think, at funerals if the elders don't agree, they could oppose it; they could choose, or specify style, as they do in some areas – but they feel obliged to go along with this new fashion, which is very compelling at the moment. Professional musicians are pragmatic. They have to make a living, like I do in England when I play Lloyd-Webber, or indeed Vivaldi. Whatever they may claim to us visiting scholars, *chuishou* have no scruples about bringing home the cash from their dates with the big band.

---

[8]   See again Jones 1998: 59–60.

We saw how poverty has long been the primary motive to take up the *chuishou* life, but as with professional musicians in many parts of the world, while musical dedication may not be immediately apparent, on closer acquaintance many *chuishou* have a real commitment; several said they began learning the music because they liked it from young. Among *chuishou* I know, Chang Wenzhou may be tough, but he believes passionately in the 'old rules', as we see below; his pupil Gao Jiu is a fine musician, and beneath his glossy veneer he too has a commitment to his art. Chouxiao is a keen musician, and Feng Xiaoping is committed; Wang Laiwa (on whom more shortly) was so excited by learning that he forgot to eat while he was learning, later giving up out of disillusionment with the superficial new style.

Chang Wenzhou's abrasive demeanour can be endearing. After a brash young new band boss leaves, he confides shrewdly: 'He's not a *chuishou*! If it's playing the trumpet you want, there are loads of 'em in Beijing who can play it well, no-one's gonna traipse all the way out here to interview us! This large shawm, only Shaanbei has it, nowhere else in the whole country has got it! If it's the small *suona* you're after, Ren Tongxiang [a famous Shandong player] plays it better than us, he's famous as a *chuishou* all over the country – but can he play this local [large] *suona*?! The common folk see this drum-kit and think it's a big deal, one guy playing all those different drums. But actually that's all there is to it – once you get used to it, it's just a fucking drum!'

But again, if Chang Wenzhou recognizes that traditional ways have been overthrown since the 1990s, he feels no mission to fight it: 'People like to listen to pop music, the old pieces are hard to understand, you can understand pieces like *Meimei zuo chuantou* ('Little sister sitting in the boat') or *Haohan ge* ('Song of the good fellow') as soon as you hear them, they like that.' We saw that Chang Wenzhou couldn't get along in the state troupe, unable to learn new pieces. But he can play any number of new pieces now, picking them up by ear, so it may be more a question of taste and incentive. While in the troupe he was on a fixed and small salary, and saw no reason to take the new pieces on board. Since the 1990s he has firm commercial incentives to learn pop music, and though the style in which he plays is partly dictated by the media, as band boss he has much more control over the repertory.

10.8 Not following fashion

Still, at least by 2001, there were still some *chuishou* doing good enough business without taking on the new style. Liu Deyi, a senior *chuishou* in Suide town (§7.2 above), commented, 'My band doesn't use Western brass instruments, but we get loads of invitations. I'll tell you why: one, people our age aren't interested in those instruments; two, our band only charges 200 or 300 *yuan*, whereas a band with trumpet can charge over 1,000, so people who are a bit better off can book a band with trumpet, people who are less well off can invite us. Tomorrow we're going to do a small temple fair for 100–150 *yuan*; the day after that we're going to play for three days at the big temple fair at Majiawa, for about 400 *yuan*.'

So less ambitious, less trendy small bands are cheaper to hire. On one hand, Shaanbei remains poor, so the small band should still be in demand; on the other hand, rituals are a time for ostentation, and the big band is becoming prestigious. It's not exactly that the members of the big band earn much more individually; rather, gigs for the small band are fewer and less promising. The big band is often employed in the towns, but it is also encroaching on the work of the traditional bands in the villages.

If the traditional style seemed to be holding its own, meetings with some other *chuishou* suggested a less positive picture – it wasn't just older *chuishou* who were giving up. In a decrepit cement factory on a dusty road near Yuhe town we tracked down the sincere former *chuishou* Wang Laiwa (b. *c*1965), from a nearby village. He spoke intensely, happy to share his disillusion with us.

'Look here, I've got seven brothers and sisters. My parents are honest folk, we were a poor family – we spent some time begging. I learnt shawm from the age of 15 [*c*1979] with a *chuishou* in my village called Zhang Deyi, then 60. I loved it – as soon as I heard the shawm I couldn't get any food down, and I used to get up at the fifth watch to practise. There were no fees, I just brought him a few eggs, little gifts, and sometimes he ate at our house. The first pieces I learnt were *Nao tiancao* (for weddings), then *Yijuban*. I could learn two or three standards (*qupai*) every day. My teacher was good to me, later he gave me his shawms – I paid him a bit for them. Business was mainly in the winter, in the summer we tilled the fields or left the village to work.'

But he went on sadly, 'Now people with money hire a brass band – the last five or six years it's become fashionable to play the trumpet, drum-kit, and sax. We feel inferior (*zibei*), so I gave up last year, and our village band stopped. I tell you, I'd been playing for 21 years. Originally everyone respected *chuishou*, but now they've got this Western trumpet, they look down on us. Myself, I never change.' Though many village *chuishou* have difficulty in investing in the new instruments, that wasn't the point for Wang Laiwa. 'It's not that we can't take out our money to buy new instruments, they just don't belong together (*peitao*)' – again, contrast Gao Zhiqiang's appreciation of the new combination (§9.5).

This suggests a rather more complex picture from that which we have gleaned so far. *Chuishou* are always thought to have been despised before, and I thought they had more prestige now, mainly from money and following fashion, but Wang seems to be pointing out a deeper morality. Though young, he was nostalgic for the old days, long before his time: 'The *chuishou* in Yuhe used to be famous. Funeral host households used to give them pearls and agate.'

Another reason why Wang gave up reveals his attachment to the music. 'I didn't take my shawm with me when I went off to work, I was afraid someone would break my reeds. I had one great reed that I used for over ten years, you could play it for several hours and it wouldn't go off. But one day I fell over and broke it – that's another reason I gave up.'

But Wang was philosophical. 'I tell you, I don't feel sad to give up. Working as a cement plate maker I get 30 *yuan* a day. Now when I'm not too tired, I still play a bit for my own pleasure.' Our brief chat with Wang Laiwa made a deep impression on us.

If some *chuishou* survived without adapting, or just gave up, others made subtle modifications. At a big funeral in a suburb of Suide town in 2001 we met a group of young *chuishou*, based in Zizhou but mainly active around Suide, led by Liu Xiong (36). His master was An the Fifth, also from Zizhou, now living in Qingjian. They described themselves to us as a traditional band, without Western brass: 'We stress tradition, and I'm dead against the way people like Chang Wenzhou add trumpet. We don't even play pop songs much. For funerals, and weddings too, you have to play the right traditional pieces, that's the only way. If you play pop songs then it's just a mish-mash (*bulunbulei*).' Again, I'm not sure how much of this was an attempt to impress us – moreover, his brother Liu Jun had recently fallen out with Chang Wenzhou (§10.5 above).

But this is not exactly a traditional Shaanbei five-man band. Also added to the band are two musicians from Xuchang in Henan province, who play small *suona* and *sheng*. We hear the small *suona* player leading the *Yuju* Henan opera piece *Qin Xuemei diaoxiao*, with two *sheng*, small drum, and woodblock; it is very effective and mournful, if not local. This band has thus reinvented itself by adding elements from outside Shaanbei, if not yet by expanding into the big band. They too use amplification.

10.9 A village struggles

If the county-towns are the hub of modernity, poor villages like Yangjiagou may be more typical of the struggle to adapt. There the remaining village *chuishou* had revived along with traditional observances around 1979. Chang Bingyou (§6.7 above) was rather too old to be active, but his son Older Brother, having studied all too briefly before the Cultural Revolution, now took up the shawm again in earnest. 'I actually set up a drum shop, going to Qingjian for a couple of years, then Yanchuan for three years, from 1981 to 1986. You don't necessarily live there all the time, usually it's just for two or three months in the winter.' Note that he still used the old term 'drum shop', which seemed to be obsolete. Back in the village, Older Brother taught the shawm to Kang Shezhang, nephew of one of the Kang family *chuishou* before Liberation.

Older Brother, virtually blind since young, has never found a wife, and is fortunate that his family has done well, and to have such a sweet personality. His older sister went to live in the county-town with her husband, who worked for the Political Department of the local government. His younger brother Yinzhang had gained admission to the Xi'an Conservatory through the 'Workers, Peasants, and Soldiers Academy' in the Cultural Revolution, where he still works as a clerk. Older Brother shares his late father's cave-dwelling with his younger sister Runlin and her resourceful husband Ma Zhihui. Having the most comfortable conditions, and affable personalities, in the village, they have become a regular hostel for scholarly visitors from Beijing and abroad. Older Brother has acquired a certain amount of standard vocabulary through the many outside guests who have stayed, and has adapted his ears and dialect, but he remains an utterly authentic informant.

Most talented musician in the Yangjiagou band is Chouxiao (Chang Jinyuan, b. *c*1960). He is at least the fifth generation of *chuishou* in his family; his predecessors were all the sole successors (*danchuan*) of their fathers. This is an important criterion: hereditary transmission (*zuchuan*) is admired more than 'seeking a teacher to learn the art' (*toushi xueyi*), like Chang Bingyou. Of course, it is not the only criterion; after all, Feng Guanglin had learnt from scratch, and was a better player than Chouxiao's grandfather. Still, as Chouxiao pointed out, kids whose fathers played had the music all around them from infancy.

He was given the small name Chouxiao ('Ugly Small') in a common practice of giving children forbidding names in the hope that evil spirits will not single them out for punishment. Typically, few know his proper name – Older Brother doesn't even know his own sister's proper name. Chouxiao graduated from junior secondary. He began playing shawm when 13 or 14, around 1974: 'We still weren't allowed to play then, so I learnt in secret at home.' Chouxiao's younger brother, just known as Wu ('Fifth') also learnt, but now only plays percussion. An older brother is also musical, having played clarinet in an army band before retiring.

Chouxiao's family lives in quite poor conditions, even by Yangjiagou standards. He is a keen musician. In his bare cave-dwelling he even has a few published scores: folk instrumental pieces from Shandong, and a 1981 mimeographed collection of shawm pieces from Mizhi. When I mention the traditional *gongche* mnemonics, which he heard when young from his father, he is keen to recall them; incongruously, I write him a score, and give him a lesson. Like Older Brother, he inherited his family's instruments, but somehow gave his father's shawms to visiting bigshot Gao Maomao (§9.3). He has kept the two *hao* trumpets, which go back at least four generations. The other instruments were bought later.

Chouxiao has a son and a daughter, 10 and 5 in 1999. His son is keen to learn when he can get his fingers round the shawm, and Chouxiao is happy to teach him. 'Learning the trade is hard work, if you can "open the crack" then you can learn quickly, if not then you don't pick it up.' Though above we saw *chuishou* discouraging their sons from learning, I deduce that for a poor family in a poor village, any extra source of income is worth trying; and Chouxiao has a certain pride in the family tradition and the music itself.

They can split into two bands if needed. Chouxiao, partially-sighted bachelor Older Brother, Yunwenr (divorced), his nephew Yang Xiaobo, and Kang Shezhang can all play shawm, adding extra percussion if needed, including partially-sighted divorcee Ma Zhenyin (§7.3 above), who is a talented drummer, and Chouxiao's taciturn younger brother Wu. Xiaobo (b. *c*1968) is the youngest, but no other youngsters are interested, unless Chouxiao's son takes to it. Lacking both reputation and transport, the band is active only within a small area of Mizhi and nearby Suide counties; they still mainly serve the home village.

For the funeral of Chang Bingyou's wife in January 1997, apart from the band from the village itself, a band from Mizhi county-town was invited, costing 450 *yuan*. For Chang Bingyou's own funeral in 1998 (also a major event) the village players made up two bands, each band earning 300 *yuan*.

Having added some vocal-derived popular pieces under the commune system, the Yangjiagou *chuishou* now played mainly the traditional repertory. As one villager observed, 'the senior musicians couldn't forget the pieces they learnt when young'. Older Brother simply said, 'What else is there to play?' The New Year's *yangge* wasn't entirely a secular repertory of four-square folk-songs; it included some of the more complex standards. The main problem is just that so few Yangjiagou villagers have taken it up since the reforms of the 1980s. The band do play some pop pieces on the two large shawms, but in 1999 they said that they couldn't afford to buy trumpet, sax, and drum-kit, didn't think they could learn them, and anyway didn't much like them. By now they were not in much demand; when poorer people in the village do invite *chuishou*, it's still usually Chouxiao they go to, but people were increasingly preferring to invite a band from outside, as they need to show off by inviting a more trendy big band with pop music.

Though Chouxiao was pretty poor, I felt he played well enough to be able to make a better living for his family somehow, but he denied any ambitions to set his sights higher than the mediocre village band. So on our next visit to Mizhi in 2001, while sitting in Chang Wenzhou's busy house, I was amazed to see Chouxiao walk in. Chang Wenzhou (a very distant uncle of his) was now booking him occasionally for 'big band' gigs, in which he mainly played sax, doubling occasionally on large shawm (⊙**D3**).

Chouxiao had bought an old sax (1959 vintage) in 2000, and taught himself. I haven't got to the bottom of the story, but Chouxiao is a bit of a loner and had been having problems in the village, so he was driven to going to ask Chang Wenzhou for work. As Older Brother observed, 'Chang Wenzhou was short of musicians – he's got a funny temperament too!'

Chouxiao is a lovely man, and I wish him well on any instrument he can make a living on. Chang Wenzhou is no charitable employer, and at the Baijiayan funeral (§11.2 below), when he sometimes got Chouxiao to play second shawm to him, he glared fiercely at him whenever their versions of the melody varied. But at least Chouxiao was now getting some work with a famous band that was widely heard around the county, enlarging his contacts.

In fact there is another band in Yangjiagou which is doing better by following fashion. In Hougou, satellite hamlet of Yangjiagou, we met Ma Qiantang above. His sons' band is more flexible. The band leader now is the oldest son, known as Hu, 'Tiger' (b.1962); the third son (b.1968) also plays. The second son (b.1964) used to be a *chuishou* too, but has become a building contractor. Hu begin playing percussion in his father's band as soon as traditional culture began reviving after Mao's death, learning shawm in 1978 when 16. Ma Qiantang commented: 'The period from 1980 to 1990 was the smoothest for *chuishou* to do business. There was so much business that sometimes there weren't enough *chuishou* to go round. Now there's a bit less business – sometimes hosts don't even hire *chuishou* for weddings any more.'

He went on, 'Five years ago the bands all added trumpet. I'm getting old, so I let my oldest son Hu go out and be band boss. They've cultivated two young kids to play the trumpet, and often go out on business.' They seem to be doing better with the big band format than before – they claimed with no small exaggeration that they are now considered the best within a 40-*li* radius of the county-town, and Hu is proud that they have been over 80 *li* (40 kilometres) on business. A fellow villager later observed that musical accomplishment was beside the point, as Hu is shrewd, and knows how to put on a show.

Anyway, even in a village like Yangjiagou, the new pop style was beginning to have an influence, but we need to remind ourselves of the enduring conservatism, and poverty, of the countryside.

One afternoon, after a couple of weeks in the countryside unable to get in touch with my partner in London, I decide to try and find a phone from where I can make an international call. Yangjiagou still has no phone, certainly not one connected to the international network, so with my colleague Guo Yuhua we set off by foot down the hill towards the district town, almost an hour's walk. We find a phone in the post office and, miraculously, I get through. As I pay the sullen assistant, she makes out a receipt, asking what name she should fill in. I tell her not to bother, but as we come out onto the street, I take a look at the receipt: she has made it out to 'WOG' (laowai). *After returning to London I framed it.*

Chapter 11

Chuishou in action

I will conclude these comments on the Shaanbei *chuishou* with some fieldnote observations on their part in some ritual activities. Calendrical and life-cycle ceremonies remain the main performing contexts for *chuishou*: most items on the traditional list (§6.3 above) still apply, notwithstanding the fundamental social change represented by the pervasive authority of the Communist Party since the 1940s. The nature of these contexts may have changed subtly, but not radically.

For some ceremonies that have continued, the hiring of *chuishou* has become optional. For instance, Older Brother observed that in the last few years around Yangjiagou, *chuishou* are booked less often for the third anniversary of the death. Nor are they always hired for the completion of a new cave-dwelling; when one family held the ceremony in 1991 they played a tape of *chuishou*.

New contexts are few. Under Maoism, *chuishou* played for secular festivals and campaigns, in both towns and villages. Since the reforms, the cultural authorities have been holding occasional '*suona* contests'. In about 2000, *chuishou* were hired to play on parade through Mizhi town by an entrepreneur whose money had been embezzled, when the police returned from a successful campaign to catch the culprit. An equivalent context before Communism is quite conceivable. 'Performances' for cadres (not exactly new, going back to the 1930s) or for secular festivals remain a minor part of the scene. I was part of the reason for one, though. The canny manager of the Black Dragon temple (Chau 2005, 2006 ch.9) put on a show of 'Shaanbei folk culture' for visiting Japanese donors, and incidentally for me and two anthropologists from the Chinese Academy of Social Sciences. Yuanr's band, with *sheng*, two shawms including one doubling on small *suona*, three trumpets, sax, and *yangge* percussion (drum, small and large cymbals), accompanied local schoolchildren and teachers performing versions of *yangge* and 'boat on water' dances; there was also accompanied singing, with mikes.

Recently, with the economic boom along the main route along the plain, particularly with the 'Open up the West' campaign, shop openings have become frequent in the larger towns – presumably these were common in the republican period, and rare under Maoism. We saw several shop openings, all with the big band style. One was for a mobile-phone shop; I still hadn't got a mobile phone, but most of the town *chuishou* had.

One afternoon in 2001 we go to see Wang Shifa's band opening a new branch of the China Post Office in Suide town (⊙**D1**). He is using his big band, amplified, with small *suona*, two trumpets, trombone, euphonium, and drum-kit, mostly playing pop pieces, with some singing too. They play one traditional suite in *fandiao* scale – I suspect for my benefit. They sit outside the post office as traffic rumbles past noisily; quite a crowd gathers to hear them, spilling out onto the road. There are no speeches or formalities.

If traditional contexts are still dominant, what they do *within* those contexts is changing, as we see from the notes below. Still, I experienced the continuing power of the traditional contexts in Yulin city (see §12.1). Here *chuishou* don't play for weddings, but mainly for funerals, and there was some debate whether it was inauspicious for me to play with my teacher for a kind of 'graduation party' in a private house. The nice host, an official in the Yulin Folk Arts Troupe, and therefore rather modern in his thinking, felt no taboos, but there was a certain anxiety. Of course, *chuishou* often play in Yulin for shop openings, so it's not entirely connected with death, but perhaps inviting them to play at a private home suggests bereavement. But it seems acceptable for the big band to play at home – it is not tainted by the associations of the traditional wailing of the large shawms.

The notes below will also allow us to glimpse some of the other kinds of music-making and practitioners, including opera troupes, beggars, and geomancers, that I mentioned in Part One. I begin by contrasting two village funerals, one using the traditional five-man band, the other with the trendy big band.

These notes are both excessively detailed and not detailed enough. I seek to hint at the complexity of ritual, or just custom – even after simplification in modern times, and even in the absence of more exalted ritual specialists like lay Daoist priests – by showing the role of the *chuishou* in a complex set of prescribed behaviours. Yet I am acutely aware of the many aspects in which one would like to know much more, such as costume, food, kowtowing, and so on; one might also wish to focus on the work of the funeral manager or the geomancer. A detailed description of all the elements of even such a simple funeral as in this next section could occupy a book on its own, so this account can only give an impression.

11.1 A village funeral, 1999

In Yangjiagou on 27th–28th October 1999, with Guo Yuhua, a fine anthropologist from Beijing, I attended a simple funeral (⊙**B2–6**).[1] Though the deceased man had died at the fine old age of 88, the family was poor, and only held a 'minor ceremony' (*xiaoban*), hiring Older Brother's five-man band in the home village. As a courtesy we paid 20 *yuan* to bring gifts of funerary incense and paper, and I later sent the family copies of my video and photos, as one should.

The main officiants are a manager (*zongguan*), a recorder of gifts (*jizhang*), and a geomancer; by contrast with many other parts of northern China, groups of lay Buddhist or Daoist ritual specialists are absent. The geomancer has been consulted immediately after the death to choose the appropriate day for burial and the proper site for the grave; he later presides over the burial itself. The coffin rests under

---

[1]   For notes on another funeral in Yangjiagou, see Fukao, Iguchi, and Kurishara 2007: 95–6, 106–7, 119–28. For funerals, see also §1.6 above.

the soul tent (*lingpeng*), an awning constructed in the courtyard of the deceased's cave-dwelling; before it is an altar table. Relatives and friends come to kowtow and pay respects before it, the female relatives periodically performing ritual wailing. The relatives wear white costumes, shoes, and headdresses of white hemp; from the headdresses hang gauze veils (*zhexiubu*), used to cover their faces when wailing. They carry funerary sticks (*zhusanggun*) decorated with white paper.

In mid-morning a grandson of the deceased, carrying the deceased's spirit tablet (*paiwei*) stuck in a dough-offering on a tray, follows the *chuishou* to the hilltop grave of the deceased's wife for the 'Inviting the Soul' (*qingling*) ritual (⊙**B2**) – later, on return to the house, the geomancer will inscribe a new spirit tablet for the couple, enabling them to be symbolically buried together.[2] The *chuishou* play briefly as they leave the village, but the procession up the narrow hill track is then silent, and quite informal. On arrival at the grave, as the grandson burns paper before the spirit tablet, kneeling before the grave, the *chuishou* play a slow stark version of the melody *Xifeng zan* in the 'basic scale' *bendiao*, repeating it many times.

As firecrackers are set off and one of the shawm players plays exorcistic fanfares on the *hao* natural trumpet, the band, still playing *Xifeng zan*, then sets off back down the hill to the village, followed by the grandson with the spirit tablet. The *hao* is only played for such liminal moments, held to be dangerous or disturbing, 'banishing evil' (*chuxie*): for the start of a ritual (*qishi*), when the spirits are moving, for entering or leaving the house, crossing a bridge or river, during the burial, for burning the paper house, and so on.

Having descended the hill in silence, as they near the village the *chuishou* strike up with the melody *Xiao Kaimen* in *fandiao* scale in slow *manban* metre. As usual, the drum leads the way, followed by cymbals and gong, the two shawms behind. Female relatives, with their funeral sticks, await on the track, kowtowing towards the procession; as the procession arrives they stand up, start wailing, and follow the *chuishou* and the grandson back to the cave-dwelling (Illustration 14, p.178), while the *chuishou* break into *Jiangjun ling* in fast *liushui* tempo. More firecrackers are let off as they climb the path up to the house. When they reach the courtyard, the *chuishou* again play the slow version of *Xifeng zan*, as relatives kowtow while wailing before the soul tent, and the wife's soul tablet is reunited on the altar table with that of her husband. The *chuishou* squat unceremoniously in a semi-circle at their place to one side of the soul tent, in front of a decrepit out-house; on their low table is a bottle of spirits from which they swig when not playing.

The paper house (*zhihuo*), costing 200 *yuan*, is displayed in the courtyard near the coffin. It will be taken to the grave and burnt to accommodate the deceased in heaven. Though complete with a car and even a latrine, it is a simple affair compared with the opulent paper houses often made in south China.

After a rest, the *chuishou* play a suite in *bendiao* scale (⊙**B3**), going through the prescribed sequence of three metres, all with the appropriate *guogu* interludes, beginning as usual with *Da Kaimen*, concluding with a fast medley. We are

---

[2] Cf. Tian 2005: 96–7, 102–3, Zhang Zhentao 2002a: 63–4.

Illustration 14   *Chuishou* lead procession on return from grave of first deceased,
    Yangjiagou 1999

otherwise engaged at lunchtime, and omit to find out if the *chuishou* played during
the midday feast. From 4pm offerings begin again, while the *chuishou* play another
suite, again in *bendiao* (though *fandiao* is commonly prescribed for the afternoon).
As usual in this band, they take turns on the various instruments. By contrast with
the common boasts of *chuishou* about playing for several hours 'in one breath', the
longest they play continuously is around 30 minutes.

After supper, for the nocturnal 'Displaying the Road Lanterns' (*bai ludeng*,
⊙**B4**),[3] the *hao* trumpet is sounded and the *chuishou* strike up as they lead the
procession off. All proceed from the house along the road to the 'front bridge' at
the entrance to the village, led by two lantern bearers and the *chuishou*, followed
by a grandson carrying a paper gateway with the deceased's details inscribed, and
lastly the relatives, again with their funeral sticks, first male then female relatives.
As tradition prescribes, the *chuishou* play in the plaintive *jiadiao* scale, first the
slow *Da Kaimen* (strikingly different from the *bendiao* version) until the procession
arrives at the bridge, whereupon 'Road Offerings' (*luji*) are made. Firecrackers
are again let off and the relatives kneel on the road, still clutching their sticks,
while a paper memorial and incense are burnt before the paper gateway, and food
offerings are made to the deceased ancestors, all directed by the funeral manager.
Once the offerings are completed the relatives kowtow, the *hao* trumpet is sounded
again, the *chuishou* break into the fast *Jiangjun ling*, and the procession begins
to return, still slowly, towards the house, the female relatives now wailing all the

---

[3]   Cf. Chau 2006: 263 n.21; Fukao, Iguchi, and Kurishara 2007: 124–5.

way. While firecrackers are again let off, corn husks soaked in tar are set down at intervals of about a metre on both sides of the road back, and they are lit from the large lanterns, showing the deceased's spirit the way back.[4]

On arrival back at the soul tent, the *chuishou* finish their suite (which they have been playing continuously since the procession set off) as the descendants of the deceased kneel in rows before the coffin and paper 'money' is burnt. While the *chuishou* repeatedly play the slow version of *Xifeng zan*, still using *jiadiao* scale, friends come to kowtow before the coffin, the relatives still kneeling; lastly the female relatives, still wailing, kowtow and hand in their funeral sticks, which are placed on top of the coffin. They stop wailing as they finish kowtowing. The *hao* trumpet is sounded as the relatives prepare to seal the coffin with glued-on paper strips.

Next morning, the burial takes place, with Taking the Soul Out (*chuling*) and Settling the Earth God (*antushen*) rituals. Before dawn (☉**B5**), the eight coffin-bearers prepare the coffin with wooden poles and sturdy ropes. A live 'cockerel to lead the soul' (*yinhunji*, also called *tizuiji* 'cockerel to replace sins') is tied to the top of the coffin, to 'lead the way' (*yinlu*); the rest of the coffin is then covered in cloth. As the coffin is raised, the *hao* is sounded and firecrackers are set off. The oldest grandson leads the way, bearing the 'soul pennant' (*lingfan, hunfan*, a multi-coloured paper streamer with a white paper inscription with the deceased's details), followed by the *chuishou* playing *Da Kaimen* in *bendiao* scale, then the coffin, and the relatives with their sticks, the female relatives again wailing.

The procession stops to make Road Offerings on the road just below the house. The *chuishou*, still playing, stand to one side, along with the grandson bearing the soul pennant, while the coffin is set down on benches before an incense table placed in the road. The *chuishou* stop playing when the coffin is set down; the female relatives continue wailing. With the funeral manager officiating, the paper gateway is placed on the table and paper 'money' is burnt in a bowl before it. The *chuishou* strike up the *bendiao* version of *Xifeng zan* in *manban* metre as the coffin bearers and other helpers kowtow before the altar table and the coffin, the close male and female relatives (the former kneeling on both sides of the coffin, the latter further to one side) kowtowing in acknowledgement.

Then all in one breath the altar table is dismantled, the coffin bearers raise the coffin again, the oldest son picks up the bowl in which the paper 'money' has been burnt and smashes it on the road, denoting the end of the relationship with his parent in *this* world. The *chuishou* are silent while this important ritual action is performed, so the sound can be clearly heard,[5] but they then begin playing *Da Kaimen* again, and the coffin-bearers begin to race up the hill (spurring on the grandson with the pennant and the *chuishou* in front of them) – some say this haste

---

[4]   This seems to be the local explanation, rather than showing the ancestors the way back to share a final meal with the deceased, as for the similar ritual in north Shanxi (Jones 2007: 66–8).

[5]   Cf. Zhang Zhentao 2002a: 71–2. For smashing the bowl in north Shanxi funerals, see Jones 2007: 70–71.

is just to get a good start, some that it helps make a distance from relatives who may seek to lean on it in their distress, making it still heavier. The relatives and bearers of the paper artefacts lag far behind. The *chuishou* stop playing once they are well outside the village, only starting again (still *Da Kaimen*) as they near the hilltop grave, a considerable climb along steep and narrow mountain tracks, most arduous for the coffin-bearers.

On arrival at the grave, the *hao* trumpet is sounded again; the *chuishou* stop playing as the coffin is set down before the grave. The poles, and the cockerel, are removed from the coffin. The geomancer is now in charge. As he prepares the tomb (a complex procedure inside the underground chamber for the coffin), the *chuishou* and others (including me) huddle round a fire – the sun is only just coming up, and it is very cold. The soul pennant is stuck in the burial mound. The *chuishou* play a brief fast piece as the coffin is lowered into the deep rectangular hole leading to the tomb, again accompanied by *hao* and firecrackers. Once the coffin has been pushed end-on into the narrow tomb itself, the geomancer continues his rituals inside the tomb.

On ascending from the tomb, the geomancer waves the soul pennant and chants fast incantations as the tomb begins to be filled in, the *chuishou* playing another brief fast piece while the relatives kneel with their backs to the scene. Then, while the tomb continues to be filled in, the geomancer performs 'Settling the Earth God', walking over to a low altar before which the grandson kneels; here paper money is burnt, liquor is offered to the earth god, and the geomancer chants fast incantations while he rings a hand-bell. The soul pennant is stuck in the new burial mound over the grave. The paper house is set out before the grave, the geomancer checking its orientation with his *luopan* compass, and then this and the other paper artefacts are burnt, the *chuishou* briefly playing a version of *Shang nanpo* in *bendiao* scale. As the sun comes up, all set off unceremoniously back downhill to the village, looking forward to breakfast.

On return to the house, all eat *gao* cake (punning on *gaoxing*, 'happiness', or just *gao* 'exalted', suggesting advancement), while the *chuishou* play another suite in *bendiao* scale, always beginning with *Da Kaimen*; they never have anything like an 'audience'. The geomancer then does another 'Settling the Earth God' ritual (☉**B6**). First he chants incantations with the hand-bell before a table altar placed in the courtyard (the two placards now for the gods and the family). Then, still ringing his bell, he makes a swift exorcistic tour of the cave-rooms (to attack evil, *da e*) with four helpers, bearing water of the five elements (*wuxing*), a vegetable cleaver, a bow, and the five grains (*wugu*), and pasting a yellow paper talisman above each doorway.[6] He then issues more talismans to all.

---

6   Cf. Chau 2006: 263–4, n.22.

11.2 A village funeral, 2001

My 2001 trip to Shaanbei was in the company of Zhang Zhentao and Tian Yaonong, colleagues from the Music Research Institute in Beijing. On 18th–19th April 2001 we attended a funeral in Baijiayan village (☉**D4–6**), in the hills some distance from Mizhi county-town.[7] The deceased woman, surnamed Du, had died aged 95 on 13th April (19th of the 3rd moon).

We arrive on the second day of the funeral. The road is not among the worst in the area, but nonetheless quite difficult to negotiate. As this is a small village (over 40 households) with the same surname (Chang), and the deceased was a much-respected old woman, her funeral involves all the inhabitants; everyone brings a gift, and therefore gets to join in the feasts.

The deceased's husband had died of illness aged only 37, so she was left to bring up her children alone. Her behaviour in 'educating her children' (*jiaozi*, as extolled in local operas) is much admired; the children have all attended school in town, going on to university or becoming cadres; the sons-in-law are also cadres. Still living at home there are only two daughters-in-law, as their husbands are both dead. This is a big funeral, with everyone coming back. The family feels proud of hosting us; guests are welcome, the more the better. We offer them a token payment for our stay and food, but they refuse firmly; I promise them a copy of my video, though a local TV man is filming anyway; later I send them photos as well.

The village's usual 'general manager' (*zongguan*) for funerals, Chang Wengang (69), is away at the moment, so Chang Wenzhong (68), a nephew of the deceased, is standing in ably. He told us that after the death, one first consults the geomancer about the right day for the funeral, then the deceased is washed and clothed. The body is 'put down on the ground' (*hadi*), placed on a doorplank, and then into the coffin. The family went to the county-town the day before yesterday (the day before the first day of the funeral) to buy liquor, meat, vegetables, paper artefacts such as the paper house, and wreaths, and to finalize details with the *chuishou*. The paper artefacts must be given by the female offspring.

Chang Wenzhou's big band has been hired. The village itself has no *chuishou*, but more importantly, the sons of the deceased have done well finding urban state jobs, and a rather lavish funeral is in order; Chang Wenzhou is from the same *wen* generation (like many) as the senior Changs in the village – *chuishou* are often invited through some family connection. So the host family sees fit to invite his big band all the way from Mizhi county-town, impressing people with his celebrity and fashionable pop music. The sons' official status, however, does not preclude the inviting of the geomancer, or the staging of religious rituals.

Before the day, Chang Wenzhou's house in the county-town is busy. Trunks with the heavy instruments (drum-kit, sound system, and so on) are prepared for the funeral family to take by tractor to the village. Though Chang Wenzhou is doing fewer jobs these days as he is in poor health, he makes an effort to turn up

---

[7]   Zhang Zhentao 2002a: 82–99; Tian 2005: 101–6.

for this funeral in person. But he has invited his star young apprentice Gao Jiu to share the burden, and does not go on procession, only playing in the open space before the family cave-dwelling.

Peasants here mainly rely on the grain harvest. Though they have planted quite a lot of trees recently, the quality of fruit is poor, it is hard to sell, and they can't transport it easily. Until 2000 the nearest water source was a donkey-ride 4 *li* away; only then did the villagers pool over 10,000 *yuan* to sink seven wells, water from three of which is drinkable. The land nearest the wells is just about irrigable, but basically they still 'rely on heaven to eat'. Du's house is right at the top of the village, with a great view but useless for fetching water. Du, as a widow, was incapable of getting to move further downhill. Her house has three caves, a fourth used for storage.

Before we arrived on the first day, the soul tent was constructed at the east side of the caves, facing west, and the coffin (costing 1,250 *yuan*) placed in it. Five tables, each seating about eight people, were set up underneath a tent-awning for the feasts. At 11am, they took Du's husband's soul tablet back from the ancestral graves, with *chuishou* and family attending, a ritual they call 'Dragging the Soul' (*che wangling*) here. After bearing the tablet back, it is placed in the soul tent, so that the couple can be worshipped together.

Chang Wenzhou's big band for this funeral has 11 musicians, including young star Gao Jiu, our friend Chouxiao on trial, a gaggle of young trumpet and sax players, and a shawm player called Zhao Maoxuan – I've heard some funky given names inspired by socialism, but Maoxuan ('Selected Works of Mao') was a new one on me. The band is allocated its own cave to sleep in. They perform in the open space in front of the family caves, overlooking the whole village and the valley (cover photo), sheltering from the sun under a tree; a thermos of hot water, bowls, and liquor are provided. They have set up their sound system, with a mike on a stand and speakers hung from trees. Their music will be perfectly audible throughout the whole village anyway, but amplification demonstrates modernity.

A paper notice is pasted on the outside wall of the cave-dwelling, with a list of helpers, their duties (as in Table 5) and their names.[8] Note another hint of aspiration to modernity there: rather than the traditional term 'looking after the drum music' (*kan guyue*), the list gives 'looking after the orchestra', *yuedui* being a modern urban term. Also displayed is a list of gifts (*lidan*). Most guests were listed as giving 5 *yuan*, though money offerings were few: most gifts were goods, converted into a currency value on the list, and often listed as 'large offerings' (*daxian*), meaning *mantou* dough shapes to display on the altar table before the coffin.

At 11.10am, for Receiving the Sacrificial Food (*ying jifan*), the *chuishou*, playing pop on small *suona*, two trumpets, sax, and large shawm, go to the kitchen (in a nearby cave) to lead one family member carrying a tray with eight dishes on

---

[8]   For similar lists, cf. Chau 2006: 130; Fukao, Iguchi, and Kurishara 2007: 95; and for a wedding, Tian 2005: 86.

Table 5   List of funeral helpers

Duty	Chinese term	numbers	explanation
organizer	*zongling* 总领	1	
recorder of gifts	*lizhang* 礼账	1	
'before the soul'	*lingqian* 灵前	1	attendant to look after the soul tent
grave diggers	*tugong* 土工	4	
meat cooks	*hunguo* 荤锅	3	
vegetable cooks	*suguo* 素锅	8	
'settling guests'	*an ke* 按客	1	arranging the seating at meals
'looking after guests'	*kan ke* 看客	4	checking the placing of dishes at table
waiters	*duanpan* 端盘	4	
fetching water	*danshui* 担水	2	
dishwashers	*xiwan* 洗碗	2	
looking after the orchestra	*kan yuedui* 看乐队	1	
cleaning the tables	*jingzhuo* 净桌	2	
looking after the geomancer	*kan pingshi* 看平事	1	

the *chuishou* stand to one side and perform even more ostentatiously, as the family prepares solemnly, oblivious to the extroversion of the band. The *chuishou* stop and return to their base, while the family members kneel, kowtow, and burn paper. Then, soon after, Visiting the Kitchen (*anchu*) is led by the *chuishou*: one family member goes to the area outside the kitchen, bringing cigarettes and liquor on a tray to thank them. The *chuishou* now play a brief and heatie *guogu* style piece with the traditional 'small-band' format; a trumpet plays a fanfare in imitation of the *hao*, though I cannot see that it is relevant here. The family member first gives a carton of cigarettes and a bottle of liquor to the cooks, and then another carton and bottle to Gao Jiu, head of the *chuishou*. Gao thanks him and the *chuishou* return to their base.

From midday to 12.30pm, the Receiving Offerings (*yingzhang*) procession parades all the way round the village. Children are called to carry 23 cloth offerings (including red and green quilts, blankets, and cloth) on bamboo poles; they are keen to do this. The *chuishou* play (in order of procession) drum, small and large cymbals, gong, one small *suona*, two large shawms, two trumpets, and sax (Illustration 12 above). Then there follow six large wreaths, the pennant (*fan*) borne by the grandson, the children with offerings, a grandson bearing a photo of the deceased, and lastly sons, grandsons, and female relatives.

Firecrackers are let off before the *chuishou* start playing. Throughout the procession firecrackers are let off regularly, to which even the *chuishou* give a wide berth. They play a series of pop pieces over and over, resting occasionally, and taking turns on different instruments. The tempo quickens as they near the home caves. First they stop and play in a circle while the procession collects itself. They then play on return to the courtyard, where the other villagers are assembled, while the family goes to the soul tent. This is the climax for the *chuishou*, now at their most virtuosic; this time they stand at their main base in the open space, not going as far as the soul tent. Again they stop playing before the relatives kneel and kowtow in front of the coffin as paper is burnt.

At 12.40pm a performing beggar shows up, to people's delight. His story is that the deceased woman was very kind, and had once given him 10 *yuan*, so he had come to repay the favour – though he is well aware that he will now earn still more. Villagers crowd round as he dons a funerary hat and veil, kowtowing before the coffin and performing melodic wails[9] with impressive theatricality. Whereas the family members wail in deadly earnest, the beggar's wailing is designed to amuse. Then he does his 'programme', which he announces: 'My second item is "At last we've found a good son-in-law" (*Renjian xundege hao nüxu*).' He uses popular devices like rhyming/punning on the numbers one to ten (such as *jiu* = nine and liquor). Between items he kowtows and wails extravagantly, still covering his face with the gauze veil, like the relatives. He goes on to perform *kuaishu* patter, 'little melodies' (*xiaodiao*), *yangge* song-and-dance pieces, and somersaults, for which the crowd has to make extra space. He takes out a yellow costume, head-dress, and two fans, as well as a small drum and hand-bell. The manager publicly gives him 15 *yuan* and two packs of cigarettes, asking him, 'Aren't the hosts good and generous?' He agrees, then says to the audience, 'Even if you've got money, it's hard to buy tunes before the coffin – I'm the Zhao Benshan of Mizhi' [Zhao is a famous sketch comedian seen on national TV]. The villagers laugh a lot, but do not applaud.

This beggar (50) comes from a village in Gaoliang district. He calls his work 'taking theatre from door to door' (*songmen xi*), for weddings, funerals, and New Year's greetings. He usually gets at least 10 *yuan* from the host; once he got 2,000 *yuan*, he claims. Once someone from Jingbian county, quite far west, invited him specially, paying his travel expenses. He never has to ask for money, people give it spontaneously by custom, and he gets fed too. He claims to earn ten or twenty thousand *yuan* per year – many times the income of a peasant.

Incidentally, we saw how both bards and *chuishou* had a close relationship with begging – bards having trained in skills that raised them somewhat above blind beggars, *chuishou* spending time begging when there was no work for them. This is a third case among performers. While urban beggars from the countryside

---

[9]   Otherwise in Shaanbei I have not heard of melodic wailing such as is common in some other parts of China, though AFS 619–20 gives a funeral lament from Fugu.

have been discussed, further study is needed of begging in rural China, such as teams of beggars migrating as entertainers under Maoism.[10]

For the feasts there are only five tables, so they need three sittings for all the guests. Lunch lasts nearly three hours, through which the *chuishou* (now led by band boss Chang Wenzhou) alternate traditional and pop pieces, mostly the latter. The *chuishou* eat last (as in the proverb 'marching before people, eating after them'), around 4.30pm. Around 5.30pm the *chuishou* play a pop session. The beggar joins in on gong, and my colleague Zhang Zhentao on drum, making a charmingly incongruous team. Chang Wenzhou plays pop songs, and is great on the small *suona*. At lunch only liquor has been provided to drink, I am bored with hot water, and the village has no general store to buy soft drinks, so I am very thirsty, but I now get to share the beer set aside for the *chuishou*. Gao Jiu sings pop and does *kaxi* opera mimicry, including the Hebei piece 'Date-picking' (*Dazao*). He also plays *sheng* with amplifying pipes. Between sets the young *chuishou* try to decipher the pop pieces they have been jotting down in cipher notation, but no-one can read or write it with any fluency. At 6pm the *chuishou* play for the simpler evening meal of noodles.

The 'Displaying the Road Lanterns' ceremony (8–9.30pm) makes an interesting contrast with that of the Yangjiagou funeral described above. Through the darkness of the mountain tracks, two large lanterns lead the way, needing refilling with oil every few minutes. First firecrackers are let off; periodically fireworks are also set off, lighting up the whole valley. The *chuishou* big band again follows the firecrackers, then a sedan with the soul tablet inside, then sons and other relatives, and other villagers. Eventually they reach an empty flat space where they make the 'Road Offerings'. The funeral manager puts offerings on a small table placed before the sedan; candles and incense are lit. The children of the deceased kowtow, pour liquor, and burn paper 'money', men first then women, the latter wailing as prescribed. The *chuishou* play a brief fast traditional piece in *bendiao* scale; the trumpets play a fanfare in imitation of the traditional *hao*.

Then on the road home, little lanterns are lit from the main lanterns, all along both sides of the road. The *chuishou* play pop again. At suitable places firecrackers and fireworks are let off, the procession stops, and the beggar, in costume, does acts including *yangge*, 'Boat on Water', and somersaults, but not singing – the *chuishou* accompany him. Villagers deliberately protract the procession, and are quite brusque with the beggar; the *chuishou* are ritually cajoled too, but they all have to put up with it. They stop four times for such acts, a long and tiring procession.

The *chuishou* only play pop music, in *fandiao* scale, not in the traditionally prescribed *jiadiao*. Again they repeat the same piece many times. The tempo begins quite slowly, gradually accelerating, but sometimes they revert to the slower tempo. One man carries a long wooden board with liquor and cigarettes to

---

[10] Cf. Fernandez-Sternbridge and Madsen 2002; Jones 2003: 329; Jones 2007: 60, 70.

give to the *chuishou* and guests, including us. The *chuishou* are busy, so they just take a swig and stick the cigarettes behind their ears.

On the return to the house, the *chuishou* go to their base, again playing exuberantly as the family goes to wail before the coffin. The funeral manager gets the male relatives to kowtow, burn paper and incense. The female relatives are wailing intensely, inconsolably, until the manager exhorts them 'Don't cry any more, life must go on!' Chang Wenzhou, who has stayed behind, now leads the traditional small band in the traditional *Da Kaimen* in *bendiao* scale. I'm not sure why: he may want to put his seal on the proceedings since he didn't go on procession, but why this piece in this scale – couldn't he choose a *jiadiao* piece to show his mastery of the 'old rules'?

Next morning, for the Burial Procession (*faling*), the *chuishou* begin playing at 6am while guests take a breakfast of auspicious *gao* cake, made by the oldest man in the village, 80 *sui* old, who always does this for funerals there. Either one or two meals are provided on the final day, depending on family circumstances. If there is to be only one meal (as in the simpler funeral above), then the burial procession is early, and the meal is given upon the return. If there are two meals, as today (the family is quite well-off), then breakfast is served first, and the burial procession sets off around 10am; lunch follows the geomancer's rituals back at the house, the whole ceremony ending around 4pm.

So after breakfast the *chuishou* lead the burial procession, with the grandson bearing the soul pennant, then wreaths, four men bearing the coffin, and finally the family. Road Offerings are made again soon after leaving the house. It is very windy, and the paper offerings are hard to control. The graveland, some distance from the village, has good *fengshui*; there are several stone steles. The grave is for husband and wife together. A 'long life lamp' (*changming deng*) is lit inside the tomb as the geomancer performs his rituals there. After clambering up from the tomb he offers to the earth god with the relatives, behind the grave. As the coffin is lowered into the grave, relatives shout to the *chuishou* to play. Then the geomancer waves the pennant to Summon the Soul (*zhaohun*), by the mound above the grave. As he throws a paper with the deceased's details into the grave, young men hasten to fill in the grave. The geomancer checks the positioning of the stele in relation to the grave with his *luopan* compass. Then the paper artefacts are burnt before the grave, and the clothes of the deceased are burnt to one side.

The *fusan* commemoration ritual should take place three days later, but as the family has all returned from outside, they are doing it immediately: they take a symbolic leave, then return to do the *fusan*.[11] On return to the house, the geomancer performs the Settling the Earth ritual (cf. §11.1 above), but we had to leave before this. The geomancer (66 *sui* old) comes from a nearby village. A senior secondary graduate, he is the seventh generation of geomancers in his family, and has inherited a volume of 'Holy incantations for settling the earth' (*Antu shenzhou*) with all the texts. He gets 80–100 *yuan* to do this kind of ritual, including calculating the 'eight

---

[11]   Cf. Chau 2006: 263 n.17.

trigrams' (*bagua*), deciding the right days for 'moving the earth' and for the ritual proper, and writing the various paper inscriptions. His grandfather and father could also cure illness, and did *fengshui* for new caves, as well as opening lockets, Crossing the Passes, and so on. They kept on practising until the Cultural Revolution, coming out in the open again afterwards. But this geomancer now depends mainly on tilling the fields, as he only gets about a dozen invitations a year.

* * *

Later, Chang Wenzhou reflects on how his young band has handled the funeral. He still has the 'old rules' of the *chuishou* at heart. He reproaches his apprentices that they sit in places where *chuishou* shouldn't sit, going into the rooms – as they're young and get bored, they tend to go inside and smoke and chat. 'You guys haven't got it sorted – you can't just go off and leave our places all empty. We have to arrive early and leave late. If the music isn't on cue, what's the host gonna think, eh?' It is important that the *chuishou* should be seen at their appointed place, not trying to mix with the guests; and it is important for them to play throughout the lengthy midday feast. Only Chang Wenzhou keeps playing, while the younger musos all find a chance to rest, smoke, sip tea, and so on.

As to the choice of repertory, 'For funerals you can't play love songs (*aiqing diao*), you should play bitter melodies (*suanku diao*). You can't play "Hold my little hand, give us a little kiss" (*Lashoushou, qinkoukou*, from the *xintianyou* folk-song genre) or "Little sister sitting in the boat" (*Meimei zuo chuantou*, from the pop song *Qianfude ai*). Today *chuishou* can only play *Zhangsheng xi Yingying* [a traditional but popular and flirtatious four-square piece], they've got a one-track mind!' Chang Wenzhou goes on: 'Now everything has become chaotic (*luanle*). Some hosts still request traditional repertory. The tradition (*lao guiju*) is that you can play some "small pieces" on the return from the burial, but even then you shouldn't play dirty (*huangse*) pieces. For funerals the old rule is that you should play *bendiao* scales in the morning, any other scales in the afternoon.'

Complaining of the fashion for merely seeking a 'red and fiery' (*honghuo*) atmosphere, he mentioned two suitably tragic and sentimental pop pieces he had chosen for the funeral. *Shishang zhiyou mama hao* ['Mummies are the only good people in the world'] is a children's song, popularized since the late 1980s in a Taiwanese TV series and a film. Its melodic structure and profile make it quite compatible with Shaanbei folk-song, but it is a far cry from the traditional shawm repertory: traditionally, not even instrumental versions of Shaanbei folk-song would feature in such a procession. Given that Liu Xin (2000: 142) notes the use of *Shishang zhiyou mama hao* at a 1992 funeral further south in Shaanxi· it may have attained a certain folk currency, even longevity by the fickle standards of pop music. Another piece Chang chose was *Xuerande fengcai* ['Blood-stained image'], a piece from 1987, describing a soldier's patriotic sacrifice – a major genre in Chinese pop. He was not to know that the song was used by Hong Kong star Anita

Mui to lament the crushing of the 1989 Tiananmen protests, later appearing on a youtube video.[12]

Yuanr has articulated a modified agenda for the big band in three-day funerals. On the first day, large shawms in the morning, then small *suona* and trumpet for the relatives' visits to the coffin, playing 'tragic music' (*aiyue*, brass band style); at lunch ('receiving guests'), use the whole set, including keyboard; for the third day, *Xia Jiangnan* and *Baichang* for the burial procession, with the traditional band. This is his own agenda, a new invention very loosely based on the old rules. Young bands are common now, alienated from the old rules, and even if old pieces aren't much needed, some senior players must be needed to maintain a vestige of etiquette. The funeral officiants aren't enough, if they are confronted by a load of musical hooligans. I deduce that even young musicians expecting to make a living mainly from the big-band style realize that some familiarity with the large shawm is desirable in order to play a few traditional processional pieces and satisfy an increasingly token demand in villages for the 'old rules', as we saw in Chang Wenzhou's comments.

11.3 A town wedding

On 26th–27th April 2001 we attended a wedding in Little Liujiagou in the suburbs of Suide town (⊙**D2**).[13] This is an entirely secular ritual: village weddings used to include 'Obeisance to Heaven and Earth' (*bai tiandi*) ritual, but this has long ceased in the towns. The civil formalities have been performed separately. Again the family has hired a local video man, but I offer to send them a copy of my video too. Wang Shifa's big band has been hired. At 5pm on 26th April they play seated in the groom's courtyard to entertain the family as they prepare.

At 7am next morning, the family and *chuishou* first drink auspicious *mitang* broth. Here there is a custom of either 'fetching' or 'awaiting' the bride (*yingqin* or *dengqin*); even if the groom does not go to fetch the bride, the procession (and the *chuishou*) must go. Today the groom is going to meet the bride. The long procession is simply called *guojie* 'passing through the streets', an ostentatious event. After the man responsible for releasing firecrackers, the big band leads the long procession, then two young men with dough offerings (in the customary form 'snake encoiling rabbit', *shepantu*, covered by red paper) on a tray, the groom, the senior male relatives, female relatives, and four cars plus a truck, decorated but as yet empty, for presents from the bride's family. One of each kind of relative comes, making a pair with the bride's family on return, called *laidan huishuang* 'arriving alone, returning in a pair'. Again, the trumpet plays C – G at liminal spaces like bridges, replacing the old *hao*, and firecrackers are set off. They play

---

[12]   Witzleben 1999: 250; http://www.youtube.com/watch?v=0NIJ9orgWks.

[13]   Cf. Tian 2005: 92–4; for weddings, see §6.3 above.

pop songs like *Qianfu de ai* ('Love of the boatman'), *Hui niangjia* ('Returning to the maternal home') and *Gesheng yu weixiao* ('Songs and smiling')

On arrival at the bride's house, the *hao* is sounded and firecrackers set off. As the relatives enter the bride's parents' house, the *chuishou* take their seats around a low table in a corner of the small courtyard. Some beggars turn up to sing a few short auspicious songs, and are paid off with a few *kuai* each. After a while the *chuishou* play a suite in *bendiao* scale, opening with the slow *manban* version of *Xifeng zan*. Meanwhile the gifts from the bride's family are brought out and displayed in the courtyard.

Then the midday feast is served inside the house – there are not too many guests, mainly the close family. The *chuishou* don't even have to play for this feast, and are fed at their place in the courtyard. After the feast, while the *chuishou* play more pop pieces outside, the bride sits on the *kang* brick-bed and is 'surrounded by buns' (*wei bobo*) made by the bride's mother, in order to bring many sons and happiness. More beggars arrive to sing short songs for a small reward, accompanying themselves on clappers or small cymbals.

At 2pm the gifts are loaded onto a truck, the trumpet plays a fanfare, and the procession sets off back to the groom's house with the bride and her family. The big band, playing pop, leads the way, followed by the groom and bride, guests of the groom, guests of the bride, then a flotilla of four cars, still empty (just for show), and the truck with the gifts. Firecrackers are again set off periodically.

On arrival back at the groom's home (Illustration 15), deafening firecrackers are set off outside the house, and as the procession enters the house the *chuishou* play the traditional *Dabaidui* in *fandiao* scale, still stipulated for this context. Then they play pop pieces as people mill around. The couple enters the marital bedroom (*dongfang*) about 20 minutes later; the *chuishou* play *Dabaidui* again. The groom's mother now presides. She brings a bowl of water for the groom, then the bride, to wash their faces in. Then she makes them 'catch the four corners' (*zhua sijiao*): the bride and groom have to search for little things like nuts and candies, all around the *kang*. Then 'surrounding with buns' again – this time the bride transfers them from a bowl to a tray, and the groom can watch, which was taboo at the bride's house. Yet another queue of beggars arrives to sing in turn and be sent off with a small payment; some are paid off without even singing. The duties of the *chuishou* will finish when they lead the guests off to the hotel where the main reception is to be held.

11.4 A small temple fair

The town of Sishilipu, on the road from Suide to Mizhi, holds its main temple fair in the 4th moon, a 'small ceremony' (⊙**A1–3**). In 2001 we visit Wang Shifa at his spacious main home there – he also rents a decrepit flat in Suide county-town. The main event for this temple fair is a *Jinju* opera troupe from Linxian in Shanxi just

Illustration 15   Wang Shifa's band nears the groom's home, Suide suburb 2001.
Wang Shifa, between the two shawm players, is holding a small *suona*.

east across the Yellow River, performing on the modern opera stage facing the temple, in a flat space further down the hill.

The *chuishou* make a base on the balcony of the temple. About five or six times a day they may have to accompany processions of Offerings (*shanggong*) to the temple. When the faithful intend to bring offerings to the temple, they first report to the chief of the temple fair committee (*huizhang*), who then requests the *chuishou* to go down the hill to play to receive them on procession. On arrival in the temple courtyard, the committee chief comes out to receive the gifts, firecrackers are released, incense and yellow paper memorials are burnt, then the offerers kowtow before the god statues, silently reciting the vow being made or fulfilled. For the Offerings ceremony we observe, the offerers are none other than Wang Shifa's family, who have made large cloaks, worth 800 *yuan*, for each of the eight god statues. The *chuishou* lead the way, followed by Wang's mother carrying the cloaks folded beneath a tray of dough offerings. The god statues are then carefully clothed in their new cloaks. The whole process lasts around 20 minutes.

The Crossing the Passes ceremony was described above (§2.3); it is accompanied by the *chuishou* from the temple balcony. In the interval between sections of the opera, the committee head comes on stage briefly to thank the guest troupe, shaking hands with the troupe boss and giving them cigarettes and liquor (offering gifts, *songli*), during which the *chuishou* play a brief piece. The atmosphere is affable, but there is no applause.

11.5 The White Cloud Mountain

I now continue my account of the week-long 4th-moon fair at the White Cloud Mountain in Jiaxian county (cf. §1.6 and §5.8 above, ⊙**A4**) with some notes on the role of *chuishou* there. As ever, they are among several types of expressive cultural forms accompanying pilgrims to the temple fair.

We got some background on *chuishou* around the Jiaxian area from Wang Shengyuan (b. *c*1922), younger brother of the famous *chuishou* Wang Shengcai (Mao Chui, *c*1920–72).[14] Their father Wang Juchun and grandfather Wang Baocheng were also *chuishou*. He recalled that originally the Wang drum shop in Jiaxian town could send out four or five bands. They were said to be the official band (*guanchui*) for the county yamen in the Qing dynasty; other bands performing in the town had to give them a cut ('management fee', *guanlifei*). But with the depression of the commune system, none of the sons took up the shawm, and they sold the family instruments.

Wang Shengyuan went on, 'The temple fair originally booked three fixed bands of *chuishou*: our Wang family band from Jiaxian; the Shen family band from Shenjiagou in Taozhen district in Mizhi, led by Shen Wujin; and the Chai family band from Linxian in Shanxi. They all had to climb the mountain by the 2nd of the 4th moon. Now the *chuishou* from Jiaxian are the band from Majiayan in Shenquan district, but the Daoists don't recognize them, as only our band was acceptable, so the Majiayan band has to ask me to escort them – it's been like that for over ten years! Now I'm too old, though, I can't go with them.' We met the Majiayan band at the fair. We had heard they were perhaps the best band in Jiaxian county; Ma Shihao (b. *c*1940), the band boss, was known as 'top drummer in Jiaxian'. They recognize their junior status to the former Wang band.

Zhang Minggui (b.1931), the ineffably wonderful abbot of the White Cloud Mountain,[15] confirmed that it had been an old custom for several decades to invite these three bands of *chuishou*, as well as three sets (*tai*, groups) of opera. They are all booked and paid by the county government's 'temple fair management office',

---

[14]   Zhang Zhentao 2002a: 162–4. For *chuishou* in this area, note the tapes of Gao Haijun and Wang Xinxi listed in §9.3 above.

[15]   Yuan, Li, and Shen 1999: 40–41; Zhang Zhentao 2002a: 153–8.

which then had a stranglehold on the running of the temple. Other bands may also turn up, but the temple office doesn't pay them. *Chuishou* aren't allowed to play inside the temples, only in the courtyards. The three bands also come for the major *jiao* community ritual in the 1st moon, and for the fairs on the 3rd of the 3rd moon and the 9th of the 9th moon.

The Linxian band told us that for the duration of the temple fair they are fed by the temple and given 700 *yuan*. They have to play before the main hall of the temple to Receive the Offerings (*yinggong*) too. They have been coming here for 20 years. We saw the Jiaxian and Linxian bands playing alternately under a portico of a side temple of the Wulonggong temple. Both can do the big band format, but they don't bring it for the temple fair – the Linxian band was even using old-style 'chicken-leg' shawms. We also found the band from Mizhi, in the courtyard of the main hall before the opera stage.

Meanwhile Chang Wenzhou had also arrived, not to play but to sell his instruments. In the new, and very clean, cave of the Mizhi pilgrim association, Chang Wenzhou, with his wife and young apprentices, were preparing to put their instruments on sale the next day. They had brought their own provisions, cooking for themselves. He began coming here with his father when he was 6 (*c*1941); they couldn't come during the Cultural Revolution, but he has come again regularly since then. He reckons on selling about 1,000 *yuan* worth of instruments at the fair.

There was another stall selling *chuishou* instruments at the fair, run by Wu Jinping from a village in Linxian county. He is the third generation of makers in his family. He told us that the national TV station CCTV had interviewed them. 'We know Chang Wenzhou very well', he said succinctly. At his stall we observed silent haggling with secret sign language, the two parties tucking their hands inside the same jacket. The bargaining was more civilized than that of Chang Wenzhou just after, when both parties were furious – again, Chang Wenzhou wasn't concerned to make friends.

Conclusion: ritual and order

The life-cycle and calendrical rituals on which *chuishou* rely remained remarkably constant throughout the twentieth century, despite drastic limitations under the commune system. Recently shop openings have supplemented these contexts, but the main work for *chuishou* is still performing for funerals. Music is now seen to reflect change in a society widely perceived as 'without order' (*mei guiju*) and 'chaotic' (*luan*). Chinese villagers, like their government, fear chaos: their traditional shawm bands create a 'red and fiery' (*honghuo*) atmosphere, but should not be 'chaotic'.

Indeed in ritual, sound – like food and costume – is a bastion of order. Though Chau does well to stress the less 'structured' social aspects of Shaanbei temple fairs, our work on temple fairs elsewhere in north China shows a rather dense ritual structure similar to that of funerals,[16] with ritual sequences complex and prescribed, notwithstanding their generally 'red and fiery' atmosphere. Particular rituals are performed in a strict sequence over the whole two- or three-day course of the event, with prescribed musical repertories – even if such sequences are known mainly by the performers, and even if the 'meaning' of the pairing of piece to ritual is rarely explicable.

Ritual sequences do seem rather less dense in Shaanbei than in some areas. Of course, the relative paucity of 'ritual specialists' in Shaanbei does not imply a lack of order: even seemingly simple sonic rituals such as wailing and releasing firecrackers have to be performed at prescribed moments, so 'structure' is always a concern. But even the traditional *chuishou* music is relatively context-light, in that while a few pieces are specific to a particular section of a particular ritual (like the scale of *jiadiao* for the rituals on the evening before the burial, or the piece *Dabaidui* on return to the groom's house), many of the same pieces may be played for both weddings and funerals, and for different parts of those rituals.

But in detail too, the traditional *chuishou* music is not just a free-for-all 'red and fiery' noise. It is prescribed in so many respects (even if, again, its detailed 'meaning' may be hard to express): the matching of scales to the time of day, the *laosangu* sequence with all its metre changes, all the tunes in each category, even the percussion patterns within each metre and the heterophony of the two shawms, all have a prescribed complexity that consolidated over a long period. Even a seemingly negligible piece like *Xifeng zan*, a short melody with 23 gong-beats, repeated over and over with variation, whether in slow *manban* or medium *duoban* metre (§8.5 above), is complex and prescribed, with its syncopations and ambiguity in scale beguiling the ear, whether or not audiences pay attention to its subtleties (cf. Jones forthcoming, analysing a shawm repertory in north Shanxi).

So here music makes a specific instance of how the 'old rules' have been relaxed in recent years. With the decline of social order and the loss of community since the 1980s, the loosening of former prescriptions such as the sequences of the shawm band, and the rapid takeover by pop music since 1995, are widely seen as an index of a chaotic society – even if the choice comes from within the society. The study of the Maoist period may suggest a preparatory basis for this readiness to abandon the old rules. It now looks as if the early reform period (c1980–1995) was one when people sought to recreate as much as possible of the old rules, before reaching a point when they felt that some of these rules could be simplified or replaced. However, we have seen hints of new 'order' emerging among big-band bosses, in their attempts to match new instrumentation and repertory to the ritual sequence, and some parts of rituals still require the traditional format.

The outcast status of the *chuishou* before Communism gradually became less relevant under Maoism, as social classes were levelled and the occasions for

---

[16]   Chau 2006a: 166–8; cf. Jones 2007. Of course, the ritual sequences described by authors in the Wang and Tsao series, or in the works of Dean and Lagerwey (all cited in the Preface above), are still more dense.

which the *chuishou* were required were anyway severely limited. The transition from exchange based on mutual aid to more monetary reward took place mainly since the 1980s' reforms. Since then, the ability of some *chuishou* to earn good money has partly cancelled out their traditional lowly status, but even in Mizhi, old prejudices remain to some extent. Becoming a *chuishou* was and is only partly a hereditary choice, with a flexible pool of players driven to it by adversity.

In instrumentation, we noted the rapid decline in the subsidiary 'fine blowing' chamber format in the 1950s. Other changes took place only from the 1980s, first the addition of small *suona* and *sheng*, and then crucially since 1995 the use of the big-band pop style.

The old repertory has doubtless been impoverished: fewer of the traditional pieces are played in fewer scales, suites became shorter – in line with simpler rituals – while simpler vocal-derived pieces related to *yangge* became more common. Since 1995 the big band format has led to the rapid spread of pop pieces. But this very recent pop revolution should not blind us to the persistence of tradition until the 1990s, and its subtle long-term modification. And indeed, the study of pop music in China should take account not only of urban trends but also observe the tastes of the majority of the population in the countryside.

Predictably, from the towns such modern influences on *chuishou* may seem quite substantial, but in the surrounding countryside they still remained slight by 2001. The *chuishou* had taken part in the rural revolution, but they maintained and then revived in impoverished fashion the old contexts, values, instrumentation, and repertory. The difficulties of rural bands in following the new market trends are now driving them out of what little business they ever had, as economic power becomes concentrated in the more fashionable bands in the main towns.

PART FOUR
Urban music in Shaanbei

Chapter 12
Musics of Yulin city

The bustling county-towns, commercial hubs dotted around the barren landscape of Shaanbei, already represent a more modern environment than the chronically poor villages and little district townships remote from the main transport arteries. But entering Yulin, the capital city of the region, one feels frankly in a different world, even if traces of tradition remain.

Yulin city, a likely starting point for forays into the countryside, lies towards the far north of Shaanxi province. From the west and north the desert is creeping up year by year. Access was difficult until very recently. The main road going south towards Yan'an, and eventually the provincial capital Xi'an still further south, has been improved since the 1990s; it is also a 20-plus-hour bus ride east to Beijing. A train runs from Shenmu, not far northeast of Yulin, east to Datong in Shanxi province; by 2002 direct train routes all the way from Beijing to Yulin, and from Yulin south to Xi'an, were promised. By 2005 there was a direct flight from Beijing, 'Opening up the West' still further.

The city has something of the feel of the wild-west frontier. Main Street (*Dagai*) retains its old-world charm, though in the evenings bikers rev up at the crossroads. There are four funeral shops (*shouyi dian*) along Main Street alone. There are also several bookshops, none of any distinction, and many shops selling CDs and cassettes; even a Buddhist shop selling CDs and cassettes as well as statues, incense, scriptures, and so on. Second Street (*Ergai*) is a kind of Wangfujing or Oxford Street, with pop music blaring from the sound-systems of shops. Away from the centre, the urban sprawl contains both new tower-blocks and rows of single-storey dwellings in traditional cave format. Even the old city walls remain. Coal bricks are piled up in courtyards to protect against the winter cold.

By the 1990s Yulin city displayed an impoverishment of traditional musical activity. Yet weddings, funerals, and temple fairs are held here too, all requiring live music. Few of the Yulin city temples have been restored to their former opulence, but the large Wuliangdian temple holds temple fairs, inviting a *Jinju* Shanxi opera troupe. The Daixingsi temple has ten Buddhist monks, staging its main temple fair in the 6th moon; nearby, two nuns staff the Guanyinsi temple. Vocal liturgy is still performed in the temples, but *sheng-guan* instrumental ensemble, once a feature of Yulin funeral ritual, has not been heard since the monks were laicized in the 1950s.

The state-funded 'Yulin Region Arts-Work Troupe' and several other opera troupes perform *Qinqiang* opera, as usual mainly for temple fairs. Towards the secular end of the continuum, the Yulin Folk Arts Troupe performs conservatory-style arrangements of local singing and dancing (§12.3 below). A genial cadre in the troupe has a few young *erhu* pupils, to whom he teaches the standard modern national repertory. There is a 'School of Arts' (*Yixiao*), teaching national styles of singing and dancing. *Yangge* dance parades are held by work-units, including schools. But with pop music now dominating the soundscape, karaoke, TV, and VCD-players are doubtless city dwellers' main exposure to music.

In July 2006 the CHIME international conference on Chinese music was based in Yulin, hosted by the Yulin Bureau of Culture. With the assistance of Beijing scholars Qiao Jianzhong (a native of Yulin), Zhang Zhentao, and Xiao Mei, Chinese and foreign participants made forays into the countryside, encountering a range of musical genres. Apart from any resulting publications (for a website, see p.xxvi n.17 above; a published collection of fieldnotes, also in Chinese, is promised), this may further stimulate the local authorities' awareness of the benefits of commodified folk performance.

In this final section, far short of attempting a thorough overview of urban musical activity such as Finnegan's for Milton Keynes (1989), I focus on three contrasting genres. First I round off the theme of the *chuishou*, with their anomalous position in Yulin; there follow brief introductions to a recreational form of vocal music with ensemble, now moribund, and vignettes on the official state-supported Folk Arts Troupe.

12.1 Yulin shawm bands[1]

Before Liberation, funerals in Yulin, as in Beijing and other northern cities, were often accompanied not only by *chuishou*, but by temple priests (both Buddhist and Daoist) performing vocal liturgy, ritual percussion, and *sheng-guan* ensemble music. One elderly citizen observed that the availability of priests who played *sheng-guan* music was one reason why the city supported rather few bands of *chuishou* – unlike in the countryside; but I questioned such a claim above (§6.8). In the period after Liberation, Yulin city still had at least two *chuishou* bands, those of Zhu Xinmin and the Ma family; both disbanded with the 1964 Socialist Education campaign.[2] Since the 1980s' reforms there has been an expansion of *chuishou* activity in Yulin city; by 2001 there were at least eight bands. But this has not been matched by a revival of priestly activity at funerals, a major change in the

---

[1]   For detail on Yulin funerals and *chuishou*, see Qiao Jianzhong 2003 and Zhang Zhentao 2002a: 62–82, 100–102.

[2]   He, Li, and Fan 1959 (mainly transcriptions of *sheng-guan* music of the White Cloud Mountain Daoists) begins with some transcriptions of shawm pieces from Yulin city, played by shawm players Ma Liang, Zhu Anmin, and Zhu Xinmin, all pupils of the same hereditary tradition. Zhu Xinmin was at least the third generation of *chuishou* in his family, and claimed that his father Zhu Shunsheng had played for the Qing military garrison in Yulin; Xinmin's older brother Fuxiang was also a fine player.

city soundscape.[3] Indeed, whereas in other parts of north China, ritual specialists in the narrow sense, like lay Daoists, practise more freely in the countryside than in the towns, in Shaanbei they are rare altogether (cf. §1.7 above).

In Yulin, funerals are organized by an occupational 'fixer' (*lantou*); this involves not only the diverse duties of the funeral manager, but acting as fixer for the *chuishou*. Yan Xiangcheng (b. *c*1920) has been a fixer in Yulin since the 1930s. 'My father was a fixer too. Our family was poor, and we didn't go to school. There were a lot of merchants in Yulin, and most people went to Inner Mongolia to trade fur-skins, so kids didn't go to school, they just learnt how to do business.'

Yan still worked as funerary fixer under Maoism. He reflected, 'I liked the age of Mao Zedong, cadres weren't corrupt – but the common people's life was too poor! Under Mao Zedong when you had a funeral you couldn't invite guests – when you only got 25 *jin* of grain a month, who dared invite? People didn't dare wear mourning clothes either. In the Four Cleanups and Cultural Revolution, the government organized funerals – when the fixer earnt money he had to give it to the government, they gave him a salary. Most people went to the local government to find a fixer, they didn't dare go to one privately.'

Since the 1980s Yan has done well. 'Deng Xiaoping let everyone get on with their own thing, anyone could do what they were good at, the government doesn't interfere.' Pointing to a bottle of fine liquor on the table, he goes on, 'Could you drink this under Mao Zedong? In those days the best you could do was scoop up dregs in a bucket! The period since the reforms is the best of my life – I can eat rice and white flour, and often eat out.'

Yulin city customs have long differed from those in the countryside. Here *chuishou* play for funerals but not for weddings: 'inviting guests' (*qingke*) means specifically for a funeral feast. Funerals only last two days instead of the three days standard in the villages. But even here, funerals are far from the secular 'memorial meetings' prescribed by state ideology. Here too burial is observed, not cremation, and 'Road Offerings' are made (cf. §11.1 above), even for the funerals of local state cadres[4] a geomancer is employed, and offerings are made to the earth god.

'In Suide and Mizhi, *chuishou* observe the custom of escorting the coffin to the grave (*songfen*), but in Yulin they don't – just the same custom as the priests in the old days. In the villages the *chuishou* sound the *hao* trumpet too; as soon as the *chuishou* enter the village, people come to mourn – it sounds from a long way away, it's used to announce the death (*jinggao*). But in Yulin city we don't use the *hao*.'

In Yulin the route of the burial procession retains an interesting vestige of tradition. It goes from the old north gate along Great Street through the south gate; though Great Street has been eclipsed in commercial importance and modern

---

[3] Zhang Zhentao 2002a: 68–74 and Qiao Jianzhong 2003: 414–15 describe recent funerals for which Buddhist priests and nuns were invited, but this was mainly at the behest of the Beijing scholars.

[4] Zhang Zhentao 2002a: 63 and n.; Qiao Jianzhong 2003: 416.

grandeur by Second Street and then Third Street, the funeral cortège must pay respects along the older route.

Today the *chuishou* bands in Yulin city are all migrants from the countryside, mainly from Mizhi and Suide. As we saw above, *chuishou* from those counties traditionally migrate, often south (to counties like Yan'an or Yichuan) or west (to Zhidan or Dingbian); but this northern migration to Yulin has only occurred since the reforms. Yan Xiangcheng reiterated the class stigma: 'Yulin people don't want to be *chuishou* – only Suide and Mizhi people do. Yulin people look down on *chuishou* – they can't get a woman to marry, people call them *guizi*, *wangba*, the lowest of the low'.

The Feng lineage of *chuishou* in Yulin came from a village in Suide.[5] Feng Shenglu (b. *c*1938) learnt when 14 or 15 (*c*1951); his father Xiuzhen and grandfather Dianyu were also *chuishou*. Feng Shenglu's third son Xiaoping (32 in 2001, cf. §10.6 above) was the first of his sons to learn, in his early teens in the early 1980s, then Jianping, the second son (37). Huiping, the oldest son (39), learnt last as he went to school in Suide town – education tends to conflict with being a *chuishou*, and urgent economic needs usually win out. Even in the early 1980s, *chuishou* were sometimes paid in kind: Xiaoping recalls going home from a funeral shouldering a sheep.

In 1987 Feng Xiaoping passed an exam to enter the Yulin School of Arts. He studied there for half a year, learning cipher notation, but they decided he wasn't their kind of material; maybe this suggests his style was still too rural. He then formed a band, renting a two-unit cave-dwelling in Yulin city for 40 *yuan* a month. He and his wife have two children, and his father and brothers have also lived in the compound since 1992. They settled in Yulin mainly because there is more business here, he says; but surely also because there are too many bands around his old home of Suide, and it is still poor. Their caves in the city may be far from luxurious, but the family can lead a relatively comfortable lifestyle. Around 1995, as the big-band pop style was catching on, Xiaoping picked up Western trumpet. His family can split into two bands.

In Yulin (and elsewhere) richer families commonly invite two bands for funerals. Xiaoping claimed that there is little rivalry in Yulin now, as they all know each other. Perhaps there is no longer such a strict division between bands, with more freelancing. The Feng band gets around 200–500 *yuan* per day before the fixer's commission. But they have had problems with fixer Yan, who was tending not to book them – and he has a virtual monopoly on business in Yulin, most families going through him.

Apart from funerals, both in town and in the countryside, Xiaoping's band is busy doing shop openings. We go to see him playing for a *yangge* rehearsal in the enormous playground at a Teachers' Training School in the city, one of many

---

[5]   Zhang Zhentao 2002a: 105–6, Tian 2005: 161–2, differing somewhat in detail. The family came from Fengjiagou village in Tudicha district, not the same Fengjiagou as the home of the celebrated *chuishou* Feng Guanglin – note that their Feng surnames are different.

secular urban *yangge* groups. The *yangge* troupe of the first-year students there has invited Feng Xiaoping and another shawm player, the students themselves playing the percussion and dancing. The shawm players play modern pieces like '*Yangge* to support the army' (*Yongjun yangge*) and 'Marching into a new age' (*Zoujin xin shidai*). Feng Xiaoping negotiates the fee; for today's rehearsal the two shawm players get 60 *yuan* each, while for the coming performance Feng recommends a third player, as it's a big space to fill.

Another band, the Liu family *chuishou*, migrated to Yulin from a Mizhi village in the mid-1980s.[6] Liu Guangli (b. *c*1932) began learning shawm when 13 (*c*1944). His father was the first in the family to learn, from a *chuishou* called Ma. Liu Guangli's son Liu Zhenlin (b. *c*1952) now leads the band. Again, the family came to Yulin partly because there were too many *chuishou* for the population of Mizhi. But also their village was in a mountain gorge, and they couldn't rely on agriculture to eat: having to ride a donkey every morning to go and fetch water, it took all morning just to fetch two pails. Again, they didn't even earn money for doing rituals – people were poor and just fed them.

We saw the Liu band in action for a funeral in the city. Liu Zhenlin also acts as receiver of guests, making the ritual calls as they kowtow and burn paper – a duty I have not seen *chuishou* fulfilling elsewhere. Today they use two large shawms with one small *suona* as their basic line-up, sometimes substituting *sheng* or trumpet for one of the large shawms. They play both traditional and pop pieces; as we saw in Part Three, pop has not yet entirely replaced the traditional repertory, it is just an extra desideratum.

But their extrovert style seems to hide a lack of discipline. Feng Xiaoping observed, 'Yulin is without order (*mei guiju*). Yulin people can't appreciate the shawm – they don't react even when we play well, and if we play badly, no-one ridicules us.' We heard an example at a funeral: the Liu *chuishou* play in *fandiao* scale in the morning, which they know should only be played in the afternoon, but they find *bendiao* 'too tiring'. Both in Yulin and the countryside, in the new undiscriminating get-rich-quick climate, ceremonial ostentation is rampant, while the 'old rules' go into further decline.

12.2 The Yulin 'little pieces'

Throughout China, many rural genres have managed to outlive Maoism, thanks largely to the continuing demand for ceremonial; in the Shaanbei countryside, opera troupes, blind itinerant bards, shawm bands, folk-singers, and spirit mediums managed to weather political campaigns before reviving more openly in the 1980s for life-cycle and calendrical ceremonies. Even in Yulin city, there is demand for occupational *chuishou*.

---

[6]   Zhang Zhentao 2002a: 106–7.

The city also had a distinctive amateur vocal music with instrumental ensemble, known as *Yulin xiaoqu*, the 'little pieces' of Yulin. Like many genres in world music, it barely had a name; like many genres in China, if people needed to call it anything, they might mention 'little pieces' (*xiaoquzi*), 'playing little pieces' (*shua xiaoqu*), 'playing silk strings' (*shua sixian*), or 'playing instruments' (*shua yueqi*). The official title *Yulin xiaoqu* was casually given in 1958.[7]

As a relatively literate genre, its popularity was largely limited to the city – unlike small-scale vocal and instrumental groups like *errentai* or *daoqing*, performed widely throughout the countryside. We saw how the literate elite patronized the music of the lowly *chuishou*, employing them as a ritual duty. But the Yulin elite supported the 'little pieces' as an amateur taste, and might even perform. The elite outside Yulin city, though thin on the ground, sometimes performed it too; in Yangjiagou village, landlord stronghold until the 1940s, young members of landlord families sometimes got together to play string and wind instruments. But in Yulin city by the twentieth century, its main clientele was among ordinary citizens, and its main performers were male manual workers.

Such genres in China, largely performed by amateurs for entertainment, are commonly called 'silk-and-bamboo' (*sizhu*). Some are mainly for instrumental ensemble (as in Shanghai or Chaozhou); in others (as in Yulin, and the *nanyin* of southern Fujian) the ensemble mainly accompanies a solo singer, and genres may be classified under narrative-singing.[8] As in Yulin, they are often linked to a literate elite background, later becoming popular among ordinary people. These 'silk-and-bamboo' genres have survived well along the southeastern coast. In southern Fujian, *nanyin* continued to enjoy wide popularity, not just in the main urban centres like Quanzhou and Xiamen but throughout the surrounding countryside. For southeastern China, music scholars have focused on such genres, but my reading of the fine ethnographic reports from the area suggests that they are only a minor part of expressive culture there – with Daoists and mediums, opera troupes and puppeteers, shawm bands and percussion ensembles dominating the rich ritual culture of the area.

Anyway, in north China, amateur silk-and-bamboo genres seem to have become musical casualties of the revolution. In Yulin city after Liberation, folk activity maintained the 'little pieces' while official efforts were made to publicize and 'develop' the music. After the end of the Cultural Revolution, as folk activity failed to revive, official control distorted the traditional features of the music, and by the 1990s it was moribund.

---

[7]   See Yulin 1994, and Huo 2005; ANS 607–15, 758–9, exx. 616–757; AFS 421–2, 464–81; AI 858–9, 878–83, 899–905. A team from the Music Research Institute in Beijing made recordings in 1977 (Zhongguo 1994: 279–80; also 115–20). It is not to be confused with the *errentai* music of Fugu and Shenmu popularized by Ding Xicai, also casually named *Yulin xiaoqu* since 1953: Hu Jingfang 1954: 1. Cf. p.17 n.31 above.

[8]   For such genres, see relevant vols. of the *Anthology* for instrumental music and narrative-singing, as well as Jones 1998; for Shanghai, note Witzleben 1995.

The imperial and republican periods

As often with folk traditions, early evidence is inconclusive.[9] By the fifteenth century regional governors were often posted from the distant Jiangnan–Zhejiang region of east China, and brief passages from the 1670s show musical activity at the Yulin court. Indeed, from the presence of many southern titles in various Shaanxi narrative-singing repertories, and indeed throughout China, one should not underestimate the influence of Jiangnan culture in imperial times.[10] Among the themes of the Yulin songs (mainly love and city life), Jiangnan scenery also features; musically too, traces of Jiangnan style may be heard, although the dominance of the *so* mode appears to be a local modification. Another theory (also said to be supported by musical similarities) is that the style was based on the opera of distant Hunan, which may have been brought to Yulin in the Tongzhi reign-period (1862–74) by a company attached to a division of Zuo Zongtang's Hunan army on campaign in the region.

The music is said to have been transmitted outside the regional court in the Daoguang reign-period (1821–50) by Li Diankui and his son Li Fang. Oral tradition names musicians since the late nineteenth century. In the early twentieth century more pieces were composed, and pieces arranged by the literatus Wang Jishi. Later a carpenter and musician called Zhu Xiaoyi (1905–88) was a popular maker of *zheng* zithers, *yangqin* dulcimers, *sanxian* banjos, and *erhu* fiddles, selling them as far afield as Shanxi and Inner Mongolia.

Musicians were amateur, and male – mainly artisans (silverworkers, watchmakers, tanners, woodworkers, plasterers, cobblers), as well as doctors and dentists. Apart from getting together for fun, musicians were also invited for life-cycle ceremonies. In 2001 I met elderly musicians Luo Xinmin and Wang Qing, who recalled: 'In the 1940s we took part in weddings, longevity celebrations (for which the piece "Rejoice in a thousand autumns" [*Xi qianqiu*] was prescribed), and first-full-moon celebrations for babies. We played seated on the host's *kang* brick-bed – the *chuishou* played in the courtyard outside. We played mainly in the evenings, the *chuishou* mainly in the daytime.'

Some children of landlord families might play music similar to the little pieces, on *pipa* plucked lute or *erhu* bowed fiddle (as in Yangjiagou village), but in Yulin the landlords and merchants didn't maintain a regular band for the little pieces, though they might have a few instruments for people to play; they just invited musicians when they held a ceremonial.

Sources barely discuss the fortunes of the music during the troubled 1930s and 1940s, though it is said – compulsorily – to have suffered in the War against Japan and the civil war. But Luo and Wang recalled: 'The War of Liberation didn't affect us – people from the Red and White areas got along quite well, going back

---

[9]   This section is based on ANS 607–8; see also Chen 1994: 126–7.

[10]   Cf. ANS 19.

and forth.' A popular venue was run by one Wang Yunxiang at the Qingxing silver furnace, by the old Drum Tower.

After Liberation

Typically, the sources stress the avuncular concern of the Communist Party for the Yulin little pieces. Along with state organization came research and control – as an urban genre it was quite susceptible to official supervision.

Still, until the Cultural Revolution, folk activity continued alongside official initiatives. Memories of old musicians suggest that the 'new life' compulsorily claimed for all genres after Liberation was in this case not so fanciful: 'After Liberation there was even more activity than before. In the evenings, because there was no electricity, and no other entertainment, people liked to get together.'[11]

I chatted with the musicians about our common friend Qiao Jianzhong, a Yulin native who had become Director of the Music Research Institute in Beijing, and whose encouragement had led me to Shaanbei. The oldest of nine brothers brought up in an old house in Main Street, his parents were typical of the city folk who enjoyed the little pieces. 'Especially in summer evenings, a lot of people came to listen, they could understand the words – Qiao Jianzhong's mother used to say "This is much better than a film!" Mostly they invited us by treating us to tea and cakes (*chayebing*).'

'In the 1950s we were active in the common hall (*jiti tingtang*) by the Bell Tower in the city centre. The silverworkers' shop next door to the Qiao family's house in Main Street was a venue – there were instruments there available to play for anyone who came along. And there was an old Chinese doctor called Lin Maosen who loved to sing – he often invited people to his house to play in the [early] 1960s.' If such recreational activity remained common, the life-cycle celebrations at which they had also participated before Liberation were now drastically reduced.

As to the more official side, in 1950 a study group (*xuexiban*) was organized in the Yulin workers' club, and musicians met three evenings a week, training over 40 performers – now including women for the first time. The genre gained a wider profile as musicians took part in festivals and won awards at provincial and national level from 1953 to 1960.

The life of the music through this period, both official and amateur, depended on a group of admired senior musicians.[12] Zhang Yunting (1900–64), a leather worker, was a fine *sanxian* player as well as singer. From 1950 he was the main teacher for the study group in the Yulin workers' club. He won awards at festivals

---

[11] Quotes here are from our chat with senior musicians Luo Xinmin and Wang Qing in Yulin in April 2001. See also Qiao Jianzhong's introduction to Huo 2005, pp.1–6, in which he gives a somewhat more optimistic picture of the prospects for the genre.

[12] For notices and photos of these and other musicians, see Yulin 1994, and Huo 2005: 311–18.

in 1956, 1957, and 1960, and recorded for provincial radio. In 1962 fieldworkers from the Shaanxi volume of the folk-song *Anthology* visited him. Bai Baojin (1914–83) was a tileworker; a *zheng* player, he also played *jinghu* and *erhu* fiddles, as well as singing. He too took part in the festivals of the 1950s.

Hu Yingjie (b.1921 or 1923)[13] is an admired singer. A manual worker, he later worked for the post office. In the 1950s some young women were recruited to sing, but most gave up after they got married. Most celebrated was Wu Chunlan (b.1930), a senior-secondary graduate, who learnt with Zhang Yunting in the first group after Liberation. She took part in a 1956 festival, going on to win an award in a 1957 national exhibition festival. Two vocal styles have been identified, mainly distinguished by enunciation: the 'Back street' (*Houjie*) style of Zhang Yunting and Wen Ziyi (1911–68), later only represented by Wu Chunlan, and the 'Front street' (*Qianjie*) style of Lin Maosen (1903–68) and Hu Yingjie.

Through the Cultural Revolution both folk and official contexts were basically silenced. There were occasional sessions on the quiet; once in the early 1970s, a general from the Lanzhou military region came and insisted on hearing the 'little pieces', so the musicians were assembled at the Hall of Culture, the gate was locked, and they performed for him in secret.[14]

Since the reforms

After the end of the Cultural Revolution, official patronage resumed, but if folk activity revived, it was short-lived; by the 1980s there was no folk counterweight to official modernization. As early as 1976, a conference on the 'little pieces' was organized by the Yulin Hall of Arts for the Masses and the Hall of Culture. In 1977 a team from the Music Research Institute in Beijing came to record (n.7 above). In 1979 a group took part in the Yulin regional folk arts festival, they recorded for provincial radio, and in 1982 they performed in Beijing. The music was featured in TV documentaries such as 'Music of the Western Regions' (*Xibu zhi yue*) for Shaanxi TV and the CCTV 'Gazing at the Great Wall' (*Wang changcheng*); a Taiwanese TV station broadcasted a programme on the music. An arrangement of the piece *Fang fengzheng* became part of the touring repertory of the glossy Yulin Folk Arts Troupe.

In 1986 a 'small research group' was formed to document texts and study the history of the genre, resulting in a useful volume (Yulin 1994). A performing group was officially set up, organizing rehearsals twice a week and cultivating new performers – including ten female singers. Hu Yingjie, who had retired in 1980, was a leading member of the group, and even sat on the Yulin city political committee. By 2001 he was no longer active as a singer. Ironically, this period of revival, like that after Liberation, is hailed as another triumph for the Party's avuncular concern for folk music. However well-meaning these efforts, since the

---

[13]   The latter date is to Yulin 1994: 13.

[14]   Luo and Wang chat 2001, as in Li Hongyue 1995: 104.

1980s there has been virtually no folk activity, and the genre was now performed mainly for visiting dignitaries. Some senior instrumentalists remained, but they rarely got together as there were few singers in the old tradition – and younger people, now mesmerized by pop music, were reluctant to take part.

The arranged sound of the fewer and shorter pieces played by the official group was increasingly remote from that of the tradition. Though the repertory had long been expanding, it was largely under Communism that pieces were incorporated from other genres, even from outside Shaanbei. As the old vocal *dadiao* were rarely performed, and changes were made in instrumentation and technique, the genre was diluted. Luo and Wang found the troupe arrangements incongruous: 'The Folk Arts Troupe plays it, but the flavour is all wrong.'

In 2000, over 30 students from the composition department of the distant Wuhan Conservatory came for a study-trip. By 2006, the keen group of elderly amateurs in the research association for the Yulin little pieces told participants at the CHIME conference that they still met informally. Though playing occasionally for life-cycle rituals and temple fairs, they now did so to scrape funds together for the group, and had to meet the tastes of audiences for other less 'refined' vocal genres, further diluting the genre. They were gloomy for the future.[15]

The kiss of death

As with other official attempts to 'improve' traditional music in China, the change of context from regular amateur entertainment to sporadic cultural showcase on the concert platform naturally led to changes in style. Instruments, technique, and structure were all modified.

Through the 1950s, despite official involvement, instruments had stayed largely immune from modernization. The basic traditional instrumentation is *yangqin* dulcimer, *zheng* plucked zither, *pipa* and *sanxian* plucked lutes, and *jinghu* bowed fiddle; the singer beats time by striking a ceramic bowl with two chopsticks. Until the 1970s all the melodic instruments were small local versions; apart from the *yangqin*, the strings were made of silk.

The *yangqin* dulcimer was a small instrument with 14 metal strings, known as 'ten-note instrument' (*shiyin qin*) after its main ten pitches. The *pipa* lute had four *xiang* frets and 13 *pin* frets. Musicians only used three fingers to stop the strings, sounded by false nails of eagle's wing-bone. Wang Qing recalled a more simple playing style: his father Wang Ziying, a great *pipa* player, used few finger-rolls (*lunzhi*). The *sanxian* banjo was quite large, tuned to the pitches *so*, *la*, and *mi*, and played in only first position, the strings sounded one at a time. Again, Luo and Wang lamented that later the common *sanxian* used for northern drum-singing was adopted, and younger conservatory-trained players used a more virtuosic, 'less rhythmical' style.

---

[15]   See under the website www.anthromusic.com, as in p.xxvi n.17 above.

In the 1980s some provincial scholars became excited about reviving the Shaanxi (Qin) style of *zheng* zither; a 'Qin *zheng*' society was founded in Xi'an. The Yulin *zheng* was perhaps the most convincing candidate.[16] It is a small instrument with 14 silk strings. A 15th string made of ox tendon, tuned very low, was only used as an effect for the piece *Jiangjun ling* to imitate the sound of percussion, but later as the piece fell from the repertory they didn't put the string on any more. Luo and Wang recalled that they still used silk strings for the 1979 Shaanxi Radio recording, and in 1980 the *zheng* teacher Zhou Yanjia, on a visit from the Xi'an conservatory, encouraged them not to change, but in 1982 the decision was taken – by whom, one wonders? – to adopt a standard national conservatory *zheng* with 21 metal strings.

False nails, again traditionally of eagle's wing-bone, are used to pluck the *zheng* strings. Luo and Wang wistfully contrasted the traditional style with that of the recent official version: 'Their playing techniques are different from ours. Our *zheng* uses no "flowery fingerings" (*huazhi*) – originally the right-hand glissandos (*guluzi, guolengzi*) were very innocent (*danchun*).' Luo Xinmin showed us his old *zheng*, made before Liberation. It has *gongche* solfeggio names for the strings on the bridge. The older generation sung *gongche* but didn't write it down; Luo had learnt the modern system of cipher notation, but knew the *gongche* names, like the string tunings.

From the republican period, *erhu* fiddle and *yueqin* plucked lute were often added to the ensemble. But since the 1970s, under official influence, again typically, further instruments were added like *dizi* flute and, to boost the bass, *dihu* cello and *zhongruan* plucked lute, as well as *zhonghu*, an alto fiddle. Call me old-fashioned, but the modern plucked bass in Chinese music is unutterably naff. Also since the 1970s, the traditional instruments themselves were modernized; as well as the *zheng*, 'national' standard versions of the *yangqin*, *pipa*, and *sanxian* were adopted, only the *jinghu* remaining traditional.

As to structure, phrases are short and four-square, with instrumental *guomen* interludes. Before Liberation, in a session of three or four hours, the instrumental ensemble usually played a few pieces before the singing began.[17] Short vocal items in simple strophic form (*xiaodiao*, 'little melodies', known as *yizidiao*) followed, and then, after a break, longer vocal sequences (*dadiao*, 'large melodies'). *Dadiao* may be either sequences of melodies, or the same melody varied in many verses,

---

[16]   AI 858–9; Yulin 1994: 131–3; Qu and Li 1999; Sun Zhuo 2001. The *zheng* is also said once to have accompanied *mihu* singing in central Shaanxi, as well as featuring in the ceremonial music of Xi'an, but neither genre appears to have any firm modern evidence – though the *zheng* was of course an important instrument in court ensembles of the numinous Tang dynasty, for what that's worth. A solo *zheng* CD by the Xi'an conservatory player Qu Yun (in the Hugo series The Treasury of Zheng Music) reveals a sanitized pan-Chinese idiom.

[17]   For full scores, see AO 899–905, ANS 614, 639–44, Yulin 1994: 115–24. Some pieces can be played solo by *zheng*, *yangqin*, or *pipa*.

or both together. Some melodies may be sung to different texts. Most pieces are sung by one singer, but *dadiao* may include some duet singing and recitation.

The *dadiao* are most complex – and, according to elderly musicians, best to listen to. Local scholar Huo Xianggui recorded all the *dadiao* from 1980 to 1982 (above we noted his work on the bards and *chuishou* – what a lot of precious recordings he made, unlikely ever to see the light of day!). By the 1990s, Hu Yingjie was the only one who still knew the *dadiao*, and he was in his autumn years. The official programme of the Folk Arts Troupe was largely limited to the shorter *xiaodiao* – the only style the women were taught.

For all the riches of Shaanbei musical life, it seemed to me that there was precious little left to study here. In chapter 5 we saw ebullient cultural pundit Meng Haiping's comments on the general cultural decline. He went on, 'If you try to force a cultural form to destruction, you can't; but some people try to protect it and end up loving it to death.' Originally the Yulin Folk Arts Troupe basically preserved the regional style, but as Meng found its recent development unsatisfactory, he went along less often.

I still don't quite understand the dynamics of official involvement. In the 1980s several senior musicians remained, and officials like Meng Haiping and Huo Xianggui seem to have their hearts in the right place. Somewhere along the line, people fall prey to the insidious conformism of modernization and 'improvement'. Recently, in Beijing at least, there have been several voices resisting this trend, but they came too late for the Yulin little pieces.

But the question remains why amateur activity in those chamber genres along the southeastern coast has remained strong through the reform period, with a spectrum of traditional and official styles, whereas the Yulin little pieces effectively died out. I surmise that in Yulin since the 1980s, the base of senior amateurs was simply too small to resist the official pressures of modernization. Musicians can typically be found to participate in the official modernizing agenda, but in this case it is hard to find anyone who believes it a success. If there are few available recordings of the *chuishou*, at least one still hears them performing for ceremonial; predictably, none of the recordings of old-time Yulin 'little pieces' have been released. The ability of cadres to 'control' the Yulin little pieces in the regional capital, and the decline of the folk base, contrast with the independence of the genres in the surrounding countryside.

* * *

On arriving at Yulin I had been sumptuously received by two brothers of my mentor Qiao Jianzhong, who had become successful businessmen with luxury jeeps and mobile phones. They were bemused to find that this 'English professor' was evidently pretty poor, especially when I sought to move out of the fancy hotel in which they installed me on the first night. We found a hostel in my modest price-range, but I was soon thrown out of it by the police, concerned for my safety – apparently not without reason. I then moved into the Qiao's lovely little house right on Main Street, which was great.

I owe you an explanation of my practices in accommodation. For many years in Hebei I have tried to stay in the villages with musicians, and when I do have to stay in a nearby town, there is usually a cheap hostel available where no-one cares much about regulations. But in Shaanbei I had less of a handle on local conditions and rarely felt inclined to stay in villages which were anyway pretty poor and where we had less of a network of friends. We found a splendid cheap hostel in Mizhi county-town, and it is delightful to stay with Older Brother's family in Yangjiagou. In Suide county-town regulations seemed stricter, and I had to keep on the move, again thrown out of several cheap hostels by local regulations, but I was eventually glad I could afford a couple of days at a more up-market hotel.

On my return to Yulin from the countryside, at my request the Qiao brothers managed to install me in a room in a typical grimy 1950s' office compound, which was very basic but just what I needed. A bit ashamed of my down-and-out clothing and frugal habits, I hung out with another less well-to-do younger brother, an affable guy basically unemployed. Meanwhile the official Folk Arts Troupe was to give a performance at the posh hotel from which I had long checked out.

12.3 The Yulin Folk Arts Troupe

Today the main official public face of folk arts in the region is the state-run Yulin Folk Arts Troupe (*Yulin minjian yishutuan*). We have already seen what it did to the Yulin 'little pieces'. As far as I know, this is the only conservatory-style troupe in the whole of the Yulin region – given that the state-run opera troupes are mostly engaged in catering for the tastes of the rural ritual market.

The main state troupe in Yulin city after Liberation was the Yulin Region Arts-Work Troupe (*Yulin diqu wengongtuan*), established in 1949.[18] From 1953 to 1969 it was called 'People's Opera Troupe' (*renmin jutuan*). Mainly performing modern versions of *Qinqiang* opera, through the 1950s it took part in provincial festivals, staging adaptations of various genres including *daoqing*, *yangge* operas, and *errentai*. Since the liberal reforms of the 1980s, the troupe has mainly performed traditional *Qinqiang* operas for the busy temple fair market.

---

[18]   AO 553–4; AO Yulin 170–71. For the Yulin opera theatre, built in 1978, see AO 609–10.

In the 1980s a new state group was formed, the 'Yulin Folk Arts Troupe', promoting a sanitized image of Shaanbei culture for the outside world. This group performs a bit of everything – highly mediated versions of local folk music, including folk-songs and dances in fancy costumes, all with 'national' orchestral accompaniment (⊙**C1**). Their relation with local folk music, as ever, is tenuous. In 1988 they toured France, Switzerland, and the USSR; from 1996 to 1999 they performed in Japan.[19] By 2000, despite the troupe's high public profile, it was in a typical state of semi-paralysis, with state salaries inadequate and performances rare. When they do perform, it is often privately for visiting dignitaries, or for 'evening gatherings' (*wanhui*) lurching towards the more pop end of the market. At the same time, as we saw, some fine music scholars have been recruited to the troupe. I am not clear how much they are responsible for the mediation of tradition.

The conflict is embodied in the characterful folk-song star Wang Xiangrong (b.1952).[20] Wang was brought up in a poor desert village with a population of only a few dozen, 45 kilometres from Fugu county-town to the northeast of Yulin. He recalls, I fear not fancifully, that he had no clothes of his own till going to school at the age of 8. The youngest of four surviving children out of nine, he was 13 when his father died. In the Cultural Revolution he managed to graduate from senior secondary. From 1971 he worked as a schoolteacher; in 1975 he toured Inner Mongolia with a band performing *errentai*. In 1977 he took part in the county band, in 1979 he was spotted by Yulin cultural cadres at a training session in Fugu county, winning a prize in a festival in 1980 and joining the Yulin Folk Arts Troupe by 1983. He has recorded for many films and TV programmes, and since 1988 has made several foreign tours, including a highly successful tour of Japan in 1999.

The kind of singing paraded by the troupe is mostly heavily mediated with kitsch orchestral accompaniment. Wang Xiangrong is perfectly aware that it is a manufactured style, attuned to the rosy official Communist image of Shaanbei. In between the extremes of that style and folk-singers performing in village life, even the few unaccompanied recordings of Wang and others show a certain refinement of rural style, such as a studied vibrato and the dramatic holding of high notes.

Wang makes something of a play of his 'shaman songs' (*shenguan diao*), learnt when he was young from two shaman uncles; he is familiar with the 'precious sword' (*baojian*) and the sheepskin drum struck with a stick. Similarly, he learnt rain songs by participation in rain ceremonies in his youth, for which a group of six villages regularly formed a 'parish' (*she*) from 1957 to 1962, and even – still more secretively – through the Cultural Revolution.

---

[19]   AD 845. For the Japanese connection, see Fukao, Iguchi, and Kurishara 2007: 135–61; some of the Japanese tours were under the banner of the 'Arts-Work Troupe'.

[20]   AFS 1466; ANS 959; Yang Cui 1995: 33–8; Zhang Peiji 1992; Huo 1996; my sessions with Wang in Yulin in 2001; and an intriguing interview under the website www. anthromusic.com (see p.xxvi n.17 above).

I get to meet the jovial Wang Xiangrong, and with the help of a friendly cadre in the troupe who is a neighbour of the Qiao family, I am surreptitiously invited to the troupe's evening concert, to be held in the great hall of the fancy hotel that I can't afford to stay in.

It's a private invitation concert for a high-ranking deputy of Li Peng, and I am not officially invited, but my new friends smuggle me in backstage to watch from the wings. If I attend formally in the audience, the bigwig will have to meet me, which would cause complications; he is happy to pretend I'm not there, and I'm happy not to get involved in courtesies. So, after all this time openly attending village rituals that some cadres might consider sensitively backward or superstitious, now that I finally find a concert showcasing the official image, I am forced to attend it in secret!

From the wings I watch the troupe go through their programme, announced suavely by a glamorous female MC in qipao *costume speaking standard Mandarin, which I haven't heard for ages, even from local cadres. Wang Xiangrong isn't singing this evening, but there are two solo singers, accompanied by a full orchestra in the pit. Introduced by the MC, a plump female singer does two sets, changing from a red ballgown with a magnificent ruff to a pink ballgown – hardly outfits that reflect the dress of the Shaanbei countryside. With the aid of a mike, she milks the songs, using all the studied hand gestures of conservatory style, backed by the orchestra in national silk-and-bamboo style, with* dizi *flute solos and* pipa *lute tremolos to the fore. A male singer in elegant white silk costume also performs a set, his songs introduced by a mellifluous* dizi *solo. The singers' facial expressions range from the smile of contentment to the longing gaze afar.*

Illuminated by fancy lighting, male and female dancers wear a variety of glitzy costumes, wielding props such as fans, umbrellas, and handkerchiefs, stock props of national dance. For one dance the girls perform acrobatics while holding aloft lotus lanterns, kitted out in green trousers, skimpy tops with fishnet midriffs, and little red floral headpieces. From my forays to the villages I have always been mystified why Mizhi county is nationally famed for its beautiful women. Now I realize they have evidently all been poached for the Folk Arts Troupe; I am reminded of the palace girls of imperial times, slave-girls at the mercy of predatory officials.

Having failed to witness shamans practising in the countryside, it is ironic to see the troupe performing a so-called 'shaman dance' for the Party bigwig, the male dancers wielding cute papier-mâché tridents, accompanied by the orchestra in pompous martial vein. In another dance the men wield cymbals, lighting effects adding to the drama.

Anyway, you get the idea: such staged performances are a world away from those I had been witnessing in the countryside. I won't go into detail, as you can see this kind of thing daily on Chinese TV; but the links with local culture are tenuous.

Whereas rural music-making depends on family and community solidarity in ceremonial traditions stretching back to imperial times, I can detect no social base for the stage performances of the official troupe, and its kitsch versions of Shaanbei culture are utterly diluted; it is contextually, historically, and musically light. I can't see whom this kind of thing satisfies; but of course one could say, as I would for the *chuishou* music, that this too is ritual, not 'merely' music; the official culture sanctioned by the state serves a need for 'civilization', for modern 'national' values on a token base of traditional local culture, on behalf of a segment of the population. And I realize there is fieldwork potential here too: these performers have lives too, doubtless a lot less glamorous than their stage personas. But if this style is part of the overall picture, it's a very small one; no-one in the countryside seems to be emulating it.

> *A few days later Wang Xiangrong takes me for a song-session in a fancy Mongolian yurt restaurant in town. His best buddy Li Yu, the charming and portly boss of the Puhui liquor factory, arrives late, having already got a considerable head start in the evening's drinking activities. Brought up in Yulin, Li recalls his time doing army service in the Cultural Revolution mainly for picking up a repertory of dirty songs, which were then all the rage – a lot of that generation will give you a similar alternative view of the period. Now doing a roaring trade with his liquor business, Li is a model capitalist, with rather good taste in music. In 2000 he organized a contest for drinking songs (jiuqu dasai) at his liquor factory, which was apparently a great success.*
>
> *Li and Wang, veteran drinking artists, are the stars of the banter over supper; other guests (including a nice academic from Yan'an, two young and distinctly nervous women, and me) are in their thrall. Wang holds court with his songs while Li Yu keeps his glass topped up with fiery* baijiu *liquor. The colourfully-costumed waitress is expected to sing for guests, and doesn't expect to be forced to drink, but with Wang Xiangrong she has bitten off more than she can chew: she is expertly, ritually, cajoled into joining in a toast after repeated verses. Wang is enjoying singing, but the fun is as much in the ritual badinage.*
>
> *Wang is a real character, but I'm not in my element. One of those pathetic English men who has never sung a song on his own in his life, in 1999 I had managed, virtually at gunpoint, to sing 'Do, a deer' and 'Rule Britannia' at a banquet in a Shaanbei temple, which still haunts me – the sacrifices we make for our art! I got away without singing that evening in the restaurant – thankfully, Wang Xiangrong had my number. Indeed, apart from rural contexts for singing, such restaurant settings may be becoming a common context for singing among the urban petty-bourgeoisie.*[21]

Conclusion: local ritual cultures

After regaling you with an all-too predictable touristy image of Shaanbei music, I can't help stressing that this is just the tip of the iceberg. As I hinted in Part One, the familiarity of literate urban culture may beguile us, with its institutional tendencies, in which music-making may revolve more around secular state-mediated events

---

[21]   Cf. Chau 2006: 152; Tian 2005: 184–6.

like concerts. In representing the culture of a region like Shaanbei, we must beware this. Having ended up in a bustling modern city, I find the perspective of the ethnographic author crucial. Basing ourselves in villages – where transport and literacy, supplies of water and electricity, remain rudimentary – may engender a very different perspective even from that resulting from a stay in a nearby city, where one's exposure to sounds, people, and ideology is very different – let alone the kind of perspective arising from our long-term base in a comfortable Western city, indeed an institutional base therein. If neither I nor many other Western scholars of Chinese music have attempted a long-term base in the countryside, we surely have a duty to reflect as much as we can glean of the peasant perspective – indeed, not only that of rural cadres, but of common folk there.[22]

Thus, notwithstanding the ephemeral links I have shown between rural music-making and state institutions and ideology, if you were one of the innumerable peasants stuck in a poor Shaanbei village perched by a barren ravine, your routine experience of music-making would be bards, geomancers reciting incantations, *chuishou* at funerals, neighbours singing at drinking parties. Sure, you would hear pop music if you switched on the TV, or blaring from sound systems and karaoke bars if you caught a rickety bus along tortuous tracks to the county-town.

Talking of rickety buses, encouraged by the claim that the long-distance bus back to Beijing would take a mere 16 hours, I embark on it naively early one morning, bidding a fond farewell to my generous hosts the Qiao brothers. On the bus I befriend a modest young guy from poor Jiaxian county, who is studying for an economics PhD at the People's University in Beijing; he is one of 15 children, of whom only three survived.

As we depart, the roof of the bus is already overladen with bulky packages lashed to the railings. I am becoming somewhat anxious when the bus makes a couple of unscheduled stops to load yet more packages onto the roof, each stop taking over an hour. This goes on, and after four hours we have still only travelled about 50 kilometres, and haven't even crossed the mountains down over the murky Yellow River into Shanxi. When we finally reach the better road surfaces of Shanxi it is already night-time.

Just as we have begun picking up speed, we grind to a sudden halt. There is a huge tailback in front of an accident, and we are stationary for several hours while the road is cleared. Before dawn, reaching Hebei province, the bus has a blowout, and we hobble along dangerously for another agonizing hour before finding a service station where tyres can be replaced. Surreally, this establishment, plonked down miles from anywhere in grimy foothills, boasts the most spotlessly clean public convenience I have ever visited in China; though I may well be hallucinating by this time, it even provides clean towels, can you imagine. If there was a Chinese truckers' Michelin guide, it would win hands down. Dazed, but in better spirits, we are on the home strait. As the sun comes up on a beautifully clear morning, it

---

[22]   Cf. Liu Xin 2000: 25, 180–81.

is not long before we join another huge tailback with the motorway ahead closed,
supposedly for fog, and at the next exit we join a million other vehicles embarking
on a lengthy detour along dirt tracks, to remind me of the countryside I thought
I had just escaped from. I am evidently the only passenger remotely taken aback
by all this. Over 30 hours after setting off from Yulin, I am relieved to get back to
Beijing at all.

In Shaanbei today, despite all the frenzied money-making activities along the plain, in the surrounding countryside poverty, the search for water and electricity, and the need for a good harvest, healthy children and livestock, are still the basic and pervasive elements in people's lives. Life expectancy may have increased, infant mortality and blindness decreased, but fear of calamity still animates much of peasant recourse to ritual practice. I have gone to some lengths to show the modern institutional connections and images of folk musicians (including singers, opera troupes, bards, and shawm bands), but my overriding musical impressions of Shaanbei, and many parts of China, are the calendrical and life-cycle ceremonies which still shield people from cultural poverty and social disorder.

Although Shaanbei is interesting by virtue of its revolutionary image, neither its poverty nor its modern history are unusual in China: we still know all too little about grass-roots music-making in vast areas like Gansu, Anhui, or Henan – in fact, almost anywhere in the Chinese countryside.

It has also been important to try and document the Maoist period. Expressive culture was certainly impoverished – not just by political campaigns, but as much by the disappearance of the more affluent patrons and sideline enterprises in what had always been a desperately poor society. Yet despite all the convulsive political campaigns, ceremonial life was maintained painfully, remaining largely resistant to central policy, enabling the more open revival of the 1980s.

Since the 1990s, ritual and musical activities have inevitably been affected more broadly by changing social conditions. The influence of market modernity and pop culture is pervasive, and new factors such as migration have further weakened local communal and cultural networks. Now not only Yulin city but the whole society is considered 'without order'; the loosening of the taboo on sighted bards, or the decline of the prescribed shawm suites, are examples. Still, cultural networks remain active; the local state has been both unwilling and unable to erase ritual life and the expressive culture that accompanies it. One may discern accommodation, as does Chau, between local folk and temple elites and the local state organs, and the local state turns a blind eye to, indeed colludes in and profits from, ceremonial contexts – precisely those of music-making. However, religious practices somehow seem in a healthier condition than music-making. Music may still accompany life-cycle and calendrical ceremonies, but under the assault of TV and pop music since the 1990s, folk-song is heard less often, bards are less popular, people are concerned for the future of opera, and shawm bands are converting to a nationally standardized repertory of pop music.

Although through the twentieth century a cultural gulf opened up between the cities and the countryside, the small towns in the Chinese hinterland are part of the whole cultural network there. In Shaanbei, while entertainment music died out with the old elite, *yangge* group dancing – whose rural performances, however ritually significant, have always been very occasional – is more prominent, and more secular, in the towns.

In ceremonial, the cast of performers includes geomancers, mediums, beggars, and funeral managers, all of whose sonic contributions deserve our attention. More conventional objects of musical study include singers, bards, opera troupes, and shawm bands. If we are to begin comprehending the sheer enormity of expressive culture in a heritage as immense in history and population as China, we must direct our attention not only to modern urban institutions, patrons, and performers, but to enduring folk ones like temple committees, shawm bands, and lay ritual specialists – and indeed individual peasants, bards, and singers.

Singers, long the pride of Shaanbei, are now elusive, at least to me. The musical activities of individual bards, blind or sighted, are a minor theme compared to opera, but the bards remain a persistent feature of Shaanbei life, maintaining their traditional story-telling among their nest of livelihoods to bring good fortune to families and the community. Though people doubt the ability of the opera troupes to withstand new commercial pressures, they too remain dependent on ceremonial, constituting the most important performance for major calendrical events.

As to *chuishou*, the exception of a few players gaining ephemeral institutional promotions proves the rule of part-time *chuishou* serving ceremonial. Now a few bands based in the towns are modernizing and claiming a larger share of the market, and their pop programme looks set to marginalize the traditional repertory more efficiently than political control ever could.

In sum, in a still largely agricultural society, despite the assaults of Maoism and pop culture on traditional contexts inherited from imperial times, music-making continues to revolve around life-cycle and calendrical ceremonies. The performers described above should not be reduced to the simplistic epithet of 'folk musicians': music-making is a vital aspect of their activities in society, and all serve different functions within the general rubric of ceremonial. And Shaanbei may be poor, but it is quite typical of vast areas of the Chinese countryside.

Finally, some succinct reflections on regional variation in the areas of Hebei, Shanxi, and Shaanbei where I have observed expressive culture since 1986. Even before attempting to account for local differences in music 'itself', ritual culture was maintained everywhere, but in different ways. The central Hebei plain has preserved amateur ritual associations, supported tacitly under Maoism by local leaderships. North Shanxi still has both shawm bands and lay Daoists, both occupational. In Shaanbei, ritual specialists are of a yet more diffused type: while geomancers, spirit mediums, bards, and shawm bands remain active, few temple or lay Buddhist or Daoist groups now perform complex rituals. And then one might look further afield, for example to areas of southeast China whose vibrant ritual cultures have been well documented. Variation in customs and music is found not just at provincial, regional, or county level, but from district to district. Ritual and musical activities are always diverse, even in the small areas I have sampled. It is not that the genres I have highlighted are the only ones active in those areas: mediums, performing beggars, lay ritual groups, opera troupes, festive dance associations, and so on, are often in evidence too.

Ritual variation is considerable; in funerals, for instance, Shaanbei is relatively less dense, partly owing to the scarcity of Daoists; for nocturnal rituals, a cart is burnt in Hebei, a treasury in Shanxi, whereas road lanterns are set out in Shaanbei. Along with all this, and not entirely related, comes musical variation: in elements such as pitch, style, scales, melodic repertory, and suite form. Shawm bands perform different sequences: in Shaanbei, the *laosangu* triple metre suite is used, whereas in north Shanxi, suite form is more diverse, and bands play entertainment sequences, including opera.

Of course, the varied local conditions we find throughout China today are obscure heritages from imperial times, complex amalgams of factors such as ecology, economy, lineage customs, and historical migration, further complicated by local histories in republican, Maoist, and reform eras (local politics and personalities, Japanese occupation, radical Communist leadership, local protectionism, and so on). It is hard as yet to explain these variations, and we need a far more detailed body of work before anyone attempts to do so, but I look forward to such studies.

Bibliography

Abbreviations

The following abbreviations are used for Shaanxi volumes of the *Anthology*. Cited volumes for other provinces are listed under Zhongguo... below.

AD   (*Anthology* dance) *Zhongguo minzu minjian wudao jicheng, Shaanxi juan* [Anthology of folk dance of the Chinese peoples, Shaanxi volumes] (Beijing: Zhongguo ISBN zhongxin, 1995).

AFS (*Anthology* folk-song) *Zhongguo minjian gequ jicheng, Shaanxi juan* [Anthology of Chinese folk-songs, Shaanxi volumes] (Beijing: Zhongguo ISBN zhongxin, 1994).

AI   (*Anthology* instrumental) *Zhongguo minzu minjian qiyuequ jicheng, Shaanxi juan* [Folk instrumental pieces of the Chinese peoples, Shaanxi volumes] (Beijing: Renmin yinyue chubanshe, 1992).

ANS (*Anthology* narrative-singing) *Zhongguo quyi yinyue jicheng, Shaanxi juan* [Anthology of Chinese narrative-singing music, Shaanxi volumes] (Beijing: Zhongguo ISBN zhongxin, 1995).

AO   (*Anthology* opera) *Zhongguo xiqu zhi, Shaanxi juan* [China opera monograph, Shaanxi volume] (Beijing: Zhongguo ISBN zhongxin, 1995).

AO Yulin (*Anthology* opera, Yulin) *Shaanxi sheng xiqu zhi, Yulin diqu juan* [Shaanxi province opera monograph, Yulin region volume] (Xi'an: San Qin chubanshe, 1998).

Other sources

Ai Keqi (1996) 'Shaanbei quxiang pipa shuo' [On the bent-necked *pipa* of Shaanbei] (handwritten MS, Zizhou county).

Apter, David and Tony Saich (1994) *Revolutionary Discourse in Mao's Republic* (Cambridge, Mass. and London: Harvard University Press).

Bai Xiaowei (2006) 'Yulinshi min'ge fenggequ huafen' [Classification of stylistic areas in folksongs of the Yulin region], *Zhongguo yinyuexue* 2006/1: 96–100.

Baptandier-Berthé, Brigitte (1994) 'The Kaiguan Ritual and the Construction of the Child's Identity', in Hanxue 1994: 523–86.

Barmé, Geremie and John Minford (1986) *Seeds of Fire: Chinese Voices of Conscience* (Hong Kong: Far Eastern Economic Review).

Baranovitch, Nimrod (2003) *China's New Voices: Popular Music, Ethnicity, Gender, and Politics 1978–1997* (Berkeley; Los Angeles, and London: University of California Press).

Belden, Jack (1973) *China Shakes the World* (Harmondsworth: Penguin; 1st edition 1949).

Bell, Catherine (1997) *Ritual: Perspectives and Dimensions* (New York and Oxford: Oxford University Press).

Bender, Mark (2001) 'A Description of *Jiangjing* (Telling Scriptures) Services in Jingjiang, China', *Asian Folklore Studies* 601: 101–33.

Booth, Gregory (1990) 'Brass Bands: Tradition, Change, and the Mass Media in Indian Wedding Music', *Ethnomusicology* 34.2: 245–62.

Cao Benye, see Tsao Poon-yee.

Cao Hongxin (1999) *Shaanbei minsu* [Shaanbei folklore], Shaanbei minjian wenhua ziliiao congshu (Yulin: Qunzhong yishuguan).

Cecchinato, Barbara (2002) *Lo Yangge dello Shaanxi Settentrionale* (Tesi di laurea, Università Ca'Foscari di Venezia, Facoltà di Lingue e Letterature straniere, Corso di Laurea in Lingue e Civiltà orientali).

Chan, Anita, Richard Madsen, and Jonathan Unger (1992) *Chen Village under Mao and Deng* (Berkeley: University of California Press) (expanded version of 1984 edition).

Chau, Adam Yuet (2003) 'Popular Religion in Shaanbei, North-Central China', *Journal of Chinese Religions* 31: 39–79.

—— (2004) 'Hosting Funerals and Temple Festivals: Folk Event Productions in Rural China', *Asian Anthropology* 3: 39–70.

—— (2005) 'The Politics of Legitimation and the Revival of Popular Religion in Shaanbei, North-Central China', *Modern China* 31.2: 236–78.

—— (2006) *Miraculous Response: Doing Popular Religion in Contemporary China* (Stanford: Stanford University Press).

—— (2006a) '"Superstition Specialist Households"? The Household Idiom in Chinese Religious Practices', *Minsu quyi* 153: 157–202.

—— (2006b) 'Drinking Games, Karaoke Songs, and *Yangge* Dances: Youth Cultural Production in Rural China', *Ethnology* 45.2: 161–72.

Chen Wangxing (1994) 'Yulin xiaoqu chutan' [Preliminary discussion of the Yulin little pieces], in Yulin 1994: 125–30.

CHIME (2008) *Chinese Shadows: The Amazing World of Shadow Puppetry in Rural Northwest China*, DVD film (Pan Records, Pan 9607).

Chow, Rey (1995) 'Silent is the Ancient Plain: Music, Filmmaking, and the Concept of Social Change in the New Chinese Cinema', in his *Primitive Passions: Visuality, Sexuality, Ethnography, and Contemporary Chinese Cinema* (New York: Columbia University Press), 79–107.

Clart, Philip and Charles B. Jones (2003) *Religion in Modern Taiwan: Tradition and Innovation in a Changing Society* (Honolulu: University of Hawai'i Press).

Crook, David and Isabel (1959) *Revolution in a Chinese Village: Ten Mile Inn* (London: Routledge & Kegan Paul).

—— (1979) *Mass Movement in a Chinese village: Ten Mile Inn* (London and Henley: Routledge & Kegan Paul).

Dean, Kenneth (1993) *Taoist Ritual and Popular Cults of Southeast China* (Princeton, NJ: Princeton University Press).

—— (1998) *Lord of the Three in One: the Spread of a Cult in Southeast China* (Princeton, NJ: Princeton University Press).

Dikötter, Frank, Lars Laamann, and Zhou Xun (2004) *Narcotic Culture: A History of Drugs in China* (Hong Kong and London: Hurst and Co.).

Dong Xiaoping and R. David Arkush [Ou Dawei] (1995) *Huabei minjian wenhua* [Folk culture of north China], Shijiazhuang:Hebei jiaoyu chubanshe, 4 vols.

Dubois, Thomas David (2005) *The Sacred Village: Social Change and Religious Life in Rural North China* (Honololu: University of Hawai'i Press).

Esherick, Joseph (1998) 'Revolution in a Feudal Fortress: Yangjiagou, Mizhi County, Shaanxi, 1937–1948', *Modern China* 24.4: 339–77.

Fan Lizhu (2003) 'The Cult of the Silkworm Mother as a Core of Local Community Religion in a North China Village: Field Study in Zhiwuying, Baoding, Hebei', *Religion in China Today*, ed. Daniel Overmyer, *China Quarterly* special issues, new series no.3 (Cambridge University Press), 53–66.

Feng Guanglin (1984) 'Feng Guanglin suona quji' [Collected shawm pieces of Feng Guanglin], ed. Liang Wenda, np, mim. [1st edn 1957].

Fernandez-Sternbridge, Leila and Richard P. Madsen (2002) 'Beggars in the Socialist Market Economy', in Link, Madsen, and Pickowicz 2002: 207–30.

Finnegan, Ruth (1989) *The Hidden Musicians: Music-making in an English Town* (Cambridge: Cambridge University Press).

Friedman, Edward, Paul Pickowicz, and Mark Selden (1991) *Chinese Village, Socialist State* (New Haven and London: Yale University Press).

Frozen Brass: Anthology of Brass Band Music, vols. 1 (Asia) and 2 (Africa and Latin America), Pan 2020 CD, Pan 2026 CD (Pan Records, 1993).

Fukao Yoko and Iguchi, Junko (1992) *Seifu shuchou* ['Music and performing arts in the Yellow River valley'], *Music of the Earth: Fieldworkers' Sound Collections*, vol. 62: China, CD in book form (Victor, Japan/Smithsonian Folkways, VCTD-62).

Fukao Yoko, Iguchi Junko, and Kurishara Shinji (2007) *Huangtu gaoyuan de cunzhuang: shengyin, kongjian, shehui* [Village life in China's yellow highlands: sound, space, and society] (Beijing: Minzu chubanshe, 2007, with CD) (translation of original Japanese edition *Koudokougen no mura: ota, kuukan, shakai*, Tokyo: Kokonshoin, 2000).

Gao, Mobo C.F. (1999) *Gao Village* (London: Hurst).

Gao Wanfei (1996) 'Suona yiren Li Qishan' [*Suona* artist Li Qishan], in Shaanxi 1996: 147–50.

—— (2000) *Shaanbei da suona yinyue* [Music of the Shaanbei big shawm] (Xi'an: Xi'an ditu chubanshe).

Garland (2002) *Garland Encyclopaedia of World Music, vol.7, East Asia: China, Japan, and Korea*, ed. Robert C. Provine, Yosihiko Tokumaru, and J. Lawrence Witzleben (New York: Routledge).

Graezer, Florence (2004) 'Breathing New Life into Beijing Culture: New "Traditional" Public Spaces and the Chaoyang Neighbourhood *Yangge* Associations', in Stephan Feuchtwang (ed.) *Making Place: State Projects, Globalization and Local Responses in China* (London: UCL), 61–78.

Grimes, Ronald (1990) *Ritual Criticism: Case Studies in its Practice, Essays in its Theory* (Columbia, SC: University of South Carolina Press).

Grove (2000) *The New Grove Dictionary of Music and Musicians*, 2nd edition, ed. Stanley Sadie and John Tyrrell (London: Macmillan).

Guo Yuhua (1992) *Side kunrao yu shengde zhizhuo* [The puzzle of death and the obstinacy of life] (Beijing: Zhongguo renmin daxue chubanshe).

—— (2000) 'Minjian shehui yu yishi guojia: yizhong quanli shijian de jieshi (Shaanbei Jicun de yishi yu shehui bianqian yanjiu, 1)' [Folk society and ritual state: an interpretation of power practice (Ritual and social change in Jicun, Shaanbei, 1)] in *Yishi yu shehui bianqian* [Ritual and social change], ed. Guo Yuhua (Beijing: Zhongguo shehuikexue wenxian chubanshe), 338–83.

Han Kuo-huang (2000) 'The Importation of Western Music to China at the Turn of the Twentieth Century', in *A Compendium of American Musicology: Essays in Honor of John F. Ohl*, eds Enrique Alberto Arias, Susan M. Filler, William V. Porter, and Jeffrey Wasson (Evanston, IL: Northwestern University Press), 229–40.

Han Qixiang (1985) *Han Qixiang yu Shaanbei shuoshu* [Han Qixiang and Shaanbei narrative-singing], ed. Yang Jingzhen and Guan Runzhuan (Shaanxi sheng qunyi guan, for internal circulation).

—— (?) *Han Qixiang chuantong shumu xuanbian* [Selected traditional stories of Han Qixiang] [details n.a.].

Hansson, Anders (1996) *Chinese Outcasts: Discrimination and Emancipation in Late Imperial China* (Leiden: Brill).

Hanxue (1994) *Minjian xinyang yu Zhongguo wenhua guoji yantaohui lunwenji*, ed. Hanxue yanjiu zhongxin (Taipei: Hanxue yanjiu zhongxin).

Harris, Rachel and Barley Norton (2002) 'Introduction: Ritual Music and Communism', *British Journal of Ethnomusicology* 11.1: 1–8.

He Jun, Fan Zhaoming, and Li Shigong [Li Shigen] (eds) (1959) 'Shaanbei Jia-Yu minsu zongjiao yinyue sanbian' [Collected folklore and religious music of Jiaxian and Yulin in Shaanbei] (Xi'an: Zhongguo yinyuejia xiehui Xi'an fenhui, mim.).

He Yutang and Wang Xiaoli (nd) *Min'ge dawang* [Great king of folk-song], audio cassette (Shaanxi sheng yinxiang chubanshe XL-1091, late 1980s).

Hequ (1956) *Hequ minjian gequ* [Folk songs of Hequ], ed. Zhongyang yinyue xueyuan Zhongguo yinyue yanjiusuo (Beijing: Yinyue chubanshe).

Herrou, Adeline (2005) *La Vie Entre Soi: Les Moines Taoistes Aujourd'hui en Chine* (Nanterre: Société d'ethnologie).

Hinton, William (1966) *Fanshen: A Documentary of Revolution in a Chinese Village* (New York: Vintage).

—— (1983) *Shenfan* (New York: Random House).

—— (2006) *Through a Glass Darkly: U.S. Views of the Chinese Revolution* (New York: Monthly Review Press).

Hockx, Michel and Julia Strauss (eds) (2005) *Culture in the Contemporary PRC, China Quarterly* special issues no.6 (Cambridge: Cambridge University Press).

Holm, David (1991) *Art and Ideology in Revolutionary China* (Oxford: Clarendon Press).

—— (1992) 'The Strange Case of Liu Zhidan', *Australian Journal of Chinese Affairs* 27: 77–96.

—— (1994) 'The Labyrinth of Lanterns: Taoism and Popular Religion in Northwest China', in Hanxue 1994: 797–852.

Hu Jingfang (ed.) (1954) 'Yulin xiaoqu' [Yulin lesser melodies] (Huadong minzu yinyue yanjiushi, mim.) [on *errentai*!].

Hu Mengxiang (1989), *Han Qixiang pingzhuan* [Critical biography of Han Qixiang] (Beijing: Zhongguo minjian wenyi chubanshe).

Huang Shu-min (1989) *The Spiral Road: Change in a Chinese Village through the Eyes of a Communist Party Leader* (Boulder and London: Westview).

Hung, Chang-tai (1993) 'Reeducating a Blind Storyteller: Han Qixiang and the Chinese Communist Storytelling Campaign', *Modern China* 19.4: 395–426.

—— (2005) 'The Dance of Revolution: *Yangge* in Beijing in the Early 1950s', *China Quarterly* 181: 82–99.

Huo Xianggui (1996) 'Nongminde zhongshi erzi: ji zhuming min'geshou Wang Xiangrong [Faithful son of the peasants: on the famous folk-singer Wang Xiangrong], *Yinyue tiandi* 1996/5: 27.

—— (1997a) 'Ta cong Luyi huilai' [He came back from the Lu Xun Arts Academy], *Yinyue tiandi* 1997/1: 38.

—— (1997b) 'Shaanbei minjian yinyue caifeng sanji' [Notes on collecting folk music in Shaanbei], *Yinyue tiandi* 1997/4: 39.

—— (2005) *Yulin xiaoqu ji* [Collected Yulin little pieces], Shaanbei wenhua yanjiu congshu series (Xi'an: Shaanxi lüyou chubanshe).

Huo Xianggui and Ai Pu (eds) (1979) *Shaanbei suona yinyue* [Shawm music of Shaanbei] (Suide: Suide wenhua guan, mim.).

Iguchi, Junko (2005) 'The Regeneration of Traditional Music in a Chinese Rural Village', *Asian Musicology* (Korea) 6: 163–73.

Jia Yu (1992) 'Xinxi huang tudi, qingman quyuan chun' [Heart belonging to the yellow earth, feelings full of the spring of the music garden], *Jiaoxiang* 1992/4: 83–5.

Jin Ting (1986) *Yan'an fengtu ji* [Record of customs of Yan'an] (Xi'an: Xibei daxue chubanshe).

Jing, Jun (1996) *The Temple of Memories: History, Power, and Morality in a Chinese Village* (Stanford: Stanford University Press).

Johnson, David (1994) 'Temple Festivals in Southeastern Shanxi: The *Sai* of Nanshe Village and Big West Gate', *Minsu quyi* 91: 641–734.

Jones, Stephen (1992) (with Chen Kexiu, Jing Weigang, and Liu Shi) 'Funeral Music in Shanxi: Field Notes 1991', *CHIME* 5: 1–28.

—— (1998) *Folk Music of China: Living Instrumental Traditions* (Oxford: Clarendon Press) (paperback edition with CD; 1st edn 1995).

—— (1999) 'Ritual Music under Mao and Deng', *British Journal of Ethnomusicology*: 27–66.

—— (2002) 'Snapshot: Yellow Earth', in Garland 2002: 257–9.

—— (2003) 'Reading Between the Lines: Reflections on the Massive *Anthology of Folk Music of the Chinese Peoples*', *Ethnomusicology* 47.3: 287–337.

—— (2004) *Plucking the Winds: Lives of Village Musicians in Old and New China* (Leiden: CHIME Foundation, with CD).

—— (2004a) *Walking Shrill: The Hua Family Shawm Band*, CD (Pan Records 2109).

—— (2007) *Ritual and Music of North China: Shawm Bands in Shanxi* (Aldershot: Ashgate, with DVD).

—— (2007a) 'Turning a Blind Ear: Bards of Shaanbei', *Chinoperl* 27: 174–208.

—— (forthcoming) 'Living Early Composition: An Appreciation of Chinese Shawm Melody', in Simon Mills (ed.) *Analysing East Asian Music: Patterns of Rhythm and Melody*, *Musiké* vol.4 (Semar).

Kang Xiaofei (2002) 'In the Name of Buddha: The Cult of the Fox in Contemporary Northern Shaanxi', *Minsu quyi* 138: 67–109.

Keating, Pauline B. (1997) *Two Revolutions: Village Reconstruction and the Cooperative Movement in Northern Shaanxi, 1934–1945* (Stanford: Stanford University Press).

Kouwenhoven, Frank (1997) 'New Chinese Operas by Qu Xiaosong, Tan Dun and Guo Wenjing', *CHIME* 10–11: 111–22.

Kraus, Richard (2004) *The Party and the Arty in China: The New Politics of Culture* (Lanham, Boulder, New York, Toronto, and Oxford: Rowman and Littlefield).

Lagerwey, John (ed.) (1996–) vols. in Traditional Hakka society series (Hong Kong: International Hakka Studies Association and École Française d'Extreme Orient).

Leung, Laifong (ed.) (1994) *Morning Sun: Interviews with Chinese Writers of the Lost Generation* (Armonk, NY: M.E. Sharpe).

Levin, Theodore (1996) *The Hundred Thousand Fools of God: Musical Travels in Central Asia* (Bloomington and Indianopolis: Indiana University Press).

Li Hongyue (1995) 'Yulin xiaoqu chutan' [Preliminary study of Yulin little pieces], *Yulin wenshi ziliao* 15: 102–7.

Li Jianzheng (1984) 'Shaanbei quxiang pipa' [The Shaanbei bent-necked *pipa*], *Jiaoxiang* 1984/2: 23–7.

Li Mei (2001) 'Jiang-Huai diqu qigai yinyue de chubu yanjiu' [Preliminary study of beggars' music in the Jiang-Huai region] *Yinyue wenhua* 2001: 201–40.

Li Runzhong (1986) *Zhongguo minzu minjian qiyuequ jicheng, Liaoning juan Panjin fenjuan* [Folk instrumental pieces of the Chinese peoples, Liaoning vols., Panjin sub-vols.] vol. 1 (Shenyang).

Li Shibin (1988) 'Minjian quxiang pipa kaocha jishi' [Fieldnotes on the folk bent-necked *pipa*], *Zhongguo yinyuexue* 1988/3: 42–6.

Liang Wenda (1953) *Shaanbei daoqing yinyue* [*Daoqing* music of Shaanbei], Xibei minjian yinyue congshu zhi san (Xi'an: Xibei renmin chubanshe).

Lin Shan (1945) 'Gaizao shuoshu' [Reforming narrative-singing], reprinted in Zhou 1946: 46–58 (also in Yan'an 1988, vol.14: 139–50).

—— (1949) 'Luetan Shaanbeide gaizao shuoshu' [On reformed narrative-singing in Shaanbei], *Wenyi bao* 1949/8, reprinted in Yan'an 1988, vol. 14: 150–54.

Link, Perry, Richard P. Madsen and Paul G. Pickowicz (eds) (2002) *Popular China: Unofficial Culture in a Globalizing Society* (Lanham, Boulder, New York: Rowman and Littlefield).

Lipman, Jonathan M. and Stevan Harrell (eds) (1990) *Violence in China: Essays in Culture and Counterculture* (Albany: State University of New York Press).

Liu Hongqing (2004) *Xiang tian er ge: Taihang mangyiren de gushi* [Eng. title Singing to the heaven: stories of blind minstrels on the Taihang mountain] (Beijing: Beijing chubanshe, with VCD).

Liu Jie (1988) 'Shaanxi zongjiao yinyue kaolue' [Outline of religious music in Shaanxi], *Jiaoxiang* 1988/3: 8–16.

Liu Xin (2000) *In One's Own Shadow: An Ethnographic Account of the Condition of Post-Reform Rural China* (Berkeley: University of California Press).

Liu Yong (2006) *Zhongguo suona yinyue yanjiu* [Study of the music of the Chinese *suona*] (Shanghai: Shanghai yinyuexueyuan chubanshe).

Luo Yang (1963) 'Geming quyijia Han Qixiang' [Revolutionary narrative-singer Han Qixiang], *Quyi* 1963/3: 48–57.

Ma Rongzhang (1995) 'Qiucixiande jianzhi shoumo jiqilishi zuoyong' [The founding of the Kucha county and its historical use], *Yulin wenshi ziliao* 15: 98–101.

McDougall, Bonnie (1991) *The Yellow Earth: A Film by Chen Kaige* (Hong Kong: Chinese University Press).

Merriam, Alan P. (1964) *The Anthropology of Music* (Evanston: Northwestern University Press).

Mizhi (1993) *Mizhi xianzhi* [Mizhi county gazetteer] (Xi'an: Shaanxi renmin chubanshe).

Mo Yan (1996), *The Garlic Ballads*, English translation by Howard Goldblatt (London: Penguin).

Myrdal, Jan (1967) *Report from a Chinese Village* (Penguin / Pelican).

—— (1973) *China: The Revolution Continued* (Penguin / Pelican).

Naquin, Susan (1988) 'Funerals in North China; Uniformity and Variation', in James Watson and Evelyn Rawski (eds), *Death Ritual in Late Imperial and Modern China* (Berkeley, Los Angeles and London: University of California Press, 1988), 37–70.

Overmyer, Daniel L. (ed.) (2002) with the assistance of Shin-Yi Chao, *Ethnography in China Today: A Critical Assessment of Achievements and Results* (Taipei: Yuan-Liou Publishing Company).

Overmyer, Daniel L. and Fan Lizhu (eds) (2006–2007) *Huabei nongcun minjian wenhua yanjiu congshu* [Studies of the popular culture of north China villages], 4 vols., Tianjin: Tianjin guji chubanshe.

Perris, Arnold (1983) 'Music as Propaganda: Art at the Command of Doctrine in the PRC', *Ethnomusicology* 27.1: 1–28.

Perry, Elizabeth (1985) 'Rural Violence in Socialist China', *China Quarterly* 103: 414–40.

Pickowicz, Paul and Liping Wang (2002) 'Village Voices, Urban Activists: Women, Violence and Gender Inequality in Rural China', in Link, Madsen, and Pickowicz 2002: 57–88.

Poché, Christian (2000) 'Surnay', in Grove 2000.

Qiao Jian, Liu Guanwen, and Li Tiansheng (2002) *Yuehu: tianye diaocha yu lishi zhuizong* [Music households: fieldwork and historical traces] (Nanchang: Jiangxi renmin chubanshe).

Qiao Jianzhong (ed.) (1996) *Tudi yu ge* [Eng. title *Songs of the Land in China: Labor songs and love songs*], 2-CD set (Taipei: Wind Records TCD 1020).

—— ed. (1998) *Jinye lai changxi* [Eng. title *The beauty of Chinese folk opera*], 2-CD set (Taipei: Wind Records TCD 1021).

—— (2002) *Zhongguo jingdian min'ge jianshang zhinan* [Guide to the appreciation of classic Chinese folk-songs] (Shanghai: Shanghai yinyue chubanshe).

—— (2003) 'Shaanxi Yulin sangzang huodong suoyi' [Recollections of funerary activities in Yulin, Shaanxi], in Tsao 2003: 404–17.

Qiao Jianzhong and Ruan Guijuan (eds) (1998) *Shiba duan quyi* [Eng. title *Shuochang: the Ultimate Art of Storytelling*], 2-CD set (Taipei: Wind Records, TCD-1022).

Qiao Jianzhong and Xue Yibing (eds) (1999) *Minjian guchuiyue yanjiu: Shoujie Zhongguo minjian guchuiyue xueshu yantaohui lunwenji* [Studies in folk wind-and-percussion music: collected articles from the first symposium on Chinese folk wind-and-percussion music] (Ji'nan: Shandong youyi chubanshe).

Qin Jianming and Marianne Bujard ['Lü Min'] (2003)*Yaoshan shengmu miao yu shenshe* [The sacred mother temple and holy parishes of Yaoshan] (Beijing, Zhonghua shuju).

Qu Yun and Li Meng (1999) *Shaanxi zhengqu* [Pieces for the Shaanxi *zheng*] (Beijing: Renmin yinyue chubanshe).

Rawski, Evelyn (1986) 'The Ma Landlords of Yang-chia-kou in Late Ch'ing and Republican China', in Patricia Ebrey and James Watson (eds), *Kinship Organization in Late Imperial China* (Berkeley: University of California Press), 245–83.

Rees, Helen (2000) *Echoes of History: Naxi Music in Modern China* (New York and London: Oxford University Press).

Ruizendaal, Robin (2006) *Marionette Theatre in Quanzhou* (Leiden and Boston: Brill).

Schimmelpenninck, Antoinet (1997) *Chinese Folk Songs and Folk Singers: Shan'ge Traditions in Southern Jiangsu* (Leiden: CHIME, with CD).

Selden, Mark (1995) *China in Revolution: The Yenan Way Revisited* (New York: M.E. Sharpe).

Seybolt, Peter J. (1996) *Throwing the Emperor from his Horse: Portrait of a Village Leader in China, 1923–1995* (Boulder and Oxford: Westview).

Shaanxi (1996) *Shaanxi minjian yishujia* [Shaanxi folk artists] (Dali [Shaanxi]: Shaanxi sheng wenhua ting and Shaanxi sheng yishuguan).

—— (1999) *Shaanxi sheng ditu ce* [Atlas of Shaanxi province] (Xi'an: Xi'an ditu chubanshe).

Siu, Helen (1989) 'Recycling Rituals: Politics and Popular Culture in Contemporary Rural China', in Perry Link, Richard Madsen, and Paul G. Pickowicz (eds), *Unofficial China: Popular Culture and Thought in the People's Republic* (Boulder, San Francisco and London: Westview), 121–37.

Small, Christopher (1998) *Musicking: The Meanings of Performance and Listening* (Hanover and London: Wesleyan University Press).

Sommer, Matthew H. (2005) 'Making Sex Work: Polyandry as a Survival Strategy in Qing Dynasty China', in Bryna Goodman and Wendy Larson (eds), *Gender in Motion: Divisions of Labour and Cultural Change in Late Imperial and Modern China* (Lanham, Boulder, New York, Toronto, and Oxford: Rowman and Littlefield), 29–54.

Sun Zhuo (2001) 'Qinzheng de lishi yuanyuan yu fuxing' [The historical origins of the Shaanxi *zheng* style and its revival] (MA thesis, Zhongyang yinyuexueyuan).

Sutton, Donald S. (2003) *Steps of Perfection: Exorcistic Performers and Chinese Religion in Twentieth-century Taiwan* (Cambridge, Mass., and London: Harvard University Press).

Tai, Jeanne (ed. and trans.) (1989) *Spring Bamboo: A Collection of Contemporary Chinese short stories* (New York: Random House).

Tan, Chee-Beng (ed.) (2006) *Southern Fujian: Reproduction of Traditions in Post-Mao China* (Hong Kong: Chinese University Press).

Tan, Hwee-san (2002) 'Saving the Soul in Red China: Music and Ideology in the Gongde Ritual of Merit in Fujian', *British Journal of Ethnomusicology* 11.1: 119–40.

Tian Yaonong (2005) *Shaanbei lisu yinyuede kaocha yu yanjiu* [Fieldwork and study of ceremonial music of Shaanbei] (Shanghai: Shanghai yinyuexueyuan chubanshe).

Tingey, Carol (1994) *Auspicious Music in a Changing Society: The Damai Musicians of Nepal* (London: School of Oriental & African Studies).

Tsao Poon-yee [Cao Benye] (ed.) (1996–2000) *Zhongguo chuantong yishi yinyue yanjiu xilie congshu* [Monograph series of studies of traditional Chinese ritual music], series (Taipei: Xinwenfeng).

—— (ed.) (2003) *Zhongguo minjian yishi yinyue yanjiu, Xibei juan* [Studies of Chinese folk ritual music, North-west vol.] (Kunming: Yunnan renmin chubanshe, with DVD).

Tuohy, Sue (1999) 'The Social Life of Genre: The Dynamics of Folksong in China', *Asian Music* 30.2: 39–86.

—— (2001) 'The Sonic Dimensions of Nationalism in Modern China: Musical Representation and Transformation', *Ethnomusicology* 45.1: 107–31.

Wang C.K. (ed.) (1997–) *Minsu quyi congshu* [Eng. title Studies in Chinese ritual, theatre and folklore series], Taipei: Shi Ho-cheng Folk Culture Foundation, ongoing [over 80 vols. planned] (Eng. *Studies in Chinese ritual, theatre and folklore series: abstracts of the first sixty volumes*, 1997).

Ward, Geoffrey C. and Burns, Ken (2000) *Jazz: A History of America's Music* (New York: Alfred K. Knopf).

Wen Xing and Xue Maixi (eds) (1991) *Shanxi minsu* [Folk customs of Shanxi] (Taiyuan: Shanxi renmin chubanshe).

Witzleben, J. Lawrence (1995) *'Silk-and-Bamboo' Music in Shanghai: The Jiangnan Sizhu Instrumental Ensemble Tradition* (Kent, Ohio and London: Kent State University Press).

—— (1999) 'Cantopop and Mandapop in Pre-Postcolonial Hong Kong: Identity Negotiation in the Performances of Anita Mui Yim-Fong', *Popular Music* 18.2: 241–58.

Wong, Isobel (1984) 'Geming Gequ: Songs for the Education of the Masses', in B. McDougall (ed.) *Popular Chinese Literature and the Performing Arts in the People's Republic of China, 1949–1979* (Berkeley: University of California Press).

Wu Fan (2007) *Yinyang yu gujiang: zai tiexu kongjianzhong* [Daoists and shawm bands in the ordering of space] (Beijing: Wenhua yishu chubanshe) (version of her 2006 PhD thesis, Zhongguo yishu yanjiuyuan Yinyue yanjiusuo).

Wu Tianming (1987) *Laojing* [The old well], film (Xi'an dianying zhibianchang).

Xiang Yang (2000) 'Music Households in Feudal China: The Data of *Yuehu* Collected in Shanxi Province', *Journal of Music in China* 2.1: 7–28.

—— (2001) *Shanxi yuehu yanjiu* [Eng. title Study of *yuehu* of feudal China in Shanxi] (Beijing: Wenwu chubanshe).

Xiao Mei (2003) 'Huwu hujie qi ganlin: Xibei (Shaanbei) diqu qiyu yishi yu yinyue diaocha zongshu' [The buzz of praying for sweet rainfall: field survey of ritual and music of rain prayer in the northwest (Shaanbei) region], in Tsao 2003: 419–88.

Xue Yibing (2003) *Shenguaide yule: Zhongguo minjian jisi yishi jiqi yinyuede renleixue yanjiu* [Holy entertainment: an anthropological study of Chinese folk ritual and its music] (Beijing: Zongjiao wenhua chubanshe).

Yan Bing (1996) 'Jianchi shuo xinshu de laoyiren Zhang Jungong' [Zhang Jungong, old folk musician determined to sing new stories], in Shaanxi 1996: 46–8.

Yan'an (1988) *Yan'an wenyi congshu* [Anthology of literature and the arts from Yan'an] (Changsha: Hunan wenyi chubanshe).

Yang, C.K. (1967) *Religion in Chinese Society* (Berkeley: University of California Press; 1st edition 1961).

Yang Cui (1995), *Loushui dili chuan hongxie: Xintianyou quji* [Collected *Xintianyou* pieces] (Beijing: Renmin yinyue chubanshe).

Yang Hong (2005) 'Xiangsu liyizhongde minjian xiban yanjiu: dui liangge minjian xibande tianye diaocha' [Study of folk opera troupes in rural ceremonial: field study of two folk opera troupes], *Zhongguo yinyuexue* 2005/3: 23–38.

Yang Mu (1994a) 'On the Hua'er songs of North-western China', *Yearbook for Traditional Music* 26: 100–16.

—— (2004b) 'Academic Ignorance or Political Taboo? Some Issues in China's Study of its Folk Song Culture', *Ethnomusicology* 38: 303–20.

Yau, Esther C.M. (1991), 'Yellow Earth: Western Analysis and a Non-Western Text', in Chris Berry (ed.), *Perspectives on Chinese Cinema* (London: BFI) 62–79.

Yu Huiyong, (ed.) (1957) *Shaanbei Yulin xiaoqu* [The Yulin little pieces in Shaanbei], Zhongyang yinyue xueyuan Huadong fenyuan minzu yinyue congkan (Beijing: Yinyue chubanshe) [on *errentai*!].

Yu Peng (1996) 'Gaoyuan geshou He Yutang' [He Yutang, singer of the high plains], in Shaanxi 1996: 141–6.

Yuan Jingfang, Li Shibin, and Shen Feixue (1999) *Shaanxi sheng Jiaxian Baiyunguan Daojiao yinyue* [The Daoist music of the White Cloud temple in Jiaxian, Shaanbei], vol.13 of Tsao (ed.) 1996–2000 (Taipei: Xinwenfeng).

Yuan Li (2001) 'Huabei diqu qiyu huodongzhong qushui yishi yanjiu' [The Fetching Water ritual in north Chinese rain prayers], *Minzu yishu* (Guangxi) 2001/2: 96–108 and 121.

Yulin (1994) 'Yulin xiaoqu' [The Yulin little pieces], special edition of *Yulin wenshi ziliao* vol. 13.

Yung, Bell, Evelyn S. Rawski, and Rubie S. Watson, (ed.) (1996) *Harmony and Counterpoint: Ritual Music in Chinese Context* (Stanford: Stanford University Press).

Zhang Jianzhong (ed.) (2000) *Shaanxi minsu caifeng: Shaannan, Shaanbei* [Collecting folklore in Shaanxi: Shaannan and Shaanbei] (Xi'an: Xi'an ditu chubanshe).

Zhang Junyi (1993) *Yulin fengqing lu* [Record of customs in Yulin] (Shaanxi renmin jiaoyu chubanshe).

—— (2000) *Xibei feng* [The northwest wind] (Xi'an: Shaanxi lüyou chubanshe).

Zhang Peiji (1992) 'Shaanbei min'geshou Wang Xiangrong fangwen ji' [Notes from an interview with the Shaanbei folk-singer Wang Xiangrong], *Yinyue xueshu xinxi* 1992/5: 10.

Zhang Qian (1965) 'Gemingde yishujia, qunzhongde yishujia: sui Han Qixiang xiaxiang ji' [Revolutionary artist, people's artist: following Han Qixiang down to the countryside], *Quyi* 71 (31 Oct): 44–7.

Zhang Yanqin (2006) 'Zhangzi shuoshu jiqi xijuhua qingxiang' [Shuoshu (story-telling) in Zhangzi and its tendency of dramatization], *Minsu quyi* 151: 31–96.

Zhang Zhentao (2002a) 'Yulin zangsu zhongde suona yueban yu chuigushou' [Shawm bands and blowers-and-drummers in Yulin funerary customs], in Zhang Zhentao 2002b: 51–173 (almost identical [*sic!*] reprint in Tsao 2003: 337–403).

—— (2002b) *Zhuye qiuyue lu: Yinyuexue yanjiu wenji* [Record of seeking music in the countryside: collected essays on musicology] (Ji'nan: Shandong wenyi chubanshe).

—— (2002c) *Yinyue hui: Jizhong xiangcun lisuzhongde guchuiyueshe* [The Music Associations: wind-and-percussion music societies in the ceremonial of the central Hebei plain] (Ji'nan: Shandong wenyi chubanshe).

—— (2003) 'Xulun: Zoujin xibu, tiyan yishi' [Introduction: Entering western China, experiencing ritual], in Tsao 2003: 27–49 (also in Zhang Zhentao 2002b: 174–225).

Zhao Jiping (1985) 'Dianying *Huang tudi* yinyue chuangzuo zhaji' [Notes on the creation of the music for the film *Yellow Earth*], *Renmin yinyue* 1985/9: 19–21.

Zhao Shiyu (2002) *Kuanghuan yu richang: Ming-Qing yilai de miaohui yu minjian shehui* [Revelry and routine: temple fairs and folk society since the Ming and Qing] (Beijing: Shenghuo duzhe xinzhi Sanlian shudian).

Zhidan (1985) 'Zhidan xian Changjia suona yinyue' [Shawm music of the Chang family in Zhidan county], draft mimeograph for *Anthology*.

Zhongguo (1983) *Zhongguo dabaikequanshu: xiqu, quyi* [Encyclopaedia Sinica: opera and narrative-singing] (Beijing and Shanghai: Zhongguo dabaikequanshu chubanshe).

Zhongguo (1989) *Zhongguo dabaikequanshu: yinyue, wudao* [Encyclopaedia Sinica: music and dance] (Beijing and Shanghai: Zhongguo dabaikequanshu chubanshe).

Zhongguo (1990) *Zhongguo xiqu zhi, Shanxi juan* [Chinese opera monographs, Shanxi vol.] (Beijing: Wenhua yishu chubanshe).

Zhongguo (1992) *Zhongguo yinyue cidian, xubian* [Dictionary of Chinese music, sequel], ed. Zhongguo yishu yanjiuyuan Yinyue yanjiusuo Zhongguo yinyue cidian bianjibu (Beijing: Renmin yinyue chubanshe).

Zhongguo (1993) *Zhongguo xiqu zhi, Hebei juan* [Chinese opera monographs, Hebei vol.] (Beijing: Zhongguo ISBN zhongxin).

Zhongguo (1994) *Zhongguo yishu yanjiuyuan Yinyue yanjiusuo suozang Zhongguo yinyue yinxiang mulu* [Catalogue of recordings held by the Music Research Institute of the Chinese Academy of Arts] (Ji'nan: Shandong youyi chubanshe).

Zhou Yang et al. (1946) *Minjian yishu he yiren* [Folk arts and artists] (Zhangjiakou: Xinhua shudian Jin-Cha-Ji fendian) (reprint 1948).

Glossary-Index

Alphabetization is by word, not by letter; thus e.g. *Da Kaimen* precedes *Dabaidui*, and Guo Xingyu precedes *guogu*. Titles of melodies are cited in the forms given by local informants, not always 'standard'. Though early sources (and often current ritual texts) use full-form characters, here simplified characters, the lingua franca of modern China, are given.

Abing 阿炳 65 n.13, 77
Ai Keqi 艾克奇 76
Ai Pu 艾谱 128
aiqing diao 爱情调 'love songs' 187
aiyue 哀乐 modern funeral music 102, 188
amateur music-making xvii, xviii, 215;
    see also dance; folk-song; *Yulin*
    xiaoqu
amplification 150, 151, 171, 175, 181, 182
Anbo 安波 50, 67
anchu 安厨 ritual 183
Ansai 安塞 6
    group drumming 12, 15, 155
    narrative-singing 67, 80 n.15, 81
    pilgrim association 85
    shawm bands 103, 104, 161
    and *Yellow Earth* 11, 12
anshen 安神 ritual 83, 84, ⊙C4
Anthology of Folk Music of the Chinese
    Peoples xxiv, xxvi, 13, 29, 139, 217
    for Shaanbei 19, 23, 29, 76, 128
    other citations xxii n.8, 23, 32 n.3, 91,
    202 n.8
antu, antushen 安土神 ritual 22, 33, 35,
    179, 180, 186, ⊙B6
Antu shenzhou 安土神咒 manual 186
army, armies 91, 92
    troupes 119, 144
    music for sending off sons to 33, 82,
    100, 119, 122
    army service and musical training 166,
    172, 212

bada paiqu 八大牌曲 'eight great labelled
    pieces' 138

badie bawan 八碟八碗 'eight dishes and
    eight plates' 122
bagua 八卦 eight trigrams 187
Bai Baojin 白葆金 205
bai ludeng 摆路灯 ritual 178–9, 185–6,
    ⊙B4, ⊙D5
bai tiandi 拜天地 ritual 188
Baichang 拜场 melody 139, 188
baishi (*laorende, mai laoren*) 白事
    (老人的, 埋老人) funerals 21;
    see mainly funerals
Baiyunguan, Baiyunshan 白云观, 山
    temples and temple fair xvi, 22, 25,
    99, 111, 118, 140 n.12
    bards at 45, 85–6
    notes from 85–6, 191–2, ⊙A4
    Mao visit 16, 17
bangu 板鼓 drum 79
banhu 板胡 fiddle 79, 106
banshi 办事 'performing ceremony' 20–21,
    95
banzhu 班主 band boss 115, 162
bao ping'an 报平安 'guaranteeing well-
    being' 33
baojian 宝剑 'precious sword' 210
baojuan 'precious scrolls' xxii–iii
Baolian deng 宝莲灯 vocal item 69
baosuo (*daisuo, guasuo*), *kaisuo*
    包(带,挂,开)锁 hanging/opening
    locket 33, 35–8
bards 4, 29–87, 93–4, ⊙A4, ⊙C3–4
bawangbian 霸王鞭 dance genre 19
bazi 八字 eight characters 36
beggars, begging 9, 25, 32, 34, 41, 47, 85,
    170, 184–5, 189, 215, ⊙D2
    chuishou and begging 96, 103, 162, 163

(beggars, begging cont.)
    funeral beggar 184–5, ⊙D4
beileyun 背了运 'down on luck' 118
benben 本本 libretto 83
bendiao 本调 scale 139, 177–80, 185, 186,
    187, 189, 201, ⊙B4
'big band' 149–53, 155–74 *passim*, 175–6,
    181–90 *passim*, ⊙D
bili 筚篥 reed-pipe 91
birth control policy 25, 64, 71, 74, 80, 166
    n.6
bisai, dasai 比赛, 大赛 contests 144;
    see also contests
Black Dragon temple, *see* Heilongtan
blind musicians 31–2, 40–41, 76–7, 85,
    87, 98
    bards 29–87 *passim*, ⊙C3
    in shawm bands 98, 106, 108, 117, 118
Braille 61, 63
brass bands 149–51, 153; *see also* 'big
    band'; pop music
Buddhism, Buddhist priests xxi, 17, 21, 36,
    45, 92, 111, 114, 140
    in Yulin 197, 198, 199 n.3
Bulala 卜喇喇 melody 138
bulunbulei 不伦不类 'mish-mash' 171
Buneng tuishe 不能退社 vocal item 61
burial 21, 176, 177, 179–80, 186, 188, 193,
    199–200, ⊙B5; *see mainly* funerals

caiquan, huaquan 猜/划拳 guessing/
    swinging fists 15, 22
Caishenye 财神爷 deity 46
campaigns, *see* Maoism
canjun 参军 joining the army 33, 100
cassette culture, *see* recordings
canshen 参神 ritual 83, 84
Cao Laiqian 曹来前 115–16, 124, 133, 168
Chang Bingyou (Chang *daye*) 常炳有
    (常大爷) 109–10, 118, 171, 172,
    173
Chang Liancheng 常连成 144, 150, 156
Chang Mao, *see* Chang Wenqing
Chang Wenjin 常文锦 113–14, 127, 129,
    131, 133, 135, 156, 168
    comments 96, 101, 103, 120, 123, 152
Chang Wenqing (Chang Mao) 常文清
    (常茆) 102, 103, 120, 133, 158, 165

Chang Wenzhou 常文洲 113–14, 128–31,
    133, 151, 155–6, 165, 166, 173,
    181–2, ⊙B1, ⊙D3
    as instrument maker 93, 131–5, 155–6.
    192
    on music 112, 122, 169, 187
    on social change 97, 114, 124, 146, 163
Chang Xinhua 常新华 107–8, 111, 152
Chang Zilin 常子林 144, 150, 156
changfa duanzhou 长法短咒 'long magic,
    short mantra' 36
changming deng 长命灯 'long life lamp' 186
changqing 常青 ritual streamers 22, 28, 37,
    38, 83, 84
Changshiban 常石畔 101, 103, 107, 108,
    109, 113, 123, 127, 129, 131, 133
chayebing 茶叶饼 'tea and cakes' 204
che wangling 撤亡灵 ritual 182
Chen Kaige 陈凯歌 4, 9, 11–12, 77
Chenghuangmiao 城隍庙 temple (Yuhe)
    22, 80
chengjia 成家 'get married' 72
chi 尺 foot (measure) 133ff.
chi shenshen 吃神神 'eat off the gods' 18
Chigui 吃鬼 vocal item 64
children, rituals to protect 11, 21, 35–8, 45,
    58, 61, 64
CHIME xxvi, 198
Chouxiao 臭小 78, 107, 112, 117, 134,
    137, 146, 167, 169, 172–3, 182
chui zidao 吹自道 'blowing your own
    way' 136
chuide mafan 吹的麻烦 'blowing a drag' 140
chuigushou 吹鼓手, *see* shawm bands
chuihao 吹号 brass instruments 164;
    see mainly 'big band'
chuishou 吹手, *see* shawm bands
chuling 出灵 ritual 179; *see also* burial
chumen jianxi, guiren fuchi 出门见喜,
    贵人扶持 slogan 40
Chunjie xuqu 春节序曲 melody 105
chushi 出师 'graduation' 136
chuxie 除邪 'banishing evil' 177
cipher notation 75, 120, 131, 158, 159,
    160, 166, 185, 200, 207
clappers 44, 65, 66, 69, 70, 84, 189
clothing and headgear 9, 81, 110, 151, 161,
    186, 210

of official troupes 11, 211

    ritual 37, 177, 184, 186, 190–91, 199

commune system, *see* Maoism

concert performances 11, 16, 18, 20, 79, 175, 206, 211, 212–13

conservatories 17 n.31, 130, 144–6, 206; *see mainly* Xi'an, Conservatory

conservatory style 65 n.13, 77, 144–6, 148, 159, 206, 207, 209–11, ⊙C1

contests 11, 51, 131, 144, 146, 156, 159, 175, 212

county gazetteers xxvi

crime 25, 86, 158, 166, 175

cuchui (dachui) 粗吹 (大吹) shawm-band style 112

cultural authorities 198, 210

    and bards 48–54, 56–65, 73–6, 80

    and opera 16

    and shawm bands 94, 112, 119–21, 128–30, 133, 144, 145, 146, 149–50, 156–7, 166

    and Yulin little pieces 204–8

    see also scholarship

Cultural Revolution 9, 12, 63, 145, 149, 150, 171, 199, 205, 210, 212

    bards in 63–5

    shawm bands in 124–5

    see also Maoism

cymbals

    in shawm bands 95, 131, 133, 136, 137

    in other genres 65, 112, 175, 189, 211

da e 打恶 'attack evil' 180

Da Kaimen 大开门 shawm melody 125, 139, 177, 178, 179, 180, 186, ⊙B3

da suona 大唢呐 large shawm 131; *see mainly* shawm; shawm bands

Dabaidui 大摆队 shawm melody 138–9, 152, 189, 193

daban 搭班 'make up a band' 106

dabanzi, (xiyang) tongguan yueqi 大班子, 西洋铜管乐器 big band/brass band 149 n.5

dadiao 大调 vocal suite (Yulin) 206, 207–8

Dagai 大街 Main Street (Yulin) 197, 199–200

Dage 大哥 Older Brother xvi, 78, 98, 107, 109, 118–19, 127, 163, 171–2, 176

on society and music 99, 100, 103, 111, 117, 119, 123, 125, 127, 128, 165, 173, 175

daike 待客 'receiving guests' 22, 35, 112

Daixingsi 戴兴寺 temple (Yulin) 197

dance 19–20, 175, 185; see also *yangge*

danchuan 单传 'sole successor' 172

danchun 单纯 'innocent' 207

dan'gan 单干 privatization 74

Dang Yinzhi 党音之 79

dangdang 铛铛 gong 112

danyin diao, shuangyin diao 单音调, 双音调 tunings 68

Daoism, Daoists xxi–xxii, xxv, 17, 20, 24 n.52, 25, 85, 86, 111, 140, 198, 215

daoqing 道情 vocal genre 16–17, 20, 53, 69, 70, 80, 106, 108, 202, 209

dashen 大神 'great god' 86

dashi 大师 'great master' 155

daxian 大献 'great offerings' 182

Dazao 打枣 melody 185

dazuoqiang 打坐腔 genre 29; see mainly *errentai*

dezui ren 得罪人 'offend people' 123

dian 点 'ordered' 84

diaokou 调口 tune, scale 70, 139

diaoyan, huiyan 调演, 会演 state festivals 65, 119, 120, 130, 131, 144, 161, 165, 204, 205, 209, 210

Dieduanqiao 叠断桥 melody 138

dietan, tiaoshen 跌坛(?), 跳神 performance of medium 24; *see mainly* spirit mediums

Dingbian 定边 6, 23 n.54, 76, 83, 106, 133, 200

dingde/qingde, songde 定的/请的, 送的 ordered (invited)/offered for free 99

dingsi 顶死 'fixed and dead' 69

'dirty songs' 187, 212

divination 35, 48, ⊙A3

dizi 笛子 flute 65, 144, 148, 159, 207, 211; see also *mei*

dongfang 洞房 marital bedroom 189

Dongfang hong 东方红 song 15

dou 斗 bowl 37, 38, 83

drum, drumming
  in shawm bands 95, 112, 117, 131, 132,
    135, 136, 137, 150, 151, 152, 159,
    163 n.5, 165, 169, 191
  in other genres 19, 23, 24, 79, 171,
    175, 184, 210
drum-kit 150, 151, 169, 170, 173, 175, 181
Du Chengzhang 杜成章 97, 104, 105, 128,
    165
Duo yin 夺印 vocal item 63
duoban 朵板 metre 136–40, ⊙B3

earnings
  of bards 33–4, 36–7, 38, 58, 60, 64–5,
    74, 81, 83
  of shawm bands 109, 114, 116, 134,
    162–4, 200, 201
  of beggars and geomancers 184, 186–7
education, formal 8, 9, 10, 40, 44, 63, 68,
    96, 109, 113, 200, 161–2, 199
  and music 149–50, 159, 160, 166, 198,
    200
  see also training
electricity xxvi, 9, 63, 78, 127, 204, 213
electronic keyboard 32, 74, 85, 150, 151, 188
erbaiwu 二百五 'thick' 130
Ergai 二街 Second Street (Yulin) 197, 200
erhu 二胡 fiddle 32, 65, 79, 85, 144, 198,
    203, 205, 207
erliushui (jiaban) 二流水 (加板) tempo 137
erpingzi 二瓶子 gongs 112
errentai 二人台 vocal genre 17 and n.31,
    29, 202 n.7, 209, 210
erwawa 二娃娃 small *suona* 146;
    see mainly small *suona*
euphonium 150, 151, 176

fagong 法功 'spiritual power' 35
fali 法力 'magic power' 36, 80
fali you daoli 法力有道理 'magic power is
    rational' 80
faling 发灵 burial procession 186;
    see mainly burial
famine 8, 47, 78, 102
fan 犯 offend 35
fan 幡 funerary pennant 179, 180, 183, 186
Fan wushen 反巫神 vocal item 58 n.4

fandiao 反调 scale 139, 175, 177, 178,
    185, 189, 201
Fang fengzheng 放风筝 melody 205
Fanshen ji 翻身记 vocal item 40 n.16,
    61–2
Feng Guanglin 冯光临 98, 107, 108–9,
    110, 119, 128, 143, 152, 172
Feng Xiaoping 封小平 167, 200–201
  on music, 124, 136, 137, 151, 169
Fengfeng ling 凤凤铃 shawm melody 102
festivals, official, see *diaoyan*
film 3–4, 11–12, 14 n.21, 22, 59, 77, 102,
    144, 145, 146, 157, 187, 210
firecrackers 21, 84, 99, 117, 177, 178, 179,
    180, 184–90 *passim*, 193
folk-song 3, 11–12, 13–15, 22, 23, 24, 32,
    34, 70, 77, 85, 129, 139, 187, 189,
    ⊙C2
  modern 12, 13–14, 77, 129, 159, 187,
    210–12, ⊙C1; *see also* pop music
food 7, 81, 85, 108, 182, 204
  ritual 21–2, 112, 122, 180, 182–3, 186,
    188, 189
fu 符 talismans 35, 58, 64, 80, 180
Fugu 府谷 6, 15 nn.23 and 25, 16, 17, 23
    n.51, 29, 83, 184 n.9, 202 n.7, 210
fuli 福利 'lucky' 36
funerals 4–5, 99, 114, 122, 138, 139, 168,
    171, 173, 199, 216
  notes from 176–88, 201, ⊙B2–6
funeral shops 17, 197
furen, xiaojie, poyi 夫人, 小姐, 婆姨
    terms for 'wife' 72
fusan 复三 ritual 186

ganda 干大 godfather 104
Ganquan 甘泉 67, 78–9
Ganzou He Shaonan 赶走何绍南 vocal
    item 50 n.12
Gao Jianxi 高建喜 101, 104
Gao Jiu 高九 138, 150, 151, 156, 168, 169,
    182, 183, 185
Gao Maomao 高毛毛 107, 145–6, 147,
    159, 172
Gao Wanfei 高万飞 101, 146, 156–7, 161,
    166
Gao Yongzhang 高永章 50
Gao Zhiqiang 高直强 59, 150, 160, 170

geju 歌剧 modern opera 20, 80

Gelaohui 哥老会 brotherhood 123

gender 23, 60, 61, 62, 106, 166 and n.6, 211
    and bards 32, 36, 57, 58
    and shawm bands 98, 106, 117, 162
    and Yulin little pieces 204, 205, 208

geomancers xxi, xxii, xxv, 21, 22, 23–4,
    64, 96, 118, 122, 124–5, 199
    and healing 35, 37
    in action 176, 177, 180, 181, 183,
    186–7, ⊙B5, ⊙B6, ⊙D5

Gesheng yu weixiao 歌声与微笑 song 189

geti minjian xiban 个体民间戏班 privately
    run folk opera troupes 15–16

gewuting 歌舞厅 song-and-dance hall 18,
    76

gewutuan 歌舞团 song-and-dance troupe
    120; *see mainly* official troupes

gong, gongs
    in shawm bands 95, 131, 133, 135,
    137, 150, 151
    in other genres 23, 79, 102, 112

gongche 工尺 solfeggio 166, 172, 207

gonggong jilei 公共积累 public assets 65

gongming 功名 official qualification 36

Great Leap Forward 62, 117, 118

gu 鼓, *see* drum, drumming

guaibing 怪病 supernatural diseases 35

guan, guanzi 管子 oboe 65, 91, 104, 112,
    122, 146; see also *sheng-guan*

guan 管 'control, look after' 74, 125

guanchui 官吹 'official blowers' 101, 191

guanlifei 管理费 management fee 191

guansha 关煞 'noxious influences' 35,
    37 n.10

guanxi 关系 'contacts' 158, 162, 165

Guanyinsi 观音寺 temple (Yulin) 197

gufangzi 鼓坊子 'drum shops'
    traditional 96, 103, 104, 105, 111, 117,
    191
    under Maoism 115–16, 120, 121, 122–3
    term persists 163, 171

Gui muqin zuo junxie 贵母亲做军鞋 vocal
    item 58 n.4

guiju 规矩 rule, tradition 187, 192, 201

guizi, guizhe, guijia 龟子/着/家 pejorative
    term 96, 102, 121, 160, 200

guluzi, guolengzi 咕噜子, 过楞子
    ornaments 207

guo manyue 过满月 1st-moon celebration
    21, 35, 45, 100, 119, 203

Guo Xingyu 郭星鹕 (兴玉) 37, 49, 56, 57,
    63–5, 74, 80
    on ritual culture 34, 35, 36, 68, 82, 84

guogu 过鼓 shawm interludes 131, 137–8,
    148, 152, 177, 183, ⊙B3

guoguan 过关 Crossing the Passes ritual
    21, 37, ⊙A3

guoguan daji 过关大吉 slogan 37

guojie 过街 'passing through the streets' 188

guomen 过门 interludes 70, 207

guo sangu 过三鼓 suite form 137;
    see mainly *laosangu*

gushou 鼓手 95; *see mainly* shawm bands

guyue ban(zi), guyue dui 鼓乐班(子)/队 95;
    see mainly shawm bands

hadi 下地 'put down on the ground' 181

haidi (*haidir, haidizi*) 海笛 (儿/子) shawm
    112, 122, 146

Han Qixiang 韩起祥 (Han *ye* 爷, Han
    zhuren 主任) 29, 43, 69 and n.18, 79
    early years 45–53, 54
    under Maoism 56, 58, 60–63, 65, 78
    after reforms 75–6

Hancheng 韩城 20, 144

hanghua, heihua, jiahuhua, jianghuhua
    行话, 黑话, 家户话, 江湖话 trade
    language 123

hao 号 natural trumpet 131, 133, 135, 172
    in ritual 21, 131, 177–80, 199; replaced
    135, 151, 183, 185, 188

Hao Yongfa 郝永发 98, 106, 128

Haohan ge 好汉歌 song 169

haozi 号子 work songs 14–15

hashou 下手 lower shawm player 136–7

He Guangwu 何光武 40, 57–8, 66, 69, 70,
    71, 72, 81–2

He Jingzhi 贺敬之 48

He Shaonan 何绍南 47–8, 50

He Siwa 何四娃 159, 166, 168

He Yutang 贺玉堂 11

He Zengrong 何增荣 106

He Zengtong 何增统 106, 120, 130, 159,
    166, 168

healing 24, 31–8, 45, 80, 82, 87
health, healthcare xxi, 10, 33, 35, 60–61,
    82, 97, 118; *see also* blind
    musicians; healing; spirit mediums
Heihulingguan 黑虎灵官 deity 19
Heihulingguanmiao 黑虎灵官庙 temple 38
Heilongtan 黑龙潭 Black Dragon temple
    xviii, xxvii, 22, 83, 160, 175
helongkou 合龙口 cave-building
    completion ceremony 21–2, 78, 175
Henan 河南 162, 171
Hengshan 横山 6, 16, 24 n.54, 33, 45, 47,
    53, 74, 76, 133, 159
heterophony 136–7, 152, 153, 193
Hong gaoliang 红高粱 film 145
hong sixian 红丝线 red thread 36
honghuo 红火 'red and fiery' 99, 150, 166,
    187, 192
hongliang 洪亮 'sonorous' 152
Hongqiqi 红旗旗 shawm melody 137
hongshi (qu xifu, yin xiuzi) 红事 (取媳妇,
    引秀子), *see* weddings
Houjie, Qianjie 后街, 前街 singing styles
    in Yulin 205
houzi 猴子 'throat' of shawm 132–3
Hu Yingjie 胡英杰 205, 208
Hu Zongnan 胡宗南 51, 116
hua 花 decorated
hua fu 画符, see *fu*
Huadaozi 花道子 melody 139
huan kouyuan 还口愿 'redeeming a vow'
    33; *see also* vows
Huang tudi 黄土地 film 3–4, 11–12, 22, 146
Huanghe jiuqu zhen 黄河九曲阵 ritual 20
huangmo 黄馍 cake 108
huangse 黄色 'dirty' 187
Huanxiang ji 还乡记 vocal item 57
huanyin 欢音 'happy notes' 70
huazhi 花指 'flowery fingerings' 207
huhu 呼胡 fiddle 104, 118, 150, 159
Hui niangjia 回娘家 pop song 189
huihui 回回 episodes 68
huishu 会书 stories for temple fairs 33,
    84–6, ⊙A4
Huixiang ji 回乡记 vocal item 62
huizhang 会长 association chief 37, 118,
    86, 190

Huo Xianggui 霍向贵 12–13, 76, 105,
    106, 128, 130, 131, 208
    influences folk musicians 65 n.13, 112,
    130, 133
huzi 户子 'fixer' 107, 162

instruments
    of bards 66–8
    of shawm bands 111–12, 131–5;
        modern, see 'big band'
    of Yulin little pieces 206–7
    see also *erhu*; *dizi*; *huhu*; *mei, meidi*;
        percussion; *pipa*; *sanxian*; *zheng*; etc.

jia heshang 假和尚 'fake priests' 25
Jia Pingwa 贾平凹 77
jiadiao 甲调 scale 139, 178, 179, 185, 193,
    ⊙B4
jiangjiu 讲究 'meticulous' 122
Jiangjun ling 将军令 shawm melody 177,
    178
    on Yulin *zheng* 207
jianpu 简谱 cipher notation 75, 120, 131,
    158, 159, 160, 166, 185, 200, 207
jiao 醮 ritual 18, 22, 192
jiaohuazi 叫花子 beggars 25; *see mainly*
    beggars, begging
jiaozi 教子 'educating children' 181
jiashi 家什 (percussion) instruments 96, 108
jiashu 家书 'stories for family' 33
Jiaxian 佳县 6, 7, 85
    bards 50, 65, 74, 82
    opera troupes 17–18
    shawm bands 92, 128, 134, 144, 191–2
    ritual 23, 25; *see also* Baiyunguan,
        Baiyunshan
Jiekazi 结卡子 'The Stammerer' 159
jietou shuochang 街头说唱 'street singing'
    62
jiguan 机关 'institutions' 33, 34
Jihua shengyu 计划生育 vocal item 64
    n.12, 74, 80
Jin Wenhua 晋文华 98, 106, 128
Jingbian 靖边 6, 68, 106, 120, 128, 133, 184
jinggao 敬告 announce a death 199
jinghu 京胡 fiddle 205, 206, 207
jingshen 敬神 'offer respects to the gods' 32

Jinju 晋剧 Shanxi opera 16, 17, 18, 77, 106, 189, 197, ⊙A1

Jinmingsi 金明寺 (Jiaxian) 25

jiqinghua 吉庆话 'auspicious phrases' 71

jishu 技术 skills 59

jiti tingtang 集体厅堂 common hall 204

jitui 鸡腿 chicken-leg (shawm) 132–3

jiuqiang shiba diao 九腔十八调 vocal repertory 41

jiuqu 酒曲 drinking songs 14, 15, 212, ⊙C2

jiuqu dasai 酒曲大赛 contest for drinking songs 212

jizhang 记账 ritual accountant 176

Jueyu fengbo 绝育风波 vocal item 64 n.12

julebu 俱乐部 club 61

jutuan 剧团 opera troupes, *see under* opera

kaichang, kaichang bai 开场白 opening of story 84

kaiji 开祭 ritual 112

kaiye 开业 'opening a business', *see* shop openings

kan 龛 shrine 45

kang 炕 brick-bed 4, 7, 9, 14, 189, 203

karaoke 17, 152, 198, 213

kaxi 咔戏 opera mimicry 151, 185

Ke Lan 柯兰 50

keban 科班 opera troupe 103

kitchen rituals 182–3

kowtowing xxii, 22, 86, 177, 178, 179, 183–6, 190, 201

Ku lingding 哭伶仃 melody 112

kuaishu 快书 patter 184

kuyin, kudiao 哭音, 哭调 'wailing' singing style 70

laidan huishuang 来单回双 'arriving alone, returning in a pair' 188

langong 揽工 temporary work 15, 109

language xv–xvi, 60, 69, 72, 95–6, 123, 131, 140, 151, 172

Langyashanshang wushenbing 狼牙山上五神兵 vocal item 50, 51

lanhale 揽下了 'guaranteeing' 36

Lanhuahua 兰花花 song 12 n.15, 14 n.21 TV film 157

lanshi, lantou 揽事, 揽头 'fixer' 107, 162, 199

lao guiju 老规矩 tradition 187, 192, 201

lao heidou 老黑豆 tuning 68

Laodong yingxiong Li Lanying/Li Ziying 劳动英雄李蓝(子)英 vocal item 50

laoguban 老鼓板 traditional shawm repertory 168

Laojing 老井 film 59

laosangu 老三鼓 suite form 124, 137, 150, 152, 193, 216

laowai 老外 'wog' 24, 160, 174

Lashoushou, qinkoukou 拉手手, 亲口口 song 187

latongtong 拉筒筒 lower shawm part 136

Lei Feng 雷峰 62

Li Bu 李卜 97

Li Daniu 李大牛 97, 98, 105–6, 115, 119, 128, 131, 133

Li Diankui 李殿魁 203

Li Fang 李芳 203

Li Huaiqiang 李怀强 37, 43–5, 53–4, 59, 64, 67, 68, 78, 80–81, ⊙C3
on healing and narrative-singing 35, 36, 69, 70, 72

Li Huanzhi 李焕之 105

Li Qishan 李歧山 116, 124, 129, 133–4, 148, 155, 157–8
on music and society 114, 134, 135, 138, 150, 151, 152, 162, 163, 164, 166

Li Shengli 李胜利 157, 158

Li Wenjin 李文金 28, 83–4, ⊙C4

Li Zichan 李子山 129, 133, 148

Li Zizhou 李子洲 8

liangdiao 亮调 prelude 137

liangfenban 两分半 division of fees 163

lidan 礼单 list of gifts 182

Lin Maosen 林懋森 204, 205

Lin Shan 林山 31, 49–52

lingfan, hunfan 灵幡, 魂幡 funerary pennant 179

lingpeng 灵棚 soul tent 177

Lingqian ku 灵前哭 melody 112

Linxian 临县 85, 92, 189–90, 191–2

lishi 历史 'history' 44

Liu Deyi 刘德义 106, 114, 115, 123, 133, 136, 169–70

Liu Qiaor tuanyuan 刘巧儿团圆 vocal item 51, 52, 75
Liu Qing niang 柳青娘 melody 140
Liu Zhenlin 刘振林 201
Liu Zhi 刘值 102
Liu Zhidan 刘志丹 8, 47, 50, 102
Liu Zhidan da Yanchang 刘志丹打延长 vocal item 50
liushui, liushuiban 流水板 metre 125, 137–8, 139, 177
lizhang 理账 ritual accountants 21, 183
longevity celebrations 15, 21, 33, 45, 100, 119, 203
Longwangye 龙王爷 deity 46; *see also* rain ceremonies
luan 乱 'chaos' 140, 187, 192
luji 路祭 ritual 178, 199
lunzhi 轮指 finger-rolls 206
luo 锣, *see* gong, gongs
Luo Xinmin 罗新民 203ff., 207
luopan 罗盘 compass 24, 180, 186
Luyi 鲁艺 Lu Shan Arts Academy 48, 105
lüjiao 驴叫 'donkey braying' 140

Ma Hu 马虎 145, 148
Ma Ke 马可 105
Ma Qiantang 马前堂 111, 112, 116, 125, 173–4
Ma Siwang 马四旺 110, 112, 117, 122, 130, 133
Ma Zhenyin 马振音 98, 109, 117–18, 172
Ma Zhihui 马智慧 xiii, 22, 127–8, 171–2
manban 慢板 metre 125, 136, 137, 139, 177, 179, 189
mantou 馒头 steamed buns 81, 182
Maoism xvii–xx, 10, 20, 26, 73, 199
　and bards 55–65
　and shawm bands 113–25, 162
　and Yulin little pieces 204–5
　see also politics
Matigou 马蹄沟 93
matong, wushen, shenguan, zouyin 马童, 巫神, 神官, 走阴, *see* spirit mediums
Mawangye 马王爷 deity 46
mazhazi 蚂蚱子 percussion 65, 66, 84
mediums, *see* spirit mediums

mei, meidi 梅（笛）flute 76, 104, 112; *see also dizi*
mei guiju 没规矩 'without order' 192, 201
Meimei zuo chuantou 妹妹坐船头 song 169, 187
meiyou guanbuliao 没有管不了 'there was nothing they couldn't control' 125
meizhi 煤汁 coal dust 35
Meng Haiping 孟海平, on folk music 55, 59, 72, 73, 74, 82, 208
menmen 门门 status 36
metres, of shawm music 125, 136, 137–8, 139, 177, 179, 193, 216
mianshao, budaishao 棉哨, 布带哨 shawm reeds 135
Miaojiaping 苗家坪 58, 150
migration 93
　before Communism 5, 8, 107, 200
　under Maoism 48, 116, 120, 121, 185
　since the reforms xi, 10, 33, 103, 107, 200, 201
　theme of songs 15
　see also *gufangzi*
mihu 眉户 vocal genre 16, 20, 48, 53, 69, 79, 80, 207 n.16
Ming ruo qinxian 命若琴弦 novel/film 77
min'ge, min'geshou 民歌, 民歌手 folk-song, folk singers, *see* folk-song
mixin 迷信, *see* 'superstition'
mixin shu 迷信书 'superstitious stories' 49
Mizhi 米脂 *passim*
　county 6, 7, 8, 53; opera 16, 150, 159; bards 50, 53, 57, 58, 59, 63, 67, 68, 73, 82
　shawm bands: in county 93, 101, 102, 121, 128, 129, 133, 146, 159–60, 161, 191, 192, 200, 201; in town 101, 103, 104, 105, 113, 131, 146, 150, 155–9, 164, 173, 175
　pilgrim association 192
　women 211
　see also Yangjiagou
Mo Yan 莫言 71
mobile phones 151, 156, 164,
motor-bikes 151, 161, 197
mu'ou jutuan 木偶剧团, *see* puppet opera

names, personal 96, 172

Nao tiancao 闹天草 melody 170

narrative-singing 29, 202; *see mainly*
bards; *errentai*; *Yulin xiaoqu*

niangniang baoyou 娘娘保佑 slogan 37

niuguisheshen 牛鬼蛇神 'ox demons and
snake spirits' 64

nongye hezuo 农业合作 collectives 59;
see also Maoism

Northwest Wind xix; *see also* pop music

notation, *see* cipher notation; *gongche*

nuanyao 暖窑 house-warming 21, 33

official involvement in folk music,
see cultural authorities

official troupes xviii, 12 n.15, 14, 24 n.54,
55, 65, 119, 205, 206, 208–12, ⊙C1
and shawm players 92, 109, 119–20,
130–31, 143–5, 149–50, 156, 159,
161, 169
see also bards; opera, state troupes;
Maoism

opera 15–19, 40, 77, 150, 161, 191, 209,
⊙A1
folk bands 103, 104, 106, 108, 115,
118, 162
state troupes 11, 15–19, 50, 80 n.15,
118, 150, 161, 189, 197
see also *Jinju*; *Qinqiang*

opium 71, 91, 97–8, 101, 105, 106, 111, 114

ostinato sections
of bards 70, 84
in shawm music, see *guogu*

pai 派 style 155

pailian 排练 'rehearse' 131

paiwei, shenweizi 牌位, 神位子 altars 38,
177

paizi 牌子 'melody' 70, 136

pao lü 跑驴 dance genre 20

peitao 配套 'make a set' 170

peixunban 培训班 training sessions 55, 144

peixunfei 培训费 training expenses 65

percussion xxii, 206
of bards 65, 66
ensemble 12, 19, 20, 92, 155, 175, 201
opera 65, 106, 159
of shawm bands 93, 95, 96, 111–12,
135, 136, 137, 148, 159, 162–4, 165

see also clappers; cymbals; drum,
drumming; gong, gongs

pianfang 偏方 'folk remedies' 35

ping'an shu 平安书 'stories for well-being'
33, 83–4, ⊙C4

ping'an xiqing shu 平安喜庆书 'auspicious
story for well-being' 34

pingdiao 平调 scale 70

pingshi 平事/士, *see* geomancers

pipa 琵琶 lute
of bards 40–41, 50, 66–8, 76, 83, ⊙C3
in Yulin ensemble 203, 206, 207, 211

Pochu maimai hunyin 破除买卖婚姻 vocal
item 64 n.12

Pochu mixin 破除迷信 vocal item 64 n.12,
70

politics xvii–xx, xxiii–xxv, 8–11, 201–16,
and *passim*
and bards 45–87
and shawm bands 102, 105, 113–25,
127–8, 143–4

polyandry 98, 106

pop music xix, 139, 149–53, 166, 168, 169,
171, 173, 182–9, 194, 197, 198, ⊙D

puppet opera 17, 18, 53, 96, 106, 108, 115,
118, 202

Pusamiao 菩萨庙 temple (Yangjiagou)
38, 45

puzhang langfei, dacao daban 铺张浪
费, 大操大办 anti-extravagance
campaigns 118, 124, 127–8

Qianfude ai 钌火的爱 song 187, 189

qiangban 抢板 metre 152

qiangjiu 抢救 'salvage' xxiv

Qiao Jianzhong 乔建中, and Shaanbei 198,
204, 209

qiao pizi 敲皮子 drum 131; *see mainly*
drum, drumming

qiban 起板 prelude of bards 70, 84

qihong 起哄 'start a fight' 166

Qin Xuemei diaoxiao 秦雪梅吊孝 opera
item 171

Qingjian 清涧 6, 16, 50, 56, 67, 68, 83, 85,
103, 160, 171

qingling 请灵 ritual 177

qingke 请客 'invite guests' 199

Qinqiang 秦腔 opera 16, 18, 20, 52 n.19, 53, 77, 150, 159, 197, 209
qishi 起事 opening of ritual 139, 177
Qiuci 龟兹 96 n.4
qiyu 乞雨, *see* rain ceremonies
Qu Xiaosong 瞿小松 77
quan 权 'authority' 36
qupai 曲牌 labelled melodies 138–40, 170
Quyi 曲艺 journal 62
quyiguan 曲艺馆 Hall of Narrative-singing 75

radio 63, 78, 129, 205, 207
rain ceremonies 12, 14, 16, 18, 19, 22–3, 52, 71, 100, 197, 210
recordings
　field 76, 128–30, 208
　commercial 11, 15, 17 n.31, 48 n.4, 77–80, 145, 146–8, 152, 155, 166–7, 175, 197, 202 n.7, 207, 210
religion and ritual xx–xxiii, xxiv, 7, 10 n.10, 23–4, and *passim*; *see also* funerals; 'superstition'; temple fairs, temples
re'nao 热闹, see *honghuo*
Renjian xundege hao nüxu 人间寻的个好女婿 vocal item 184
Rensheng 人生 film 157
ritual, *see* religion and ritual
rivalry between shawm bands 155, 165–6

Sanbian 三边 sub-region 6–7
sancai ban 三才板 genre 19
Sanda jilü baxiang zhuyi 三大纪律八项注意 song 64, 75
sanfenzhang 三分帐 division of fees 163
sanhuang 三皇 three emperors 33, 40 n.17
sanshandao 三山刀 medium's ritual 24
Sanshilipu 三十里铺 song 15
sanxian (*xianzi*) 三弦 (弦子) lute 40, 41, 47, 59, 66–8, 69, 77, 79, 84, 85
　in Yulin 203, 204, 206, 207
sao 搔 'strike' (percussion) 96
saxophone 150, 151, 158, 160, 164, 170, 173, 175, 182, 183
scales
　of bards 69–70

of shawm bands 139, 177–80, 185–9, 193, 201
scholarship xvii–xxvii, 29, 76, 91, 128–30, 156–7, 198, 205; *see also* cultural authorities
Shaan-Gan-Ning bianqu wenxie shuoshuzu 陕甘宁边区文协说书组 Shaan-Gan-Ning Border region literary association narrative-singing group 50–51
Shaanbei 陕北 xix, 5–11, 146, 215–16
　images of xvii, xix, 3–5, 77, 110, 155, 161, 209–13
Shaanxi 陕西 5
Shachangwei 杀场尾 shawm finale 137
shandian 闪点 cymbals 131; *see mainly* cymbals
Shandong 山东 120 n.4, 169
Shang Airen 尚爱仁 12, 56, 58
Shang nanpo 上南坡 melody 138, 180, ⊙B3, ⊙B5
Shang tiantai 上天台 melody 138
Shangganling 上甘岭 film 102
shan'ge 山歌 'mountain songs' 15
shanggong 上供 Offerings 190–91, ⊙A2
shangshou, hashou 上手, 下手 upper and lower shawm parts, *see* heterophony
shangxi 上席 'sit up at table' 160
shanqu 山曲 'mountain songs' 15
Shanxi 山西 215, 216
　bards and beggars 25 n.55, 32, 48 n.10, 50 n.12, 55 n.1, 59, 71 n.23, 74 n.2, 85, 87 n.23
　daoqing, errentai 16 n.30, 17 n.31
　opera 16; *see mainly Jinju*
　rain ceremonies 23 n.51
　saisai 19 n.36
　shawm bands 92, 95, 96, 133, 159, 191
　song 15 n.24
　links with Shaanbei 5, 85, 92, 159
shawm, shawms 91, 131–5; *see also* small *suona*
shawm bands 91–4, ⊙A2–4, ⊙B1–5, ⊙D1–3, ⊙D5
　before Maoism 95–112
　under Maoism 113–25
　since reforms 127–94

in Yulin city 198–201

she 社 parish 19 n.38, 22, 33, 34

shehuo 社火 'parish bands' 19, 20; see also *yangge*

sheng 笙 mouth-organ 112, 146, 148, 149, 151, 158, 159, 160, 171, 175, 185, 201

sheng-guan 笙管 ensemble 25, 92, 112, 114, 122, 166, 197, 198

shengtong 升筒, *see hao*

shenguan 神官, *see* spirit mediums

shenguan diao 神官调 'mediums' songs' 210

shenhan, shenpo 神汉, 神婆, *see* spirit mediums

Shenmu 神木 6, 15 nn.23 and 25, 16–17, 29, 68, 81, 83, 197, 202 n.7

shepantu 蛇盘兔 'snake encoiling rabbit' 188

sheshu 社书 'parish stories' 33; see also *she*

Shi Tiesheng 史铁生 9, 77

Shi Weijun 石维君 51, 52, 56, 64

Shi Weiren 石维仁 159–60

shicha hui 施茶会 pilgrim associations 85

shichuanbuliao 失传不了 'can't be lost' 168

shifenzhang 十分帐 division of fees 163

shifu 师傅 'master' 109, 158

Shishang zhiyou mama hao 世上只有妈妈好 pop song 187

shop openings 100, 164, 175–6, 192, 200, ⊙D1

shoukuren 受苦人 'people who endure suffering' 11, 45

shouwa 手瓦 gong 112

shouyi dian 寿衣店 funeral shops 197

shuaban 刷板 percussion 65, 66, 70, 84

shuichuan, hanchuan 水船, 旱船 dance genre 19–20, 175, 185

shujiang 书匠, *see* bards

shuochang 说唱, *see* narrative-singing

shuofa 说法 'expound magic' 36

shuoshu 说书 story-telling 29; see mainly bards

shuoshude 说书的 story-teller, *see* bards

shuoshu xunlianban 说书训练班 narrative-singing training band 51

shuoshu yiren xuanchuandui 说书艺人宣传队 narrative-singing artists' propaganda team 55

shuoxi, nianxi 说喜, 念喜 'reciting joy' 34

si 死 'dead', inflexible 69, 137

Siji facai, shengyi xinglong 四季发财, 生意兴隆 motto 84

Sishilipu 四十里铺 78
 shawm bands 114, 115–16, 120, 150
 temple fair 37, 84, 189–91, ⊙A2, ⊙A3

sizhu 丝竹 'silk-and-bamboo' genres 202

small *suona* 144, 146, 150, 151, 152, 156, 159, 164, 169, 171, 175, 182, 183, 185, 188, 190, 201

SOAS, shawm band 167

songfen 送坟 'escort to the grave' 199

songli 送礼 'offering gifts' 191

songmen xi 送门戏 'taking theatre from door to door' 184

songshen 送神 ritual 38, 83, 84

sound systems, *see* amplification

spirit mediums xvii, xx, xxii, 24, 32, 36, 37, 49, 58, 70, 96, 215
 in concert representations 210, 211

stammering 106, 159

status, of musicians 36, 82, 96–8, 105, 113, 119–21, 160–62, 170, 187, 193–4, 200

suangua 算卦 fortune telling 33; *see also* divination

suanku diao 酸苦调 'bitter melodies' 187

Suide 绥德 6, 7, 8, 48, 53, 58, 209
 bards 30, 32, 33, 50, 51, 56, 58, 64, 65, 67, 68, 74, 80, 82
 opera and other troupes 19–20, 106, 109, 159
 shawm bands: in county 93, 101, 102, 105, 110, 121, 124, 128, 134, 160, 200; in town 105, 106, 111, 115–16, 150, 164, 169, 171, 175, 188–9

suiji yingbian 随机应变 improvising 69

suite form, of shawm bands 124, 130, 137–8, 152, 177, 194, 216, ⊙B3, ⊙B4

suona 唢呐 91, 95; *see mainly* shawm

suona xiehui 唢呐协会 *suona* associations 144, 148, 167

'superstition' xxvii, 8, 18, 19, 37, 86, 127–8
 and bards 35, 49, 51, 52, 53, 55, 59, 61, 64, 69, 70, 87
 and shawm bands 113, 124, 125

tai 台 opera set 18

tai Longwang, tai shenlou 抬龙王, 抬神楼,
　　see rain ceremonies

Taihangshan 太行山 metaphor for firm
　　metre 137

tanbulai 谈不来 'can't agree' 166

tao 套 suite 130; *see mainly* suite form

temple fairs, temples xvi, xviii, xx,
　　xxi–xxii, 7, 22, 23, 25, 127
　　and bards 33–4, 45, 69, 80, 81–2, 83,
　　　　84–6
　　and opera 17–19, 103
　　shawm bands at 99, 100, 160, 170,
　　　　175, 189–92
　　in Yulin 197, 209
　　notes from 37–8, 84–6, 189–92, ⊙A

Tian Zhizi 田志子 33, 34, 58, 61, 63, 74,
　　81, 82

tiaoniuchang 跳扭唱 'dancing, twisting,
　　and singing' 150

titoude 剃头的 barbers 96

tong (*tonggu*) 通鼓 knobbed gong 131;
　　see also gong, gongs

touhui 头会 first association 85

toushi xueyi 投师学艺 'seeking a teacher
　　to learn the art' 172

tuozai miannan 脱灾免难 'avert calamity'
　　86

training, traditional
　　of bards 31, 44, 47, 56, 57, 58, 64, 80,
　　　　83
　　of shawm bands 98, 109, 135–7, 138,
　　　　166–7, 170, 172

transport xxvi, 7–8, 103, 107, 197, 213–14

trombone 150, 151, 152, 164, 175

trumpet, Western 135, 150–51, 158, 160,
　　164, 169, 170–75, 182–5, 188, 189,
　　200, 201

TV 10, 11, 40, 77, 78, 79, 86, 144, 146,
　　152, 157, 184, 187, 192, 205, 210

violence 32, 165–6, 185

vocal music, *see* bards; folk-song; opera;
　　pop music; *Yulin xiaoqu*

vows xxi, 18, 21, 31, 32–4, 36, 45, 81, 86,
　　190

wailing, funerary 177, 178, 179, 184, 185,
　　186, 193

Wang changcheng 望长城 documentary
　　205

Wang Gui yu Li Xiangxiang 王贵与李香香
　　vocal item 56, 58, 79, 80 n.15

Wang Jinkao 王进考 56, 57, 64, 67, 68,
　　⊙C3

Wang Laiwa 王来娃 150, 161, 163, 169,
　　170–71

Wang Piqin zou nanlu 王丕勤走南路
　　vocal item 58

Wang Qing 王青 203, 206

Wang Shifa 汪世发 114, 124, 164, 175–6,
　　188–90, ⊙A2, ⊙D1–2
　　on music and society 93, 115, 136,
　　　　150, 168

Wang Shushan (Mao Xiao) 汪树山 (毛小)
　　115, 122

Wang Xiangrong 王向荣 210, 211, 212

wangba 王八 pejorative term 96, 200

wanhui 晚会 'evening gathering' 18, 210

Wanhun ji 晚婚记 vocal item 80

Wannan shibian 皖南事变 vocal item 50
　　n.12

wanwan 碗碗 bell of shawm 133

wanwanqiang 碗碗腔 puppet opera 17, 18,
　　53, 106; *see also* puppet opera

wazi, nazi, wawa 瓦子, 呐子, 娃娃 shawm
　　95, 131, 146; *see also* shawm

weddings xx, 3, 14, 15, 17, 21, 24, 182 n.8,
　　184, 188–9, 190, 203
　　bards and beggars at 33, 34, 82
　　shawm bands at 99, 100, 103, 116, 117,
　　　　122, 125, 127, 164, 170, 174, 199,
　　　　⊙D2
　　posthumous 86

wei bobo 围饽饽 'surrounding with buns'
　　189

wei shengling 喂生灵 'feeding livestock' 33

Wen Ziyi 文子义 205

Wendai dahui 文代大会 Great Assembly
　　of Cultural Representatives 60

wengongtuan 文工团 arts-work troupes 16,
　　55, 119, 209

Wenhuaguan 文化馆 Hall of Culture 55;
　　see mainly cultural authorities

Wenjiaoju 文教局 Cultural Education
      Department 12 n.16

wenshu, wushu, xianjia shu, shenshen shu
      文书, 武书, 仙家书, 神神书 types
      of story-telling 69 n.19

White Cloud temple, *see* Baiyunguan

women, *see* gender

Wubu 吴堡 6, 7, 14 n.21, 63, 81, 85, 92,
      101, 128, 133, 148

Wu Chunlan 吴春兰 205

wudiao 武调 'martial tunes' 70

Wuding river 无定河 7, 106

wugu 五谷 'five grains' 22, 180

wuguan buquan, renjia bugen 五官不全,
      人家不跟 'people won't follow
      you if your five organs aren't
      complete' 32, 83

Wuliangdian 无量殿 temple (Yulin) 197

Wulonggong 五龙宫 temple (Baiyunshan)
      85, 192

Wunü xing Tang zhuan 五女兴唐传 vocal
      item 59

wushen 巫神, *see* spirit mediums

wuting 舞厅 dance hall 76

wuxing 五行 five elements 180

Wuzhuangbu 武装部 Armed Forces
      Department 124, 128

Xi qianqiu 喜千秋 melody 203

Xi ying chun 喜迎春 melody 130

Xia Jiangnan 下江南 shawm melody 188

xiajiuliu 下九流 social dregs 161

Xi'an 西安 63, 106, 109, 113, 131, 197
      Conservatory 11, 120, 143, 148, 159,
      171, 207

xian jutuan 县剧团 county opera troupe
      16; *see mainly* opera, state troupes

xiang 乡 township xxv

xiang, pin 相, 品 frets on *pipa* 68, 206

xiangda, xiangshou 响打, 响手 95;
      see mainly shawm bands

xianghuo 相伙 mutual aid 97

Xiangma zhuan 响马传 vocal item 84

xiangsheng 相声 dialogue skit 18

Xiannü pei 仙女配 vocal item 69

xiansheng 先生 'master' 31

xianzhi 县志 county gazetteers xxvi

xiao cha 小镲 small cymbals, *see* cymbals

xiao suona 小唢呐, *see* small *suona*

xiaoban 小办 'minor ceremony' 176

xiaodiao 小调 'little melodies' 14–15, 138,
      140, 184, 207, 208

xiaomi 小米 grain 36

xiaoming 小名 nickname 96

xiaoxi 小戏 'little operas' 16–17

Xibei quxie 西北曲协 Northwest
      Storytelling Society 60

Xibei yishu zhuanke xuexiao 西北艺术转
      科学校 Northwest Arts Training
      School 120, 148

Xibu da kaifa 西部大开发 Opening up the
      West 10, 175

Xibu zhi yue 西部之乐 documentary 205

Xichuan 西川 45, 53

xichui (xiaochui) 细吹 (小吹) shawm-band
      chamber style 112

xiebing 邪病 'irregular illness' 45

Xifeng zan 西风赞 melody 125, 137, 139–
      40, ⊙B2, ⊙B4, ⊙B5, ⊙closing
      credits

xingmenhu, huanmenhu 行门户, 还门户
      'going from door to door' 31 n.1

xingmu, jingtangmu 醒木, 惊堂木
      woodblock 65, 66

xinpu 新谱 'new scores' 160

xintianyou 信天游 song genre 3, 15, 53,
      69, 187

Xitian gufo jing 西天古佛经 scripture 36

xizi 戏子 'opera performers' 96, 161

Xu Wengong 许文功 63, 68, 83, 85–6, ⊙A4

xue chuishou 学吹手 learning to be
      shawm-band musician 95; *see also*
      training, traditional

Xuerande fengcai 血染的风采 song 187–8

xuexiban 学习班 study group 130, 204

xunlianban 训练班 training sessions 51, 144

yahe 牙合 livestock intermediary 105

Yan Xiangcheng 严向成 199, 200

Yan'an 延安 6, 8, 48, 51, 52, 53, 58, 60, 62
      bards 48, 52, 53, 67, 75, 78, 79, 81,
      shawm bands 92, 96, 104, 105, 161
      'the Yan'an way' 8, 11

Yan'an Song-and-Dance Troupe 14 n.21,
      79, 120, 145

yanchu 演出 'perform' 130

Yang Hongyou 杨红佑 106, 118

Yang Shengfu 杨生福 50, 51

yangge 秧歌 dance 14 n.21, 19, 20, 23, 48, 61, 69, 77, 175, 198, 200–201, 209, 215

　　shawm bands and 100, 114, 118, 119, 122, 124, 125, 138, 145

　　funeral beggar performs 184, 185

Yangjiagou 杨家沟 xiii, xvi, xxvi–xxvii, 2, 46, 78, 120, 124, 171–2, 202, 203

　　bards 36, 38, 43–5, 53–4, 59, 64, 81, ⊙C3

　　shawm bands 90, 92, 97–100, 107–11, 112, 115, 116–19, 123, 127–8, 129, 133–9 *passim*, 145–6, 163, 167, 171–4, 175

　　funeral 176–80, ⊙B2–6

　　rain ceremonies 23 n.51

Yangjiajiang 杨家将 opera item 51

Yanglaozhuang 养老庄 60–62

yangming 扬名 'making a name' 150

yangqin 洋琴 dulcimer (*shiyin qin* 十音琴) 203, 206, 207

Yankoudai 烟口袋 vocal item 58 n.4

yanyan 燕燕 dough figure 37

yaofan 要饭 33; *see mainly* beggars, begging

yaofan dui 要饭队 'beggars' team' 74

yaogu, naogu 腰鼓, 闹鼓 percussion ensemble 12, 19, 155

yaxiaqu 压下去 'put someone down' 165

Yazhiyou 压指游 shawm melody 137

Yellow Earth, see *Huang tudi*

Yichuan 宜川 52, 145, 200

Yichuan da shengli 宜川大胜利 vocal item 52

Yijuban 一句半 melody 170

yiming 艺名 'art name' 96

Yinchuan 银川 45, 53, 67, 83

ying jifan 迎祭饭 ritual 182

yinggong 迎供 ritual 99, 192

Yingqin 迎亲 erhu solo 65

yingqin, dengqin 迎亲, 等亲 fetching or awaiting the bride 188

yingzhang 迎帐 procession 105, 183

yinhunji (tizuiji) 引魂鸡, 替罪鸡 funerary cockerel 179

yinlu 引路 'leading the way' 179

yinyang 阴阳, *see* geomancers Daoists 24 n.52

yiren 艺人 'artist' 31 n.2, 35, 55

yishu 艺术 'art' 150

Yixiao 艺校 School of Arts (Yulin) 198, 200

yizidiao 一字调 term for 'small melodies' in Yulin 207

Yongjun yangge 拥军秧歌 song 201

youdaolide 有道理的 'rational' 64

Youxiu tuanyuan 优秀团员 vocal item 58 n.4

yuanjia 冤家 'enemies' 166

Yuanr 勇儿 134–5, 159–60, 164, 175, 188

yuanshu 愿书 stories for vows 33

yuehu 乐户 'music households' 96

Yuejin ji 跃进记 vocal item 62

yueqin 月琴 lute 207

Yuhe 鱼河 town 22, 80, 101, 170

Yulin 榆林 region 6–8, 53–4, 92, and *passim*

Yulin city 149, 176, 197–212

Yulin diqu renmin jutuan 榆林地区人民剧团 Yulin Region People's Opera Troupe 209

Yulin diqu wengongtuan 榆林地区文工团 Yulin Region Arts-Work Troupe 130, 197, 209

Yulin minjian yishutuan 榆林民间艺术团 Yulin Folk Arts Troupe 144, 156, 205, 208, 209–12

Yulin xiaoqu 榆林小曲 genre (*xiaoquzi, shua xiaoqu/sixian/yueqi* 小曲子, 耍小曲/丝弦/乐器) 41 n.18, 201–208

yunluo 云锣 gong-frame 112

zaofan 造反 'rebellion' 64

Zaoyuan laile yanggedui 枣园来了秧歌队 melody 145

Zhang Heping 张和平 79

Zhang Hulin 张虎林 134, 150, 158, 164, 165

　　comments 103, 123, 138, 146, 161, 163

Zhang Jungong 张俊功 65, 77–80

Zhang Lu 张鲁 102, 105

Zhang Yulan canjia xuanjuhui 张玉兰参加选举会 vocal item 58 n.4

Zhang Yunting 张云廷 204–5

Zhangsheng xi Yingying 张生戏莺莺 song 187

Zhao Fuying (Zhao Wu) 赵福英 (赵五) 104

Zhao Jinrang 赵锦让 104, 128, 131

Zhao Jiping 赵季平 11, 12

Zhao Laixi 赵来喜 150, 151, 164

Zhao Suotong 赵所同 104, 105, 120
    comments 97, 103, 112, 114, 124, 137,
      165

zhaohun 招魂 ritual 186

Zhenchuan 镇川 7, 78, 93, 159–60

zheng 筝 zither 203, 205, 206, 207

zhengben shu 正本书 'story proper' 83

zhengxi 正席 feast 112

Zhenniantaisui 贞年太穗 deity 38

zhenshanmeixiao 真善美孝 'truth,
    goodness, beauty, and filial piety' 72

Zhenwu 真武 deity 86

zhexiubu 遮羞布 funeral veil 177, 184

zhibing 治病 healing illness 33

Zhidan 志丹 county 6, 45, 53, 68, 81, 102,
    103, 120, 200

zhidaoyuan 指导员 political instructor 74

Zhihui, *see* Ma Zhihui

zhihuo 纸活 funerary paper artefacts 177

Zhishi qingnian huixiang ji 知识青年回乡
    记 vocal item 64 n.12

Zhongguo quyi gongzuozhe xiehui 中国曲
    艺工作者协会 Chinese narrative-
    singing workers association 62

zhou, zhouyu 咒语 incantations 24, 35, 36,
    38, 180, 186

Zhu Guomin 朱国民 96, 103, 104

Zhu Xiaoyi 朱学义 203

Zhu Xinmin 朱新民 128, 198

zhua sijiao 抓四角 'catch the four corners'
    189

zhuan jiuqu 转九曲 ritual 20, 22 n.50, 104

zhuang 壮 'robust' 68, 133, 140

zhudi 竹笛 bamboo flute 79; see also *dizi,
    mei, meidi*

zhuidao yinyue 追悼音乐 memorial music
    102

zhusanggun 柱丧棍 funerary sticks 177ff.

zhusha 朱砂 cinnabar 35

zhutou, zhunao 猪头, 猪脑 woodblock 66

zibei 自卑 'feel inferior' 170

Zichang 子长 6, 61, 62, 67, 78, 93, 128,
    144, 148

Zizhou 子洲 6, 7
    bards 30, 33, 34, 58, 66 n.15, 67, 74,
      76, 82,
    shawm bands 92, 93, 101, 128, 135,
      144, 150, 158, 162, 171
    pilgrim association 85

zongguan, zongling 总管, 总领 ritual
    manager 21, 176, 181

zou xikou 走西口 song genre 15

zou zai renqian, chi zai renhou 走在人
    前, 吃在人后 'marching before
    people, eating after them' 96, 117,
    185; *see also* status

Zoujin xin shidai 走进新时代 song 201

zoulu diao, zhanshi diao, weiwang diao
    走路调, 战士调, 为王调 styles of
    singing 70 n.22

zuchuan 祖传 hereditary transmission 172

zuoshou 做寿, *see* longevity celebrations